WARMACHINE

ESCALATION

PRIVATEER
PRESS

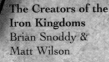

CREDITS

The Creators of the Iron Kingdoms
Brian Snoddy &
Matt Wilson

Game Design
Matt Wilson

Lead Developer
Jason Soles

Creative Director
Matt Wilson

Editor-in-Chief
Joe Martin

Contributing Editor
Bryan Cutler

Development Team
Rob Baxter
Steve Benton
Rob Stoddard

Rules Editors
Bryan Cutler
Andrew Daniels

Rules Development
Rob Baxter
Steve Benton
Andrew Daniels
Chris Such

Writers
Ed Bolme
Rob Baxter
Peter Flannery
Chad Huffman
Jessica Kristine
Joe Martin
Jason Soles
Bryan Steele
Matt Wilson

Text Proofing
Alex Badion
Kevin Clark
Bryan Cutler
Dominick DiGregorio
Rob Hinds
Rob Stoddard

Privateer Playtesters and Additional Development
Alex Badion
Alex Chobot
Mark Christensen
Kevin Clark

Douglas Colton
Dominick DiGregorio
Rob Hinds
Adam Johnson
Tom Paton
Jon Rodriguez
Brian Snoddy

Art Direction
James Davis
Matt Wilson

Cover Illustration
Matt Wilson

Illustration
Chippy Dugan
Jeremy Jervis
Alison McVey
James Ryman
Brian Snoddy
Matt Wilson

Graphic Design
James Davis

WARMACHINE Logo and 3D Art
Daniel Gelon

Faction Symbols
Todd Gamble

Miniatures Direction
Mike McVey

Sculpting
Gregory Clavilier
Christian Danckworth
Roy Eastland
Chaz Elliot
Peter Flannery
Will Hannah
Jason Hendrix
Bobby Jackson
Mike McVey
Jerzy Montwill
Paul Muller
Kev White
John Winter

Miniature Painting
Todd Arrington
Dominick DiGregorio
Tammy Haye
Joshua Howdeshell
Finn Kisch
Alison McVey
Mike McVey
Aaron Nissen
Dave Perotta

Eric Roof
Jason Soles
Rob Stoddard

Painting Guide Text
Mike McVey

Terrain
Todd Gamble
Rob Hinds
Alison McVey
Mike McVey
Jason Soles
Rob Stoddard

Photography
James Davis
Craig Gibson
Alison McVey
Mike McVey

President
Sherry Yeary

Operations Manager
Rob Stoddard

Executive Assistant
Nicole Remacle

Customer Service
Erik Fleuter

Press Gang Coordinator
Rob Hinds

Shipping & Packing Manager
Mark Christensen

Shipping & Packing Team
Bryan Cutler
Doug Colton
Alex Badion
Kevin Clark
Nathaniel Williams

Production Master
Kelly Yeager

Mold Maker
Jason Hendricks

Casting Team
Alex Chobot
Dominick DiGregorio
Ryan Gatterman
Adam Johnson
Tom Patton

Jon Rodriguez
Bob Traylor
Tom Williamson

Web & Forum Support
Corbin Cook
Andrew Daniels
Erik Lakin
Alun Gallie
Nathan Letsinger
David Ray

Escalation Playtesters
Amanda Adams
Scott Barber
Erik Bridenstein
David Cordy
Matt Crain
Scott Curness
Andrew Daniels
Keiron Duncan
Alun Gallie
Craig Gibson
Vince Hoogendoorn
Matt Hoskins
Tony Jones
Kevin Kennedy
Chris Keimig
Eric Lakin
Dave Larson
Jon Linder
Jon Luckhaupt
Brian Martin
Ken Metcalf
Iain A. McGregor
Kai Nesbit
John Newman
Pete O'Carroll
Chris Oakley
Ray Peng
Dave Perrotta
Darren Pettrey
Geoff T. Roscoe
Dan Smith
Bryan Steele
Sarah Steele
Chris Such
Riley Vickrey
Brent Walder
Josh Weinberg
Juan Zapata
Tony Zoltai

Special Thanks
Brush Thralls
Press Gang
Seattle Combat-Monkeys
Steam Dogs

CONTENTS

Visit: www.privateerpress.com

Pivateer Press, Inc.
2601 NW Market St. •Seattle, WA 98107 • Tel (206) 783-9500 • Fax (206) 783-9502

For online customer service, email: frontdesk@privateerpress.com

First Printing, July 2004. Printed in Canada.

ISBN: 0-9706970-8-2   PIP 1002

What you hold in your hands is the culmination of a year's worth of work that has consumed the efforts of literally dozens of people. This end product, a book of a couple hundred pages, is only the tip of an iceberg that just a short time ago was nigh unfathomable.

In April of 2003, WARMACHINE: PRIME entered game stores. At the time, Privateer Press consisted of less than ten people. While many people contributed to the creation of the original game, all production of models was outsourced and everyone, as we like to say, wore many different hats. Today, Privateer Press has become largely self-sufficient, having grown to over 30 crew members, and while the duties of the individuals have become more specialized, every Privateer has played an essential role in the end product before you—a book called ESCALATION, and the models therein.

Game design, writing, artwork and sculpting are the core of any game product, but nothing would exist without the crew of supporters that have gathered under our banner. From customer service, to our production team, to the very folks who hand pack each and every single component of a model into blisters and boxes—the success of WARMACHINE is dependent on a dedicated collection of people who believe in the mission of Privateer Press and our commitment to quality.

A quick perusal of our credits list will show that the daily duties of the Privateer Press crew are not the only aspect of their involvement with our products. Many Privateers from all corners of the company participate in the ongoing playtest and development sessions held outside of normal office hours. Their dedication to WARMACHINE, simply for the love of the game, has lead to fantastic developments and an achievement in quality that would otherwise be impossible.

Two other major components in the propagation of WARMACHINE are our crack line-up of out-of-house playtesters, and a phenomenal group of enthusiasts known collectively as the Privateer Press Gang. Our playtesters generate, quite literally, reams of data that is critical to the balancing of this game. And while the playtesters do their best to wreck our work (for the better, of course!) the Press Gang works equally hard to introduce and promote WARMACHINE to those who have not yet experienced the glory of this metal mayhem. The Press Gang also provides amazing convention support to Privateer on the road, and organizes events so numerous they can't be calculated. They are almost completely responsible for the exponential growth of the WARMACHINE player community.

WARMACHINE would scarcely be a ripple among an ocean of games, were it not for the tireless efforts of our crew at home, and our many supporters abroad. We are blessed as a company to have attracted such distinguished individuals underneath our flag, and hope that in future years, we will be fortunate enough to continue to grow our association as we have in the past year.

It's a good time to be part of this crew—Privateer Press.

It started as a manifesto of our disposition—the philosophy with which we created WARMACHINE. We never expected it to be the pavement of our common ground, the doctrine of a movement of players, or the center of controversy and a source of unlimited debate. Love it or hate it, though, you can't avoid it.

Is it about sexism? An anatomy lesson for the testicularly impaired?

No.

Page 5 is about honesty. It's a self awareness of what we're doing, why we're doing it, and who we're doing it for. It's a declaration of our stance, the 10-40 on our attitude. It's about the kind of people we are and the kind of people we want to face across the table.

We pour blood and sweat into this game, into the stories, into the art, and into the metal. We want to see WARMACHINE experienced the way we intended it.

Escalation takes it to the next level and we're piling it on heavy. We've spent a year hammering away at this gallery of ass kickers and ensuring that everything you see is as borken as you expect it, but nothing here stands alone. Escalation raises the bar, but it stands on the shoulders of the nine-ton giants who came before it.

This is the triple shot in your 8 AM espresso. This is the nitrous injection in your 426 Hemi. This is the depleted uranium tip on your armor-piercing round. We threw out anything that slowed down the fight. This is the final cut—pure grain, grade A, distilled aggression.

You're going to need a hernia belt to lift these new warjacks. They're bigger, badder, and pissed off. They don't fill the cracks in your armies; they work your opponent over like a school girl who wandered into a back-alley cage match. We've given you the warcasters to lead them too—professional name-takers specifically designed to kick your foe in the nuts and bolts while a procession of solos, troops, and blazing field artillery run through his back-entrance like a freight train on a mission from God.

Still, the new models are only half of the pants-soiling experience found within these pages. The Escalation campaign pitches you headlong into a conflict between four nations that will leave no one unscarred or uncharred. If you like piña coladas, getting caught in the rain, show tunes, romantic comedies, and happy endings, then you're crying into the wrong Kleenex™, pink boy. This is a story about war. It's 87 pages of mud-slogging, blood-drenching, mind-blowing brutality. We've given you the lenses to see the Iron Kingdoms through our eyes. Better wear a helmet.

Page 5 was only a page number in a freshly printed book a year ago. Now it's the creed for a new era in wargaming, the banner for players looking for a challenge, and the battle cry for a game with serious stones.

You just hefted two scoops of whoop-ass for your Wheaties™, Waldo. Remember to lift at the knees. We've given you a year to master the basics, and it's time to do your business or get off the pot.

And now that we're all on the same page—

Play like you've got a pair.

KINGS, NATIONS AND GODS

PART I

High atop the crenellated watchtower of the Cygnaran fortress of Northguard, a soldier nudges her fellow guard. "You hear something?" she whispers.

"Huh? What?" The second soldier stands up. They are surrounded by darkness, broken only by the stars overhead. They can see the lights in the fort, the shadows of the nearby hills, and the rippling reflection of the stars in the lake to the east. "I can't see nuffin'," he says. "Calder ain't out. Too bloody dark."

"Clear your lug-hole and listen up," says the first, a sneer in her voice. "I said I *hear* something… out there."

The second soldier leans through a crenature over the parapet, one hand cupped to an ear. He pauses for a moment, then snorts, "You mean the water?"

She nods. "Yah."

"'Course you hear water," he says, sitting back down. "It's a bloody lake. Now, lemme rest."

"No, it's too loud, like. I think there's something out there."

"Right then, so some gargling fish is keeping me from my sleep. Stuff it."

"No, like a boat."

"Now what kind of bloomin' idiot would be out in a boat in this darkness? Huh? Answer me that, schoolmarm!"

"I dunno. Smugglers, mayhap?"

"Hey, yah, now that would make sense, now wouldn't it?" He rolls his eyes but stands up and cups his hand again. After a moment, he looks at her more seriously. She's right. He nods. "I hear what you mean, now. Kinda like someone's swimmin' or somethin'."

"Paddlewheel, you reckon?"

He squints into the dark, still listening, then says, "No engine, but rowers mayhap. I'll pass the word; we'll get a launch out there." He starts to disappear down the trapdoor, then pauses. "Good ears, mucker."

"Ta. Now hurry up."

She turns and peers back out over the battlements, wishing for more light on this dark night. She hears the soldiers below, speaking, first casually, then in muffled voices. *Good, mates,* she thinks, *keep the chatter down. Noise travels over water too easily.*

She barely hears a squad moving stealthily down to the lake's edge, and she sees the dim glow of a shuttered lantern. The soldiers push a launch into the water, and the wood creaks as they clamber in, one at a time. The last soldier pushes the launch out, his feet splashing the water. On the lake, she still hears the steady splash-splash of the mysterious intruder. Nearer at hand, she begins to hear the subtle groaning of oarlocks.

Suddenly, a beam of light pierces the night as the guards open the lantern's shutter. The beam sweeps slowly across the lake, looking for a target. To the right of the launch, she hears a quick commotion on the water, and then a shower of sparks flies up into the air.

"Stack flare!" someone bellows. "There they are!"

The boat's lantern swings about to rest squarely on the intruder vessel. It's a sidewheeler galley, long and slim with a large, trim paddlewheel on each side. Its narrow, sharp bow indicates that the ship is built for speed, probably for the express purpose of running past fortifications like this. And the size of the stack flare indicate that it's about to show what it can do. With no more need for stealth, the oars run in and the engines begin to sputter and churn.

6

Forgelock fire splits the night, illuminating the launch in a spatter of flashes. "Row, you manky gits, row!" the Cygnaran sergeant yells.

The sidewheels start turning, sending a spray of water into the air. The blockade runner lunges forward like a hound, almost slipping out of the lantern's beam.

"Oh, bloody bum," mutters the guard, thumping her fist on the merlon. "There they go."

Grand Scrutator Severius rises from his knees and bows before the altar to Menoth, thick with burning candles. He steps backward, his robes whispering on the marble floor. As he reaches the great double door to his private sanctum, he bows again, slowly and reverently. Then he reaches for his mask—a custom-fit gilded steel plate shrouded with an ivory hood—takes it off its stand, and places it over his head.

Reaching behind him, he undoes the latches that hold the doors closed. Immediately, servants on the outside pull the heavy oaken doors open, and he backs out of the room.

Once the doors have been quietly closed again, he turns about. "I have had a revelation," the scrutator's voice resonates through the chamber. "As our efforts near their fruition I am compelled to inspect the progress of our armories."

"With the crusade growing near, and the words of the Harbinger guiding our wisdom as Menoth's willing vessel, diligence is our shield while we forge our own spears. The servants nod, dumb to the true meaning of the words Severius has spoken. The aged scrutator beckons to a single servant,

"I leave within the hour. Ensure that my vassals are prepared for travel to Tower Judgment."

At this pronouncement, the room bursts into activity, as servants and acolytes hustle to prepare everything that such a trip requires. Severius moves through the bustle like a swan amongst chickens, his red-trimmed ivory robes trailing elegantly behind him. He pauses at the rack that holds his staves. Ordinarily, he would take up the Staff of Wisdom, but he will be traveling to Tower Judgment, near enough to the Bloodstone Marches and Cygnaran outposts that there might be trouble. His hand passes over the Staff of Wisdom, the Staff of Penance, and the Staff of Purging, coming to rest at last on the Staff of Judgment.

His hand closes about the gnarled grip, and he hefts the heavy staff from the rack. Its spiked handguard glistens, and the iron blade on the butt of the spear shines from fresh sharpening. The head of the staff is heavy, and bears the mark of Menoth; an ancient and revered pendant has been permanently mounted there to help attract Menoth's gaze. He needs the extra attention; the older he gets, the harder it is to wield such heavy equipment effectively. Thankfully, he'll be wearing his warcaster armor by the time he gets to Tower Judgment, and the faithful will not have to endure a display of the weakness of mortal flesh.

"My lord Menoth," he pleads, whispering, "please take me ere the flesh fails. Grant that I die in combat, serving your cause."

Dawn breaks in the east, staining the cloudy skies red and blue. The *Lady of Llael* moves quickly downstream. It's an easy pace for the trim vessel, and only a very little smoke escapes the ship's stack.

Captain Hugh climbs to the deck, buttoning his coat with one hand and rubbing the sleep from the corner of his eye with the other. He shuffles over to his first mate, yawning. The mate has a sour expression, more so than usual.

"What's she want now, Rosado?" he asks his mate quietly, gesturing slightly with his head to the tall, thin Khadoran woman who stands at the vessels' prow.

"To go faster."

"Why is that? We're goin' faster than all but the bestest horses can do."

"She says the horses don't have to follow the river, like we do. She says we wind back and forth, but they can go straight across fields and such. So, she wants us to go faster."

"What a potful," grumbles Hugh. He glowers at the woman's back as she watches the sun break the horizon. She had insisted on shipping two damnably huge crates. The massive wooden boxes sat on the deck like barrels on a donkey's back, making the ship top heavy and hard to handle. Too much more speed and they'd capsize on a sharp turn if they were lucky. "Very well then, let's shovel on some more bloody coal."

"Cap'n, why should we put up with all this rot, eh?" Rosado mutters conspiratorially. "I say we weigh the wench, sell the blag in those crates and pocket the full purse. With that money we could buy ourselves a tavern on a river somewheres."

"I wouldn't talk like that now," says Hugh quietly. "There's a good chap."

But the mate persists. "And if'n we goes deep into Cygnar, them Khadorans'll never find us. Too many guards at the borders. There's so many sabers rattling, nobody'd have their eyes out for a couple o' smugglers. They say there's a war comin' and all."

"Shh!"

"What, you think she's gonna hear?"

"No, but—"

"But what then? What's wrong with that plan?" asks the first mate, a bit of a whine in his voice.

"Well…" the captain looks back over his shoulder for a trice, then fixes Rosado with an intense look. "I think she's one o' them warcaster types."

The two sailors cast sidelong glances at the woman. The wind starts whipping up across the vessel's brow, ruffling the woman's hair beneath her winter cap.

A sudden chill gust billows the first mate's jacket. "They wouldn't waste a warcaster guarding a boatload of gears and such. C'mon," he adds with a wink, "I gots a plan on how to off her." He takes the captain by the elbow and turns toward the stern, and finds the Khadoran woman standing directly in their path.

"Wh—" stammers Rosado. He and Hugh both glance over their shoulders at the bow again. No one is there. "H—how did you—"

The woman smiles. "I am not a wench," she says in her fine Khadoran accent, and she grabs the first mate by the neck. "And you are no more a sailor."

Even as she speaks the words, the captain feels the wind change unnaturally. It whirls around them, fast and cold. The captain glances at his mate and sees the man transfixed, the wind whipping his hair tightly around his head in a speeding vortex. Rosado gurgles in pain between chapped lips. Right before the captain's eyes, Rosado's skin blisters with frostbite, then turns black and begins shredding beneath the punishing wind. His eyes frost over.

The woman lets go of the first mate's neck and the wind dies away in an instant. Rosado slumps to the deck, and Hugh dares not move to see if he yet lives.

The tall Khadoran woman turns to face the captain. "You," she says, poking him in the forehead. "Increase our speed."

A palanquin moves steadily through the badlands near the edge of the Bloodstone Marches, borne by eight strong bearers who move in perfect stride across the uneven terrain. To jostle the heavy litter would be unthinkable, a heresy.

It's a warm day for late autumn. Inside the palanquin, a bead of sweat makes its way down the nose of Grand Scrutator Severius. Deep in devoted prayer to Menoth, he does not note its passing, nor feel it drip onto the gilded menofix clutched tightly in his penitent hands. The gentle sway of the palanquin sets the rhythm of his prayers, and his lips move silently as he steps his soul through the rituals of supplication.

At last, he feels Menoth's peace wash over him. His spiritual flagellation is complete. His evils have been atoned for. Menoth's fire burns brightly in his soul. He raises his head reverently. His eyes have been tightly closed for so long that he squints at even the few stray beams that pierce the closed windows of his transport. He blinks a few times, a minor scowl on his face, until his eyes adjust. Then, squinting again, he slides back the wooden panel that seals the window at his left hand.

Severius immediately sees two of the forty guards that encircle him, carefully watching the empty terrain about. Bright sunlight reflects off their shining helmets, and the Grand Scrutator bows his head until his eyes can withstand the assault. He looks again, past the glinting helms of his escort. But a bowshot away, he spies the camp.

Camp indeed, he thinks. The facility sprawls with metalworks, boilers, and smelting furnaces running in unison; the largest concerted effort of mechanikal manufacturing the Protectorate had ever undertaken. The armory is no mere camp; it is the forge of the Protectorate's main battle force, complete with warjacks built and designed by the faithful, and soon to be guided into battle by their own warcasters.

The Priestess of the Flame would be waiting, having guided the efforts of the facility for over two months now. The scrutator frowns at the thought of having to endure Feora's petulance. He would not enjoy seeing her. She was always a challenge. Still, her value to Hierarch Voyle was not without merit, and so they must all tolerate the woman.

As his palanquin draws close to the camp, he can see the runner approaching, an envoy sent to receive news of his arrival and set preparations for his reception into action.

Severius smiles, a faint gesture of pleasure that rarely graces his face, and reaches for his mask. Menoth's timing is perfect as ever. He sequesters his menofix properly and arrays himself for his duties. His anticipation of seeing the efforts of their planning firsthand urges an invocation to Menoth, and then he watches the runner sprint back toward the facility.

A rider bearing the standard of a Cygnaran messenger gallops hard down the King's Highway from Corvis. To his right are leagues of scrub-filled plains and to his left are the rolling waters of the Black River. As he rides, he keeps glancing nervously across the river at the wasteland beyond. Though he has seen nothing on this ride, he remains alert.

His face relaxes a bit when he sees the bastions of Fort Falk, Cygnar's easternmost outpost. Fort Falk sits on the banks of the Black River, and overlooks the forbidding hills of the Caerlys Craig, the frontier of the Bloodstone Marches. Knowing he's close, protected under the watchful eyes of Cygnaran guards, he whispers a few encouraging words to his mount.

He sees a group of soldiers awaiting his arrival by the open doors to the fort. He rides up, dismounts quickly, stumbles over to them and offers a perfunctory salute. "Smugglers on the river, sirs, a rapier-thin sidewheeler. Fast as salts through an ol' lady."

The soldiers nod. "Aye," says one.

"Aye?" says the messenger, as understanding dawns on him.

"We sent a ship to try to run 'em down," adds the guard.

"Bloody hell," says the rider. "My arse is chafed and my legs are raw, and all that for nothin'."

Some guards lead away his lathered mount for a well earned meal and some rest. Meanwhile, one of the guards remains with the rider.

"Don't fret, man," he says politely. "Whenever I'm on duty, I think of the options."

The rider gives him a weary-eyed glance, and the guard continues while ushering them both toward the mess hall. "I could take a plague-ridden arrow in the throat fired by some leering thrall, I could get flattened by some clapped out Khadoran 'jack, some mad Menite could lob a firebomb in me lap, or some freakish creature from me worst nightmare could cross yon river and eat me head. Then I thinks to meself that wastin' me time is a fair option, and I get paid a mite or two just to be bored silly."

At all that, the rider chuckles tiredly. "I suppose you're right," he admits as they ascend some steps. "Well, friend, here's to a right boring winter, then."

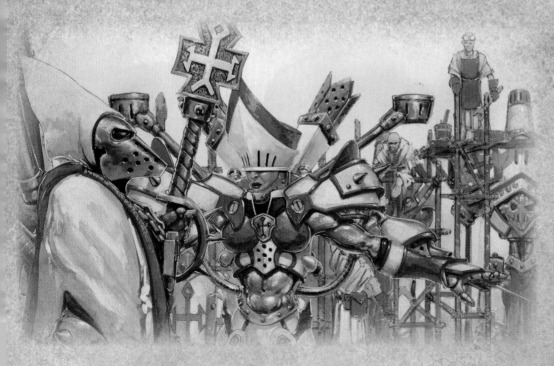

The first guard claps the rider on the shoulder as they enter the kitchens. "Aw, now. Don't jinx it," he replies with a scraggly-bearded grin.

Feora, Priestess of the Flame, watches as Grand Scrutator Severius steps down from his palanquin. As soon as his foot touches the earth, she bows, precisely as deep as required by the rituals and not one inch more. Behind her, two squads of Flameguard, totaling a score, and a collection of zealots, vassal mechaniks, and other staff remain deeply bowed in reverence. Beyond them, inside the workings of the facility, numerous others toil, their work too critical to interrupt even for the scrutator's visitation.

"Rise," he says gently, and Feora bridles at the gentleness of his tone. "Show me how Menoth has blessed our work here."

As they tour the facility, the Grand Scrutator begins to feel his flesh grow weary from the heat. Damning his age, and asking Menoth for strength, he stands taller. Not wanting to let Feora see him in a moment of weakness, he changes his approach. He keeps his questions fast, often complex, and sometimes direct in order to keep her attention off his condition and on answering his inquiries.

Finally, after long moments of observing gearwrights, mechaniks, and weapons manufacturing, they arrive to the foremost reason he has come—warjacks. Feora steps aside and gestures toward the main work area.

"If you please, your eminence," she says, and escorts him to a cluster of completed 'jacks. Their fresh paint glistens, blood-hued menofixes stark and powerful against the ivory background. Set in rows, the constructs serve as silent sentinels to the ongoing labor of the workers. Each completed warjack stands ready, hoppers full, boilers stocked with pure water, awaiting anointment by a cleric designated to call upon Menoth's favor.

"These are complete," she says, not bothering to mask the pride in her voice. "They stand ready for service."

"Ah, Reckoners," says Severius. "Field tested?"

"The prototype, yes," she answers. "Quite thoroughly."

She points across the open ground, to where another dozen warjacks stand beneath a scaffolding

of cranes and winches. Their torsos are laid open like eggshells, and small parts and large assemblies litter the ground around each of them. "Those are nearly finished, and then all shall be complete." She waits a half heartbeat to finish. "We only await the needed parts from those of the north sympathetic to our cause."

"Very good," nods the Grand Scrutator. "We shall take our crusade to the threshold of our oppressors and see them fallen for all time. I look forward to seeing them proven in battle."

"As do I," Feora says. "It shall not be much longer now. Shall we continue, your eminence?"

"Later," Severius replies, then clears his voice in order to hide his weariness. "First, to my chambers. I wish to cleanse myself and offer supplication for the grand things I have seen this day."

The steamship's wheels reverse with a resounding bang, followed by a familiar series of rhythmic clunks from somewhere in the vessel's guts. It drifts to the pier, slowing its speed, while the captain at the helm begs a silent prayer to Morrow for saving his soul from a frosty death. *Poor Rosado*, he thinks, then observes as two of his "riverdogs"—riffraff hired out of Five Fingers—moor the *Lady of Llael* to the dock with lines built to hold fast and cut fast.

The ramp lowers, the dark-haired and dangerous Khadoran beauty standing at the top of it ready to meet a gathering of men at the stone pier. Judging from their garb, they are Menites from the Protectorate, a score or more at first count. *Cortex smuggling. It figures*, Captain Hugh thinks. *No wonder the pot she offered was so sweet.*

He watches the woman stride smoothly down the ramp, her cloak flaps open to reveal her Khadoran attire.

"You're late." The man in charge steps forward. "Do you not realize the importance of what we do? The season draws to a close and soon winter will be upon us…" He pauses and looks about for a moment, checking the ship's deck. The man's brow furrows. "Where is Dragosni? It was he we were to meet. Not some girl!"

"I do apologize. Captain Dragosni has another commitment." Her voice draws the supervisor into silence. "He has found new employment, in some western gulag, I do believe."

At that news, the Menites draw blades from sheaths, muskets from holsters, and Captain Hugh ducks low in the steering house behind a metal box. He's seen what the woman can do. He has no doubt she can handle twenty as easily as one, and having dodged stray fire before, his survival instincts take over. Several among the crew follow their captain's example, while others stand about, stupidly looking on.

"So, girl, what did you think to bring in those crates? Cortexes or no, you'll be coming back with us... a scrutator will wipe that smirk off your pretty face." The man moves forward threateningly.

"Twice you have called me 'girl.' You will not do so a third time, do you understand? My name is Kommander Kratikoff." Her voice cuts through the men, drawing them silent. The Menites pointing muskets at the woman lower their weapons upon hearing her name, fearing to draw the renowned warcaster's ire.

"I am here to deliver a proclamation. Listen and mark my words. Her majesty Queen Vanar formally requests that the Protectorate immediately cease calling upon her subjects to assemble in their damnable theocracy. No matter their faith, they are Khadorans first."

With those words, she levels her gaze at the supervisor. "You," she points at him. "Tell your overseer there will be no more cortex deliveries from Khador. From this day forward, Khadoran labors are not for the Protectorate to exploit. Consider our gates and factories closed. Do you understand?"

The man appears baffled. He hesitates, his mouth moving as if struggling to form words, but no sound comes forth. A muffled, clanking noise emanates from the deck of the river vessel, grabbing the attention of most of the crew, as well as the Menites on the pier. The noise yields an unpleasant familiarity.

Sorscha Kratikoff's eyes bore into the man, bringing him back to focus on her hardening face. "Do you understand, you fool?"

The man swallows and nods awkwardly. "Y-yes. But—"

The woman does not allow him to say more. "Best to run quickly if you wish to avoid the fate of your comrades. Go now."

The noises on the deck increase in volume, and the crew is now moving away from two massive crates. The supervisor turns to face his men, then begins running back down the pier at top speed. The others watch him retreat, then catching on, they, too, begin running; for them, however, it is too late. An icy wind, colder than the bite of deepest winter, envelopes them. Captain Hugh, from the steering house, blinks in disbelief as he witnesses all of the Menites immediately frozen in place, save one, their leader, who has nearly cleared the pier in his flight.

"Tell your warcasters to stay out of Llael!" Sorscha yells after the fleeing Menite.

She turns and strides back up the ramp and onto the deck of the *Lady of Llael*. The two massive crates burst open, and a pair of Destroyer warjacks emerges from the ruined tinder. The constructs' torsos pivot toward the pier, and they aim their weapons. The low thumps of the bombards precede the explosive shells that rain death onto the helpless Menites, turning each man into icy, bloody shards. From the bank, the supervisor watches, aghast, and once the carnage is complete, he scrambles away from the river as fast as he possibly can.

Ten days after his arrival, the Grand Scrutator strides across the factory quad, his boots imparted seemingly with the will of Menoth as clouds of dust rise with each step. His impatience grows as he paces, and the anger inside of him boils. Had he the men to do so, he would strip Feora of her rank and put her screaming on the menofix right now, but he keeps himself in check.

The Priestess of the Flame emerges from her quarters. A group of Flameguard immediately snaps to attention and moves to escort her. She navigates across the quad, meeting the Grand Scrutator halfway.

"You wished to speak with me, Severius?" Her address, calling him by his proper name, shows such disrespect for his station he can barely contain himself. They had not gotten along well, as he had anticipated, during his stay. He forces his emotions down like angry dogs, and composes himself.

"You have done nothing about this Khadoran kommander's message. Nothing!" He feels his rage rise again.

"Perhaps because, in your zeal, you wracked the messenger before I could gather much needed information. We have no way of proving anything to the Hierarch save for the fact that we are more than two dozen cortexes short and our efforts are now delayed by months! At least the man lasted long enough for us to determine it *was* a Khadoran

kommander, and a woman I might add, but any other information died with him on the wrack."

The Grand Scrutator begins to speak, but Feora cuts him off. "Consider your words carefully, your eminence. You don't run this facility, and you are not my commander, not in times of war or peace, and certainly not here. My faith is as strong as yours; however, my inner fire tempers my wrath. You should look to your inner fire, as well."

The Priestess hesitates for Severius to respond, but the masked scrutator merely stares at her. She can see the wrath in the eyes of his mask, and she can only imagine how contorted the remainder of his face may appear. He is a sermonizer, and not one given to being preached to, even by a priestess of the same faith.

Feora realizes that she needs to distract his attentions, if but a little, to soothe the man's rage. She looks about the factory and shakes her head. "Set back at least three months, perhaps six. I imagine the Hierarch will call for flensing all around. With so few Reckoners in the arsenal, we'll need more cortexes to complete our army."

Severius's masked countenance looks away from her, taking in the goings-on about them. Slowly, he nods in agreement, and Feora can feel his anger washing away with the waters of reason. "We shall have to raid for cortexes," he speaks softly. "If possible, we must seize more of those who can create them… Heed me, Feora… I have just had a vision…"

Feora steps closer, and begins to listen to Severius' plan.

"Why in damnation are they sending a bloody warcaster after bloody smugglers?" the sergeant asks his lieutenant, voice low to avoid being overheard. "This don't seem right to me, takin' over your command like this, sir."

Captain Gormleigh casts a sidelong glance at the warcaster who stands yards away at the bow of the warship before he answers his infuriated sergeant. "I reckon it's because we're not chasing your regular rumrunners, sergeant. We're likely after something larger."

"So wot's all so bloody important then I wonder?" asks the sergeant, wiping his nose with a heavily soiled rag.

"Scuttlebutt is that smugglers had a fallout with some Menites, could be some warjacks is involved," says Gormleigh. "That might be what we're after. I can't say for certain."

"Blimey! Double-crossin' rotgut bastards! Curse them and their—"

"That will be all, sergeant," says the captain tersely, his eyes narrowed. The man salutes and steps away, leaving the captain to finger the tiny golden menofix he keeps hidden in his pocket.

Rather than try to unravel the conflicting emotions of Cygnaran patriotism and Menite spiritualism that twist his guts, Gormleigh walks across the deck to stand beside the warcaster, who is scanning the left bank.

"Sir," begins Gormleigh, but before he can continue, the warcaster spins about.

"Hard over!" the lean warcaster shouts. "Helmsman, make for that stone pier! Soldiers on deck, weapons and ammo only! Everyone debark as soon as we drop anchor! I mean everyone! Move!"

The warcaster begins stomping aft but Gormleigh bellows after him, "Lieutenant Caine! Might I inquire, sir, what this is about?"

"That's where they unloaded," replies Allister Caine, aiming a gloved finger to the starboard shore. "The bodies, captain. You can't smell them? Doesn't look like the smugglers left much more than gibbets for the ravens."

Caine snorts sharply, clearing the stench of rotting flesh from his nostrils. "I hope your tracker's up to the task; I doubt there were survivors, but you never know."

As the ship lands ashore, long gunners and trenchers hop into the shallow waters of the riverbank, scanning the shattered corpses with rifles at the ready. Caine and the captain leap from the deck as well, their boots splashing in the thick silt. The bodies around the stone pier are ripped apart. Large craters leave a telltale sign. Caine grunts in recognition.

"Lieutenant?" Gormleigh inquires.

"These craters, pretty distinct… I'd be a fool for saying, but these were bombards. No mercs in this territory that I know of have access or use bombards."

"Khadorans, then? Here?"

"I doubt it. Likely just a salvaged bombard riveted to a Nomad by some dodgy junker. It definitely looks like the smugglers weren't on the side of the Menites, that's for damn sure. Poor sods." Caine chuckles, while Gormleigh feels a flush of anger. Calming himself, he attends to Caine while carefully hiding his displeasure.

Off in the distance a long gunner yells something indistinct, then from a group of nearby trenchers a trooper runs over to the lieutenant. "Sir, we've found something."

"What?" Caine expects a dead smuggler. Maybe a priest.

"Tracks, sir. Prolly a survivor. Dead run, due east... trail is a day old, maybe two."

"Let's get a move on then, soldier! Let's go."

As the two warcasters huddle over maps and go over Severius' strategy, a lone man runs past them yelling over the din of the manufacturing efforts. "Now, what might that be about?" inquires the Grand Scrutator, raising his head.

Feora looks in the same direction. She spies the lone Menite running in a most unecclesiastical fashion, waving his arms and yelling something that is inaudible over the hissing, pounding, and rattling sounds of mechanikal industry. She turns to one of her aides, but the man is already moving to intercept the panicked disciple.

The priestess confers with Severius for a few more minutes, speaking loudly to be heard over the work, and explains the nuances of navigating the route north to Llael. She pauses, and glances up to check on the progress of her aide.

He is already returning, crouching low, and zigzagging as he closes. Further on, Feora sees the formerly panicked disciple lying face down, a pool of blood encircling his head. She glances to her aide in time to see him stumble and fall. He gets back up, limping badly, blood spattering his white robes. He jerks to the side, falls once more, and does not move.

"To arms!" she bellows, and the force or her voice carries over the din. "To arms!"

She flexes the grotesque fingers of her mechanikal gauntlets and mentally commands her warcaster armor to run at full power. "Now, your eminence," she says, "permit me to demonstrate."

"But the boilers—" the Grand Scrutator protests but, in defiance of decorum, Feora takes immediate leave, not allowing him to finish. She runs purposefully across the grounds to where the completed Reckoners stand inert. Faithful vassals swarm around each one, igniting the pilot fires, stoking the furnaces, and pulling off the transport locks, but the desperation in their eyes betrays the futility of their work. It takes a long time to properly heat a steam boiler to proper operating temperature—far too long if Cygnaran long gunners are nearby.

Feora intones a prayer to Menoth, begging his intervention to assist in the destruction of Morrowan heathens. Then she opens the valves on her gauntlets and bathes a chosen warjack's burner and boiler with a blast of Menoth's Fury from her gauntlets. The flame burns brightly, too brightly to be natural, and engulfs the warjack entirely. In a few moments, the fires fade and the warjack lumbers to life, steam wisping away from its vents. Feora watches the boiler cool from its red-hot state, dumping its heat into the water. The metal pings and creaks with thermal stress, but the boiler holds and the great mechanikal warjack steps forward.

The priestess scans the battlefield. Ahead, she sees a line of long gunners aiming their weapons in preparation for another volley. No sign of other forces save a few trenchers scattered about. While trenchers, with their dirty tricks, ordinarily give her pause, this is her battlefield, not theirs.

Among the Menite faithful, workers scatter back and forth, one step away from panic. Around the camp, loyal Flameguard return from their posts to assist in defending the camp, but they won't arrive at her side for several moments. Behind her, Severius raises his arms to heaven, beseeching Menoth's aid. She has little to back her counterattack, but then, it appears the Cygnarans have no warjacks.

She reaches out with her mind and touches the cortex of her warjack, then also takes control of a Vanquisher that had just been completed and moved into position. Although neither is running at full power, Feora is confident that they will be enough for her to crush the Cygnarans.

She boldly strides toward the foe, her faith well placed in both Menoth and her warcaster armor. The new warjacks take their positions, one to each side of her. She'd rather charge the enemy line outright, but she can sense the warjacks' boilers haven't built up enough pressure to sustain such a long run.

Feora watches the line of long gunners erupt in cottony blossoms as they let loose another volley. She staggers slightly as the lead projectiles impact her armor's protective field, and she hears the whistle of other missiles just missing her. Suddenly,

surprisingly, she feels a burning sensation in her left shoulder. She glances down and sees welling blood staining her pristine robes.

"Menoth's stripes!" the incredulous priestess chants beneath her breath a common soldier's curse. Then, she sets her jaw and unloads twin blasts of Menoth's fire at her warjacks' boilers, praying that her god will help the flames stoke them to a full head of steam. She urges her warjacks in front of her as protection from further sniping, slipping portions of her will into their cortexes, goading them to charge. *Menoth, let them have enough to last*, she prays silently.

Feora runs just behind them, her eyes absently taking in the terrain; keeping her focus on the warjacks like this makes her feel like she is in a stupor. Only her rigorous training keeps her moving. As the trio reaches the enemy, she hears the long gunners cry out. The Vanquisher warjack unloads a heavy blast of Menoth's fire, and their agonized screams harmonize wonderfully with the crackle of the fire and the sizzle of body fats. The Reckoner's condemner cannon fires a hot shell into a trencher, sending him burning to Urcaen. As the trenchers pull back, the Reckoner closes in and smashes two of them into bloody meat with the heavy Consecrator mace in its left hand. A thick cloud of incense begins to surround it as the Consecrator emits choking smoke partially concealing the warjack from enemy fire.

A blow from behind penetrates her armor's field and impacts heavily on her burnished helmet. She turns to see a trencher looking with surprise and dismay at the butt of his firearm, broken by its impact with her blessed armor. She lashes out with one hand and opens the flue of her gauntlets, letting fire purify his heathen soul.

Glancing around, Feora spies some survivors fleeing away from her and the 'jacks. She indicates for her Flameguards to intercept the survivors before they can get away and they begin pursuit. In mere moments, just like that, the skirmish is over. Feora breathes a sigh of relief, becoming more aware of the rising pain in her shoulder. She stops short. "Those heretic dogs will pay for this," the priestess vows.

"Indeed they will," comes Severius' voice as approaches from several yards away.

The Grand Scrutator arrives at her side, leaning heavily upon his staff. In the bright light of day, she sees nothing behind the glossy reflections of his mask but dark shadows.

"Cygnar will *indeed* pay for their temerity, Priestess," he says coldly.

Feora nods her approval and looks over the camp, her eyes finally coming to rest on the smoldering corpses of the enemy. "As you say. It appears our testing is suddenly ahead of schedule."

She looks back at the Grand Scrutator's masked visage. "I shall accompany you on your return to Imer. I must prepare the Flameguard."

It will be a long trip home, the scrutator thinks.

Lieutenant Allister Caine lies concealed by a thin shrub growing along the bank of the river. It is scant cover, so the majority of his body is in the water, slowly growing more chilled as time passes. Only his head, shoulders, and one arm are above the water's surface, and he watches the events downstream with bitter self-loathing.

He'd expected to find Menite warjacks, to be sure. He just hadn't expected to find them fully assembled and under a head of steam. He also hadn't expected to find two warcasters. Two! If only he'd had more soldiers, if only there'd been just one warcaster, if only his shot had been on the mark and struck the Menite wench in the throat, if only…

Caine grimly clenches his jaw. The sacrifice of his entire detachment was a hard price to pay for his near escape, but the knowledge he now had from witnessing the facilities size must reach the ears of the Royal Assembly. The Protectorate was gearing up for war like never before, or at least not since the Civil War. *Damned bloody zealots! First unsanctioned warjacks, now a standing army. Evidently, treaties lose power over time.*

Caine still has the tang of his own blood in his mouth. He spits softly. His gaze scans for enemies in the pre-dusk. They had abandoned the search for him, no doubt thinking he was long gone. He watches, quiet and motionless, as workers carry the bodies of the Cygnaran soldiers and sailors aboard the river vessel, dropping them in a haphazard heap. Their grisly task done, they cast the ship adrift on the river, while the warcaster wench burns away any last vestiges of Cygnaran blood.

Soon there will be no trace of the group that debarked here in pursuit of the smugglers.

Nothing left… but Caine.

As the last of the Menites leaves the area, he pulls himself out of the muck of the riverbank and begins walking purposefully in the direction of Fort Falk, his mission not yet ended. In fact, it appears for Cygnar things have only just begun.

Under a starlit sky, crisp with the promise of winter, a ship drifts slowly downstream. Its canted rudder causes the vessel to spin ever so slightly as the current carries it along. A Cygnaran flag hangs limply from its stern, as if the flagpole itself is shrouded in mourning for the dead soldiers carelessly piled on its deck.

belly. Slowly, several shapes emerge from the water and work their way up the sides, over the gunwale, and onto the deck. Their bare, dead feet flap wetly in the darkness as they move over to the pile of corpses. One-by-one they haul the carcasses to the railing, thoughtlessly pulling them by limb, clothes, or hair.

Floating above them on wings of gossamer shadow, a figure in iron and black cloth descends to the steering house. As he lands, a ghostly wisp resembling a woman in dark armor settles to the deck beside him. Slowly solidifying in the cold night, the warwitch called Deneghra stands beside Asphyxious

No sound breaks the funereal silence; even the river frogs have stilled their incessant croaking as the ship passes by. The water stirs beneath the ship's keel, an unnatural welling that spreads across the glassy river like a rash. The shift sets the ship to rocking, and its timbers creak as it rolls. Then it slows to a stop, and the passing current trickles and burbles past the now-stationary hull.

Hands paw their way to the surface of the river, then dig unfeeling claws into the wood of the ship's

to witness the work of their minions on the deck of the leaning riverboat.

"So silent and diligent in their tasks, so perfect in their function… beautiful really, the order of undeath itself." Deneghra looks upon the thralls laboriously working to salvage the remains on the deck.

"Yes, and as war takes its toll, our numbers shall grow, filled with the reanimated dead of our enemies."

The lich says in a voice like an iron grate. "We gather an army from beneath them."

Deneghra gazes at Asphyxious, looking upon the face of her mentor. "We shall swell up from below and consume them all."

The iron lich nods silently in agreement, satisfied with the work of the thralls. Turning to face the shore he signals to Deneghra that it is time to leave the boat. His dark wings take light again, carrying him to the silent shore of the Black River. Deneghra follows closely, her ghostly form flitting across the deep cold waters.

Splashes break the darkness as the dead are tossed into the dark water. The bodies float for an instant before unseen hands tug them down, leaving nothing but a few tiny bubbles to mark their existence to the surface world.

Once the decks are cleared of all but blood, the thralls lumber back off the deck and let themselves drop into the water's icy embrace. They sink to the bottom as the derelict vessel is released to the current once more. Then, as a group, the dead creatures move away with their grisly burden, toward a rendezvous with their masters.

As WARMACHINE continues to grow and evolve, regular model releases will introduce exciting new elements and options to the game including new unit types and abilities. WARMACHINE: Escalation adds dozens of never-before-seen models such as weapon teams, jack marshals, and unit attachments. This section details the new rules required to play with the models introduced in Escalation.

JACK MARSHAL

A rare combination of mage and warrior not common in the Iron Kingdoms, warcasters are elite military leaders. Supporting their armies are capable soldiers specially trained to command warjacks without the benefit of magical skills. These specialists, called jack marshals, can control warjacks using gestures and commands shouted out across the battlefield. While this is not as efficient as using focus, the jack marshal can guide a warjack to perform maneuvers it normally would not be able to do on its own. Though they are not warcasters, jack marshals may begin the game controlling one or more warjacks. These warjacks are not part of any warcaster's battle group.

The number of warjacks a jack marshal can control is listed in parenthesis beside the Jack Marshal special ability in the model's description. For example, *Jack Marshal (2)* can be found in the Man-O-War Kovnik's model description, so he may begin the game controlling two warjacks. Each jack marshal has a marshaling range equal to his CMD stat in inches. A controlled warjack within marshaling range of its controller may run, charge, or boost an attack or damage roll once per activation. A warjack gains these benefits even if its controlling jack marshal is stationary.

If the jack marshal is destroyed or removed from play, his warjacks become *autonomous* but do not become inert. Autonomous warjacks remain active but do not have a controller. An autonomous warjack acts normally but may not be marshaled or allocated focus, though it may receive focus from other sources. A warjack must have a controller at the start of the game and may not begin autonomous.

A jack marshal may reactivate one friendly inert warjack of the same faction per turn in the same manner as a warcaster. The reactivated warjack comes under the jack marshal's control unless he already controls his limit of warjacks. If the jack marshal already controls his limit, the warjack becomes autonomous. Likewise, if an opposing player takes control of a jack marshal, with the use of the Convert or Dark Seduction spells for example, a warjack controlled by the marshal remains under the control of its original player and becomes autonomous. If control of the jack marshal is returned to his original player, the jack marshal resumes control of the warjack.

A warcaster or jack marshal who does not already control his limit of warjacks may take control of an autonomous friendly warjack of the same faction. To take control of the warjack, the warcaster or jack marshal must be in base-to-base contact with the jack and forfeit his action but may still cast spells and use special abilities. The warjack must forfeit its activation and cannot channel spells on the turn it becomes controlled. Beginning with the next turn, it may be marshaled or allocated focus.

MERCENARY WARCASTERS, JACK MARSHALS, AND WARJACKS

Mercenary warjacks may only be included in a battlegroup controlled by a mercenary warcaster or assigned to a mercenary jack marshal. Warcasters belonging to a faction may not control mercenary warjacks. Mercenary warcasters and jack marshals can only control mercenary warjacks and cannot control warjacks belonging to a faction. Mercenary warcasters may only give orders to mercenary units and may rally only mercenary models.

REPLACING MODELS

When replacing one model with another, place the new model so that the area covered by the smaller of the bases is completely within the area covered by the larger. If two bases are the same size, place the new model in the same location as the one being replaced.

UNIT ATTACHMENTS

Unit attachments are made up of one or more models that may be added to a unit specified in the unit attachment's description. Only one unit attachment may be added to any unit. A model in the unit attachment with the Officer special ability becomes the new unit leader. The original unit leader remains part of the unit but loses the Leader ability while the officer is in play. The original unit leader cannot issue orders without the Leader ability but may use all of its other abilities. If the new unit leader is destroyed or removed from play, the original unit leader regains its Leader ability.

For instance, if a Monolith Bearer unit attachment is added to a Holy Zealot unit, the Monolith Bearer becomes the new unit leader. The Priest is no longer the unit leader and may not issue commands to the unit but may still use Prayers of Menoth. If the Monolith Bearer is destroyed or removed from play, the Priest becomes the unit leader again.

A unit attachment increases the victory point value of the unit to which it is added by an amount detailed in the description of the unit attachment.

Weapon Crews

Weapon crews are small units that operate large or cumbersome weapons. Weapon crews are made up of a Gunner and one or more Crewmen. Unlike other units, weapon crews do not have leaders. A weapon crew cannot run or charge. The Gunner gains +2" of movement for each Crewman from his own unit in base-to-base contact with him when he begins his activation. If the Gunner takes sufficient damage to be destroyed, a Crewman within 1" can take the destroyed Gunner's place immediately, becoming a new Gunner. Remove the Crewman from the table instead of the Gunner. The damaged Gunner is destroyed. Any effects or spells on the damaged Gunner expire. Any effects or spells on the removed crewman are applied to the new Gunner.

Even though the Gunner is on a larger-sized base, it is treated as a small-based model. A Gunner only blocks line of sight to models with small bases. It does not block line of sight to a model with a medium-sized base or larger, nor does it screen such a model from a ranged or magic attack. Intervening models of any base size block line of sight to a Gunner and screen him.

CYGNAR

PROGRESS

Commander Coleman Stryker strides toward the small group gathered in the proving grounds, his battered greatcoat swaying with his confident gait. The grass is all but gone from the rocky soil, killed by iron feet, electric strikes, and magical explosions, and the hobnails in Stryker's boots scratch and clack on the multitude of exposed stones in the dirt.

A hundred yards beyond the group, a warjack stands immobile, un-powered, stark against the overcast autumn sky.

Stryker heads for the silver-haired man at the center of the assembly. As he draws near, the others gathered about nod in greeting to him as they move respectfully aside, continuing to excitedly talk amongst themselves.

Stryker stops and hails his fellow warcaster, the renowned Sebastian Nemo. "Sir, I heard you were looking for me?" he asks casually.

Nemo watches the group move away from them a few more yards, then turns to regard Coleman Stryker over the rim of his spectacles. "Looking? You heard wrong. I *summoned* you."

Stryker frowns. "After all this time and me even a commander, you still insist on treating me like an apprentice."

Nemo's blue eyes become as cool as a mountain lake in winter. Stryker immediately ducks his head and holds up a hand. "No! No stare downs. Please."

Nemo smiles thinly. "I am a commander adept. My apprentice you'll remain until you have the iron to—"

"I know, I know. Don't bother saying the rest, lest either my ears or your tongue develop a repeated stress fissure."

At that, Nemo's countenance cracks, and the two laugh together. They clasp forearms. "How have you been, my boy?"

"Well enough for six months busting hump in the field. Knackered, flea bites to last me all winter, and I think I'll have to chisel the mank from my pits." Stryker stretches his shoulders back. "Thank Morrow winter will end the campaign season."

Nemo smiles. "Aye that. The Assembly has me on winter watch this year. A couple patrols, a lot of grog by the fire. They must think the years are catching up to old Nemo."

Stryker shakes his head and merely grants his mentor a barely audible snort.

The older man seems to take note of the younger one's reticence, but decides it's not much of an issue for debate. Whatever the Royal Assembly wants. For king and country and all that. Nemo nods and moves the conversation along. "So... how're those borders?"

"Secure enough. Although the smugglers are making a killing."

Nemo nods sagely. "Spill it, boy."

"It's tense out there," Stryker replies. "Khadorans angling for a scrum to prove their mettle, Menites who'd knife you in the back as soon as spit on you, and always reports of black ships off the coast. Everyone wants something, and they're all ready to carve it out of our hide, seems like."

They pause for a moment, and then Stryker asks, "So what have you been doing up here all this time?"

Nemo smiles thinly. "I knew you'd ask. I think you'll want to see this. My latest experiment in warjack mechanika."

Stryker scratches the side of his head as he looks out at the behemoth in the field. "Looks like a clapped-out Ironclad to me."

"It's one of the first," says Nemo. "You recall the one with the warble in its cortex? The mechaniks wanted to scrap it, but I asked them to let me have it instead."

"Oh, aye?"

"Aye. So I put a little time into it and swapped out the furnace for a storm chamber."

"What?" Stryker raises his eyebrows appreciatively. "Like in a storm glaive?"

"Something like that... on a much larger scale. I reckon this old 'jack should bust out a lot more power now. More than what coal can provide. Better yet, no coal, no need for a steam boiler. It's proven more responsive, more reliable. With a company of these, Coleman, we can have the best military tool in the world.

"Think of it," whispers the commander adept. "No smoke plumes to give away our position. Operating for days away from base camp—*days*, my boy! No need to depend on supply trains for coal. Our first-strike capability will be top crack, and the enemy will never know where our strongest defenses are lurking.

"*That*," he closes, poking Stryker in the chest with one gnarled finger, "is what I've been doing up here... and it's all for hotshot upstarts like *you*."

Nemo stands up straight, a smug smile on his face. "I asked you to be here because, my boy, I wanted you to be present for the first field test. Apprentice."

Stryker rubs his chin. "If it's all that you say it is, the Khadorans are going to be spitting teeth over it. They'll say we're gearing up for a scrum. You're not concerned that Queen Ayn won't use the deployment of this warjack as an excuse to attack us again?"

Nemo snorts and waves a hand dismissively. "Stuff that. I've never known a war to start because Cygnar was too strong. Now, pay attention." Nemo gestures and a nearby aide waves a red flag.

Out on the field, a gobber sidles up to the warjack. He leans gingerly forward, reaches with his left hand toward a bright yellow lever on the warjack's back, then inches forward again until his hand can grasp the handle. After a moment's hesitation, the gobber thinks better of it and grasps the handle with his right hand. He then pulls his hand back, wipes the sweat off on his jersey, then grips the handle one more time. To his right, Stryker hears Nemo murmur impatiently.

Then, in one fluid motion, the gobber throws the switch and dashes madly for cover, arms covering his head.

Stryker hears a howl, sounding like a gale through tree branches, as the 'jack powers up. The howl rises in pitch to a whine, then to a sort of whistle. The warjack comes to life, its eyes and vents glowing with a powerful ice-blue light, not the customary coal-fire red that Stryker is used to seeing. The behemoth starts quivering like it's ready to surge forward, and even from that distance, Stryker's hair starts to stand on end.

"Goggles," says Nemo.

"Right," says Stryker distractedly as he fumbles in the pockets of his greatcoat for his goggles and puts them on, as do the other lookers-on clustered to their far right.

There is a long pause, and Stryker hazards a glance at his mentor. Nemo wears a wry smile.

"Sir?"

"Let's see what this great bucket of dregs can do, shall we?" says the commander adept.

Stryker plugs his ears. If Nemo intends to test the 'jack the way he gambles, well...

Nemo stretches out his arms and forms his fingers and thumbs into a diamond shape, his eyes glowering with concentration. As he exhales, the warjack bursts into action. It steps back, swings a left backfist at an imaginary target, and follows immediately with a right hook. The momentum of the swings pulls the warjack forward, and

it stumbles a little. Stryker hears the familiar clangor as the warjack's leg or arm piston rends loose from its housing cylinder.

"Sir—"

"Stuff it!" Nemo's face breaks into a combat smile, and Stryker can feel the arcane power the commander adept is pumping into the machine. It starts to charge across the open ground.

The warjack abruptly explodes—a single high-pitched concussion of intense blue energy.

Stryker winces with the flash and sound, hears a large shard of the warjack's armored hull whistling as it spins past, mere feet over the group. The pattering of iron rain thuds all about them, and the commander looks skyward to ensure that no large pieces are destined to fall near him, his mentor, or any of the others. He realizes then that he is the only one standing; the rest of the assembly are prone, their arms covering their heads... except for Nemo, who lies flat on his back, a rivulet of blood draining from one nostril.

"Sir!" Stryker drops to his knees beside the older man. He bites the fingertips of one glove and yanks it off, then gently presses his fingers to Nemo's neck to check for a pulse.

"Get your filthy hands off my gizzard," groans Nemo.

Stryker leans back on his heels as Nemo pulls off his goggles, rubs his temples, then smears the blood across his face with the back of his hand. With a long exhalation, he rolls to his knees, then uses Stryker's extended arm to stand upright on wobbly legs.

He squints out at the ruined warjack, little more than a pair of arms and legs attached to a smoldering bowl of twisted metal.

"The storm chamber must have overloaded," he grimaces. "Feedback blew the cortex. Bloody near fried mine, too."

"Well," says Stryker helpfully, "I have to admit it certainly has more power than what I'm used to seeing. Have to be able to control it better... maybe throttle it back some."

Nemo looks at Stryker and snorts. "That's funny," he says. "Listen to you, my boy."

"Funny?"

"Throttle it back?" he says, poking Stryker in the chest, "You saying *that* to *me*."

Stryker laughs, and then helps a shaken looking man nearby to his feet. "We'd best see to this wreckage, sir. Good thing you have a long, quiet winter ahead of you to work out all the kinks."

Nemo surveys the smoking ruin of his latest project with a scowl and grumbles.

COMMANDER ADEPT SEBASTIAN NEMO

WARCASTER

*"The grandeur of Cygnar will not long be forgotten. On the face of Immoren, it is legendary.
It is certainly the most powerful… the wealthiest… but because of this, we have a responsibility
to uphold, to protect the people, especially the poor, the underprivileged, the weak, and the young…
great is the nation that looks to its future."*

—Excerpt from Commander Adept Sebastian Nemo's graduation speech adressed to the Strategic Academy graduating class, Solesh of 604 AR

Commander Adept Sebastian Nemo has served the nation he loves well into his twilight years, becoming the most famous warcaster in Cygnaran history. The magelock-toting Allister Caine has been overheard referring to Nemo as "a relic whose reputation eclipses his fading power." Despite views by some self-styled radicals such as Caine, the Commander Adept is a potent and welcome presence on any battlefield and a man who has had a legendary effect on the Cygnaran Royal Army.

Sebastien Nemo had a keen insight beyond his years from an early age. His heart was stirred by tales of turmoil and glory, and as a youth he was close to his grandfather who had fought and lost two brothers in the legendary Battle of the Tongue during the Thornwood War. Nemo showed a proclivity for magic early on as well, but rather than be apprenticed to one of his wealthy family's wizards, he requested enrollment in the Royal Cygnaran University's Strategic Academy. In Caspia, Nemo excelled as a student of the sciences as well as in the arts of both war and magic. He eventually graduated with honors and chose to stay on at the Academy to become one of the very few to bear the title of commander for his martial prowess and adept for his mystical abilities.

Over his lifetime he has endured several hardships, not the least of which was the loss of a brother during a secret mission under Nemo's command. The next year, he lost one of his best friends in a similar situation. A few years after that, his wife took their daughter and left him because he could not pull himself away from his work. She died just months later of the disease rip lung, and the guilt of not being there for her with all of his family's resources and connections haunts him still. He was saved from the bottle by the survival of his little girl, but he soon enough became engrossed with his duties again and sent her away from Caspia to be raised by his family in the Shieldpoint province.

During Vinter the Elder's reign, Nemo became rather embittered with the Crown, although he was wise enough to keep most of his opinions to himself on how he felt about the despot Raelthorne's treatment of the kingdom and its people. Indeed, Nemo's continued service had him rising rapidly in the ranks, yet he chose to pass up the position of general to focus on weapon research and development—neither choice sat well with him at the time, but he preferred to be away from the atrocities committed in the field by Vinter's hand-picked troops. Decades later, no one denies that Nemo's inventions are changing the way Cygnar fights its battles. In addition to many experimental devices, he is credited with the development of the infamous storm glaive.

Nemo was roused from his work during the Scharde Invasions of 584–588 AR. He took to the years-long struggle in a suit of warcaster armor of his own design, based

22

on electromagnetic power rather than steam, and was instrumental in pushing the intruders back from Cygnar's shores during that bloody, horrific campaign in which he witnessed "untold brutality and horrors beyond mention."

A few short years thereafter, the graying warcaster made the decision to lend his hand against his own King Vinter in lieu of his brother, the usurper Leto the Younger. It is a decision he does not regret. Since King Leto's rulership, Nemo has once again taken to the battlefield with a renewed commitment. In combat, he relies primarily on his magical prowess. His ability to control and influence warjacks is legendary, as is the variety and power of his arcane repertoire. Though he prefers to rely on his magic, he carries his lightning rod for when the battle gets personal. His armor makes him a curious sight as well: while most warcasters are demarked with a red furnace glow and smoke plumes, Nemo crackles with crawling static releases and, in the darkness, emits a faint nimbus of light.

For the past decade and a half, several high thinkers have denigrated many of Nemo's theories, calling them madness induced by tireless decades of over-study—and perhaps a touch of combat neurosis—but like his namesake, the legendary Sebastien Kerwin, he has proven himself the rarest of creatures: a visionary who forges his dreams into reality. Nevertheless, there may be a kernel of truth to their claims. The fervor with which Nemo hones his inventions indicates he may well be, at the core of his being, a madman—although certainly a genius one.

Many say he throws himself into his work because of the loss of so many of those who were dear to him. True or not, today his only true friend seems to be Commander Coleman Stryker, whom he mentored through his journeyman days. Nemo sees great potential in Stryker and he constantly belittles his "apprentice," goading him to excel ever more. Stryker responds with mock sarcasm, but Nemo can see his good-natured badgering has instilled a burning desire in Stryker to surmount all barriers, be they personal or in the field.

Commander Stryker aside, Nemo is misunderstood for the most part by the rest of his contemporaries. He is viewed as harsh, arrogant, demanding, and an eccentric visionary lacking social refinement, but the truth is quite different. Despite his fortunate birth into a wealthy, connected family, he has a deep sense of noblesse oblige—he started with more than most, so he feels he must give all of himself to his country. If his standards are soaring, it is because he drives himself as hard as he can and expects his subordinates to keep up. If he flaunts his power, it is to show others what they can achieve if they persevere. If he has few friends, it is because he has embraced Cygnar itself as his one and only love.

FEAT: ELECTRICAL STORM

Commander Adept Nemo can exert control over the forces of voltaic energy, and is capable of bending electro-magnetism to his will with the advanced mechanika packed into his warcaster armor. By attuning the coils and resonant accumulators in his warcaster armor, and summoning a sufficient amount of arcane energy into the coils, he can unleash a dynamic storm of intense static energy. The resonating pulse of electrical force released destroys foreign warjack cortices and irreparably damages their mechanikal systems.

All enemy warjacks currently within Nemo's control area suffer a POW 14 damage roll and Disruption. This damage may be boosted. A warjack damaged by Electrical Storm takes one additional point of damage to its first available cortex system box. Mark this damage after marking the normal damage from Electrical Storm.

FOCUS	7	CMD	8

SPD	STR	MAT	RAT	DEF	ARM
5	4	5	5	14	14

ELECTRICAL BURST

	RNG	ROF	AOE	POW
	8	1	3	14

LIGHTNING ROD

	Special	POW	P+S
	Disrupt	7	11

Damage	14
Point Cost	75
Field Allowance	C
Victory Points	5

Base Size: Small

SPECIAL RULES

- Arcane Accumulator — When another model casts a spell within Nemo's control area, Nemo gains a power token—max 3. On his next control phase, replace each token with a focus point.
- Overpower — During each of his control phases Nemo can increase his control area by 1" per focus point spent for one round.
- Rapid Recharge — For every focus point Nemo spends to regenerate his power field he removes 2 damage points instead of 1.
- Supercharge — During each of his control phases, Nemo may allocate up to 5 focus points to one of his battle group's warjacks within his control area.

ELECTRICAL BURST

- Critical Disruption — On a Critical Hit, target warjack model suffers Disruption. A warjack suffering Disruption loses any unused focus points and cannot be allocated focus points or channel spells for one round.

LIGHTNING ROD

- Disruption — A warjack suffering Disruption loses any unused focus points and cannot be allocated focus points or channel spells for one round.

Spells	Cost	RNG	AOE	POW	UP	OFF
Accelerate	Spec	6	—	—	No	No
Increase target warjack's movement by 1" per focus point spent for 1 round.						
Ball Lightning	4	8	4	13	No	Yes
On a Critical Hit, all warjacks within AOE take one additional point of damage to their first available cortex system box, before marking normal damage.						
Blinding Flash	2	Caster	CTRL	—	No	No
All enemy models within AOE when spell is cast suffer −2 RAT for one round.						
Chain Lightning	3	10	—	10	No	Yes
Lightning arcs from target model to d6 additional models. The lightning arcs, automatically hitting the nearest model within 4" of the last model hit, but cannot strike the same model more than once. Each model hit suffers a POW 10 damage roll.						
Disruption Field	3	6	—	—	Yes	No
Target friendly warjack gains +1 STR and its melee attacks cause Disruption.						
Electrify	2	6	—	—	Yes	No
If target model is hit by a melee attack, after damage is dealt the attacker is pushed back d3" and suffers a POW 14 damage roll which may not be boosted. The spell then expires.						
Voltaic Snare	5	8	*	—	No	Yes
Target warjack cannot move and suffers −4 DEF. While within 3" of target warjack, warjacks cannot run, charge, or slam and can only move directly toward the target warjack. Voltaic Snare lasts for one round.						

STORMCLAD
WARJACK OF RENOWN

"As you stood beside me through tyranny and fear, so shall these tokens of my gratitude stand beside you, lending their strength through the trials to come."

— King Leto Raelthorne, to the assembled Stormblades of Caspia at the Stormclad dedication ceremony

SPD	STR	MAT	RAT	DEF	ARM
5	11	6	5	12	18
					19

GENERATOR BLAST

	RNG	ROF	AOE	POW
RIGHT	6	1	—	14

OPEN FIST

	Special	POW	P+S
LEFT	Buckler	0	11

GENERATOR BLADE

	Special	POW	P+S
RIGHT	Critical	8	19

DAMAGE GRID

SYSTEMS	1	2	3	4	5	6
Left Arm (L)						
Rght Arm (R)		L			R	
Cortex (C)	L	L	M	C	R	R
Movement (M)		M	M	C	C	

Point Cost	128
Field Allowance	2
Victory Points	3

Base Size: Large

In the aftermath following the bloody coup that resulted in Leto Raelthorne's rise to power, there was much dissension amongst those troops who were asked to fight against their own countrymen. Soldiers had cut down friends and neighbors in battle, and Cygnar had some very open wounds to heal. Even King Leto had suffered the loss of his beloved wife to his brother's outlaw forces. Turning from sorrow, the new king set his mind toward rebuilding his country and honoring those heroes who had stood by him.

During the overthrow, few of his supporters showed as much devotion as the knightly Stormblades. Without their sacrifice, Leto doubted if his coup would have met with success. To bolster their ranks, as well as thank them personally for their vigilance in the face of the Exile's tyranny, Leto felt he needed to bestow unto them a special reward. Such patriotism required more than just a medal or a commendation. For their integral role in overthrowing Vinter Raelthorne, Leto set his greatest engineers to the task of developing a grand new weapon to serve the Stormblades in the field, and the Stormclad was the resulting masterpiece and a suitable addition to the ranks.

By taking the impressive bulk and chassis of the Ironclad and arming it with an enormous mechanikal energy weapon, the King's engineers constructed a walking tempest of iron and lightning. Leto gathered his troops in Caspia to witness the Stormclad's presentation to the remaining twelve units of his elite Stormblades. The knights cheered their new king with such feeling that it is said all of Cygnar seemed to be present that day.

A constant nimbus surrounds each massive Stormclad. Thick bolts of blue energy cascade down from the tip of its mighty generator blade, supercharging nearby storm chambers. Energy flows through the generator blade making it unto a force of nature that melts and cleaves through armor like a storm splitting a tree. With ease, the weapon is capable of projecting electrical singularities of raw cataclysmic power, leaping at times from target-to-target.

The Stormclads stood shining and new at their unveiling, each one bearing the sleek banner of the unit to which it was assigned. Since that day, they have become a reminder of good King Leto and his faith in his troops. Now, though patched and worn, the banners rising above the Stormclads have come to represent the struggle to defend all of Cygnar, and each soldier feels that proud surge of patriotism in his heart when they look up to find one of the Stormclads marching alongside them into battle.

SPECIAL RULES

- **Battle Standard** — Friendly Cygnar models/units within 10" of the Stormclad never flee. Fleeing friendly Cygnar models/units within 10" of the Stormclad immediately rally.
- **Chain Reaction** — After a successful blast attack made by a friendly Stormblade within 3" of the Stormclad, lightning arcs from the target model to the closest non-Stormblade model within 4". The model suffers a POW 10 damage roll.

GENERATOR BLAST & GENERATOR BLADE

- **Critical Chain Lightning** — On a Critical Hit, lightning arcs from target model to d3 additional non-Stormblade models, ignoring the Stormclad. The lightning arcs, automatically hitting the nearest model within 4" of the last model hit, but cannot strike the same model more than once. Each model hit suffers a POW 10 damage roll. Critical Chain Lightning is not a melee attack.

OPEN FIST

- **Buckler** — The Buckler adds +1 to the Stormclad's ARM. The Stormclad loses this bonus if its left arm system is disabled.

Armament	Generator Blade (right arm), Buckler (left arm)
Fuel Load/Burn Usage	120 Kgs / 6 hrs general, 1 hr combat
Initial Service Date	597 AR
Cortex Manufacturer	Fraternal Order of Wizardry / Cygnaran Armory
Orig. Chassis Design	Engines East, commissioned by order of King Leto under instruction from Commander Adept Nemo

"Victory and the smell of burning powder are linked to the trigger's pull."

—Captain Adept Everett Wallis, Militant Order of the Arcane Tempest

CAPTAIN ADEPT				CMD	8
SPD	STR	MAT	RAT	DEF	ARM
6	4	5	8	15	12

MAGELOCK PISTOL

	RNG	ROF	AOE	POW
	12	1	—	10

SWORD

	Special	POW	P+S
	—	3	7

Damage	5
Point Cost	32
Field Allowance	1
Victory Points	1

Base Size: Small

SPECIAL RULES

- Commander — A Gun Mage Captain Adept has a command range equal to his CMD in inches. Friendly Cygnar models or units within command range may use the Adept's CMD when making a command check. The Adept can rally and give orders to friendly Cygnar models within command range.
- Field Officer — An additional Arcane Tempest Gun Mage unit may be fielded over normal Field Allowance limitations for each Captain Adept included in the army.
- True Sight — A Captain Adept ignores Camouflage, Concealment, and Stealth.

MAGELOCK PISTOL

Arcane Effect — Each time the Magelock Pistol is used to make a ranged attack, choose one of the following effects:

- Blaze — Add an additional die to the damage roll for this attack.
- Flash Fire — Target any model within range regardless of line of sight. Flash Fire ignores cover, obstructions, and intervening models.
- Long Shot — The range of the Magelock Pistol is increased to 18".
- Shocker — Target Warjack hit by this attack automatically takes one point of damage to its first available cortex system box. Mark this damage before making the damage roll.
- Thunderbolt — Target model hit by this attack is pushed back d3". On a Critical Hit, target model is also knocked down.

The journey to becoming a gun mage is difficult and long, and few are good enough to take so much as the first step. Of those who survive the trials and have what it takes to take up the coveted magelock pistol, only a very few make the rank of captain, and fewer still of captain and adept. Gun mages this powerful are rare, and the army reserves them for the most crucial battles and demanding missions. Their skill and prestige is such that they are often given command of additional gun mages in the field, typically a unit of eager young "spell-slingers" always keen to impress.

Many a poor fool has taken cover, thinking himself safe from the deadly aim of a gun mage, but a captain adept need not see his quarry to place a shot in them. Who knows what naked landscape they see when they close their eyes and level the muzzle of their Rhulic-steel pistol? Nevertheless, sure and certain is their aim, and neither concealment nor stealth aids their intended mark. Indeed, several soon-to-be corpses have peered from the trenches to taunt a gun mage for the modest reach of his pistol and swiftly obtained a "blackpenny" between the eyes. The arcane words they speak into their rune-cast rounds greatly increase their range with the famous long shot, and the flash fire bullet is like a thing possessed as it zings from wide to true in the beat of a ruptured heart.

For services rendered, gun mages of this level of power typically earn the title "favorites of the King," but if they are vaunted by those who brought them into being, then they are doubly reviled by those who have the misfortune to face them in the field.

STORMBLADE OFFICER & STANDARD BEARER
STORMBLADE UNIT ATTACHMENT

"Stormblades are the sons of thunder, and their commanders, the eye of the storm."

—Stormblade Lieutenant Vincent Redstrom

It is rare for warriors to enter into legend while they live and breathe and walk upon the earth, but so it is with those known throughout the kingdoms as Stormblades. These renowned Cygnaran knights hold the elemental force of lightning in their grasp and unleash it through the enchanted mechanika of their stormglaives. A single Stormblade is an awesome sight, but to witness them en masse fighting under the banner of the Royal Knights of Cygnar is to glimpse the ancient force that ravaged the bedrock of the primal world.

Fierce winds tear at their banner, but the standard bearer holds fast. He is in his element, raising his standard in salute to the storm as black clouds gather over him like the very embodiment of fury. He plants his feet in the earth and prepares to embrace the terrifying energy that would render to ash any mortal of lesser steel. Then the sky tears open and a searing bolt of lightning forks down from the boiling clouds to engulf him. He is not consumed; he stands there, harnessing the power, until the standard pulses with light, and then with a

unified cry, his blade-brothers come forward. As they raise their glaives, the crackling energy arcs from one to the other and energizes each in turn. Fully charged, the Stormblade Lieutenant calls his knights into line—it is a line that might look thin before the massed ranks of the enemy, but it is the thinness of a cutting blade.

The Lieutenant's subordinates are not the only things he commands, for he is also trained to give orders to warjacks in order to rouse them to battle. Many a foe has been sent to flight by the sight of a warjack lumbering forward to the commands of a Stormblade Lieutenant, and while the Stormblades live, no warjack attacks alone. With a slash of his stormglaive the Lieutenant unleashes the 'blades, and they roll forward with the heavy tread of doom. Forks of energy blast forward as they make controlled fire attacks, and as they close on the enemy, the Lieutenant bellows the final command, "Lightning, strike!" and incandescent spikes lance from their glaives as they lead the charge to victory.

LIEUTENANT				CMD	9
SPD	STR	MAT	RAT	DEF	ARM
5	6	8	6	13	15

STANDARD BEARER				CMD	6
SPD	STR	MAT	RAT	DEF	ARM
5	6	7	4	13	15

STORM GLAIVE BLAST

	RNG	ROF	AOE	POW
	4	1	—	12

STORM GLAIVE

	Special	POW	P+S
	—	7	13

Lieutenant's Damage	5
Lieutenand & Standard Bearer	43
Field Allowance	1
Victory Points	+1

Base Size: Small

SPECIAL RULES

LIEUTENANT

- Controlled Fire (Order) — When issued this order, Stormblades may combine their attacks at the same target instead of making ranged attacks separately, so long as they are in open formation or closer. The Stormblade with the highest RAT in the attacking group makes one ranged attack roll for the group, adding +1 to the attack and damage rolls for each Stormblade, including itself, participating in the attack. Controlled Fire may not target a model in melee.
- Jack Marshal (1) — The Lieutenant may start the game controlling one warjack. The Lieutenant has a marshaling range equal to his CMD in inches. If the controlled warjack is within the Lieutenant's marshaling range, it can run, charge, or boost an attack or damage roll once per activation. If the Lieutenant is destroyed or removed from play, the warjack does not become inert. The Lieutenant may reactivate one friendly inert Cygnar warjack per turn in the same manner as a warcaster. The reactivated warjack comes under his control unless he already controls another warjack.
- Officer — The Lieutenant is the unit leader.

STANDARD BEARER

- Conduit — All Stormblades within open formation gain +1" range and +1 to the POW of their weapons.
- Lightning Strike — Once per game, as part of a Charge, after moving, each Stormblade may make a ranged attack followed by a charge attack with his melee weapon. A Stormblade is not considered to be in melee when making the Lightning Strike's ranged attack.
- Unit Standard — When the Standard Bearer takes sufficient damage to be destroyed, a non-leader trooper model of this unit within 1" of the Standard Bearer may take up the standard. Remove the trooper model from the table and replace it with the Standard Bearer model. Any effects or upkeep spells on the replaced trooper are applied to the Standard Bearer model. Effects and upkeep spells on the destroyed Standard Bearer expire.

UNIT

- Combined Melee Attack — Instead of making melee attacks separately, Stormblades in melee range of the same target may combine their attacks. The Stormblade with the highest MAT in the attacking group makes one melee attack roll for the group, adding +1 to the attack and damage rolls for each Stormblade, including itself, participating in the attack.
- Fearless — Stormblade units never flee.
- Unit Attachment — The Stormblade Unit Attachment can be added to any Stormblade unit. The unit's Victory Point total is increased by 1.

STORMSMITH

SOLO

"…in this enlightened age, even the forces of nature answer our call."

—Commander Adept Nemo, after the unveiling of the first Stormcaller

When the Stormblades first strode across the field of battle, the enemies of Cygnar retreated from the crackling energy of their blades, but now there is nowhere left to run, since from those mighty knights now come the Stormsmiths, and they are terrifying to behold. Stormblade ranks part when the Stormsmiths advance. They come on slow as clouds gather above them, rising up in a bruise-black thunderhead, and the smell of ozone surrounds them like the miasma of impending doom.

A blast of cold air precedes their march like a force of nature as closer they come. Then, standing alone before the enemy, they raise up their dire countenance and electrical light flickers in their eyes. They carry neither arrow nor bow, neither pistol nor long-barreled rifle. They do not need such weapons, for in their mortal hands they hold Stormcallers, mechanikal staves of power able to call down fire from the heavens.

Planting their feet in the earth, they raise their Stormcallers high. They cannot be heard over the rising gale, but their lips move as they form the words of arcane power and call upon the latent charges of the air. Suddenly the sky splits in fury. Dark clouds are rent apart by incandescent bolts that lance down to blast asunder those foolish enough to remain when Stormsmiths are abroad. Do not think it sufficient to duck from view and hide. The Stormsmiths need not see the flesh of the enemy to sear it from their bones. The sky is their eyes, and the twisting forks of light, their wrath. So flee… and pray that the Stormsmith comes alone, for when two or three combine their might, the firestorm that ensues can rage so fierce as to scar the earth for years.

STORMSMITH				CMD	7
SPD	STR	MAT	RAT	DEF	ARM
6	4	5	4	13	11

SWORD			
	Special	POW	P+S
	—	3	7

Point Cost	12
Field Allowance	3
Victory Points	1

Base Size: Small

SPECIAL RULES

Stormcall [8] — As a Special Action, the Stormsmith may call down one of the following lightning strikes. Stormcall lightning strikes are not considered ranged attacks and do not require line of sight. Models hit by a lightning strike suffer a POW 10 damage roll and warjacks are Disrupted. Warjacks suffering Disruption lose any unused focus points and cannot be allocated focus points or channel spells for one round.

- **Single Strike (★ Action)** — With a successful skill check, the Stormsmith calls down a single lightning strike hitting any model within 10".

- **Surge (★ Action)** — A Stormsmith may make a Surge special action if there is another friendly Stormsmith within 20". The Stormsmith may target up to two models whose bases intersect any line drawn between the bases of the two Stormsmiths. Make a skill check to hit each model with a lightning strike. Models may only be targeted once per Surge special action.

- **Triangulation (★ Action)** — A Stormsmith may make a Triangulation special action if he and two other friendly Stormsmiths are within 20" of each other. The Stormsmith may target up to three models whose bases are at least partially within the triangular area between the three Stormsmiths. Make a skill check to hit each model with a lightning strike. Models may only be targeted once per Triangulation special action.

SWORD KNIGHTS

UNIT

"Once taught how to work with the warjacks, we learned how to work against them."

—Captain Fend Hawkwood, Sword Knight

The legendary Sword Knights are masters of the Caspian battleblade. Every knight practices tirelessly with the weapon until it becomes an extension of his will. Upon dubbing, each knight is bestowed a ceremonial battleblade to be kept with him at all times. He is expected to maintain this weapon throughout his life. It is never to be drawn in battle, and upon a valiant knight's death, the blade is buried alongside him to keep him safe in the wilds of Urcaen.

For centuries, the Sword Knights have served as part of the Royal Knights of Cygnar, keeping the realm free of brigands and rampaging beasts, but since the dawn of the warjack, the Sword Knights have also adapted their time-honored tactics to deal with monsters of metal as well as flesh. Upon achieving mastery of the sword, the knights are expected to study the internal workings of warjacks. The intimate knowledge of a 'jack's inner mechanisms allow a knight to pick and choose his targets at openings and joints to wreak considerable damage where it is most effective.

Sword Knights who remain in the service for long tours are rewarded with private tutelage in 'jack marshalling, and esteemed units are often granted warjacks of their own. Because of this practice, these knights are well-versed in maneuvers alongside their 'jack, using their massive counterpart as a spearhead and often fanning out to flank the enemy—a successful tactic they put to use with other friendly warjacks as well if given the chance. The knights accompany their warjack into battle and hold their shields in a fashion to maximize protection from the hail of enemy attacks—no doubt headed for their metal comrade. Long-standing knights often see their unit's 'jack as a battle brother and have been known to lay their lives down for it just as they would any other warrior of flesh and blood that marches under the banner of the Cygnaran Swan.

CAPTAIN				CMD	9
SPD	STR	MAT	RAT	DEF	ARM
6	6	7	4	13	14
KNIGHT				CMD	7
SPD	STR	MAT	RAT	DEF	ARM
6	6	6	4	13	14

BATTLE BLADE			
	Special	POW	P+S
	—	4	10

Leader and 5 Troops	56
Up to 4 Additional Troops	9 ea.
Field Allowance	2
Victory Points	2

Base Size: Small

SPECIAL RULES

CAPTAIN

- Jack Marshal (1) — The Captain may start the game controlling one warjack. The Captain has a marshaling range equal to his CMD in inches. If the controlled warjack is within the Captain's marshaling range, it can run, charge, or boost an attack or damage roll once per activation. If the Captain is destroyed or removed from play, the warjack does not become inert. The Captain may reactivate one friendly inert Cygnar warjack per turn in the same manner as a warcaster. The reactivated warjack comes under his control unless he already controls another warjack.
- Leader

UNIT

- Defensive Line —Any Sword Knight in tight formation with one or more Sword Knights in the unit gains +2 ARM.
- Flank — When attacking enemy models that are within melee range of a friendly Cygnar warjack, Sword Knights gain +2 on attack rolls. Add an additional damage die to successful attacks.
- Penetrating Strike — After a successful attack against a warjack or warbeast, a Sword Knight may automatically inflict one damage point instead of making a damage roll.
- Swordmaster — Sword Knights may make one additional melee attack.

TRENCHER CHAIN GUN CREW

UNIT

"Raise yer mugs high, blokes. This one's for the chainers — the toughest sods I ever seen.
May we see 'em again tomorrow!"

— Victor Terrell, Cygnaran long gunner

GUNNER				CMD	8
SPD	STR	MAT	RAT	DEF	ARM
2	6	6	5	13	14

CREWMAN				CMD	8
SPD	STR	MAT	RAT	DEF	ARM
4	6	6	5	13	14

CHAIN GUN (GUNNER)				
	RNG	ROF	AOE	POW
	10	2	—	10

MILITARY RIFLE				
	RNG	ROF	AOE	POW
	10	1	—	11

TRENCH KNIFE			
	Special	POW	P+S
	—	2	8

Gunner and Crewman	28
Field Allowance	2
Victory Points	1

Base Size: Large (Gunner and Chain Gun), Small (Crewman)

Before Cygnar commits the bulk of its forces to battle, it sends in the trenchers. Unable to quickly lug their heavy equipment around the battlefield, the gritty chain gun crew know they must hold the line even at the cost of their own lives. It's a dangerous existence for Trenchers and few return home—at least in one piece. Those who do make it back to the homestead usually bless the courage of the chain gun crews, or "chainers," for the opportunity.

So far ahead of the rest of the army, the Cygnaran chain gun—originally developed for the Sentinel 'jack—may be the only thing that stands between the crew and death. Their guns lay down a hail of shot to cover advancing forces as the gunners crank away at the firing pin while crewmen feed belts of pre-packed rounds into them. Every chainer team carries a great deal of ammunition into battle, and prays that they will live for the chance to use each and every shot.

Even with the protection of shoveled out trenches and a devastating rate of fire, chain gunners know the odds are stacked against them. Trencher platoons often treat their chainers with a bit of reverence and prestige, knowing that their stalwart partnership might one day buy them enough time to live beyond a battle gone sour. A round of drinks and a hot meal are never bought at so high a price. Hard-nosed and grim, the chainers eat their supper, gulp down their drinks, and savor each mouthful… as it may well be their last.

SPECIAL RULES

CREWMAN

• Ammo Feeder (★Action) — The Gunner can make an additional ranged attack with the Chain Gun during his current activation. The Crewman must be in base-to-base contact with the Gunner and not engaged to use Ammo Feeder.

UNIT

• Advance Deployment — Place Trencher Chain Gun Crew after normal deployment, up to 12" beyond the established deployment zone.

• Dig In (Action) — The Trencher Chain Gun Crew can dig a hasty battle position into the ground, gaining cover (+4 DEF) and +4 ARM. The Chain Gunners remain dug in until they move or are engaged. Chain Gunners cannot dig into solid rock or man-made constructions. Chain Gunners may begin the game dug in.

• Weapon Crew —The Trencher Chain Gun Crew is made up of a Gunner and Crewman. The Gunner is mounted on a large base with the Chaingun. A weapon crew cannot run or charge. The Gunner gains +2" of movement if he begins activation in base-to-base contact with the Crewman. If the Gunner takes sufficient damage to be destroyed and the Crewman is within 1", the Crewman is removed from the table instead. Any effects or spells on the damaged Gunner expire. Any effects or spells on the removed Crewman are applied to the new Gunner.

CHAIN GUN 〜GUNNER ONLY〜

• Light Artillery — The Chain Gun cannot be used to make ranged attacks if the Gunner moves. The Gunner does not receive an aiming bonus for forfeiting movement when attacking with the Chain Gun. The Gunner cannot make ranged attacks with the Chain Gun and another ranged weapon during the same activation.

• Strafe — A single attack with the Chain Gun has the potential to hit the target and several nearby models. First, make a normal ranged attack against an eligible model. If the initial attack hits, roll a d3 to determine the total number of Strafe attacks the initial attack generates, then divide the result between the original target and any models within 2" of it. Each model may receive more than one attack, but cannot receive more attacks than allocated to the initial target. Make separate hit and damage rolls for each Strafe attack generated. Completely resolve each attack individually, applying the targets' special rules immediately as each attack is resolved.

HUNTER
LIGHT WARJACK

"Bear a wary eye the Hunter. You become aware of its reach, then it's already too late. Best then to call for your chief mechanik, and hope to the hells your cortex's still together."

—Khadoran kapitan advising a junior officer

Height /Weight	8' 5" / 2.75 tons
Armament	Long Arm Cannon (left arm), Battle Axe (right arm)
Fuel Load/Burn Usage	75 Kgs / 10 hrs general, 1.5 hr combat
Initial Service Date	603 AR
Cortex Manufacturer	Cygnaran Armory
Orig. Chassis Design	Cygnaran Armory

The Hunter is a 'jack assassin. Ranging far ahead of warcaster and company, it is the unknown element lurking in any mountain pass or forest valley. Acting as its master's eyes, the Hunter is equipped with advanced mechanika relays developed to increase range, effectively doubling the distance at which a warcaster may control it, as well as an innovative gyroscopic device to stabilize its gun. Its lightened chassis and armor permits it to pass through challenging terrain, and an inventive boiler design incorporates a reserve steam tank that can be expelled for a short burst of impressive speed. A favored combat tactic is to use this accelerated movement to withdraw quickly from combat and retreat into cover to strike again from afar. This impressive array of features allows the pioneering Hunter to deploy well in advance of its battle group.

The Hunter's Long Arm cannon is designed for a specific task: penetrating heavily-armored opponents over distance. The gun relies on alchemically hardened rounds to punch through thick armor as easily as a hammer shatters clay. For situations where a Hunter might be trapped in melee, or for the clearing of paths in particularly difficult terrain, it is also outfitted with a weapon resembling a woodsman's axe.

The Hunter is a recent addition to the ranks, but it has already made a name for itself in the field. More than one border incursion has ended due to well-placed Long Arm fire incapacitating incoming 'jacks before they ever reach their intended targets. Indeed, few military developments have been so disquieting to Cygnar's rivals.

SPD	STR	MAT	RAT	DEF	ARM
6	7	5	6	14	14

LONG ARM

	RNG	ROF	AOE	POW
LEFT	14	1	—	6

BATTLE AXE

	Special	POW	P+S
RIGHT	—	4	11

DAMAGE GRID 1 2 3 4 5 6

SYSTEMS

Left Arm (L)						
Rght Arm (R)		L			R	
Cortex (C)	L	L	M	C	R	R
Movement (M)		M	M	C	C	

Point Cost	88
Field Allowance	U
Victory Points	2

Base Size: Medium

SPECIAL RULES

- **Advance Deployment** — Place the Hunter after normal deployment, up to 12" beyond the established deployment zone.
- **All Terrain** — The Hunter ignores movement penalties from rough terrain and obstacles. The Hunter may charge or slam across rough terrain.
- **Extended Control Range** — When checking to see if the Hunter is in its controlling warcaster's control area for the purpose of allocating focus, double the area for this check.
- **Pressurized Reserve Tank** — Once per game the Hunter can make an additional move at the end of its activation. After completing its normal activation, the Hunter can Advance an additional 6", ignoring free strikes during this movement.

LONG ARM

- **Armor Piercing** — Targets with medium-sized or larger bases have their ARM stats halved when calculating damage from the Long Arm. Effects that further modify ARM are not reduced. The Long Arm gets +2 POW against models with small bases.

CENTURION
HEAVY WARJACK

"Place a Centurion at each flank and you can be certain, none shall pass."

—Commander Coleman Stryker

Cygnaran military doctrine is grounded in advanced technological development over brute force, yet sometimes fire must be fought with fire. As warfare evolves in western Immoren, Cygnar's mechanikal engineers continually develop wondrous innovations and always push their art to greater levels. Challenged to design a warjack to rival the size and strength of Khadoran heavy 'jacks, the engineers of Caspia developed a heavy, sturdy chassis and outfitted it with some of the most advanced mechanika available, dubbing it the Centurion. This steam-belching behemoth of iron is the heaviest warjack in Cygnar's formidable arsenal, and though the increased bulk of its chassis makes it Cygnar's slowest warjack, what it lacks in speed it makes up in durability.

Unassailable to frontal assault, the Centurion is both immovable and nearly invulnerable from behind its mechanikally-enhanced magno shield. Powerful electrical coils embedded in the shield are capable of two unique effects: it can stop charging attackers dead in their tracks by emitting a repellent field powerful enough to slow a running warjack, forcing most effective attacks to circumvent the shield and come from behind—no mean feat—and also, when the shield's polarity is reversed, it is a powerful magnet able to latch onto an enemy's arm or head, often locking its weaponry tight and rendering it useless.

Even the hardest targets are ground to scrap at the working end of the Centurion's piston spear. The wickedly sharp point, crafted for piercing layers of armor, is hydraulically-powered to rip through anything in the warjack's path. Once activated, the spear's piston hammers away relentlessly at anything within striking distance.

Height /Weight	12' 7" / 8.5 tons
Armament	Magno-Shield (left arm), Piston Spear (right arm)
Fuel Load/Burn Usage	180 Kgs / 5 hrs general, 1 hr combat
Initial Service Date	599 AR
Cortex Manufacturer	Cygnaran Armory
Orig. Chassis Design	Cygnaran Mechaniks Coalition at the Royal Cygnaran University

SPD	STR	MAT	RAT	DEF	ARM
4	12	5	4	11	19
					21

MAGNO SHIELD

	Special	POW	P+S
LEFT	Multi	0	12

PISTON SPEAR

	Special	POW	P+S
RIGHT	Multi	6	18

DAMAGE GRID

SYSTEMS	1	2	3	4	5	6
Left Arm (L)						
Rght Arm (R)		L			R	
Cortex (C)	L	L	M	C	R	R
Movement (M)		M	M	C	C	

Point Cost	113
Field Allowance	U
Victory Points	3

Base Size: Large

SPECIAL RULES

MAGNO SHIELD

- Electro-Lock (★ Attack) — The Centurion can use the powerful magnet in its shield to tie up an enemy warjack's arm or head to prevent its use. Declare which component the Centurion is attempting to lock before making the attack roll. On a successful hit, the targeted component is locked with the same effects as an Armlock/Headlock power attack. The Centurion gets +2 on its STR roll to maintain the lock. The Magno Shield cannot generate a Polarity Field while maintaining an Electro-Lock. The Centurion does not gain an ARM bonus for the shield while using Electro-Lock.

- Polarity Field —The Centurion cannot be charged or power attack Slammed by a model that began its activation in the Centurion's front arc.

PISTON SPEAR

- Critical Sustained Attack — On a Critical Hit, additional attacks with the Piston Spear against the same target this turn automatically hit. No additional attack rolls are necessary.

- Reach — 2" melee range.

The Protectorate

DEVOTION AND DUTY

High Exemplar Mikael Kreoss moves easily through the city streets of Imer, his armor, blazoned with the Holy Menofix, clanking slightly with every step. As is traditional, a mask covers his face, a depiction of the stern face of Menoth the Creator.

The ragged crowd, mostly Idrian and lowborn Sulese, parts for him as he walks, the people shuffling aside to open a clear path for him down the center of the cobbled street. Even carts and carriages pull to the side of the road as he approaches. His path is clear, although it is also constantly surrounded by whispers, pointing fingers, fearful and devoted gazes, and the occasional brave soul crying out for his blessing. The crowd closes again in his wake, covering his path behind him. Some of the faithful continue following.

Originally, Mikael Kreoss found the crowds that gathered about him whenever he went abroad to be disconcerting, but he eventually came to accept them as an allegory for his life: although his way might not seem clear, Menoth shall free his every step of the many distractions and temptations that endeavor to lure him aside. So long as he ignores the world, as he ignores the crowds, the way will open up before him. Now, he is used to the fame, the notoriety, the privilege and isolation of his status. Now, he moves with grace and purpose in the knowledge that he is a powerful agent of Menoth and a reflection of his glory.

Kreoss' fingers are intertwined, both hands raised to his breastbone as he strides to the Sovereign Temple of the One Faith. He petitions Menoth to free his heart from uncertainty. He has doubts, dark fears in the corners of his soul, that some of those who direct the temple may not, in fact, truly be its servants. "Menoth," he says aloud, "divine Creator, search our hearts. Flense the weak and impious in your clergy. Turn each heart to you or to dust, as you will."

As if in answer, one person in the crowd stands in his path. It is the Priestess of the Flame, of course; no one else has Feora's untamed will. She is arrayed in full battle armor, far heavier than the peacetime gear that Kreoss wears, and wisps of steam vent from the rear grates. A stray lock of long, black hair shows from beneath her mask, and Kreoss surmises that she donned her armor in haste.

He stops, his countenance darkening beneath his mask. *She is trouble*, he thinks. Although Feora is generally calm and placid, even congenial, she has a famous temper. Every moment in her presence is like holding a rifle with a hang-fire, wondering whether or not any given words or actions will end in an explosion.

Kreoss says nothing for a long moment, forcing her to hold her tongue lest she undermine her argument by breaching etiquette. However, if she waits too long, the same effect shall be had. Finally, the Priestess speaks nonetheless, her voice as smooth as softened butter: "What is the meaning of this?"

The High Exemplar shrugs nonchalantly. "I'm sure I have no answer, for I've no idea what *'this'* might be." He steps past her as if he has nothing more to say. For some reason, the high exemplar derives pleasure from treating Feora like an impertinent child. He considers it only fair; she acts that way much of the time.

Instead, she reaches out and grabs his arm with one of her massive gauntlets, forcing him to turn and face her… *as she would a servant.* Kreoss' eyes narrow menacingly behind his golden mask. He peers down at her hand, still gripping his arm.

She remains placid. Holding a finger from her remaining hand aloft like an instructor, she asks, "Why have I been removed from my temple?"

Kreoss shrugs her restraining hand away. "You are no god," he growls. "Therefore, you have no temple."

"You know what I mean. Why have I been removed as commander of my Flameguard? I've overseen the security of the Sovereign Temple for years."

"*Your* Flameguard? They are not *your* Flameguard, Feora, nor is it *your* temple," says the High Exemplar. "The temple is Menoth's. The Flameguard are Menoth's. Even your service belongs to Menoth. And the Creator's highest servant, the Hierarch Voyle, will personally direct security of the temple, now that *she* is here. If you take exception to this, I suggest you ask the Hierarch to petition Menoth directly for judgment."

Exemplar Seneschal
SOLO

"This blade is named Law. This one, Order. I am their wielder, their master. May my grip upon them fail only when my life does. They are to me as I am to the Creator."

— From the *"Oath of Devotion"* sworn by every exemplar seneschal

The power of belief is never in question among Menoth's congregation. Never more than forty-eight in number, the seneschal is both knight and priest with stronger faith than the common example of either. These holy knights are living pillars of faith, and where they go the Will of Menoth follows. They are among the Creator's most diligent followers, and duty sends them to wherever the Hierarch's orders are, to be carried out with the highest priority.

The seneschal is nothing less than a force of nature on the battlefield. Upon rising to the rank of seneschal, the knight is granted a second relic blade pried from the fingers of one of the seneschal's fallen exemplar brethren. With his twin blades the seneschal wades through the enemy tirelessly, sowing death with every step. Those unfortunate enough to be caught between the onslaughts of blades are smote by the sheer power of Menoth's holy fury which sunders even the largest of opponents like waves against the shore.

Most notable is a seneschal's inherent bond with his fellow Menites. Like the exemplar knights who rage at the sight of a fallen battle-brother, the seneschal feels the demise of every Menite like the cutting of his own flesh. Indeed, one tale relates the saga of a seneschal charging from the very gates of Urcaen to avenge the deaths of his Menite brethren at heathen hands. Such is their conviction the seneschal will never relent from his holy duty until his broken body can carry him no further, and sometimes his will goes even beyond this, for as the tale relates, their broken bodies will undertake a last ditch effort to avenge the transgressions of the unenlightened, whereupon they can finally move on from this world to join Menoth's forces in the hereafter.

EXEMPLAR SENESCHAL				CMD	9
SPD	STR	MAT	RAT	DEF	ARM
6	6	8	4	13	15

RELIC BLADE			
	Special	POW	P+S
	—	5	11

RELIC BLADE			
	Special	POW	P+S
	—	5	11

Damage	5
Point Cost	34
Field Allowance	2
Victory Points	1

Base Size: Small

SPECIAL RULES

- **Aegis of Faith** — An Exemplar Seneschal is not affected by continuous effects.
- **Chain Attack-Smite** — If the Exemplar Seneschal hits the same target with both his initial Relic Blade attacks during the same activation, after resolving the attacks he may immediately make an additional melee attack against the target. If the attack roll succeeds, the target is slammed d6" directly away from the Seneschal with the same effect as a Slam power attack, suffering a POW 11 damage roll. Do not roll an additional damage die for Weapon Master on successful Smite attacks.
- **Commander** — An Exemplar Seneschal has a command range equal to his CMD in inches. Friendly Protectorate models or units inside his command range may use the Seneschal's CMD when making a command check. The Seneschal can rally and give orders to friendly Protectorate models within his command range.
- **Fearless** — An Exemplar Seneschal never flees.
- **Field Officer** — An additional unit of Knights Exemplar may be fielded over normal Field Allowance limitations for each Exemplar Seneschal included in the army.
- **Restoration** — An Exemplar Seneschal regains one wound, up to his maximum, each time a friendly Protectorate model within his command range is destroyed. When the Seneschal loses his last wound, he is knocked down instead of being destroyed. If he has not been restored to at least one wound by the controlling player's next maintenance phase, the Seneschal is destroyed.
- **Righteous Fury** — An Exemplar Seneschal gains +2 STR and ARM for one round when one or more friendly Protectorate models are destroyed within a range equal to his CMD in inches.
- **Weapon Master** — An Exemplar Seneschal adds an additional die to its melee damage rolls.

Monolith Bearer

HOLY ZEALOT UNIT ATTACHMENT

"Look! Look upon the power of Menoth and tremble! In His will, all things are made possible!"

— A holy zealot acolyte, as he first lifted his Menofix monolith

The Menofix is a powerful icon to any Menite. It is a symbol of past pains, ancient history, and the future, and its very presence on the battlefield can sometimes sway the actions of faithful troops to greatness. Some of them feel the Menofix's call more than others, and in a show of tremendous faith these zealots bear massive holy symbols to the field in order to encourage their fellow Menites. These hulking granite or basalt monoliths weigh thousands of pounds, but the holy zealots bear them up nonetheless as if taking on but a fraction of their actual burden. Such is their drive, they heft this great weight and go before the throngs of their brothers and sisters, praying loudly and singing the hymns of the Shaper of Man.

To the teeming masses, the monolith bearer is a powerful reminder of Menoth's awesome power and strength. The presence of the bearer extends a divine vigor into his peers and inspires unwavering loyalty as the bearer shrugs off otherwise mortal wounds. When the bearers do finally succumb to the damage wrought upon them, their monoliths topple from their grasp and they lie in an unbelievable ruin of blood-soaked flesh and bone. Their loss is just as moving as their march into combat, even more so it might seem, for the zealots that followed the monolith bearer drive themselves ever harder into the fray so that they, too, might receive a likewise and honorable demise in the ultimate service of their great god.

MONOLITH BEARER			CMD	9	
SPD	STR	MAT	RAT	DEF	ARM
6	6	5	4	12	13

HEAVY MACE

	Special	POW	P+S
	—	4	10

Damage	5
Point Cost	24
Field Allowance	1
Victory Points	+1

Base Size: Small

SPECIAL RULES

- Fiery Assault — If the Monolith Bearer is destroyed by an enemy model, all models in the Holy Zealot unit can run without being ordered to do so and perform a combat action after running. This ability lasts for the remainder of the game.
- Greater Destiny (★ Action) — Models in the Monolith Bearer's unit do not take damage and cannot be destroyed for one round. Greater Destiny may be used once per game.
- Holy Monolith — While the Monolith Bearer remains on the table, models in the unit never flee. When one or more models in the unit are destroyed, the remaining models gain +4 DEF and ARM for one round.
- Officer — The Monolith Bearer is the unit leader.
- Tough — Whenever the Monolith Bearer takes sufficient damage to be destroyed, the controlling player rolls a d6. On a 5 or 6, the Monolith Bearer is knocked down instead of being destroyed. If the Monolith Bearer is not destroyed, he is reduced to one wound.
- Unit Attachment — A Holy Zealot Unit Attachment can be added to any Holy Zealot unit. The unit's Victory Point total is increased by 1.

Flameguard Cleansers
Unit

"All the world's execrations must be bathed in the flames of purity."

—Feora, Priestess of the Flame

Never intended for foreign fields of war, the role of the cleansers was originally seeded in domestic conflict. Much feared as the disciplinary arm of the Flameguard Temple, the infamous cleansers are merciless and unyielding. It is their job to sanctify the land from the touch of accused heretics or practitioners of witchcraft. With blessed fire they scour those places touched by heresy burning the accused and their homes to the ground along with all of those too close to the source of the heresy. The sight of a cleanser unit solemnly marching through a Protectorate city is enough to make anyone cringe, let alone those of weak faith.

Once called to duty, they saturate the heretic home or hiding place with purifier flamethrowers, reducing the building, the inhabitants, and—as the scrutators decree—the taint of corruption to ash. As their fires begin, cleansers stand watch over the blaze and cut down those who might try to escape—most cleansers choose to merely wound or hobble a burning escapee before tossing them back into the inferno, thus carrying out their sentences to the letter of the law.

Though they were created for domestic purposes, the expansion of hostilities has called for the deployment of cleansers against heretics outside the Protectorate borders. Their highly-shielded armor protects them as they stand vigil over the blazing buildings they immolate, but it also offers protection from their enemies in the field. Evidently, the armor is less effective from behind—where the fuel for their purifiers is stored in tanks that can explode when ruptured—but what god-fearing Menite is found with their back to the enemy?

ARMS MASTER				CMD	8
SPD	STR	MAT	RAT	DEF	ARM
5	4	5	6	12	14/11

CLEANSER				CMD	6
SPD	STR	MAT	RAT	DEF	ARM
5	4	4	5	12	14/11

PURIFIER				
	RNG	ROF	AOE	POW
	Spray	1	—	12

PURIFIER BLADE			
	Special	POW	P+S
	—	3	7

Leader and 5 Troops	54
Up to 4 Additional Troops	8 ea.
Field Allowance	2
Victory Points	2

Base Size: Small

SPECIAL RULES

ARMS MASTER

- Incineration (Order) — When issued this order, every Cleanser in the unit may combine his fire at the same target within 5″. This attack requires at least three eligible models, which must be in open formation with another participant, able to declare a ranged attack against the intended target, and be in range. The Cleanser with the highest RAT in the attacking group makes one ranged attack roll for the group, adding +1 to the attack roll for each Cleanser, including itself, participating in the attack. Incineration is a POW 12, AOE 4″ attack which leaves a cloud effect that remains in play for one round. Increase the POW by +1 for each Cleanser participating in the attack. Models moving through or ending their turns within the cloud suffer a POW 12 damage roll. Incinerate may not target a model in melee.
- Leader

UNIT

- Irregular Armor — Cleansers have ARM 14 against attacks that originate in their front arc and ARM 11 against attacks that originate in their back arc.

PURIFIER

- Critical Fire — On a Critical Hit, target model suffers Fire. Fire is a continuous effect that sets the target ablaze. A model on fire suffers a POW 12 damage roll each turn during its maintenance phase until the Fire expires on a d6 roll of 1 or 2.
- Explosive— If a Cleanser is destroyed by an attack originating in his back arc, he explodes. All models within 3″ suffer a POW 12 damage roll and are set on Fire.

The Wrack
SOLO

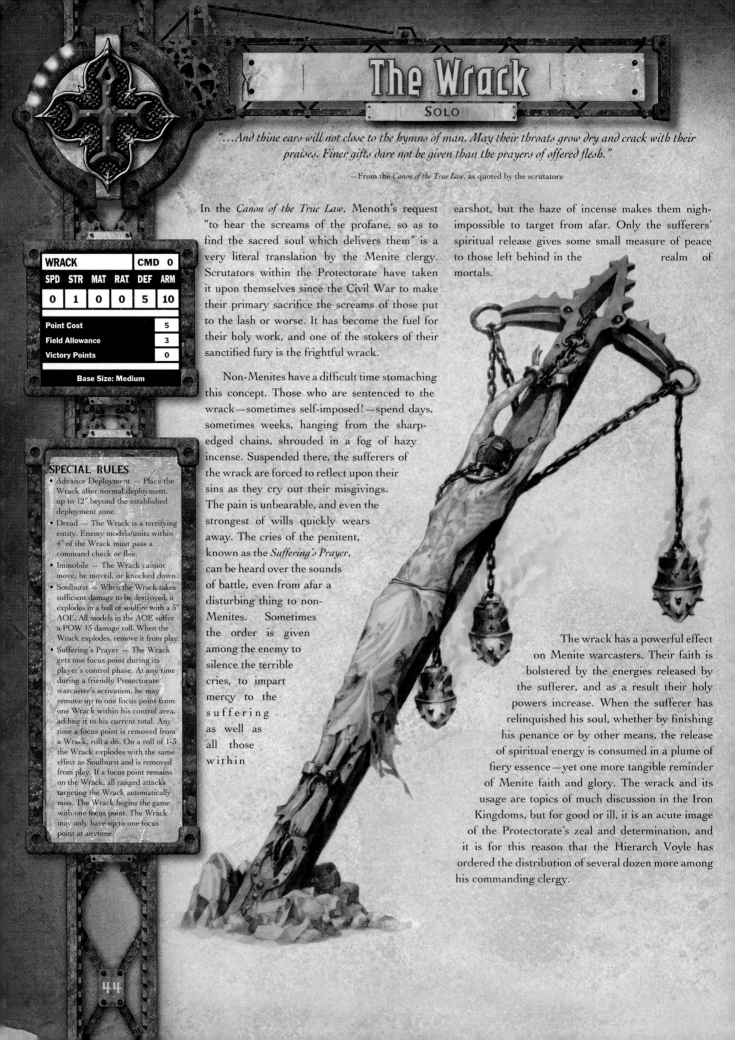

"...And thine ears will not close to the hymns of man. May their throats grow dry and crack with their praises. Finer gifts dare not be given than the prayers of offered flesh."

—From the *Canon of the True Law,* as quoted by the scrutators

WRACK				CMD	0
SPD	STR	MAT	RAT	DEF	ARM
0	1	0	0	5	10

Point Cost	5
Field Allowance	3
Victory Points	0

Base Size: Medium

SPECIAL RULES

- Advance Deployment — Place the Wrack after normal deployment, up to 12" beyond the established deployment zone.
- Dread — The Wrack is a terrifying entity. Enemy models/units within 4" of the Wrack must pass a command check or flee.
- Immobile — The Wrack cannot move, be moved, or knocked down.
- Soulburst — When the Wrack takes sufficient damage to be destroyed, it explodes in a ball of soulfire with a 5" AOE. All models in the AOE suffer a POW 15 damage roll. When the Wrack explodes, remove it from play.
- Suffering's Prayer — The Wrack gets one focus point during its player's control phase. At any time during a friendly Protectorate warcaster's activation, he may remove up to one focus point from one Wrack within his control area, adding it to his current total. Any time a focus point is removed from a Wrack, roll a d6. On a roll of 1-3 the Wrack explodes with the same effect as Soulburst and is removed from play. If a focus point remains on the Wrack, all ranged attacks targeting the Wrack automatically miss. The Wrack begins the game with one focus point. The Wrack may only have up to one focus point at anytime.

In the *Canon of the True Law*, Menoth's request "to hear the screams of the profane, so as to find the sacred soul which delivers them" is a very literal translation by the Menite clergy. Scrutators within the Protectorate have taken it upon themselves since the Civil War to make their primary sacrifice the screams of those put to the lash or worse. It has become the fuel for their holy work, and one of the stokers of their sanctified fury is the frightful wrack.

Non-Menites have a difficult time stomaching this concept. Those who are sentenced to the wrack—sometimes self-imposed!—spend days, sometimes weeks, hanging from the sharp-edged chains, shrouded in a fog of hazy incense. Suspended there, the sufferers of the wrack are forced to reflect upon their sins as they cry out their misgivings. The pain is unbearable, and even the strongest of wills quickly wears away. The cries of the penitent, known as the *Suffering's Prayer,* can be heard over the sounds of battle, even from afar a disturbing thing to non-Menites. Sometimes the order is given among the enemy to silence the terrible cries, to impart mercy to the suffering as well as all those within earshot, but the haze of incense makes them nigh-impossible to target from afar. Only the sufferers' spiritual release gives some small measure of peace to those left behind in the realm of mortals.

The wrack has a powerful effect on Menite warcasters. Their faith is bolstered by the energies released by the sufferer, and as a result their holy powers increase. When the sufferer has relinquished his soul, whether by finishing his penance or by other means, the release of spiritual energy is consumed in a plume of fiery essence—yet one more tangible reminder of Menite faith and glory. The wrack and its usage are topics of much discussion in the Iron Kingdoms, but for good or ill, it is an acute image of the Protectorate's zeal and determination, and it is for this reason that the Hierarch Voyle has ordered the distribution of several dozen more among his commanding clergy.

Devout
LIGHT WARJACK

Height /Weight	8'7" / 3.90 tons
Armament	Pole Axe (right arm), Great Shield (left arm)
Fuel Load/Burn Usage	60 Kgs / 7 hrs general, 2 hrs combat
Initial Service Date	579 A.R.
Cortex Manufacturer	Vassals of Menoth
Orig. Chassis Design	Sul-Menite Artificers / Cygnaran Armory

The Order of the Wall has been in decline for over a generation. It struggles to remain significant to the Protectorate, but every year their numbers wane. Indeed, the Order's role—that of guarding Menoth's clerical elite—has begun passing to the mechanikal masterpiece known as the Devout.

Every component lends to the Devout's ability to protect its controller. It is are light enough to keep up with the fleet-of-foot warcasters and uses its enhanced mechanikal reflexes to intercept attacks or bring weapons to bear against a foe drawing too close to its ward. Its massive shield is layered with protective spells and durable armor plates capable of shrugging off a great deal of damage. The true power of the shield's enchantments is to protect its nearby controller from the accursed magic of outsiders. For its size, the Devout can withstand a heavy amount of damage and will certainly perform its duties until the last smoky sigh drifts from its heartfire.

While some older Menites remember the glory days of the Order of the Wall, most cannot argue their replacements are not an improvement in many ways. The Devouts are ever ready to defend their commanders. They do not sleep, eat, or balk morals at wartime decisions. In truth, they are perfect Protectorate soldiers to stand guard over the elite.

SPD	STR	MAT	RAT	DEF	ARM
5	9	5	4	13	16
					18

GREAT SHIELD
	Special	POW	P+S
LEFT	Barrier	0	9

POLE AXE
	Special	POW	P+S
RIGHT	Reach	4	13

DAMAGE GRID 1 2 3 4 5 6

SYSTEMS

Left Arm (L)
Rght Arm (R) — L — R —
Cortex (C) — L L M C R R
Movement (M) — M M C C —

Point Cost	69
Field Allowance	U
Victory Points	2

Base Size: Medium

SPECIAL RULES
- **Defensive Strike** — The Devout may make a Defensive Strike against an enemy model that ends its movement within the Devout's melee range. Resolve the Defensive Strike immediately after movement ends. The Devout may make a Defensive Strike with a single melee weapon and gains +2 on the attack roll. If the attack succeeds, add an additional die to its damage roll. The attack and damage rolls may not be further boosted. Models hit by Defensive Strike suffer –2 MAT until the end of the turn. Models involuntarily moving into the Devout's melee range do not suffer a Defensive Strike. If the Devout makes a Defensive Strike, it may not make another until after its controlling player's next turn.
- **Shield Guard** — Once per round, when the Devout's controlling warcaster is directly hit by a ranged attack during an opponent's turn, it may move to intercept the attack. The Devout must be within 2" of its warcaster and be able to position itself as an intervening model between the warcaster and the attacker using its normal movement. The Devout then moves and is hit automatically by the attack, suffering full damage and effects. If the Devout uses Shield Guard, it may not use it again until after its controlling player's next turn. If the Devout is denied its full normal movement it cannot use Shield Guard.

GREAT SHIELD
- **Spell Barrier** — During its activation the Devout may spend one focus point to activate Spell Barrier if its controlling warcaster is within base-to-base contact with the Devout. Once Spell Barrier is activated, the warcaster cannot be targeted by enemy spells for one round.

POLE AXE
- Reach — 2" melee range.

45

Reckoner
Heavy Warjack

"Under a veil of flame and a shroud of ash, He will walk amongst them, and their flesh will be as dust on the winds"

—An excerpt from the *Canon of the True Law*, inscribed upon the first Reckoner warjack

Height /Weight	12' / 8.6 tons
Armament	Consecrator (right arm), Condemner Cannon (left arm)
Fuel Load/Burn Usage	110 Kgs / 5.5 hrs general, 1 hrs combat
Initial Service Date	604 AR
Cortex Manufacturer	Vassals of Menoth
Orig. Chassis Design	Sul-Menite Artificers

As tensions between the Protectorate and Cygnar move toward open conflict, the great power of Menoth's warjacks have become manifest. Yet, even the formidable Crusaders and the powerful Vanquishers remind Hierrach Voyle of the Protectorate's impure dealings with the heathen northlanders of Khador. His nation needed something of its own—a symbol of the faith and dedication to the holy war effort and a testament to the Creator. The first solely Menite warjack—devoid of the impurities of outside design—was to become one of the faces of the Lawgiver as foretold in the *Canon of the True Law*.

According to the Codex: "He who is the Grand Reclaimant is, too, the reckoner of man, burning away the sins of the faithful with but the merest glance." Designed with this image in mind—said to be an agent of Menoth in the End Times—the Reckoner is a monstrous hulk of iron and bronze. The warjack's powerful Condemner cannon—able to fire even as it charges into combat—launches pyromite-filled shells and yields brilliant fiery displays that often blind and disorient the enemy. These shells burn so hot that armor literally liquefies like molten lava upon impact, wreathing its target in a cloak of flame. The blaze frequently acts as a beacon to the Menite troops and attracts their combined fury. The Reckoner's o t h e r weapon is its smoke-belching consecrator. Heavily reinforced and banded in iron, it emits a thick cloud of holy incense that chokes heathen enemies approaching too near and makes the 'jack's location difficult to pinpoint from a distance. Indeed, among the forces of the Protectorate, the massive Reckoner stalks the battlefield within a burning miasma, bringing reality and mechanikal motion unto the damning prophecies of the *Canon*.

SPD	STR	MAT	RAT	DEF	ARM
5	11	5	4	10	19

CONDEMNER

	RNG	ROF	AOE	POW
LEFT	12	1	—	12

CONSECRATOR

	Special	POW	P+S
RIGHT	Veil	6	17

DAMAGE GRID

	1	2	3	4	5	6
SYSTEMS						
Left Arm (L)						
Rght Arm (R)		L			R	
Cortex (C)	L	L	M	C	R	R
Movement (M)		M	M	C	C	

Point Cost	126
Field Allowance	U
Victory Points	3

Base Size: Large

SPECIAL RULES
- Assault — As part of a charge, after moving, the Reckoner may make a single ranged attack followed by a charge attack.

CONDEMNER
- Critical Splash — On a Critical Hit, target warjack or warbeast suffers 1 point of damage to each column of its damage grid or branch. If a warjack damage column is full then apply the damage to the next column to the right. If a warbeast branch is full then apply the damage to the next branch in order.
- Flare — Models hit by the Condemner suffer –2 DEF for one round. This penalty is not cumulative with itself.

CONSECRATOR
- Choking Veil — Living non-friendly models within 2" of the Reckoner suffer –2 to all attack rolls. The Choking Veil provides concealment to the Reckoner.

KHADOR

ELEVENTH HOUR

It's cold and wet in the foothills above Laedry. A light drizzle falls from the low-hanging clouds and drips from the short needles of tall pine trees and leafy cedars, landing on the packed dirt with small, wet thumps.

Within the trees and the mist, an army is on the move. Several lengthy columns meander carefully down a hillside, the brown, dead needles of the forest floor clinging to their water-spattered boots, concealing the once spit-polished black sheen and camouflaging it to match the color of the ground. Likewise, the precipitation has turned brown leather greatcoats to a darker hue. The faces of the soldiers are grim, fatigue showing on some of their features from the bone-wearying pace set by their kommandant, but in spite of the size of the army and its exhaustion, they make as little noise as possible.

Just behind the van, a Khadoran kommand group winds among the trees. Walking at the center of this group is the heralded Kommandant Irusk, stern, professional… and restless, awaiting word on the enemy disposition.

The campaign has already begun, although the Llaelese don't know it yet. To the south, Kommanders Kratikoff and Zoktavir strike eastward to Elsinberg and Redwall, several divisions of troops and heavy contingents of warjacks in tow. The inclement weather should obfuscate the steam plumes of their 'jacks, granting them the element of surprise and a few days' grace before anyone knows the Motherland is reclaiming its rightful lands. If all goes well, Kratikoff's and Zoktavir's sieges should both conclude within a week's passing.

Irusk's offensive, however, is the hammer strike to absolutely squash the enemy—seizing the nation without resorting to a prolonged siege. Once Laedry falls, they will march east across the North Road, isolating Rynyr and assaulting the town of Riversmet. And once Riversmet falls, the trade route to and from Rhul will be cut off, not only crippling the rest of Llael, predominantly the capital city of Merywyn, but also their hegemonic puppet master, Cygnar. Controlling the Black River is a major stride in the total domination of the Iron Kingdoms and, hence, the rebirth of the Khardic Empire.

This assault across the north is the most difficult of the tasks, which is why among all the High Kommand, the queen appointed Kommandant Irusk to the operation. It was a challenge that, in many ways, he relished. He needs to ensure that the three northern bastions are isolated or defeated swiftly, and he must do so with troops weary from weeks of marching and a light contingent of warjacks when compared to Kratikoff's and Zoktavir's forces. It would be nigh impossible if he didn't have two batteries of long-range siege guns deploying on the escarpment to the north. Firing from such an advantageous spot, they can rain down shells anywhere in Laedry, using angles and charges carefully calculated by the best ballistic mathematicians in Khador. Irusk has planned several barrage patterns, and will choose the one best suited to disrupt the enemy formations. Once he has that information, the Llaelese garrison will vanish in a rain of fire.

Suddenly, a perimeter guard on the north side of the van crouches low behind a fallen cedar's trunk, raising one hand. Irusk and his retinue scatter behind trees, and the columns of soldiers halt. Footsteps approach and a scout appears, trudging up the slope toward the kommandant. A Winter Guard lieutenant and a kapitan of the Widowmakers break formation and sidle up to the kommandant, as well.

As the scout comes near, Irusk recognizes the man in spite of the black mud and pine needles adhering wetly to his uniform. The kommandant pauses for the man to catch his breath, then asks, "What news, soldier?"

"The town garrison is as you predicted, sir," the old man rumbles through a mouth half empty of teeth. "Fire Pattern A will serve well. But there are mercenaries. Many. A heavy battalion at least, maybe more… They are Thunderhelms, I believe, Kommandant."

"Indeed? Where?" asks Irusk, pulling out a campaign map from his coat. The Thunderhelm Irregulars was a storied mercenary company, known for their part at the Ironfields in dealing Khador a major loss. It was a long time ago. Just over three centuries. But not a single Thunderhelm was about to let anyone forget that momentous time, when they fought alongside Cygnaran troops and the first major deployment of warjacks since the Colossal Wars.

"Beyond the town," says the hunter, pointing to a spot on the kommandant's map. "They camp in these rolling ridges."

Irusk crinkles the map, closes his eyes, removes his fur cap, and tucks it in his armpit to free up a gloved hand so that he can run it slowly through his gray-spangled hair and down the back of his neck. The nearby kapitan and lieutenant move in closer, concern clearly etched on their veteran faces, while the scout takes a step back and looks aside at some nearby troopers.

"We march into the proverbial lead furnace, fellow patriots," says Irusk quietly, as he dons his cap once more. "I suspected they may have reinforcements stationed here, but had hopes that I was wrong. I am not. We attack a numerically superior foe."

"But we never concern ourselves with numbers, sir," says the lieutenant. "Our troops will slay them by the cartload. Thunderhelms or not, they are mercenaries, not Khadorans."

Irusk smiles grimly. The lieutenant had roughly quoted—a bit out of context—from the kommandant's own book on Khadoran tactics, *Irusk on Conquest*. "True, but we will not make the same mistake our brothers made long ago. The city will have their own 'jacks stationed there, as will the Thunderhelms. Always, they are said to have their 'jacks, at least a dozen, likely more. Our siege guns have no trajectory plotted to the mercenary camp. If we bombard them, we fire blind, and the uneven terrain protects the enemy from shells that fall off target. Pointless.

"Instead, we shall hit Laedry as planned. Then… we will retreat. This will draw out the mercenaries. I have not known one that will not take the opportunity to harry a retreating army. Once they are out, I will mire them in the open. I shall hit them first with an airburst, then you fire the guns and crush them. Timing is everything, patriots. Understand? We must draw them into the target zone. It is dangerous… but we must look like we break."

The officers nod.

"Very good. Deploy your troops," he orders, waving his arm. "I must study the maps a few moments more."

As the soldiers depart, Irusk sits on a sodden cedar log, soft with moss, and opens his map. He pores over it as the columns move along. Three divisions of Winter Guard. A Widowmaker battalion. An Iron Fang battalion. A raucous unit of Man-O-War

shock troopers with three aides each to lug sections of their inert armor and, intermingled among them, ten warjacks—seven Juggernauts, two Destroyers, and one Marauder. The march had begun with eight Juggernauts and two Marauders, but a rotted, outworn bridge had collapsed beneath their weight, hastening a Juggernaut and a Marauder, their respective carts, and their drivers several hundred feet to a rocky demise. Their salvaged cortexes were presently housed inside an enclosed carriage near the rear of the column.

One warjack to a 1,000 soldiers, Irusk thinks. The pulsing of cortexes hum in his head as he watches the 'jacks and Man-O-Wars tread by, trampling through the brush and snapping branches, trailing two grim-faced 'jack marshals, bold men who had without question descended the cliffs to appraise the fallen constructs.

Last comes the baggage train, the noisiest portion of his army: cooks, launderers, battle mechaniks and 'jack stokers struggling with muddy-hoofed mules and their cumbersome cartloads of coal and water, more beasts, surgeons, even Morrowan and Menite priests alike—at opposite ends, of course—to sanctify the dead of their respective clergies. The kommandant pays them little heed as they move by, once again lost in his maps. He looks up only when he realizes the sounds of his troops are diminishing.

Irusk watches the last of the train and the rearguard dissolve into the misty drizzle to his right and, after several moments of sitting alone, stands and rearranges his gear. He is just about to follow the jink and jingle of the fading army, when an intuitive awareness flares in the back of his skull. A rhythmic pulse, not unlike the heartbeat of a man or beast. *Cortexes*, he thinks, *but not mine. These are unfamiliar… and there is something else…*

He lingers, breathing softly, peering into the dark trees to the south, and the feeling grows in clarity and strength. He realizes he is practically alone, although a forceful bellow would surely grab the attention of the rearguard, now well over a hundred yards away. The kommandant tenses, his eyes narrowing into slits. *What warjacks are these? It cannot be… no, it is too unlikely… impossible even. Yet who else can it be?*

A lone figure emerges from the shadows of a dark pine. It takes but an instant for him to recognize the impressive, armored figure. It is as he suspected.

"Prince Tzepesci," Irusk says with a puckered brow.

The Umbrean prince approaches and nods, a hint of a smile playing at the corners of his thin lips. "Kommandant Irusk," he says with a voice like black satin.

"The queen assigned you to protect the Cygnaran border."

"Quite true."

"It is dangerous to defy the queen, Prince," says Irusk, adding an extra plosive to the noble title.

"I defy nothing," replies the dark-eyed warcaster. "I vill be at the assigned place on the assigned day."

The kommandant raises his brow. "Then what are you doing *here*?"

Vladimir offers a lopsided smile and ignores the question, instead saying, "It is vasteful to tie down varriors like us vis purse strings. Victory requires speed. It requires power. It is not had through the counting of coins, like others in our High Kommand believe.

"Between your great guns and my varjacks, there is no doubt Laedry will fall. After that, you take your troops through the pass and seize Rynyr boldly. Meanvile, I push my varjacks to Riversmet and take it ahead of schedule. Once done, I board a ship down the Black River to Ravensgard, arriving there on time and as promised. In fact, Laedry may not be as vell garrisoned as vee are led to believe. Llael's Prime Minister has plans that are, shall vee say, not quite in alignment vis that of his fellow countrymen."

Irusk knew as much, having heard from Queen Ayn's own lips that the Prime Minister Glabryn had been trimming garrisons in the west for quite some time. His scout so much as confirmed the situation in Laedry, although the mercenaries and their warjacks admittedly made things more difficult.

As they talk, the distinctive sound of mechanika, the heavy tread and rhythmic hissing of warjacks on the move, is on the rise. The trees tremble, shedding sheets of rain droplets like veils. The ground, built up through years of slowly decomposing evergreen needles, vibrates, and for a moment Irusk fancies that the mountain itself has a heartbeat. Then he sees them, lighter shadows against the darker gray of the drizzle-masked trees. They move swiftly, brushing aside branches and even small saplings. Their rain-slicked armor shells reflect the light that scatters through the cloud cover. Steam vents from engines, blending with the low-hanging clouds. The shadows resolve into shapes.

"Those are Berserkers," he says. When the prince does not acknowledge the comment, he presses the issue. "Their cortexes are… they are unstable. Perhaps they blow in the heat of combat?"

Prince Vladimir favors him with a pointed look. "There are those who think I am unstable," he says.

"The Berserkers know their duty, just as any son or daughter of the Motherland should."

The words do little to alleviate Irusk's concerns. "I already have warjacks."

"Clearly you do, Kommandant. I have more. So does Laedry. So do the mercenaries. You do not have enough for this siege."

"It can be done."

"Perhaps, yes. If anyone stands a chance, it is the mighty Kommandant Irusk. But vie take the chance? Vie not be sure of victory?"

His personal distaste for Tzepesci aside, Irusk could not debate the prince's logic. "Very well. How many do you have?"

"All of them."

"Twenty-seven? Only a *fool* would think to control that many!"

The prince fixes Irusk with a stare and the tension between them is as palpable as ever, but suddenly Tzepesci waves his hand dismissively. "I can control enough. The others replace those destroyed. You may field as many as you vish, Kommandant. Together vee launch a new type of var the Iron Kingdoms has not seen before."

"Six suit my needs," says the kommandant. "Tell me… how did you get them here? It is leagues from the nearest supply center, and—"

"I make my own plans. Betimes, they run deeper than those of our beloved queen's."

"Or perhaps… 'not quite in alignment?'"

The prince shrugged. "If you mean to imply something, Kommandant, then by all means—"

"No matter, Prince. I do not mean to imply anything, or to be impolite. So, how *did* you foresee this?" asks Irusk. "You would need coal cached throughout these mountains. Spare parts, as well. Assuming you knew we would attack through this pass? If we had attacked Rynyr directly—" And then realization dawns on him, and he stops dead in his tracks, eyes narrowing.

Prince Vladimir laughs, and he trudges on through the rain. It is an eerie sound in the dark forest. "That is right, Kommandant Irusk," he calls out, without looking back. "If vee had made to attack Rynyr, I vould *still* have brought you as many Berserkers as you needed! Now, shall vee continue bandying vords, or shall vee attack?"

KOMMANDANT IRUSK

WARCASTER

"Kommandant Irusk, allow me to say you are a living legend, sir… and it does the Motherland proud to have you lead it into war."

—Queen Ayn Vanar XI to the Kommandant at a recent summit of the High Kommand

Kommandant Gurvaldt Irusk was born to make war. His mother died when he was young, leaving his father, a retired veteran officer, to raise him. In spite of a crippling battle wound sustained right around the time Irusk was born in 550 AR, the old soldier imbued his son with his knowledge of battle, his martial skill, and his ruthless persistence, so when Irusk was sent to Volningrad at the young age of 12 to train as a Winter Guard, he swiftly became an accomplished soldier in order to make his father proud.

More than soldiering came naturally to young Irusk. His superior officers recognized his arcane potential during his training and dispatched him to the Druzhina—the elite military academy in Korsk—at the age of 17. Without his arcane abilities, Irusk was already a formidable soldier; with them, he was soon to become an unstoppable machine. His instinctive grasp of tactics saw weaknesses where others did not, his commanding presence rallied and organized troops to press the attack, and his spells exploited every situation to its utmost. An officer at 19,

he became a vested warcaster by 21 and reached a staff position in the High Kommand by age 25.

As he rose to even greater power, he left in his wake a growing number of admirers, enemies, and grieving families. One thing is certain, however, and that is that to the common soldier in Khador's army, Irusk is nigh unto a god. Troops are never more fearless than under his order, for they know for certain that if they die, theirs will not be a useless death.

Over the last twenty years or so, he has moved up through the High Kommand to become Queen Ayn Vanar XI's chief advisor on military matters. In his new position, he has begun his personal dream: building a new Khadoran military, modernizing and enhancing it to conform to his vision. His connection to the common soldier led him to oversee the development of an improved blunderbuss for military use as well as its recent adoption by the troops of the Winter Guard. His eye for utility led him to order the development of the mortar based on the specs of the Destroyer's bombard, and his tactical brilliance literally wrote the book on Khadoran tactics, a startlingly insightful tome on combined arms entitled *Irusk on Conquest: How to Fully Subjugate Your Enemy*.

Due to his success in life's undertakings, most notably his victory at Tverkutsk, the Kommandant is a popular man. Irusk's reputation has transformed him into a famed personality throughout the Motherland, and he is often surrounded by hangers-on and the upwardly-mobile. Still, he does not brook ignorance in his company. During his rise through the ranks, he focused solely on the art of war. All his magical training is bent toward war, and for leisure he reads old texts by a variety of military geniuses such as Baromitzk and Zerkova. He depends upon those who gather around him to have like interests.

In Queen Ayn's hall during her various summits, he negotiates the subtle interplay of politics like a warjack barreling through a haze of mirrors. His brusque manner promotes an air of arrogance, of which he is self-admittedly guilty but for good reason. His battlefield prowess and flawless reputation place him above his peers in many ways, and those who might try to stab him in the back politically find their own careers ended first, if not their lives.

Irusk's loyalty is to the Motherland only; he is truly beholden to his profession. In truth, it matters little to him who rules Khador so long as he is able to direct the defense of his beloved country. In such defense he carries Onslaught, a cannon-sword that is as unsubtle as he is. His magical abilities change the battlefield to suit his strategies, causing havoc among enemy lines and providing his troops with fervor and protection.

FEAT: UNDYING LOYALTY

With his reputation as a fearless and loyal Khadoran Kommandant, Irusk has gained the eternal respect and devotion of the entire Khadoran military. His orders, his words, even his very steps into battle inspire men to view him as a paragon of soldiering, an iconic representation of everything that they strive to be. As a national hero and military mind held in the highest esteem, troopers will follow Irusk into battle without hesitation, bolstered by his words of inspiration they leave doubt behind. In doubts place, a relentless courage exists that defies fear, injury, and even death.

For one round, all friendly Khador warrior models currently within Irusk's control area become fearless, gain +2 on attack rolls, and if they take sufficient damage to be destroyed, the controlling player rolls a d6. On a 4-6, the model remains in play but is reduced to one wound.

FOCUS	7	CMD	10

SPD	STR	MAT	RAT	DEF	ARM
6	6	7	6	15	15

SWORD CANNON

	RNG	ROF	AOE	POW
	10	2	-	13

ONSLAUGHT

	Special	POW	P+S
	Slaughter	6	12

Damage	17
Point Cost	78
Field Allowance	C
Victory Points	5

Base Size: Small

SPECIAL RULES

- Assault — As part of a charge, after moving, Irusk may make a single ranged attack followed by a charge attack with Onslaught. Irusk may not spend focus points to make additional ranged attacks this turn.

ONSLAUGHT

- Slaughter (★ Attack) — If Onslaught damages a target, immediately make an additional POW 13 damage roll against the target. This additional damage roll is caused by the Sword Cannon. The damage roll may be boosted.

Spells	Cost	RNG	AOE	POW	UP	OFF
Airburst	4	CTRL	3	8	No	Yes
Airburst may target any model in Irusk's control area regardless of LOS. Airburst ignores intervening models, cover, concealment, and elevation. All models within the AOE suffer a POW 8 damage roll.						
Battle Lust	3	6	—	—	No	No
Target warrior model/unit becomes fearless and gains an additional damage die on all melee attacks for 1 round.						
Confusion	3	10	—	—	No	Yes
Target non-character warrior model/unit must pass a command check during its next Maintenance Phase at CMD −2 or forfeit its activation.						
Grind	3	10	—	14	No	Yes
Target warjack damaged by Grind takes one additional point of damage to its first available movement system box. Mark this damage after marking the normal damage from Grind.						
Inhospitable Ground	3	Caster	CTRL	—	No	No
While in Irusk's control area, all enemy models treat open terrain as rough terrain. Inhospitable Ground has a duration of 1 round.						
Iron Flesh	2	8	—	—	Yes	No
Target warrior model/unit gains +3 DEF and suffers −1 SPD.						
Superiority	3	6	—	—	Yes	No
Target warjack gains +2 SPD, MAT, and DEF and cannot be knocked down.						

KODIAK

"They are like the cave bears trained by our ancestors. With them, we will shred the enemy. These 'jacks remind us the Motherland does not forget her fallen! The education our legion received at the Tongue is not long forgotten, either. Today, our bears are forged in iron and steel!"

—Kapitan Gerla Petrovich of the 5th Border Legion to her troops

SPD	STR	MAT	RAT	DEF	ARM
4	12	5	3	10	20

ARMORED FIST

	Special	POW	P+S
LEFT	Multi	2	14

ARMORED FIST

	Special	POW	P+S
RIGHT	Multi	2	14

DAMAGE GRID

SYSTEMS	1	2	3	4	5	6
Left Arm (L)						
Rght Arm (R)			L		R	
Cortex (C)	L	L	M	C	R	R
Movement (M)		M	M	C	C	

Point Cost	117
Field Allowance	2
Victory Points	4

Base Size: Large

After their heinous defeat in the Thornwood War at the Battle of the Dragon's Tongue at the hands of Cygnaran and Llaelese troops in 513 AR, tempers flared high for many of the Khadoran soldiers when orders came from Korsk to withdraw—some units lingered and others refused outright to give up land they had fought so hard to take. One such unit was the 5th Border Legion. These mighty veterans of the Winter Guard were some of the first soldiers to hit Cygnaran soil in the beginning, and they refused to acknowledge defeat for years after the war had ended. When they returned to Volningrad, the tales of their grisly successes behind enemy lines had them regarded by many as heroes.

As a reward for their duty, King Sagriv Vanar II ordered the Khadoran Mechaniks Assembly to refit a handful of Juggernauts specifically for the 5th Border Legion. With the woodland legion in mind; they received heavier payloads of fuel, larger boilers for extended (or fervent) use, and a lack of bulky weaponry that would otherwise hinder a 'jack in the thick wilderness. The Kodiaks must have been a sight to behold—those enormous powerhouses of iron and steam—when they first paraded down the avenues of Volningrad in front of the assembled Guard and the King himself.

The Kodiak takes a utilitarian look at the battlefield using only a pair of reinforced fists to pummel the enemy like an eleven-ton barroom brawler. To cull such a devastating, pugilistic effect out of the creation, the Greylords Covenant had instilled specialty melee strikes as routine patterns in their cortexes.

When a Kodiak is set into action, nothing can withstand its steam-driven assault; obstacles and other impediments of terrain are barely noticed as the 'jack rushes over or through them with ease, unfettered by snapping branches or grabbing vines. To achieve such speeds and surges of titanic power, the Kodiak has been fitted with a multi-walled boiler, reinforced with bands of armor-grade iron which are still not always enough to contain the pressure. To compensate the 'jack has a "dragon vent" to exhale clouds of superheated vapor—often scalding nearby troops and enveloping the warjack in a hazy fog. With its concentrated energy store, the Kodiak places legendary amounts of force into its every movement. Those unlucky enough to suddenly fall under the shadow of this warjack are not long for this world, for its hammer-falling fists are powerful enough to powder marble and shatter steel.

The Kodiak was never mass-produced due to the extreme cost of its specialized cortex and multi-walled boiler apparatus. In fact, only a small number of them ever saw service and those who command them must spend large amounts of resources keeping them in working and battling condition. Today, they are produced—albeit rarely—as a reward for loyalty to the Motherland and are typically assigned solely to the most prestigious of warcasters.

SPECIAL RULES

- **All Terrain** — The Kodiak ignores movement penalties from rough terrain and obstacles. The Kodiak may charge or slam across rough terrain.
- **Chain Attack-Spine Crusher** — If the Kodiak has both arm systems functional and succeeds with both initial Armored Fist attacks against the same warjack or warbeast, after resolving the attacks it may immediately make an additional melee attack roll against the target. If the attack succeeds against a warjack, the target suffers one damage point to the first available box of each system, including its hull, and is knocked down. If the attack succeeds against a warbeast, the target suffers one point of damage to every aspect and is knocked down.
- **Heavy Boiler** — The Kodiak can run without spending a focus point.
- **Vent Steam (★ Attack)** — The Kodiak creates a cloud effect with a 3" AOE centered on itself that remains in play for one round. The cloud remains at the spot placed even if the Kodiak moves. Warrior models within the AOE when the cloud is put in play suffer a POW 12 damage roll. All damage rolls must be boosted seperately. The Kodiak does not get an additional damage die on charge attacks with Vent Steam. The Kodiak can spend focus points to make additional fist attacks after a Vent Steam attack.

ARMORED FISTS

- **Fist** — Both the Kodiak's Armored Fists have the abilities of an Open Fist.
- **Hammerfist** — Add an additional die to damage rolls against knocked down targets.

Ryman

Height /Weight	11.7' / 11.2 tons
Armament	Armored Fists (right and left arm)
Fuel Load/Burn Usage	240 Kgs / 6 hrs general, 1.5 hr combat
Initial Service Date	547 AR
Cortex Manufacturer	Greylords Covenant
Orig. Chassis Design	Khadoran Mechaniks Assembly

GREYLORD TERNION

Unit

"Fear us, they do. Their weak blood turns to ice before our spellwork even begins."

—An unnamed Greylord, making a remark to his ternion comrades

The wizards of Khador are true battle-mages. It has been many years since the war-wizards of the Greylords Covenant forsook the walls of the Fraternal Stronghold in Ceryl and turned their backs upon the Fraternal Order of Wizardry. Their duty to Khador was paramount, and the call of the Motherland was too strong to deny. Now many of them ride along with the armies of Khador, and the bitter laws of winter are theirs to command. Their enchanted plate armor shimmers with the rime of diamond frost, and the blades of their rune axes are deeply etched with arcane lines and symbols of power.

Mighty is the army that counts Greylords among its ranks, and now they have found a new way to enhance their power. No longer do the wizards enter the battlefield alone. Recently, they have formed into triptychs known as ternions: three wizards bound together as one. Where one can slow an enemy with a blast of freezing air, two or three together can hold them

fast in a crystal fist of ice. They render the strongest warrior or finest marksman powerless by surrounding them in a blizzard of sleet and driving snow. Unable to see and unable to fight, their victims simply hunker down and shield their eyes from the nipping teeth of cold. The wizards' breath ghosts before their lips as they channel the element of ice, and thrusting out their arms they project a storm of blade-sharp hail, blasting from their gauntleted hands in a killing stream known as the Frost Bite.

Fear of the Greylord ternions is not restricted to the enemy, and while the simple folk of the Motherland might be grateful for their protection, cheering at the sight of these wizards of war, they spit all the same to divert the evil eye. As the wild stallions appear to bear the wizards off, talk of familiars and suspicions of dark magic are slow to fade from the murmurings about the hearthfire's glow.

KOLDUN				CMD	9
SPD	STR	MAT	RAT	DEF	ARM
5	5	5	4	14	13

MAGZIEV				CMD	7
SPD	STR	MAT	RAT	DEF	ARM
5	5	5	4	14	13

RUNE AXE			
	Special	POW	P+S
—	—	5	10

Koldun and 2 Magziev	43
Field Allowance	2
Victory Points	2

Base Size: Small

SPECIAL RULES

KOLDUN
• Leader

UNIT
Magic Ability [7] — As a combat action, each Greylord can make one of the following magic attacks during his activation. Instead of making a skill check, determine the success of a magic attack by rolling 2d6 and adding the Greylord's Magic Ability score of 7. If the roll equals or exceeds the target's DEF, the attack succeeds. The Greylord cannot make a melee attack after making a magic attack or make a magic attack after making a melee attack. Greylord magic attacks are considered spells.

• Blizzard — Target model within 10" is surrounded by a Blizzard cloud effect with AOE 3" for one round. The cloud remains centered on the model even if it moves. Models within the cloud suffer –2 SPD and RAT. If the magic attack roll fails nothing happens; do not roll for deviation. If target model is destroyed or removed from play, the effects of Blizzard immediately expire.
• Frost Bite — Frost Bite is a POW 12 spray attack.
• Ice Cage — Target model within 10" suffers a cumulative –2 DEF for one turn to a minimum of DEF 5. Apply this penalty before any other DEF modifiers. If a model is hit with three or more Ice Cage attacks in the same turn, it becomes stationary for one round.

Ryman

IRON FANG OFFICER & STANDARD BEARER

IRON FANG UNIT ATTACHMENT

"Vee are Iron Fangs. Vee fear nothing. Tell us destroy enemy 'jack… is done. Vee do not falter… veecause there is no fear in Iron Fang, no sense of dread that normal man feels ven he sees fighting voorjack. Zis means nothing. Is only something vee destroy… Is simple thing."

—Kapitan Dobrik Govorko, 603 AR

standard. A rallying point on the field, the bearer holds high the banner of the Motherland and fills the hearts of his countrymen with pride and determination. Under the striking red Khadoran colors, the Iron Fangs truly become men of iron. Signaled into motion by the standard bearer, the unit swiftly forms a shield wall in the thick of battle. Since these soldiers are respected veterans of countless frays, they drive their expertly-drilled units to excellence. Amid the compelling hue and cry of the kapitans and the valiant beckon of the company standard bearers, no enemy exists the Iron Fangs cannot overcome.

KAPITAN				CMD	9
SPD	STR	MAT	RAT	DEF	ARM
6	6	8	4	13	14
STANDARD BEARER				CMD	7
SPD	STR	MAT	RAT	DEF	ARM
6	6	6	4	13	14

BLASTING PIKE			
	Special	POW	P+S
	Multi	7	13

Kapitan's Damage	5
Kapitan & Standard Bearer	35
Field Allowance	1
Victory Points	+1

Base Size: Small

The Iron Fangs are devoted to being the finest examples of martial prowess in all Immoren. Their recruiting regimen borders on superhuman and ensures that those who "earn their fangs" are pikemen without equal and the men who bear the honor of commanding them as kapitans are consummate leaders. When Iron Fang units charge into action, they are spurred ever onward by the calls of their kapitans, double timing toward the enemy across any terrain no matter how difficult—trained as they are to weather the elements and to brave the harshest of conditions. Once the Iron Fangs are within striking distance, the kapitans lead them in skilled precision attacks with their blasting pikes intended to dismantle their targets where they stand, specifically the iron-hulled warjacks of the enemy.

Some revered veterans among the Iron Fangs are bestowed with the honor of carrying the unit's

SPECIAL RULES

KAPITAN

- Combined Melee Attack — Instead of making melee attacks separately, Pikemen in melee range of the same target may combine their attacks. The Pikeman with the highest MAT in the attacking group makes one melee attack roll for the group, adding +1 to the attack and damage rolls for each Pikeman, including itself, participating in the attack.
- Furious Charge (Order) — When this order is given, every Iron Fang may charge at +5 SPD across rough terrain though they suffer normal movement penalties.
- Officer — The Kapitan is the unit leader
- Precision Strike — When he damages a warjack in melee combat, the Iron Fang Kapitan chooses which column takes the damage.
- Shield Wall (Order) — When this order is given, every Iron Fang who moves into tight formation gains +4 ARM against attacks from his front arc. Models that do not end their movement in tight formation do not benefit from the shield wall. This bonus lasts for one round even if adjacent models are destroyed or removed from play. Troopers in tight formation can perform combat actions as normal.

BLASTING PIKE ⟦KAPITAN ONLY⟧

- Critical Knockdown — On a Critical Hit, target model is knocked down.
- Reach — 2" melee range.

STANDARD BEARER

- Defensive Formation — After all Iron Fangs in the Standard Bearer's unit complete their combat actions, immediately move all models in the unit within open formation up to 6" into tight formation with the Standard Bearer, forming the Shield Wall order, as above. The Standard Bearer may not move during Defensive Formation. Defensive formation may be used once per game.
- Unit Standard — Models in the Iron Fang unit do not flee while the Standard Bearer remains in play. When the Standard Bearer takes sufficient damage to be destroyed, a non-leader trooper model of his unit within 1" of the Standard Bearer may take up the standard. Remove the trooper model from the table and replace it with the Standard Bearer model. Any effects or upkeep spells on the replaced trooper are applied to the Standard Bearer model. Effects and upkeep spells on the destroyed Standard Bearer expire. If the Standard Bearer is not replaced, the unit must immediately pass a command check or flee.

UNIT

- Unit Attachment — An Iron Fang Unit Attachment can be added to any Iron Fang unit. The unit's Victory Point total is increased by 1.

KOSSITE WOODSMEN

UNIT

"No matter. Is fine by us. We take you anywhere you want, long as you pay. Fool's coin spends as well as clever man's."

—Kossite scout Norek Volgotskyev to a potential customer

SERGEANT				CMD	7
SPD	STR	MAT	RAT	DEF	ARM
6	5	5	4	12	10
WOODSMAN				CMD	5
SPD	STR	MAT	RAT	DEF	ARM
6	5	4	3	12	10

RANGED ATTACK

	RNG	ROF	AOE	POW
	10	1	—	10

HAND WEAPON

	Special	POW	P+S
	—	3	8

Leader and 5 Troops	55
Up to 4 Additional Troops	9 ea.
Field Allowance	2
Victory Points	2

Base Size: Small

Some call the port city of Ohk the gateway to Khador, and for those newly arrived and planning to make for the interior, they would do well to take a guide. In those lands, Kossite woodsmen are the scouts of choice, but one must take care, for the rumor is that these natives of the northern mountains cannot be trusted too far or too much—it is said they serve the Khadoran regime with an uneasy sufferance. Their knowledge of tracking and the art of ambush are renowned, but so, too, is their reputation for being shrewd and devious, sometimes returning from the mountains without the people they were hired to lead. Truth be known, this is because they have the skills to survive whereas others die for want of hearth and home.

These woodsmen know the ways of the wind and the earth and the creatures that move upon it. Tireless trackers and deadly hunters, they trust in no one and nothing save their own abilities. Their clothes are motley, but their minds are sharp, and while their muskets and elk-horn short bows might resemble antiques and bear the patina of years, they can kill just the same. Many is the army that thought itself well deployed only to be undone by hidden Kossites who laid in ambush, waiting with the patience and the instincts of the wild to strike.

Some folk mistake them for barbarians in their winter furs. Some folk think they are mad when they speak of death's voice upon the wind. Some folk think a deal paid in silver is enough to earn the loyalty of these fell hunters, but the Kossite sense of duty was learned in the school of tooth and claw and in the merciless freeze of winter. They might lead a column of warjacks through the treacherous gullies of Hellspass or shadow the enemy for days without ever being seen, but those who think they own the Kossite woodsmen are fools indeed.

SPECIAL RULES

SERGEANT
• Leader

UNIT
• Ambush — Kossite Woodsmen do not have to be put in play at the start of the game. The Kossites' controlling player may put one or more units of Kossite Woodsman in play during his control phase during any turn. When put into play, place Kossite Woodsmen in skirmish formation within 3" of any table edge except the back of the opponent's deployment zone. Kossite Woodsmen gain +2 on attacks during their activation the turn they are put into play but do not gain an additional aiming bonus if they forfeit their movement that turn.
• Camouflage — Kossite Woodsmen gain an additional +2 DEF when benefiting from concealment or cover.
• Pathfinder — Kossite Woodsmen ignore movement penalties from rough terrain and obstacles. Kossite Woodsmen may charge across rough terrain.
• Trail Blazer — Friendly models ignore movement penalties for rough terrain while remaining within 3" of a Kossite Woodsman but may not charge or slam across rough terrain.

Ryman

MAN-O-WAR KOVNIK

SOLO

"My metal brothers and I have an understanding... so long as they remain steadfast and stalwart, I will lead them, and they, in turn, will be led well."

— Kovnik Rolf Dovyetsk, Man-O-War

The Man-O-War armor allows some of the bravest—some say maddest—men of Khador to walk alongside warjacks as virtual equals. These strong, proud Khadorans in their sweltering iron skins, like any unit among the armed forces of western Immoren, have an established rank and file, and among them the kovniks are dedicated officers who have worked their way up the ranks due to their shining records. They lead the Man-O-War troops into battle and, almost always in their armor, are truly living machines of war.

Rare military-grade cortexes are only assigned to the most trusted officers, and who better to control a warjack than someone who lives like one? Hence,

kovniks are not only troop leaders, but master 'jack marshals. The kovnik also carries specialized armaments more suited to his battlefield role than the weapons carried by his subordinates. His cannon is fixed with a heavy mechanikal axe blade powerful enough to cleave through a 'jack's hull, and his great shield can even batter aside these constructs with as much sheer motive force its boiler can muster. It is no small wonder these hard-arsed veterans think themselves living warjacks—for all intents and purposes, they are indeed.

KOVNIK				CMD	9
SPD	STR	MAT	RAT	DEF	ARM
4	9	8	6	12	18

CANNON SHOT				
	RNG	ROF	AOE	POW
	8	1	—	14

AXE CANNON			
	Special	POW	P+S
	—	6	15

Damage	10
Point Cost	34
Field Allowance	2
Victory Points	1

Base Size: Medium

SPECIAL RULES

- **Commander** — A Man-O-War Kovnik has a command range equal to his CMD in inches. Friendly Khador models or units within his command range may use the Kovnik's CMD when making a command check. The Kovnik can rally and give orders to friendly Khador models within command range.
- **Fearless** — A Man-O-War Kovnik never flees.
- **Field Officer** — An additional Man-O-War unit may be fielded over normal Field Allowance limitations for each Man-O-War Kovnik included in the army.
- **Jack Marshal (2)** — The Man-O-War Kovnik may control up to two warjacks at the start of a game. The Kovnik has a marshaling range equal to his CMD in inches. If a controlled warjack is within the Kovnik's marshaling range, it can run, charge, or boost an attack or damage roll once per activation. If the Kovnik is destroyed or removed from play, his warjacks do not become inert. The Kovnik may reactivate one friendly inert Khador warjack per turn in the same manner as a warcaster. The reactivated warjack comes under his control unless he already controls two other warjacks.
- **Melee Attack (Drive)** — A Man-O-War Kovnik can attempt to Drive each warjack under his control within his marshaling range. To Drive a warjack, the Kovnik must make a CMD check at any time during his activation. If the check succeeds, the warjack can make an additional melee attack with any weapon during its activation this turn. If the check fails, the warjack does not benefit from Jack Marshal this turn.
- **Slam** — A Man-O-War Kovnik can make Slam Power Attacks. Do not roll an additional damage die for Weapon Master on successful slam attacks.
- **Weapon Master** — A Man-O-War Kovnik adds an additional die to his melee damage rolls.

WINTER GUARD MORTAR CREW
UNIT

"Hail them. Let mortar fire signal the Fifth's arrival."

—Kapitan Gerla Petrovich of the 5th Border Legion

The mortar was developed under the direction of Kommandant Irusk in an attempt to further modernize the military and is the latest addition to the Winter Guard's arsenal. This new weapon has added considerable firepower to the Guard. It is already proven in combat, and the troops are grateful for the long-range covering fire provided by the mortars.

The mortar is a man-portable variant of the bombard used on the Destroyer warjack. While heavy, it is simple to operate, easy to maintain, inexpensive to build, and it fires very large projectiles. In short, like the blunderbuss, it is an ideal weapon for the Khadoran military: cheap and effective.

The weapon is new enough that Khadoran officers are still developing tactics to integrate the mortar into use with infantry and warjacks. The favorite tactic to date is the so-called "Thundering Barrage" in which several mortar teams lay down fire on the enemy lines and create a series of explosions reminiscent of a raging storm—if such a storm spewed chunks of rock and meat in the air, of course. Winter Guard troops charge from behind this curtain of covering fire as the mortar crews sustain fire until just before the Guard reaches the opposing line. Truth be told, the mortar's inaccuracy and the crew's lack of expertise has led to a number of deaths in friendly fire, but most officers shrug off these additional casualties as the price of war.

Irusk has proposed a massed volley of mortar fire as an effective alternative to sieges and has reportedly commissioned the development of incendiary ammunition. No doubt other developments are already in the works.

GUNNER				CMD	7
SPD	STR	MAT	RAT	DEF	ARM
2	5	5	4	12	13

CREWMAN				CMD	7
SPD	STR	MAT	RAT	DEF	ARM
4	5	5	4	12	13

MORTAR (GUNNER)

	RNG	ROF	AOE	POW
	20	1	4	16

BLUNDERBUSS

	RNG	ROF	AOE	POW
	8	1	—	12

AXE

	Special	POW	P+S
	—	3	8

Gunner and Crewman	25
Field Allowance	2
Victory Points	1

Base Size: Large (Gunner and Mortar), Small (Crewman)

SPECIAL RULES

CREWMAN

• Range Finder (★ Action) — The Gunner gains +2 RAT for one round. The Crewman must be in base-to-base contact with the Gunner and not engaged to use Range Finder.

UNIT

• Weapon Crew — The Winter Guard Mortar crew is made up of a Gunner and Crewman. The Gunner is mounted on a large base with the Mortar. A weapon crew cannot run or charge. The Gunner gains +2" of movement if he begins activation in base-to-base contact with the Crewman. If the Gunner takes sufficient damage to be destroyed and the Crewman is within 1", the Crewman is removed from the table instead. Any effects or spells on the damaged Gunner expire. Any effects or spells on the removed Crewman are applied to the new Gunner.

MORTAR ⚙GUNNER ONLY⚙

• Arcing Fire — When attacking with the Mortar the Gunner may ignore all intervening models except those that would normally screen the target.
• Inaccurate — The Gunner suffers a –4 penalty to his attack rolls with the Mortar.
• Light Artillery — The Mortar cannot be used to make ranged attacks if the Gunner moves. The Gunner does not receive an aiming bonus for forfeiting movement when attacking with the Mortar. The Gunner cannot make ranged attacks with the Mortar and another ranged weapon during the same activation.
• Minimum Range — Attacks made with the Mortar cannot target any model within 8".

Ryman

BERSERKER

HEAVY WARJACK

"Respectfully, Kommandant, I must submit that even Zoktavir has questioned the Berserker's stability. Need there be more evidence they are too dangerous to use?"

—Excerpt from a report by Kommander Sorscha Kratikoff to Kommandant Irusk

Height /Weight	10' 11" / 8.4 tons
Armament	Twin War Axes (right and left arms)
Fuel Load/Burn Usage	75 Kgs / 10 hrs general, 1.5 hr combat
Initial Service Date	430 AR
Cortex Manufacturer	Greylords Covenant
Orig. Chassis Design	Khadoran Mechaniks Assembly

Among Khador's earliest warjack designs, the Berserker has come to exemplify its name in a manner that even Khadoran warcasters find unsettling. First manufactured well over a century ago, the primitive Berserker cortexes have become unstable over the years. Repeated deployments in a variety of border skirmishes have left the cortexes skewed toward aggression, or "ionized ire," as Khadoran battle mechaniks refer to it. The bloodthirsty manner with which it slaughters opposing infantry has long been legendary.

Incombat situations, Berserkers are prone to charge without orders, drawn to the frenzy of combat. Some warcasters refuse to use Berserkers simply for the risk that they will, at some point, charge into the field heedless of the warcaster's intentions. About the best one can say of the Berserkers is that they rarely attack friendly forces.

Worse yet, their cortexes' metal alloys have grown brittle and are prone to concussive overload if stimulated with too much arcane energy. While most soldiers and many warcasters fear an accidental detonation, the most canny warcasters consider this another weapon at their disposal.

Armed with a pair of immense axes, the Berserkers are ruthless in close combat. They are protected with as much armor as other Khadoran warjacks, although the aging iron plates are not fitted together with quite the same precision (nor do mechaniks wish to try to replace them).

The success of the Berserker chassis determined the development of Khador's modern warjack forces. As such, this warjack holds a revered place in the history of Khadoran technical development—if current events don not forever tarnish its reputation. Most civilized nations would have retired the Berserker long ago, but Khador's traditional disregard for human life has kept them in the field where they will continue to serve until they cause more losses to Khador than to the nation's enemies—at which point the Khadoran High Kommand may reevaluate their deployment.

SPD	STR	MAT	RAT	DEF	ARM
4	11	4	3	9	18

WAR AXE

	Special	POW	P+S
LEFT	–	5	16

WAR AXE

	Special	POW	P+S
RIGHT	–	5	16

DAMAGE GRID — 1 2 3 4 5 6

SYSTEMS

Left Arm (L)			L		R	
Rght Arm (R)					R	
Cortex (C)	L	L	M	C	R	R
Movement (M)		M	M		C	

Point Cost	84
Field Allowance	U
Victory Points	3

Base Size: Large

SPECIAL RULES

- **Berserk** — The Berserker can Charge without spending a focus point. Each time the Berserker successfully hits a target during its activation, it gains a cumulative +1 to its attack and damage rolls for all subsequent attacks that turn.
- **Chain Attack-Brutality** — If the Berserker hits the same target with both of its initial War Axe attacks, after resolving the attacks it may immediately make a Head-Butt Power Attack against the model without spending a focus point.
- **Decayed Cortex** — The Berserker begins with one cortex damage box filled. The damaged cortex box cannot be repaired by any means.
- **Head Spike** — While not a weapon on its own, the Head Spike gives the Berserker POW 2 for Head-butt attacks.
- **Unstable** — The Berserker's cortex is dangerously unstable and can explode catastrophically. Roll a d6 at the end of any activation the Berserker spent one or more focus points. If the roll is equal to or less than the number of focus points spent, the Berserker explodes. All models within 3" of the Berserker suffer a POW 14 damage roll and the Berserker is removed from play. A Berserker that explodes in this manner does not leave a wrecked warjack marker.

DEVASTATOR

HEAVY WARJACK

"If we are being pushed back, let loose the Devastators. Let us push forward… always forward."

— Prince Vladimir Tzepesci, deep in enemy territory

With the notable exception of the Widowmaker's hunting rifles, Khadoran ballistic science remains several steps behind Cygnar. Khador's chief mechaniks have favored pursuing the development of precise long-range warjack firearms for quite some time, but Queen Ayn has a differing opinion, regarding such projects too expensive. Instead, she has ordered the improvement of ballistic protection for her 'jacks. Not so very long ago, engineers unleashed the Devastator, and the 'jack has proven better than anticipated, and also less expensive, much to the Queen's approval.

The Devastator's massive arms are covered with a series of thick armor plates designed to fortify it with sturdy coverage. However, the true ingenuity of the design reveals itself when the warjack brings its arms defensively in front of its torso: the armor plates interlock to give the Devastator fully-armored protection nigh impossible to breach. As a result, the warjack does weigh almost half again as much as any other, but due to this, it can push aside nearly anything in its path using this ability to wade into the thick of the opposing lines. Early on, the added heaviness proved too great for the prototype's chassis to handle effectively—especially on any

kind of grade more than ten degrees—and the 'jack proved unstable. The designers lightened the load by scaling back the torso armor, stabilizing the 'jack, but also making it more vulnerable when its arms are in combat position.

The Devastator is equipped with a series of short range grenade launchers. It can fire these when it extends its arms, unleashing what the Khadoran troops like to refer to as the "Rain of Death." The resulting blasts tend to ravage enemy units, clearing the battlefield so the 'jack can finish its devastating work. It goes without saying that this recently fashioned warjack is a cause of great concern to enemy forces.

Height /Weight	11' 5" / 16 tons	
Armament	Twin Shield Fists (right and left arms), Rain of Death Short Range Grenade Launchers (integral)	
Fuel Load/Burn Usage	220 Kgs / 4.5 hrs general, 1 hr combat	
Initial Service Date	598 AR	
Cortex Manufacturer	Greylords Covenant	
Orig. Chassis Design	Khadoran Mechaniks Assembly	

SPD	STR	MAT	RAT	DEF	ARM
4	12	5	3	10	17
					21
					25

SHIELD FIST

	Special	POW	P+S
LEFT	Fist	2	14

SHIELD FIST

	Special	POW	P+S
RIGHT	Fist	2	14

DAMAGE GRID

	1	2	3	4	5	6
SYSTEMS						
Left Arm (L)						
Rght Arm (R)		L			R	
Cortex (C)	L	L	M	C	R	R
Movement (M)		M	M	C	C	

Point Cost	122
Field Allowance	U
Victory Points	4

Base Size: Large

SPECIAL RULES
- **Armored Shell** — The Devastator is protected by a cocoon of heavily-armored plates giving it ARM 25. The Devastator's ARM is reduced by 4 for each disabled arm system. If the Devastator makes an attack, its ARM drops to 17 until the start of its next activation. The Devastator may not be arm-locked. The Devastator's Armored Shell is not a shield.
- **Bulldoze** — If the Devastator moves into base-to-base contact with another model, the other model is moved up to 2" in the direction the Devastator is moving as the Devastator continues its movement. A model can only be moved by Bulldoze once per activation and cannot move through or over another model. Models moved by Bulldoze are not subject to free strikes during this movement.
- **Head Spike** — While not a weapon on its own, the Head Spike gives the Devastator POW 2 for Head-butt attacks.
- **Rain of Death (★ Attack)** — All models in base-to-base contact with the Devastator suffer a POW 18 damage roll. All other models within 3" of the Devastator suffer a POW 9 damage roll. All damage rolls must be boosted separately. The Devastator does not get an additional damage die on charge attacks with Rain of Death. The Devastator can spend focus points to make additional fist attacks after a Rain of Death attack.

SHIELD FIST
- **Fist** — Both the Devastator's Shield Fists have the abilities of an Open Fist.

Cryx

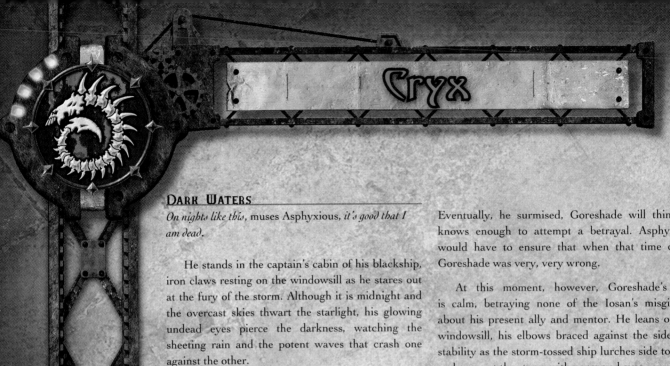

DARK WATERS

On nights like this, muses Asphyxious, *it's good that I am dead.*

He stands in the captain's cabin of his blackship, iron claws resting on the windowsill as he stares out at the fury of the storm. Although it is midnight and the overcast skies thwart the starlight, his glowing undead eyes pierce the darkness, watching the sheeting rain and the potent waves that crash one against the other.

Had he been alive, he would surely be seasick, perhaps even fearful for the safety of his pitiful life, at the mercy of his living weakness. Instead, he is able to enjoy the dark energy of the storm, draw some cold pleasure from its terror. He doesn't even need to attend to the salty spray or raindrops that splash his grinning skull: they are inconsequential.

He hears his cabin door slam open as the ship lurches to port, then slam shut again as the waves roll the ship to starboard. Uncertain footsteps walk across the pitching deck to stand a respectful distance behind him.

"Attend, Goreshade," commands Asphyxious. He takes a step away from the sill. "Gaze thee out upon the sea."

"As you wish." Goreshade stalks up to Asphyxious' side and looks out.

Meanwhile, Asphyxious looks Goreshade over. Though he shares the lithe shape of the Iosans, his heavy armor makes his frame seem massive. His natural grace belies any unease he may experience by the rolling deck. Goreshade is striking, even beautiful in a feral, alien way. His catlike eyes have power and confidence, and seem to burn like embers in his once elegant face. His formerly feminine skin has puckered and turned pallid with his descent into undeath. Framed by his ebon hair, every feature of his face demands attention.

No one alive knows what Goreshade has done to transform himself into an eldritch. No one at all, save Asphyxious. And when the last of Goreshade's soul slipped away during the transformation, Asphyxious tasted the bitterness of distrust and ambition therein.

Eventually, he surmised, Goreshade will think he knows enough to attempt a betrayal. Asphyxious would have to ensure that when that time came, Goreshade was very, very wrong.

At this moment, however, Goreshade's face is calm, betraying none of the Iosan's misgivings about his present ally and mentor. He leans on the windowsill, his elbows braced against the sides for stability as the storm-tossed ship lurches side to side, and gazes at the storm with narrowed eyes.

"What seest thou?" asks Asphyxious.

"Just a storm," replies Goreshade. "Waves, rain, lightning that splits the sky."

Annoyed at the apparent thickness of his apprentice, Asphyxious presses onward. "I see a metaphor. Waves slapping each other into foam. Sound and fury, force and drive, and ultimately what changeth? Nothing! The sea is as it is, and the waves be but afterthoughts of the storm.

"We, however, use the storm to press forward," continues Asphyxious, warming to his subject. "We ply across the waves. They carry our ship to its goal.

"The sea is Caen, and the waves are the Iron Kingdoms. They fancy their petty clashes to be the storm, but they are wrong, pitifully wrong. The storm is history, and history pusheth us forward. We must sail upon the wars of the living to the complete and utter conquest of all Caen, the slaughter of the living, and the death of Lord Toruk's insolent brood."

Asphyxious sees the fire of pride and conquest fill Goreshade's slitted eyes. His mouth draws into a wry smile, and the eldritch straightens up. "I see it, my lord," he says, "It is beautiful."

"Excellent," says Asphyxious. "Now, for thy first assignment: we must redirect the wind of the storm."

The iron lich ambles across the swaying deck to the heavy table in the center, his mechanikal body hissing and whirring as he walks with the surefootedness of a veteran sailor. The iron soul cages at his waist sway and clank at the end of their chains, scattering green speckles across the walls of the cabin. Goreshade follows after, careening slightly as the floor lurches beneath his feet.

Asphyxious reaches his right hand down to one of the soul cages and loosens the valve at the top. With his left, he makes several mystical passes, and his iron talons leave gossamer trails of flickering motes in their wake. The slight hiss from the soul cage's valve grows in strength into an echo of a scream filled with agony and despair. It is the cry of an old man, a wizened and loving grandfather, as his essence is siphoned off to fuel the caster's whim. Truth be told, Asphyxious no longer hears the screams.

As the iron lich makes the last few passes, bright light illumines the table and the maps tacked to its surface.

Goreshade leans over the table, legs spread apart and hands gripping the table's edge. "Where am I going, my lord?" he asks.

Asphyxious stabs the table with one iron talon, piercing the map. "To the Protectorate of Menoth. We will drop thee here, by the coast, this very evening."

"It will be a dangerous landing," observes Goreshade.

"Land? Nonsense. I've too much necrotite on this ship to gamble it among the shoals. Thou shalt be weighted by thy ankles to sink, and thou canst walk to shore."

Goreshade pauses, then snorts in amusement. "As you wish," he says. "It seems the most expedient solution. When I reach shore, what is my assignment?"

Again the iron lich stabs the parchment map. "In Imer, in the great temple of the Menites, they hold a young woman. She is barely beyond her youth, and hardly a woman. The words of Menoth fill her ears; her lips are a spigot, spilling his commands. This cannot continue."

"I shall kill her, then?"

"No," says Asphyxious, "rather thou shalt change her song. Let her be the mouthpiece for Cryx. Let the words she hears come from me, not from him. Let her words subvert the Menites and work our will among them."

Goreshade smiles. "Twisting a young Menite girl will pleasure me," he purrs. "She shall be ours. But how to penetrate the temple? Surely they shall sense the perfidy with their foul magic."

Asphyxious shakes his head. "Can a wizard read the cortex of a warjack?"

"Nay," says Goreshade.

"Wherefore not?" counters Asphyxious. "It thinks, does it not?"

Goreshade starts to reply, but realizes he has no answer.

"A warjack," says Asphyxious levelly, "hath no soul. Neither dost thou. Thy brain is no more alive than a cortex. They will not detect impure thoughts in thee. Merely shroud thyself like a pious servant of Menoth, and all shall go well."

"As you wish," says the eldritch with a dark smile. "I go to prepare." He turns and leaves the cabin. Asphyxious watches him depart.

A few minutes pass, then Asphyxious strides across the cabin and bars the door. He glides to the window and does the same. He casts an abjuration against magical scrying, fueled by the soul cage, then lets the soul leak out for a few extra moments.

He moves across to the back wall of the cabin, a wide expanse of polished black cherry studded with brass fixtures. He casts another spell, touches three brass bolts that protrude from the wall, then presses on a wooden panel. The panel slides in and Asphyxious reaches up inside the wall to release a catch. He then moves to his right and taps on another piece of dark wood, and the panel falls open, revealing a small compartment.

Inside is a piece of intricate mechanika, quietly generating a magical field that evades detection, arcane or mundane. Even though he created it, Asphyxious has a hard time looking at the machine; it blurs itself to evade his gaze, redirecting his eyes to the back panel of the compartment.

The iron lich reaches in and gently takes hold of the other item in the small compartment: a large, golden soul cage decorated with a pattern of eight-pointed stars. The interior of the cage glows brightly, casting stars on the iron lich's desiccated skull. He cradles the cage in his arm, and reaches one iron talon through the perforations to caress his own soul.

Someday, he thinks, *someday I shall be whole again.*

Goreshade the Bastard & Deathwalker

WARCASTER & SOLO

"Souls make war in the hereafter. I have seen the death of gods. 'Tis no different whether you die and your soul passes on to fight their war... or is bound here to fight mine."

—Goreshade the Bastard

Since nightmares and ill omens are more commonplace than daylight in Cryx, the ominous mysteries surrounding the helljacks were paid little mind, yet the early trials ended in bloody disaster. The Seethers were erratic and hard to control. Worse yet, they seemed to possess a level of awareness that bordered on sentience. Cryxian warcasters complained bitterly that keeping control over the Seethers was a continuous struggle of will; if their attention lapsed, even for an instant, the machines would brutally lash out at anything that crossed their path. All that could be done was to wait for their furnaces to go cold and hope the destruction they wrought was acceptable.

After losing a small army of thralls to the Seethers' murderous tendencies, the decision was made to seal

Height /Weight	12' / 6.5 tons
Armament	Twin Death Claws (right and left arms), Tusks (head)
Fuel Load/Burn Usage	45 Kgs (necrotite) or 120 Kgs (coal) / 12 hrs general, 2 hrs combat
Initial Service Date	566 AR, decommissioned 567 AR
Cortex Manufacturer	Master Necrotech Verrik Kurr
Orig. Chassis Design	Unknown

them away in the vaults beneath Skell where they have been ever since. In recent days, preparations for war have brought renewed attention to the Seethers, moldering away in their tombs. It may not be long before these inhuman atrocities walk the earth once more.

Bloat Thrall

Solo

"The survivors' wounds are too horrific. We can but offer them a prayer and a quick death."

—Kommandant Irusk, after his first meeting with bloat thralls in the field

BLOAT THRALL				CMD	5
SPD	STR	MAT	RAT	DEF	ARM
4	7	4	3	10	14

DESPOILER

	RNG	ROF	AOE	POW
	12	1	5	14

BLUDGEON

	Special	POW	P+S
	—	3	10

Damage	10
Point Cost	28
Field Allowance	2
Victory Points	1

Base Size: Medium

Cryxian engineers are always exploring new and more atrocious methods of slaughter, forever twisting their trademark blasphemies of flesh and iron into fresh applications of the mechanikal art. Obsessed with their fluids, necrotechs are ever seeking the perfect concoction. Hence, a recent crew of insidious engineers has struck upon a most volatile recipe indeed—a gelatinous muck so potent that the tanks in which it is stored must be alchemically treated lest they dissolve into molten sludge.

Pleased with this latest compound, they have fashioned a creative delivery system for the wretched chemical. Assembled from crudely amputated body parts, bloat thralls are stitched together and fitted with a thick iron valve mounted directly into its bowels. Before each battle, massive storage tanks are latched to the valve and their bodies are pumped full of the caustic sludge.

The bloat thralls, rife with livid, weeping seams and oozing sores, their turgid forms bulging with the acidic ooze nearly to the bursting point, shamble into combat and with seizure-like quivering expel their contents through a brass cannon. Upon impact, the viscous fluid hungrily devours both flesh and iron, and those who are struck endure screaming, bubbling deaths as the flesh sloughs from their bones. If a bloat thrall is ruptured, it explodes and showers the surrounding area in corrosive foulness. The ultimate irony in battlefield design, this type of thrall is as dangerous to destroy as it is to leave whole.

SPECIAL RULES

- Rupture — When the Bloat Thrall takes sufficient damage to be destroyed, it explodes in a shower of boiling filth with a 5" AOE. All models in AOE suffer a POW 14 damage roll. If the Bloat Thrall explodes, remove it from play.
- Terror — Enemy models/units within melee range of the Bloat Thrall must pass a command check or flee.
- Undead — A Bloat Thrall is not a living model and never flees.

DESPOILER

- Arcing Fire — When attacking with the Despoiler, the Bloat Thrall may ignore intervening models except those that would normally screen the target.
- Horrific Attack — Models/units within Despoiler's AOE must pass a CMD check or flee.

Machine Wraith

SOLO

"Until I saw the corpse fire burning in the Defender's eyes, I would have sworn they were nothing but a mechanik's drunken delusion. At that moment, I became a believer."

—Lieutenant Allister Caine, at a debriefing following a costly battle

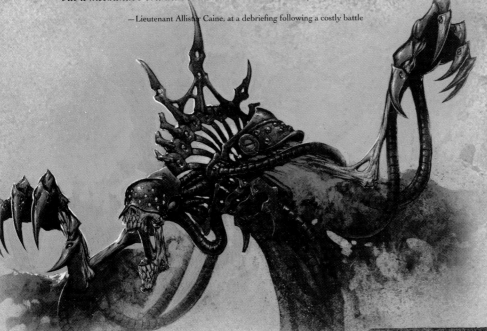

MACHINE WRAITH				CMD	7
SPD	STR	MAT	RAT	DEF	ARM
7	4	6	0	14	12

MECHANO-CLAWS			
⚔	Special	POW	P+S
	—	4	8

Point Cost	21
Field Allowance	3
Victory Points	1

Base Size: Medium

Little is known about the nightmarish apparitions called machine wraiths. That they are some deviant warping of mechanikal artifice is certain, though their origin remains a mystery. Some folks whisper they are the bitter ghosts of arcane mechaniks, some say they are priests of Cyriss, and others maintain they are fallen warcasters, but all of these rumors are mere speculation. What is known is that the sound of their arrival strikes a chill into the marrow of even the staunchest warrior; it is a keening screech that serves as the machine wraith's clarion call—something between the howl of a banshee and the straining of massive, rusty gears.

The ethereal forms of the machine wraiths are both ghostly and mechanikal, and lacking corporeality, they drift as insubstantial specters amongst the rank and file of the Cryxian armies. Only arcane methods are proof against such beings, and their unlife is driven by one obsession: the possession of warjacks. Preferring to ignore the physical world entirely, a machine wraith seeks to dominate the cortex, severing any warcaster's link and seizing control of the construct, although they are adequately capable of dealing with the living with their rending claws.

When the machine wraith seizes control of a 'jack, it pits it against its former comrades and intends nothing less than the summary destruction of all enemy warcasters. Indeed, these great wielders of magical energies are anathema to the machine wraith, for on occasion warcasters have been known to exorcise a machine wraith from its mechanikal host through a concentrated effort of will and the use of powerful magic. A machine wraith thus exorcised becomes corporeal, if but for a short time, and is exposed to the mundane but all-too-real dangers of killing forces on the battlefield. Thus, machine wraiths quickly and unerringly seek the destruction of warcasters who wield such magic as to threaten their very existence.

SPECIAL RULES

- **Incorporeal** — While Incorporeal, the Machine Wraith ignores movement penalties from rough terrain and obstacles. It can move through obstructions and other models if it has enough movement to move completely past the obstruction or model's base. A model may move through the Wraith without effect if it has enough movement to move completely past the Wraith's base. The Wraith does not count as an intervening model. The Wraith cannot engage models or be engaged. The Wraith only suffers damage and effects from spells and feats and is not affected by continuous effects. Continuous effects on the incorporeal model expire during its controlling player's maintenance phase. The Wraith cannot be charged, slammed, or pushed. Slammed and thrown models move through the Wraith without effect. The Wraith cannot charge. When the Wraith makes an attack it loses the Incorporeal ability for one round.

- **Machine Meld (★ Attack)** — The Machine Wraith may possess inert or enemy warjacks. The Wraith may not possess a warjack with a disabled Cortex. The Wraith must succeed in a melee attack to possess a warjack. A successful attack causes no damage, but the Wraith's controlling player takes control of the warjack. Remove the Machine Wraith model from the table. Any upkeep spells on the Wraith expire when it is removed. The controlling Cryx player may not activate the warjack for one round after it is possessed. A possessed warjack cannot be allocated focus points. A controller with the Focus Manipulation ability may attempt to regain control of his possessed warjack within his control area by spending a focus point during his activation. The controller then makes an unboostable magic attack roll (2d6 + FOC) against the Wraith's DEF. If successful, the Wraith is expelled. The controller can spend a focus point to re-roll failed checks. Each time a possessed warjack suffers one or more damage points, the Wraith must make a CMD check. If the check fails, the Wraith exits the warjack. The Machine Wraith may exit the warjack during its Maintenance phase at will. If the Wraith leaves a warjack for any reason, control of the warjack returns to its controller. The Wraith is placed in play within 3" of the warjack and loses the Incorporeal ability for 1 round. If an exited warjack's controller has been destroyed or removed from play, the 'jack becomes inert unless it was controlled by a model with Jack Marshal. The Wraith is destroyed if the possessed warjack is disabled or destroyed.

- **Undead** — The Machine Wraith is not a living model and never flees.

73

Necrosurgeon & Stitch Thralls
MECHANITHRALL UNIT ATTACHMENT

"We use only the best meat."

—A nameless Cryxian necrosurgeon

NECROSURGEON			CMD	7	
SPD	STR	MAT	RAT	DEF	ARM
6	6	6	3	12	13
STITCH THRALL			CMD	4	
SPD	STR	MAT	RAT	DEF	ARM
6	4	3	3	14	12

GUT SPLITTER			
	Special	POW	P+S
	—	5	11

Necrosurgeon's Damage	5
Necrosurgeon & 3 Stitch Thralls	31
Field Allowance	1
Victory Points	+1

Base Size: Small

Frequent battles throughout the borderlands of the west have left behind bloody trails of human debris. For leagues around, heaps of the dead and dying are attended by carrion scavengers of a grisly kind. Stitch thralls move slowly through this charnel realm of flies and moans, crunching their way over ribcages and out-flung hands and carefully taking in every detail. Like patrons at a fruit stall, they pause amidst the fallen to gather the best bits—arms, legs, torsos, and heads—and, if need be, severing them. Then, the stitch thralls gather the parts and deliver them to their ghoulish masters, the necrosurgeons.

As bands of mechanika-enhanced necrotic soldiers campaign from one killing field to the next, the necrosurgeon often calls for a halt to evaluate the troops, and usually some kind of spontaneous surgery is required on various thralls in states of disarray. As a specialist among necrotechs, the necrosurgeon favors one instrument in its occupation above all others: the gut splitter. Bent over carcasses and attended by stitch thralls bearing fresh parts, the necrosurgeon drills, digs, and sews enthusiastically. Any thrall that disrupts the grotesque industry with an unsatisfactory delivery— the parts they have chosen spoiled, indiscriminate, or too small—receives a hiss and a backhand, sometimes atoning for the difference with one or more of its own limbs.

Incessantly mumbling as it toils over its task, the necrosurgeon works with a child's glee. "You're a fine one… Does this hurt…? Not yet? How about this? You felt that? Wonderful… yessss…."

Quickly, the surgeon opens each body, living or dead, adds steamwork tubes and pumps and stitches together limbs of flesh and steel before finally bolting a grease-stained furnace into place. Once the lump of necrotite therein is ignited, the conglomeration abruptly rises in undeath as an awkward and menacing mechanithrall—a flesh and metal soldier of the Nightmare Empire of Cryx. Thereafter each mechanithrall is quickly led to formation, ready to march for war.

SPECIAL RULES

NECROSURGEON
- Body Snatcher (3) — Gain a corpse token each time a Mechanithrall or living model is destroyed within 3" of the Necrosurgeon. If more than one model is eligible to claim a corpse, the model nearest the destroyed model receives the corpse token. The Necrosurgeon can have a maximum of 3 corpse tokens at any time.
- Officer — The Necrosurgeon is the unit leader.
- Reanimate [8] (★ Action) — With a successful skill check, the Necrosurgeon creates one Mechanithrall for each corpse token it possesses. Discard its corpse tokens and place an equal number of Mechanithralls within 3" of the Necrosurgeon. These Mechanithralls are part of the Necrosurgeon's unit but cannot activate in the turn they are put in play.
- Terror — Enemy models/units within melee range of the Necrosurgeon must pass a command check or flee.

GUT SPLITTER ⟐NECROSURGEON ONLY⟐

STITCH THRALL
- Body Snatcher (1) — Gain a corpse token each time a Mechanithrall or living model is destroyed within 3" of the Stitch Thrall. If more than one model is eligible to claim a corpse, the model nearest the destroyed model receives the corpse token. A Stitch Thrall can have a maximum of 1 corpse token at any time. If a Stitch Thrall with a corpse token ends its activation within 1" of the Necrosurgeon, give its corpse token to the Necrosurgeon (unless the Necrosurgeon already has 3 corpse tokens).

UNIT
- Undead — The Necrosurgeon and Stitch Thralls are not living models and never flee.
- Unit Attachment — A Mechanithrall Unit Attachment can be added to any Mechanithrall unit. If the Necrosurgeon is destroyed or removed from play, remove the Stitch Thralls in the unit from play. The unit's Victory Point total is increased by 1.

Pistol Wraith

SOLO

"I seen one once at the crossroad. There ain't no shame in telling, me mucker, I turned tail and made a good run of it."

— Adolphous Monk, sergeant of the watch in Corvis

If the mask of a skull is said to wear a grin then 'tis doubly so for those called pistol wraiths, for smile they do… and they murder while they smile. Throughout the kingdoms, few inhabitants dare to meet the challenge in those dead-black eyes. No one knows from where they came, but some say they rose in the coiled streets of Skell. Those who have seen the pistol wraiths in the dark hours of the night speak of gaping holes in the swirling smoke of their flesh, the wounds of their demise preserved like a curse in their incorporeal bodies.

Some say the very first pistol wraith was a legend of the Broken Coast and a favored minion of the Pirate Kings, and it was they who petitioned the necromancers of the Dragonfather to bring him back from the fate of a coward's bullet. Those who were forced to accept the challenge of this first wraith always fell and then rose again on the next eve, seeking out mystical forgelocks called wraith pistols and wandering the world in search of other pistoleers

to slay. Indeed, it could be that these monstrosities were born of dark sorcery, for only sorcery can harm them. They do not bleed nor fear the cutting of their flesh, for no earthly blade or bullet can harm these ethereal gunmen… unless they draw first.

And there's the rub, for to render a pistol wraith susceptible to attack one must allow him to attack first and pray that the shots from his wraith pistols fly wide. Then one must retaliate quickly because their forms only coalesce for a short time, becoming solid and vulnerable to the dull weapons of steel and powder-driven lead. Dragged into the material world by their carnal desire for revenge, the pistol wraith can be killed or rather dispatched into eternal exile. However, should one tarry, the wraiths dissolve once more into smoke and malice, raising their pistols, pulling back the spectral hammers, and leveling the barrels upon one's very soul.

PISTOL WRAITH				CMD	7
SPD	STR	MAT	RAT	DEF	ARM
6	4	4	7	14	12

WRAITHLOCK PISTOL				
	RNG	ROF	AOE	POW
	10	1	—	12

WRAITHLOCK PISTOL				
	RNG	ROF	AOE	POW
	10	1	—	12

Damage	5
Point Cost	33
Field Allowance	2
Victory Points	1

Base Size: Small

SPECIAL RULES

- **Chain Attack-Death Chill** — If the Pistol Wraith hits the same target with both Wraithlock Pistols during the same activation, after resolving the attacks it may immediately make an additional ranged attack against the target. If the attack succeeds, the target must forfeit either its movement or action on its next turn. This attack does not inflict any damage.
- **Crack Shot** — The Pistol Wraith's targets do not benefit from being screened.
- **Incorporeal** — While Incorporeal, the Pistol Wraith ignores movement penalties from rough terrain and obstacles. It can move through obstructions and other models if it has enough movement to move completely past the obstruction or model's base. A model may move through the Wraith without effect if it has enough movement to move completely past the Wraith's base. The Wraith does not count as an intervening model. The Wraith cannot engage models or be engaged. The Wraith only suffers damage and effects from spells and feats and is not affected by continuous effects. Continuous effects on the incorporeal model expire during the controlling player's maintenance phase. The Wraith cannot be charged, slammed, or pushed. Slammed and thrown models move through the Wraith without effect. The Wraith cannot charge. When the Wraith makes an attack it loses the Incorporeal ability for one round.
- **Undead** — A Pistol Wraith is not a living model and never flees.

WRAITHLOCK PISTOL

- **Body Count** — A Pistol Wraith gains a soul token each time it destroys a living model. A Wraith may have a maximum of 3 soul tokens at any time. Soul Tokens may be spent to boost attack or damage rolls.

Revenant Crew of the Atramentous

UNIT

"Give us storms and rocks, give us mutiny and plague, but save us from the Atramentous."

—Casper Avery, captain of the *Magnificent*

"To sail in the wind of the dragon's wings is to sail into greatness…" Thus say the corsairs of renown and thus say the Revenant Crew of the *Atramentous*, the cinder-ship that was baptized in the fiery breath of Lord Toruk Himself. To spy the blackened timbers of this deathly ship is enough to sink the heart of many a brave captain. The coastal watches cry out in fear at the sight of their black funereal galleon, and even on the battlefield the brave retreat before these apparitions. They fly the flag of the Dragonfather and the mystical flames of his breath lick around the scorched sails that belly out in the slightest wind. Indeed, such is the enduring heat of the Dragon's fire that the very sea boils in the wake of the *Atramentous'* black hull.

And what prize for service to the Lord of Dragons? What gift for those who looted in his name and bathed the deck of their ship in the blood of innocents? Why, to pass through the furnace of undeath into His service! Those who served the Dragonfather in life, sailing the waters that lesser pirates feared to sound, return as His servants in death, and terror fills their sails. They may die a thousand deaths in the service of their lord all the while watched over by the Quartermasters, the custodians of the Revenants' service and rebirth, and when Lord Toruk is victorious over the world, then Meredius and all who sail upon its vast deeps shall belong to the Revenants.

They advance with deliberation. In one skeletal fist, the Revenants wield their vicious cutlasses filled with the ghostly light of the crescent moon. In the other they hold antique pistols loaded with necrotite harvested from many a scuttled wreck. They come on slowly. They cannot be destroyed… at least not while the Quartermaster lives. Indeed Revenants have but one life to offer, and to kill one is to waste a bullet, but to kill the Quartermaster? That, it is said, is perhaps the only way to sever the Revenant crew's undead cord of life.

QUARTERMASTER			CMD		7
SPD	STR	MAT	RAT	DEF	ARM
6	6	6	5	13	12
PIRATE			CMD		5
SPD	STR	MAT	RAT	DEF	ARM
6	6	5	4	13	12

NECROTITE PISTOL				
	RNG	ROF	AOE	POW
	8	1	—	10

CUTLASS			
	Special	POW	P+S
	—	3	9

Leader & 5 Troops	77
Up to 4 Additional Troops	11ea
Field Allowance	2
Victory Points	2

Base Size: Small

SPECIAL RULES

QUARTERMASTER
- Deathbound — Pirates in the unit destroyed within 7" inches of the Quartermaster return to the table during the controlling player's maintenance phase if the Quartermaster has not been destroyed or removed from play. Place the models anywhere within 3" of the Quartermaster.
- Leader
- Tough — Whenever the Quartermaster takes sufficient damage to be destroyed, the controlling player rolls a d6. On a 5 or 6, the Quartermaster is knocked down instead of being destroyed.

UNIT
- Deathstroke — After a successful melee attack roll, a Revenant can make a Deathstroke, doubling its STR to 12 for the damage roll. The Revenant is destroyed immediately after the attack is resolved.
- Terror — Enemy models/units within melee range of a Revenant must pass a command check or flee.
- Undead — Revenants are not living models and never flee.

NECROTITE PISTOL
- Critical Wasting — On a Critical Hit, target model suffers an additional damage point.

Stalker

BONEJACK

"These abominations only strengthen our resolve to bring His light into dark places."

—High Exemplar Kreoss, standing bloodied over the wreckage of a Stalker

Height /Weight	8' 10" / 2.2 tons
Armament	Twin Eviscerators (right and left arms)
Fuel Load/Burn Usage	15Kgs (necrotite) or 30 Kgs (coal) / 16 hrs general, 2 hrs combat
Initial Service Date	Unknown
Cortex Manufacturer	Unknown
Orig. Chassis Design	Unknown

The battlefield breeds superstition. Some soldiers believe that the souls of the fallen remain behind to watch over their comrades until the battle's end. Others believe that fighting on grounds once bloodied by war is to tempt ruin, and some speak of unseen horrors skulking out of view, reaping all manner of misfortune upon the living. Those warcasters who have fallen prey to the Stalker's scything blades know that at the heart of every tale is a spark of truth.

The Stalker is a thing out of nightmare, an insidious fusion of shadow and steel designed but for one purpose: to butcher those who oppose the will of Cryx. Nearly invisible at a distance, the surfaces of their shadow-forged hulls appear to ripple continuously with twisted, formless shapes gazing out balefully through their black metal environs.

Moving at blinding speeds, they vault effortlessly over anything in their path like great black-iron insects. Once within reach of their prey, they lash out savagely with their dreaded eviscerator blades. Warcasters wounded by such malefic weapons find not only their flesh rent but also their arcane defenses, for eviscerators draw more than blood; the Stalkers feed on the mystic energies of their victims, expending it in relentless attacks.

For the better part of a century, Stalkers have unfailingly served the dark designs of Cryx by brutally murdering their victims from shadow. Like an apparition of death, the Stalker is something the enemy cannot see, cannot study, and cannot hope to predict. Thus, the Stalker shall never become obsolete, but remain a killing machine of timeless design.

SPD	STR	MAT	RAT	DEF	ARM
7	7	6	4	16	13

EVISCERATOR

LEFT	Special	POW	P+S
	Multi	5	12

EVISCERATOR

RIGHT	Special	POW	P+S
	Multi	5	12

DAMAGE GRID 1 2 3 4 5 6

SYSTEMS

Left Arm (L)		□		□			
Rght Arm (R)		L			R		
Cortex (C)	L	L	M	C	R	R	
Movement (M)		M	M	C	C		

Point Cost	64
Field Allowance	U
Victory Points	2

Base Size: Medium

SPECIAL RULES

- **All Terrain** — The Stalker ignores movement penalties from rough terrain and obstacles. The Stalker may charge or slam across rough terrain.
- **Leap** — After moving but before performing an action, the Stalker can spend a focus point to leap an additional 5". The Stalker cannot leap if it runs, charges, or slams. When leaping, the Stalker can move over other models if it has enough movement to move completely past their bases. It ignores free strikes, rough terrain and obstacles, and all other movement penalties and effects. The Stalker may attack normally after leaping. Any effects that prevent charging or slamming also prevent the Stalker from leaping.
- **Stealth** — All attacks against the Stalker from greater than 5" away automatically miss. A Stalker greater than 5" away from an attacker does not count as an intervening model.

EVISCERATOR

- **Arcane Interference** — A model with a Power Field damaged by an Eviscerator cannot recharge its Power Field for 1 round.
- **Power Sink** — Each time the Eviscerator hits a model with the Focus Manipulation ability, the Stalker gains a power token and the model hit receives one less focus point on its next turn. On the Stalker's next control phase replace each power token with a focus point; these focus points are in addition to any focus points allocated to it from its controlling warcaster.

Leviathan

"We didn't stand a chance... It rose from the water and cut us down where we stood...."

— Last words of a dying long gunner

As Cryxian raiding parties thrust further and further into the belly of western Immoren, they found it increasingly difficult to move in secrecy. Their helljacks were simply ill-suited to negotiate the treacherous landscapes at any kind of speed. Thus, Cryxian warcasters turned to the gristle-and-grease workshops of their necrotech engineers and demanded a solution. The Dragonfather's engineers gleefully accepted the challenge and in due time unleashed the Leviathan—a creeping black-iron atrocity of unparalleled mobility.

An amphibious horror, the Leviathan is favored among the reaver captains of the nightmarish blackships. Their watertight furnaces seal for a short time, allowing the helljack to be deployed at sea, whereupon it is shoved overboard and left to scuttle to shore. Once on dry land, there is no place where men can hide that the diligently murderous Leviathan cannot track them.

Once the helljack finds its prey, Morrow help them, for it bears an array of truly gruesome weapons effective even against the durable design of warjacks themselves. A massive pinching claw adorns one of the Leviathan's arms, alchemically treated to withstand immense force while inflicting grievous mechanikal devastation. The claw clamps down upon the limbs of the enemy 'jack and holds it immobile and constricts it. Then, like some sadistic child pulling the legs from an insect, the Leviathan is able to tear limbs clean from their chassis. Additionally, the other arm bears a cannon born of vile engineering called a spiker. When the Leviathan's soul forge begins to flare, it builds up an excess of steam. Its hopper feeds crude but effective necrotite-tipped spikes into the steam driven repeating cannon. Then, with a steam whistle howl, it unleashes a barrage of black iron, riddling its victim and dismantling any system be it made of gears and metal or the much more vulnerable flesh and bone.

Height /Weight	10'5" / 7 tons
Armament	Spiker Cannon (left arm), Crushing Claw (right arm)
Fuel Load/Burn Usage	45 Kgs (necrotite) or 120 Kgs (coal) / 12 hrs general, 2 hrs combat
Initial Service Date	Unknown, first documented sighting 586 AR
Cortex Manufacturer	Unknown
Orig. Chassis Design	Necrotechs of Cryx

SPD	STR	MAT	RAT	DEF	ARM
5	12	5	4	12	18

SPIKER

	RNG	ROF	AOE	POW
LEFT	13	3	—	13

CRUSHING CLAW

	Special	POW	P+S
RIGHT	Multi	5	17

DAMAGE GRID

SYSTEMS	1	2	3	4	5	6
Left Arm (L)						
Rght Arm (R)		L			R	
Cortex (C)	L	L	M	C	R	R
Movement (M)		M	M	C	C	

Point Cost	125
Field Allowance	U
Victory Points	3

Base Size: Large

SPECIAL RULES
- **All Terrain** — The Leviathan ignores movement penalties from rough terrain and obstacles. The Leviathan may charge or slam across rough terrain.
- **Amphibious** — The Leviathan's furnace is not extinguished if it moves into deep water. The Leviathan may move through deep and shallow water without penalty. While completely within deep water, the Leviathan cannot make ranged attacks or be targeted by ranged or magical attacks.
- **Spider Legs** — The Leviathan cannot be knocked down.

CRUSHING CLAW
- **Critical Crushing Grip** — On a Critical Hit, the Crushing Claw can seize another warjack's arm or head system, crushing it and preventing its use. Declare which system has been seized after the attack roll. The selected system takes an additional d3 damage points and is automatically locked just as if the Leviathan had made a successful Armlock/Headlock power attack. Mark this damage before making the damage roll.
- **Fist** — The Leviathan's Crushing Claw has the abilities of an Open Fist.

OLD DEBTS

A mercenary stalks the avenues of Point Bourne, limping heavily on his right leg, a detached expression on his face. The air is crisp with the coming winter, bringing with it the metal tang of imminent snow. Furled in his nondescript travel-worn cloak, little about the man save his awkward gait invites attention from others walking the street. A group of them loudly carouse nearby in some personal celebration, but as they happen to the man's eyes, they sober and move quickly aside, for lethal venom lurks in the darkness of that gaze.

The mercenary keeps his head slightly canted to one side, as if assessing ways to kill each person that crosses his path. He limps noticeably but swiftly and with purpose. In his wake he leaves hearts chilled and fearful, at least until the night's passing cajoles the revelers to forget the cold shadow that crossed their path.

He moves through the crowd, glowering and ignoring the various sounds and voices. Here, at least, he is unknown. He turns down a second less-frequented thoroughfare, then again onto an even slighter filth-strewn avenue populated by unsafe—or unmoving—shadowy figures, but they ignore the limping man, as he does them. At last, he pauses at the entrance of a large plaza, and glances at an inn at the far side of the square.

Fewer people seem to be gathered outside this building than any other tavern in the city, and those who stand outside swilling their mead sing songs that are far bawdier and violent than the ditties favored elsewhere. For the first time, the mercenary presents the merest hint of a smile. It is the expression of one who has returned at last to familiar surroundings.

He hobbles directly across the plaza, timing his uneven gait to slide between the passing carriages. As he approaches the building, he extracts his left arm from beneath his cloak and, per superstition, taps the bottom of the inn's sign as he enters, setting it swaying.

The sign features a faded picture of a fat blunderbuss and a small pile of large ammunition, and is emblazoned with the words *The Iron Balls*.

Inside *The Iron Balls*, the crowd is more hushed than on the streets. They do not celebrate the harvest's closing as fervently as the rest of the city, for they are mercenaries—swords and guns for hire—and their harvest is far more grisly than the wheat and chaff gathered by the farmers. Most of the patrons hunker over their steins and talk quietly amongst themselves, although in one corner a pair of loud-mouthed mercenaries holds a gathering of avid listeners in thrall by virtue of their exaggerated stories and a keg of free-flowing ale.

The mercenary moves across the tavern floor and stands at the bar, keeping his cloak furled about him. A sunken-eyed barfly moves over to him, then thinks better of it and leaves him in peace so she can pursue easier game. He orders a tall glass of potent brandy, then leans against the bar and watches the patrons as he drinks.

They appear to be, most of them, in good spirits. The campaign season had been fair enough, leaving them with rousing tales to share and the memories of many comrades to toast in bittersweet remembrance. Now they're looking forward to a long, quiet winter, carelessly spending the coin they've earned while the rulers of the nations fret and stew about the next year and the next war.

The mercenary snorts. *They are happy just to fight and drink*, he thinks. *They care not for the plots of nations… That's what makes them such excellent tools.*

He downs the rest of his drink and moves to the stairs that lead to the second floor. The old wooden boards creak under his weight as he climbs. His limp makes the ascension difficult, so he grips the rail with one arm, half pulling himself up the steps. He navigates the balcony that circles the tavern floor, ignoring the patrons who lean on the railing and absently watch the crowd below.

On the far side of the balcony from the stairs he comes to a hallway that leads deeper into the inn, back to the suites. Many of these are de facto bunkhouses for the more famous mercenary companies, while others are all but owned by famous mercenary leaders.

He walks down the hallway, his heavy boots scraping an uneven cadence on the dirty wooden floorboards. It sounds almost like the last heartbeats grinding out from a decrepit battle-damaged warjack. He stops at the second door from the end, opens it, and hobbles inside.

The front room has a solitary table bedecked with cards, coins, several empty tankards, and a tarnished brass lantern with dirty glass panes. Two trollkin sit at the table; one rises from his chair, while the other gathers the cards and shuffles the deck.

The trollkin lurches into the mercenary's path. The lantern light makes his gray skin seem more the color of pus. "Got ye an appointment, eh?" he asks, his voice filling the room with the well-known trollkin resonance.

"No."

"Right, then. Lessee yer chops," adds the trollkin, holding out one meaty hand for the certificate that recognizes the bearer as a recognized soldier-for-hire.

"Never signed any buggered charter," replies the mercenary levelly.

The trollkin snorts, an alien sound squeezed through his teeth. "Cor, we don't wants yer type o' coin-filchin', meat-lootin' corpse-thumpers 'round here. Git off wit' ye."

Instead, the mercenary steps around the trollkin and toward the room's other door.

The second trollkin quickly stands, knocking his chair over, and boldly interposes himself between the mercenary and the door that leads further into the suite. "Right, mate," he growls, the rumble in his voice darkening the room with danger, "ye've done asked fer it…"

The mercenary's right arm shoots out from beneath his cloak, a huge mechanikal appendage built for extreme violence. Its open paw strikes at the trollkin, catching his throat in its viselike grip and slamming him back against the wall. The wood cracks with the impact. Turning quickly, the mercenary throws an underhanded gesture at the other trollkin, and a black-hued magical ray thrusts out of the man's palm and smites the trollkin square in the face, sending him sliding across the room. The fallen creature writhes on the floor, clutching at his eyes and grinding his teeth, his booted feet kicking at the floor in unbridled pain.

The mercenary turns his baleful gaze back to the trollkin against the wall.

"M—Magnus…" stammers the trollkin guard, "I'm sorry, I din't know… thought ye was dead…"

"Care to join me, then?" asks Magnus, his iron hand tightening.

The trollkin shakes his head, clutching at the mechanikal paw as it cuts off his windpipe. "The boss'll… see ye now," he gasps as blackness fills his eyes.

Magnus lets him drop to the floor, spittle drooling from his mouth as his lungs labor for air. "Thank you," he says with a wan smile.

Magnus opens the door to the interior rooms and enters. He utterly ignores the seven firearms aimed at his head. As he crosses the common room, doing his best to conceal his limp, the weapons lower one-by-one as the bearers opt for the better part of valor.

Several tables fill the room, and Magnus stops at the only table that still has someone seated at it: the trollkin mercenary captain, eating a late dinner. He pulls up a chair and seats himself opposite.

"Magnus," says the trollkin, munching his food. He doesn't even look up to meet the man's gaze.

"Boomhowler," says Magnus, imitating the trollkin's tone. He lets silence settle in for many long minutes.

At last, Boomhowler speaks. "What news?" he asks, feigning indifference.

"The time has come."

Boomhowler glances at his lieutenants. "I… we have other commitments," he says, too nonchalantly.

Magnus points to Boomhowler with his mechanikal arm. "I paid you very well, long ago. The rules of the charter state you *will… serve me… now*."

The trollkin captain meets Magnus' stare for a long moment, then he simply nods.

Magnus smiles. *It's a good time to be a mercenary.*

GORTEN GRUNDBACK
WARCASTER

"I knew ol' Grundback when he was a mine foreman back in Rhul. When I heard he was following the Code, I almost choked on me own tongue… but, ta know he does our people proud as a warcaster—that nearly brings a tear to me eye."

—Herne Stoneground, dwarven mercenary

Gorten Grundback of Clan Dohlan grew up quickly in the mines of Rhul. He knew at a young age of his inherent abilities to wield the magics of earth and stone. His clan, a long-storied family of ore-smithing miners, saw great potential in the young dwarf, and he rose quickly in the hierarchy of his clan's mining conglomerate. The higher he rose in station, the more dwarves and tools he had at his disposal.

Eventually he began to commission mining steamjacks to further his work, and that is when a whole new world opened up for Gorten Grundback.

The dwarf found he had a knack for manipulating arcane energies associated with mechanika. As a trader of materials and labor with the dwarves beyond Rhul in the lands of Llael and Khador, he familiarized himself with the mechanikal constructs, spending much time around them on his many treks. From the resonance their multi-ton steps made in the tunnel floors to the miniscule tunes within their cortexes, Gorten taught himself how to push and pull their vibrations just as he could the tremors of the earth itself, and in time, his inherent powers gave him a honed command of his steamjacks.

One day Gorten had a revelation. He realized his own potential as a self-styled warcaster, and he felt his talents were wasted in the stone bowels of Rhul.

He had heard tales amongst men and dwarves about the great honor and glory of the warcasters, so he made the decision to leave the mining life behind. Gorten turned foremanship over to his nephew, took a handful of his own personal steamjacks with him, and ventured forth to become one of the few dwarven warcasters in the Iron Kingdoms. For a while, he lived as any mercenary does: sometimes his coffers were full and his tankards overflowing, while at other times he had barely a scrap to speak of—but after proving the worth of his Rhulic warmachines a time or two, his services became highly regarded by those able to afford them.

Gorten brings a mighty command of stone and earth to the battlefield, causing walls of rock to rise from nowhere, molten ore to slag the enemy, or rooting allies to the ground so nothing short of death can move them. Such is his command of the earth's crust. He can even focus his will into a gigantic landslide of stone and soil that careens through the enemy and leaves his allies virtually untouched.

Gorten's magic is powerful and relentless, and so are his combat abilities. Physically, the dwarf is a block of armor and muscle. He plods through battle ignoring most blows in order to close quarters and level a foe with Forgefather, his mechanikal maul made to withstand terrible impacts and counter-balanced to add titanic force behind its blows. A single strike with this hammer can knock anyone off balance—men, warjacks, and even warcasters. In case Gorten's foes are too cowardly—or he too slow—to meet in battle, he also carries a double-barreled Stoneground original pistol modified to his specifications. Gorten Grundback is a skilled technician, a masterful manipulator of the elements, and a proud and mighty dwarven warrior; all available for a few thousand gold coins. Not many can pass on such an opportunity.

FEAT: LAND SLIDE

Gorten's command of the element of earth extends to an uncanny mastery of tectonic forces. The powerful warcaster can actually force the earth to shift and slide creating areas of telluric interference that can draw his enemies closer or push them away. Gorten can quickly turn an enemy offensive into a scramble for escape.

All enemy models currently within Gorten's control area are moved up to 8" toward a table edge selected by Gorten's controlling player. All models must be moved the same distance. Models moved cannot be moved over anything but open terrain and stop if they run into obstacles or other models. Gorten's controlling player chooses the order in which the models are moved. Models moved by Land Slide cannot give or receive orders and suffer –3 SPD, RAT, and DEF for 1 round.

FOCUS	5		CMD		8
SPD	STR	MAT	RAT	DEF	ARM
4	7	7	5	13	19

DUAL HAND CANNON

	RNG	ROF	AOE	POW
	12	2	—	12

FORGE FATHER

	Special	POW	P+S
	Critical	7	14

GUTTER

	Special	POW	P+S
	—	2	9

Damage	18
Point Cost	60
Field Allowance	C
Victory Points	5

Base Size: Small

SPECIAL RULES

Mercenary—Gorten will not work for Cryx or the Protectorate

Mercenary Warcaster — Gorten counts toward the maximum number of warcasters allowed in an army. Only mercenaries may be included in a force if the only warcasters are mercenaries. Gorten can only give orders to mercenary units. Only mercenaries may use his CMD when making command checks.

Rhulic Mercenary Warcaster — Gorten can only have Rhulic Mercenary warjacks in his battle group.

DUAL HAND CANNON

Both Barrels (★ Attack) — Gorten simultaneously discharges both barrels for a devastating attack. Make one roll for the attack. If it succeeds, target model suffers a POW 16 damage roll. Gorten cannot spend focus to make additional ranged attacks after a Both Barrels attack.

FORGE FATHER

Critical Concussion — On a Critical Hit, target model suffers Concussion. A model suffering Concussion forfeits its next activation and cannot allocate focus for 1 round.

Spells	Cost	RNG	AOE	POW	UP	OFF
Crater	3	8	4	13	No	Yes
Models within AOE cannot run, charge or slam for 1 round.						
Molten Metal	2	10	—	—	No	Yes
Target warjack suffers 1 point of damage to every column on its damage grid. If a damage column is full then apply the damage to the next column on the right.						
Rock Wall	2	10	Wall	—	Yes	No
Gorten creates a wall of stone. The wall template cannot be placed touching a model's base or an obstruction or obstacle. The wall template is a linear obstacle, providing cover.						
Solid Ground	2	Caster	CTRL	—	Yes	No
While in Solid Ground's AOE friendly models cannot be knocked down and do not suffer blast damage from AOE attacks.						
Strength of Granite	3	6	—	—	No	No
Target model in Gorten's battlegroup gains +5 STR and Critical Knockdown on melee attacks for one round. On a Critical Hit, target model is knocked down.						

GRUNDBACK GUNNER
LIGHT WARJACK

"Leave it to a dwarf to put such power in something so small."

—Commander Coleman Stryker, regarding the Grundback Gunner

SPD	STR	MAT	RAT	DEF	ARM
5	6	4	5	12	18

CANNON

	RNG	ROF	AOE	POW
HEAD	10	1	—	12

DAMAGE GRID

	1	2	3	4	5	6

SYSTEMS

Head (H)
Cortex (C)
Movement (M)

		H	H	C	M	
	H	H	C	C	M	M

Point Cost	48
Field Allowance	U
Victory Points	1

Base Size: Medium

The Grundback Gunner was originally intended to carry messages quickly (a relative term for the long-lived dwarves) through tunnels and mines rather than perforate the enemy with cannon fire. Named after Gorten's family, it was actually a cousin of his who first crafted the "tunnel runner"—something Gorten's own fame as a warcaster has diminished over the years.

After crafty mechaniks added a powerful cannon to the chassis, the "Grundback Runner" became a security 'jack known as the "Grundback Gunner." The cannon can even be prompted to add more punch if a warcaster feels the need. To make room for more fuel and efficient mechanisms, the Gunner is spared a great deal of the extra internal reinforcement under its thick armor plating, so although it is completely encased in steel, once its armor gives way there is little inside to protect its precious components.

Height /Weight	4'10" / 3 tons
Armament	Rhulic Cannon (head)
Fuel Load/Burn Usage	75 Kgs / 24 hrs general, 5 hrs combat
Initial Service Date	513 AR (Runner) / 526 AR (Gunner)
Cortex Manufacturer	Varies (each clan relies on their own manufacturers)
Orig. Chassis Design	Aruhn Grundback

As with much of Rhul's finest technological wonders, their 'jacks tend to be far more utilitarian and efficient than anything dreamed of by human minds. The Gunner takes the firepower of larger human machines, adds the ingenuity of the Rhulic engineers, and bolts on a touch of Grundback pride to forge out one of the most interesting warjacks to lumber through the smoke and fire of Immoren's battlefields.

SPECIAL RULES
• **Rhulic Mercenary Warjack** — The Grundback Gunner may only be included in a Rhulic Mercenary warcaster's battle group.

CANNON
• **Powerful Blast** — Spending one focus point boosts both attack and damage rolls.

GHORDSON DRILLER
HEAVY WARJACK

"Warjack armor is made from metal. Metal is made from ore. Ore is found in the stone beneath the mountains. Drills are made to break that stone and grind that ore. So what happens if we advance the whole process a bit, eh? Go straight to grinding armor?"

—Gorten Grundback, discussing some advantages of the Ghordson Driller to a potential customer

Height /Weight	11'6" / 9.5 tons
Armament	Grappler Hydraulic Claw (left arm), Rock Drill (right arm)
Fuel Load/Burn Usage	225 Kgs/ 14 hrs general, 3 hrs combat
Initial Service Date	446 A.R.
Cortex Manufacturer	Varies (each clan relies on their own manufacturers)
Orig. Chassis Design	Unknown (attributed to Varl Ghordson)

The Ghordson Driller has been in use in Rhul for well over a century. Unlike human engineering, the Rhulic approach does not just design warjacks solely for use in battle. They are a multi-purpose people with multi-purpose tools that can be called upon in times of war if need be. In such a manner, Rhul can be protected by all of its creations at any given time. A mainstay of Rhulic mercenaries on the road, surplus Drillers have been purchased by enterprising warcasters at substantial discounts.

The Driller is, not surprisingly, a mining steamjack used to break down heavy stone walls and embankments. It is a massive monster of iron and hydraulics designed to withstand falling stone or mineshaft collapses. Because of these factors, the Driller makes for a devastating combatant. Its armor is heavy and thick, and the Driller itself is a behemoth of iron and steel. It can suffer terrible attacks and shrug them off while bringing its own relentless assault to bear.

The Driller is equipped with a great rock drill that bores holes through the toughest of armor and leaves behind tatters of scrap inside and out. It is also equipped with the Grappler hydraulic claw, a powerful clenching pincer used to clear and remove rubble from work areas. It also serves as a very effective method of holding a target still long enough to bring the rock drill to bear. While not as "fast" or as "nimble" as its ponderous Khadoran cousins, the Ghordson Driller is an unyielding metal monster. Whether it is clearing the mine of obstacles or the battlefield of enemies, it does so tirelessly and efficiently.

SPD	STR	MAT	RAT	DEF	ARM
4	12	5	4	9	19

GRAPPLER		
	Special	POW	P+S
LEFT	Multi	3	15

DRILL		
	Special	POW	P+S
RIGHT	Critical	5	17

DAMAGE GRID	1	2	3	4	5	6
SYSTEMS						
Left Arm (L)						
Rght Arm (R)		L		R		
Cortex (C)	L	L	M	C	R	R
Movement (M)		M	M	C	C	

Point Cost	112
Field Allowance	U
Victory Points	3

Base Size: Large

SPECIAL RULES
- **Rhulic Mercenary Warjack** — The Ghordson Driller may only be included in a Rhulic Mercenary warcaster's battlegroup.

GRAPPLER
- **Fist** — The Driller's Grappler has the abilities of an Open Fist.
- **Grip** — After a successful Grappler attack, all Drill attacks made by this Driller against the same target this turn hit automatically. Grip only affects the last model hit by a Grappler attack.

DRILL
- **Critical System Failure** — On a Critical Hit, every warjack system damaged by the Drill, except the Hull system, is automatically disabled. After marking regular damage, those systems that took damage have their remaining system boxes marked as well.

MAGNUS THE TRAITOR
WARCASTER

"Sometimes the machinations of fate conspire to bring down great men, and no amount of valor or loyalty to king and country can excuse bloody deeds committed in a tyrant's name."

—Commander Adept Sebastian Nemo, speaking against Magnus' pardon, 595 AR

A relic of the dark days before good King Leto took the throne of Cygnar, the war criminal called "Magnus the Traitor" is among the most wanted men in the known world. With a broken body and will of iron, he wages a vendetta against his former homeland. A warcaster on the run, Magnus finances his private war with mercenary contracts, spending the bulk of his spoils on repairs and supplies to keep his ragtag battle group in fit condition. He is infamous for his sheer brutality and callous disregard for life, and only gains employment from the desperate or the ruthless.

He was not always a man without a country. Years ago, Commander Asheth Magnus was privileged to serve Vinter Raelthorne IV the Elder as an elite soldier, a canny inventor, and a much-favored battle leader. He fought with reckless abandon and directed several border campaigns against Khador. He was known for sacrificing the lives of his troops to ensure victory but, to this, Vinter paid little heed—after all, life was cheap, warjacks were not.

After usurping his brother's throne, King Leto Raelthorne sought to heal his country's wounds by offering a hearing for a full pardon and military commission to any officer who had been loyal to Vinter. Magnus refused. Instead, he led some remnants of the Royal Knights of Cygnar who still claimed loyalty to the Elder in a bloody guerilla war that went on for months. Finally, starving and wounded, he was forced to surrender to Leto's terms at sword point.

Rather than be imprisoned, after a hearing Magnus was demoted—and disgraced. He was stationed at a remote garrison along the Khadoran border where

old tactics born of a darker time eventually cost him dearly. After a daring raid against Khador's renowned 5th Border Legion, Magnus tortured to death a number of officers to gather information. His actions were immediately reported by an aspiring journeyman warcaster named Coleman Stryker. Though the sensitive information proved vital in halting Khadoran operations in the region, his superiors were appalled by his methods. He was subsequently demoted and endured six months in the brig.

Insult compounded injury when he was afterward given over to the command of the recently promoted Captain Stryker. He was obstinate, often contradicting the young Stryker's orders, and with each passing day Magnus grew progressively insubordinate. He crossed the line when he ignored direct orders in the field and forced Stryker to abandon carefully-laid battle plans to rush to Magnus' aid. Arriving just in time to keep a Crusader from landing a killing blow, Stryker sent the brutish warjack sprawling to the ground with an arcane tremor. By mere misfortune, the 'jack landed on top of Magnus and crushed his body beneath it. His arm was severed, his leg was ruined, and for weeks, he lay in the infirmary, clinging to life only through sheer hatred. To this day, he gets by with a brace on his hobbled leg and a powerful mechanikal arm replacing the one he had lost, but in many ways Magnus never fully recovered from that day.

When he was fit enough to stand, Magnus rode to the front lines, revenge heavy on his mind. The day after his arrival, he joined the unsuspecting Stryker on the battlefield, and when Magnus saw his chance, he struck. He buried his blade in Stryker's back and sent him into the dust. He reveled as Stryker sputtered blood, but before he could land the finishing blow, Magnus was battered aside by a stormglaive blast. Realizing he was outgunned, the Traitor fled the field, sacrificing warjacks under his command to block the path of his pursuers.

Since that day, Magnus has served any master who could afford his price, often bartering Cygnar's secrets with his services. A branded war criminal, Magnus bears a heavy price on his head. Commander Stryker has sworn personally to bring the villain to justice by any means necessary.

Fresh rumors concerning Magnus have begun circulating. It is said in hushed whispers that the Traitor is commissioning mercenaries for missions of his own. Some go so far as to claim Magnus gathers a secret army about him, but the sellswords who have entered his employ refuse to comment on their activities, further fueling the conjecture from dingy saloons and back alley establishments into the city streets of Caspia and beyond.

FEAT: HIT & RUN

Insanely reckless and uninhibited, Magnus has learned that motion in combat is the key to maintaining a superior initiative. By overexerting his warjacks in combat, Magnus can close in, attack, and then distance himself from an enemy while exploiting his foes' inability to adapt to the changing tides of the battle.

Magnus and all warjacks in his battlegroup currently within his control area may make an additional movement at the end of this turn. After all friendly models have completed their normal activation, models affected by Hit and Run may make an additional advance or run, ignoring free strikes during this movement. Warjacks do not have to spend a focus point to run during this movement.

FOCUS	6	CMD	7

SPD	STR	MAT	RAT	DEF	ARM
5	6	6	5	14	17

SCATTERGUN

RNG	ROF	AOE	POW
Spray	1	—	12

FOECLEAVER

Special	POW	P+S
Multi	6	12

MECHANIKAL ARM

Special	POW	P+S
Knockdown	5	11

Damage	17
Point Cost	69
Field Allowance	C
Victory Points	5

Base Size: Small

SPECIAL RULES

Mercenary — Magnus will not work for Cygnar

Backstab — Magnus gains an additional die to his Back Strike damage rolls.

Feign Death — Magnus cannot be targeted by ranged or magical attacks while knocked down.

Mercenary Warcaster — Magnus counts toward the maximum number of warcasters allowed in an army. Only mercenaries may be included in a force if the only warcasters are mercenaries. Magnus can only give orders to mercenary units. Only mercenaries may use his CMD when making command checks.

FOECLEAVER

Powerful Attack — When attacking with Foecleaver, spending one focus point boosts both its attack roll and damage roll.

Two-handed Strike (★ Attack) — Magnus can make a sword strike with all the force of his mechanical arm behind it for a combined POW + STR of 17. Two-handed Strikes benefit from the Powerful Attack ability, but the target is not knocked down.

MECHANIKAL ARM

Knockdown — On a hit, target model is knocked down.

Spells	Cost	RNG	AOE	POW	UP	OFF
Arcane Bolt	2	12	—	11	No	Yes
Magical bolts of energy streak towards the target model.						
Blur	2	6	—	—	Yes	No
Target model/unit gains +3 DEF against ranged attacks.						
Disruptor	3	8	—	—	No	Yes
Target warjack loses any unused focus points and cannot be allocated focus points or channel spells for one round.						
Frenzy	3	6	—	—	Yes	No
Target warjack gains +2 MAT and may charge without expending a focus point.						
Raining Steel	4	10	5	13	No	Yes
Wreckage from the battlefield rains down on Magnus' enemies.						
Temper Metal	2	6	—	—	Yes	No
Target warjack gains +2 ARM and is not affected by continuous effects. Continuous effects on target model when this spell is cast are removed from play.						

RENEGADE
LIGHT WARJACK

"Keep yer bloody heads down! If that thing fires, we're done for!"

—Sergeant Blake Warrant of the Eastwall trench platoon, upon being assaulted by Magnus the Traitor

Another of Magnus's infamous creations since his escape from Cygnar, the Renegade is his idea of the perfect support warjack. When designing the Renegade, Magnus wanted something that could perform a variety of battlefield roles. The result was a sort of "'jack of all trades."

For close-in armament the Renegade uses a savage chain-driven scrapsaw called a shredder which tears holes in armor while the angled teeth bite in further and deeper. It causes horrible wounds in both metal-and-steam and flesh-and-blood troops. To support the need for long-range attacks, Magnus concocted the alchemical Obliterator rocket. Made of heavy scrap-chaff and expensive chemicals wrapped in a deadly segmented shell, the rocket takes up a great deal of space and finances, but the result is a far-reaching attack that explodes powerfully in all directions, showering the area with "deadly metal hailstones."

The powerful concussive blast tosses troops about like rag dolls, if not obliterating them outright.

Height /Weight	Average 8'7" / 3.75 tons
Armament	Shredder Scrapsaw (right arm), Obliterator Rocket (left arm), Reconstructed Grade IV Arc Node
Fuel Load/Burn Usage	Average 80 Kgs / average 7 hrs general, 1 hr combat
Initial Service Date	599 AR
Cortex Manufacturer	Fraternal Order of Wizardry/ Cygnaran Armory/ Magnus the Traitor
Orig. Chassis Design	Engines East/ Cygnaran Armory/ Magnus the Traitor

SPD	STR	MAT	RAT	DEF	ARM
5	8	5	5	11	17
					18

OBLITERATOR

	RNG	ROF	AOE	POW
LEFT	14	1	4	16

SHREDDER

	Special	POW	P+S
RIGHT	Shred	4	12

DAMAGE GRID

SYSTEMS	1	2	3	4	5	6
Left Arm (L)						
Rght Arm (R)		L	A	A	R	
Cortex (C)		L	L	M	C	R	R
Movement (M)		M	M	C	C	
Arc Node (A)						

Point Cost	65
Field Allowance	2
Victory Points	2

Base Size: Medium

SPECIAL RULES

Custom Warjack — The Renegade may only be included in a battlegroup controlled by Magnus the Traitor.

Faulty Arc Node —The Renegade may channel spells but every time it does so there is a chance it will backfire causing damage to Magnus the Traitor. Each time the Renegade is used to channel a spell, roll a d6 after resolving the spell's effects. On a roll of 1-3, Magnus takes one damage point, plus an additional point for every focus point used in boosting the spell's attack and damage rolls. On a 4-6 Magnus takes no damage.

OBLITERATOR

Arcing Fire — When attacking with the Obliterator, the Renegade may ignore all intervening models except those that would normally screen the target.

Buckler — The Buckler add +1 to the Renegade's ARM. The Renegade loses this bonus if the warjack's left arm system is disabled.

Knockdown — All models in AOE are knocked down.

One Shot — The Obliterator can only be used once per game.

SHREDDER

Shred — The Renegade may immediately make an additional attack against any model it damages with the Shredder. Separate attack and damage rolls are required for each additional attack. Completely resolve each attack individually, applying the targets' special rules immediately as each attack is resolved.

Magnus mastered the assembly of the arc node at a young age. It is a talent that allows him to do the unthinkable: re-assemble a functioning arc node from damaged or destroyed ones. Arc nodes are too rare and expensive for most mercenaries to purchase on the black market, so the Renegades are scrap-built and, hence, can sometimes be dangerous. Magnus doesn't fret about such things; nosebleeds and migraines from magical feedback are worth the price of victory—and to Magnus, the Renegade is well worth the cost.

TALON
LIGHT WARJACK

"Would someone like to tell me why we stopped using those things?"

—Captain Victoria Haley, during a thwarted capture attempt upon Magnus the Traitor

Height /Weight	9' / 3.25 tons
Armament	Stun Lance (right arm), Shield (left arm)
Fuel Load/Burn Usage	75 Kgs / 7 hrs general, 1.5 hrs combat
Initial Service Date	522 AR, decommissioned 579 AR
Cortex Manufacturer	Fraternal Order of Wizardry
Orig. Chassis Design	Engines East

Originally developed as a frontline 'jack by Cygnar, the Talon is a common sight in today's black markets and salvage yards. After years of service, the Cygnaran Royal Armory had the chassis decommissioned when newer models took their fancy. Despite retirement, the Talon has remained a black market favorite among those with the gold or influence to acquire them.

The Talon uses a predecessor to cortex-shock technology in its stun lance. "Stalling" is based around a negatively tuned apparatus in the head of the spear which sends confusing commands into any cortex-driven mechanika upon striking it. These confusing commands cause warjacks to falter and palsy and makes movement difficult or even impossible. Eventually the commands will be overridden by the cortex itself, but sometimes a few moments are all the Talon needs to cause a critical blow with its lance or spiked shield.

While newer, more technologically advanced 'jacks are in production throughout western Immoren, those who do not have access to royal coffers or governmental taxes must rely on that which is available. Although expensive, the Talon is numerous and effective and will no doubt be part of many mercenary and freelance charters for a long time to come.

SPD	STR	MAT	RAT	DEF	ARM
6	8	5	4	12	16
				⛊	18

SHIELD		
	Special	POW	P+S
LEFT	–	0	8

STUN LANCE		
	Special	POW	P+S
RIGHT	Multi	4	12

DAMAGE GRID   1   2   3   4   5   6

SYSTEMS

Left Arm (L)						
Rght Arm (R)		L			R	
Cortex (C)	L	L	M	C	R	R
Movement (M)		M	M	C	C	

Point Cost	61
Field Allowance	2
Victory Points	2

Base Size: Medium

SPECIAL RULES

STUN LANCE

- Powerful Charge — A Talon making a charge attack with the Stun Lance gains a +2 bonus to its attack roll.
- Reach — 2" melee range.
- Stall — A target warjack hit by the Stun Lance becomes Stalled. Stall is a continuous effect that reduces the warjack's base SPD to 1 and DEF to 7. Stall will expire in the model's maintenance phase on a roll or 1 or 2.

MANGLER
HEAVY WARJACK

"That hideous device tore through some of the Motherland's finest like it was toppling a house of cards. Were I not avowed to avenge my Khadoran brothers, I might admire such strength and ferocity."

—Prince Vladimir Tzepesci, commenting on the Mangler during a Llaelese border skirmish

SPD	STR	MAT	RAT	DEF	ARM
5	11	5	4	11	19

PUNCHING SPIKE

	Special	POW	P+S
LEFT	Fist	2	13

WRECKER

	Special	POW	P+S
RIGHT	Multi	6	17

DAMAGE GRID	1	2	3	4	5	6
SYSTEMS						
Left Arm (L)						
Rght Arm (R)		L			R	
Cortex (C)	L	L	M	C	R	R
Movement (M)		M	M	C	C	

Point Cost	105
Field Allowance	2
Victory Points	3

Base Size: Large

When Magnus fled Cygnar after his brutal attempt to kill Stryker, he was forced to sacrifice his own 'jacks to ensure his escape. Following that, he needed replacements for when the day would come when he could go back to finish what he started. Obviously, Magnus couldn't steal fully-functional warjacks—their installed cortex locks make such a thing quite difficult indeed. It was apparent that he would need to create a new force from salvaged parts using a new brand of bloody ingenuity.

As an inventor for the former king of Cygnar, Magnus was up to the task, and his first—and some say greatest—creation was the Mangler. Using components looted from Protectorate and Cygnaran stockpiles, Magnus assembled what he considered to be the deadliest combination of strength, ability, and durability he could afford and he soon enough had several powerful scrap-giants assembled. Made almost entirely of salvaged or stolen bits and scrap, fused together with the Traitor's driven genius, Magnus' Manglers are as formidable as any warjack created by Cygnar's fine engineers.

Height /Weight	Average 12' / 8 tons
Armament	Wrecker (right arm),Punching Spike (left arm)
Fuel Load/Burn Usage	Average 120 Kgs / average 5 hrs general, 1hrs combat
Initial Service Date	598 AR
Cortex Manufacturer	Fraternal Order of Wizardry/ Cygnaran Armory/ Magnus the Traitor
Orig. Chassis Design	Engines East/ Cygnaran Armory/ Magnus the Traitor

Manglers make use of a wrecker which is a thick chain—often nabbed from ship's anchors or drawbridges—used to swing a massive spiked or studded ball of riveted iron in wide sweeping arcs that can smash through a dozen or more men in a single swing. They are also armed with a massive three-foot-long spike of tempered metal attached to the knuckles, making them deadly in close combat as well. It was crucial to Magnus that the spike did not impair the 'jack's ability to open and close its hand, as he also uses Manglers for labor and for hauling ordnance and supplies—essentially a standard ten-ton mule able to level an entire town unaccompanied.

SPECIAL RULES
- **Custom Warjack** — The Mangler may only be included in a battlegroup controlled by Magnus the Traitor.

PUNCHING SPIKE
- **Fist** — The Punching Spike has the abilities of an Open Fist.

WRECKER
Circular Strike (★ Attack) — The Mangler may make a separate melee attack roll against every opponent in melee range of its front and back arcs. Completely resolve each attack individually, applying the targets' special rules immediately as each attack is resolved. Determine damage normally.

Reach — 2" melee range.

NOMAD
HEAVY WARJACK

"Oh, it may be simple, yah, but we dogs like the Nomad. Tough, tenacious, really bears down and tears things up… heh, just like us, eh boys? Why, even the name suits our way of life!"

—Samantha MacHorne, leader of the Devil Dogs mercenary company, talking about her preference for the Nomad warjack

Height /Weight	12.1' / 10.5 tons
Armament	Battleblade (right arm), Buckler (left arm)
Fuel Load/Burn Usage	120Kgs / 5 hrs general, 1 hr combat
Initial Service Date	455 AR, decommissioned 563 AR
Cortex Manufacturer	Fraternal Order of Wizardry
Orig. Chassis Design	Engines East

Before disruption, alchemical freezing, and technological development became the deciding factor in 'jack warfare—the sword was law. In those days it was not the efficiency of an engine or the composition of the frame; it was how much wreckage a warjack could create before becoming a wreck itself. That was the era of the Nomad, but the old 'jack never did say quit, and it can still be found in service today.

The Nomad is a simple but effective monster of bolted iron and reinforced frame. It is a reminder of Cygnar's storied history, wielding an oversized version of the Caspian battleblade employed by the Sword Knights for centuries. While not as sophisticated as some of the weapons of its descendants, the

Nomad's blade delivers mighty blows just the same. A small buckler above the Nomad's open hand grants it additional protection, while not affecting its ability to open and close. The hands of a 'jack are especially important to mercenary companies who use them as a labor force to make up for their lack of manpower. Indeed, the Nomad has become a mainstay for many mercenary companies throughout western Immoren. It is reliable and easy to repair for less-than-savvy mechanics, and even though its design predates anyone living today, it is doubtful the Nomad will ever truly be retired. It is an iron token of days past and a reminder that newer does not always mean better.

SPD	STR	MAT	RAT	DEF	ARM
5	11	5	4	10	18
				◡	19

OPEN FIST		
	Special	POW	P+S
LEFT	Buckler	0	11

BATTLE BLADE		
	Special	POW	P+S
RIGHT	–	7	18

DAMAGE GRID

	1	2	3	4	5	6

SYSTEMS

Left Arm (L)						
Rght Arm (R)		L			R	
Cortex (C)	L	L	M	C	R	R
Movement (M)		M	M	C	C	

Point Cost	82
Field Allowance	U
Victory Points	3

Base Size: Large

SPECIAL RULES

OPEN FIST
• Buckler — The Buckler adds +1 to the Nomad's ARM. The Nomad loses this bonus if the warjack's left arm system is disabled.

CAPTAIN SAM MACHORNE AND THE DEVIL DOGS

UNIT

"Cross the devil and ye'll get her hornes."

—Lieutenant Grebbel Bhug, Devil Dogs mercenary

SAM MACHORNE			CMD	9	
SPD	STR	MAT	RAT	DEF	ARM
6	6	7	6	15	12

DEVIL DOG			CMD	6	
SPD	STR	MAT	RAT	DEF	ARM
6	6	6	4	13	13

HAND CANNON

	RNG	ROF	AOE	POW
	12	1	—	12

SLUG GUN

	RNG	ROF	AOE	POW
	4	1	—	14

STUN SWORD

	Special	POW	P+S
	Stall	4	10

PICK AXE

	Special	POW	P+S
	Trash	4	10

Sam's Damage	5
Sam and 5 Devil Dogs	76
Up to 4 Additional Devil Dogs	11 ea.
Field Allowance	C
Victory Points	2

Base Size: Small

With a history entrenched in warfare, it is no wonder the mercenary trade is such a lucrative profession in western Immoren. Some might even call it an industry. "Kingdoms crumble and empires fall, and only the mercs shall survive it all," is a popular cadence sung by these sellswords, and with the great number of mercenary companies throughout the Iron Kingdoms, it may well be true. In fact, many companies have charters longer than the royal dynasties they have served.

One such company bears the red-blazoned insignia of a ferocious horned hound. They are called the Devil Dogs, or "Dog Company" as they often refer to themselves. This company was established over 180 years ago by Grigor Dorenski, a former kapitan of the renowned Winter Guard, and they benefited from several decades as a successful army-for-hire often on the Khadoran payroll, participating in some noted campaigns as well as a few sorties into Llaelese territory.

However, during the Second Expansion War, the Devil Dogs would rewrite their charter with a declarationnever to accept Khadoran coin again. As Kommander Zerkova pounded the northern Ordic borders season after season in 464 AR, the lives of Khadoran soldiers disintegrated like ocean waves crashing against rocky cliffs. Mercenaries were contracted from wherever they could be found—among them, Dorenski's Devil Dogs. Proud to be in the hire of his homeland again, Dorenski faithfully carried out orders to take Boarsgate as Zerkova led his army once more against the walls of Midfast. Unknown to Dorenski, the Kommander never expected the Dog Company to succeed—only to sap forces from Midfast as Zerkova made his grand entrance. Still, the all-too-capable mercenary army toppled the fort in a single night and day, sending most of the Boarsgate garrison retreating for Midfast, which ultimately succeeded in reinforcing the defenders and repelling Zerkova's army once again. Embarrassed by this folly, Zerkova withheld payment

from the Devil Dogs. Upon learning of this, Dorenski rewrote the company's charter in his own blood, stating that the Devil Dogs would never again fight on Khador's behalf even if they were the last paying kingdom on Caen.

Nearly a century-and-a-half later, Dorenski's great, great nephew wagered and lost ownership of the Devil Dogs to an enterprising Thurian female by the name of MacHorne. The former owner of the Devil Dogs later claimed he threw the game intentionally as an excuse to retire from "years of mud-slogging," but it mattered little to Samantha MacHorne who had keenly perceived the negative impact of impending war upon her river trade business and saw an opportunity to line her purse with the gold of restless governments possessing more wealth than diplomacy.

Though the Devil Dogs enjoyed a respectable reputation as a reliable mercenary company, MacHorne's upbringing in Ord had taught her to be wary of the dangers of falling behind the times. The weapons and tactics of Dog Company were antiquated by modern standards, and after selling off her trade outfit, she quickly invested great sums,replacing crossbows with firearms and upgrading her new troops' armor to something capable of weathering the current mode of warfare.

Two years later, Captain Sam MacHorne and the Devil Dogs hired themselves out as the best professional anti-jack unit gold could buy. Newly-equipped with custom-built, armor-blasting slug guns, warmachine entangling chains and nets, and heavy pick axes designed to dismantle warjacks plate-from-piston, the Dog Company re-entered the mercenary market as a force to be reckoned with. Today, the Devil Dogs preserve the ancient Iron Kingdoms mercenary tradition upon which they were established, and the blood of their founder still reads red on their vintage charter: "Grigor V. Dorenski, 464 AR. Khador Beware."

SAM MACHORNE

Jack Marshal (1) — Sam may start the game controlling one mercenary warjack. Sam has a marshaling range equal to her CMD in inches. If the controlled warjack is within Sam's marshaling range, it can run, charge, or boost an attack or damage roll once per activation. If Sam is destroyed or removed from play, her warjack does not become inert. Sam may reactivate one friendly inert mercenary warjack per turn in the same manner as a warcaster. The reactivated warjack comes under her control unless she already controls another warjack.

Leader

HAND CANNON
➤Sam Only⬅

STUN SWORD
➤Sam Only⬅

Stall — A target warjack hit by the Stun Sword becomes stalled. Stall is a continuous effect that reduces the warjack's SPD to 1 and DEF to 7. Stall will expire in the model's maintenance phase on a roll of 1 or 2.

DEVIL DOGS

Combined Ranged Attack — Instead of making ranged attacks separately, Devil Dogs in open formation may combine their attacks against the same target. The Devil Dog with the highest RAT in the attacking group makes one ranged attack roll for the group, adding +1 to the attack and damage rolls for each Devil Dog, including himself, participating in the attack.

Entangle (★ Attack) — Instead of attacking normally, 2 or more Devil Dogs may attempt to entangle a target warjack or warbeast within 2". The model with the highest MAT in the attacking group makes one melee attack roll for the group, adding +1 to the attack for each Devil Dog, including himself, participating in the attack. If the attack is successful, the target is knocked down but suffers no damage.

PICK AXE
➤Devil Dogs only⬅

Trash — Double POW of this weapon against knocked down targets.

SLUG GUN
➤Devil Dogs only⬅

UNIT

Mercenary — The Devil Dogs will not work for Cryx or Khador.

GORMAN DI WULFE, ROGUE ALCHEMIST
SOLO

"The Wolf…? Hmmm, I don't know… Why? He's a madman. I think there is not a finer alchemist for leagues around… but… like I said, he's a madman."

—Commander Coleman Stryker, when asked about the employ of Gorman di Wulfe

GORMAN				CMD	8
SPD	STR	MAT	RAT	DEF	ARM
6	4	5	5	14	12

ALCHEMICAL GRENADES

	RNG	ROF	AOE	POW
	6	1	*	*

STILETTO

	Special	POW	P+S
	—	2	6

Damage	5
Point Cost	28
Field Allowance	C
Victory Points	1

Base Size: Small

Born to wealth in Leryn, Gorman di Wulfe showed great interest at a young age in the path of scholars. He was eventually sent to Merywyn Academy and was a fine student, but he soon waned from other subjects to become wholly enveloped in the Crucible's teachings. He left the Academy and returned to Leryn to study alchemy at the Order of the Golden Crucible's Thunderhead Fortress.

Gorman was enthralled as an apprentice. Every other facet of his life fell to the wayside in his pursuit of alchemical mastery, and he surpassed his mentors' expectations, decorated with the mantle of an expert by his fifth year. Regarding the mixing of agents to create wondrous effects, nothing seemed beyond Gorman's skills and imagination. From invisibility to bottled luck to concentrated longevity, naught was too challenging for him—except dealing with the Crucible's politics, that is.

Just recently, troops retreating from the west brought news of the fall to Khadoran forces of Laedry and Rynr and of the imminent assault upon the town of Riversmet mere leagues away. Gorman beseeched his superiors to allow him to direct his potions against the invaders, but he was denied. Undeterred and used to getting his way, he suited up regardless. The alchemist grabbed a bandolier of his most powerful tinctures, threw on a wide-brimmed hat to cover his face, and rode hard for the endangered Three Rivers Town. He arrived just as the assault had begun. Selflessly consumed with the thrill of it all, Gorman rode hard into the city under fire, weaving through the enemy and hailstorms of deadly shot. Soon enough his horse went down, but he continued the fight, running on foot from spot-to-spot, tossing jars of his deadly acid and metal-weakening salves at Khador's finest. Gorman's potions worked marvelously, and he celebrated their success with howls of fervor. Whether it was the fumes or the frolic, the young alchemist noble had become euphoric in the carnage unfolding around him.

While Gorman was bounding around the battlefield, a rocket suddenly exploded nearby and buffeted him aside like a rag doll. When he came to, the assault had ended. His body was undiscovered, having been sheltered in a pile of debris, but the near-death experience caused him to see clearly for the first time in his pampered life that he wanted to live on the edge forever. Gorman di Wulfe never returned to Thunderhead Fortress. He let them believe whatever they wished—he could be dead, rogue, or a deserter. He did not care. All he wanted was to feel alive.

Now the rogue alchemist has taken his skills on the road. He is keen on the Cygnaran translation of his family name and has taken to calling himself "the Wolf." Under that name, he happily hires himself out to anyone promising an exciting battle, sometimes working for next-to-nothing in the service of both king and tyrant, and of course, he brings his powerful potion-grenades with him. Obfuscated by alchemy and ingenuity, Gorman darts from battle-to-battle, mixing just the right amount of obsession with a healthy portion of dedication for powerful results.

Sometimes the Wolf's explosive reputation precedes him, and some commanders have become reluctant to hire him at all. He is called a "lunatic" and a "loose cannon;" someone who can't be counted on for anything save the swirling storm of entropy that follows in his wake. If there is a method to Gorman's madness, it lies somewhere deep in the equations of the alchemist's mind—a labyrinth best left unexplored.

SPECIAL RULES

Mercenary — Gorman di Wulfe will work for any Faction

- **Bushwhack** — Gorman may make a ranged attack before moving. After attacking, Gorman can Advance normally, but can take no additional actions.
- **Invisibility** — Gorman can forfeit his activation to become invisible. While invisible, Gorman cannot be targeted by ranged or magic attacks, cannot be charged, and gains +4 DEF against melee attacks for one round. Gorman cannot become invisible if engaged at the start of his activation. While invisible, Gorman does not block line of sight or provide screening.
- **Smoke Bombs (★Action)** — Gorman may place a Smoke Bomb centered anywhere within 3" of himself. A Smoke Bomb creates a 3" AOE cloud effect that remains in play for one round.
- **Stealth** — All attacks against Gorman from greater than 5" away automatically miss. If Gorman is greater than 5" away from an attacker, he does not count as an intervening model.

ALCHEMICAL GRENADES

Gorman may throw one of the following Alchemical Grenades per attack:

- **Acid Bomb** — The Acid Bomb has a 3" AOE. All models within AOE suffer a POW 12 damage roll and Corrosion. Corrosion is a continuous effect that slowly erodes its target. Corrosion does one point of damage each turn during the model's maintenance phase until it expires on a d6 roll of 1 or 2. Corrosion is not affected by water.
- **Black Oil** — Black Oil has a 3" AOE. All models within AOE suffer blindness for one round. Blind models cannot make ranged or magical attacks, suffer -4 MAT and DEF, cannot charge, run, or slam, and must forfeit either movement or action during activation.
- **Rust** — Target warjack suffers -4 ARM. Rust is a continuous effect that remains in play until it expires during the model's maintenance phase on a d6 roll of 1 or 2.

RUPERT CARVOLO, PIPER OF ORD
SOLO

"Aye, I recognize him. 'Tis said the people of Ord are among the bravest of all. I dinnae 'bout that…
but I know ye could scour the land for heroes and not find a greater nor sadder one than yon
Piper o' Sorrows, that's for damn sure…"

—Captain Victoria Haley, when asked about a mercenary with Ordic pipes entering a Cygnaran bivouac

CARVOLO				CMD	8
SPD	STR	MAT	RAT	DEF	ARM
6	6	6	4	13	14

SWORD			
	Special	POW	P+S
	—	3	9

Damage	5
Point Cost	22
Field Allowance	C
Victory Points	1

Base Size: Small

SPECIAL RULES

Mercenary — Rhupert Carvolo will not work for Cryx or Khador.

SONGS

As a Special Action, Carvolo may play one of the following songs, affecting himself and a target unit within 3". All songs last for one round. Carvolo may not play the same song two rounds in a row:

Dirge of Mists (★ Action) — Carvolo and target unit are wrapped in obscuring mists, gaining +1 DEF and Terror. All enemy models/units within melee range of models with Terror must pass a command check or flee.

Heroic Call (★ Action) — Carvolo and target unit gain the Tough and Fearless abilities. Whenever a Tough model takes sufficient damage to be destroyed, the controlling player rolls a d6. On a 5 or 6, the model is knocked down instead of being destroyed. Models not destroyed are reduced to one wound. Fearless models never flee.

March (★ Action) — Carvolo and target unit gain the Pathfinder ability and either +2" of movement or an additional melee attack with any weapon. Pathfinder allows models to ignore movement penalties from rough terrain and obstacles. Models with the Pathfinder ability may charge across rough terrain.

The courage of Rupert Carvolo is truly appalling to those who do not know the depth of his suffering. To go on living after what befell him is more than the stoutest heart can bear, but to suffer so and still retain one's sanity is simply asking too much. How does a man give voice to the torment in his soul? The weak may bite a bullet. The strong might take a sword to seek peace through a warrior's bloody death. But not Carvolo…

They call him the "Piper of Sorrows," and the tunes that he ushers forth from his pipes have the force of compulsion in their lilting melodies. To hear him is to forfeit reason and embrace despair, for it is said his playing can leave a brave man weeping in the street, fill his mind with a nightmare's dread, or even stop his heart dead. This is not mechanika. This is not "the Gift." This is the power of desolation, and strong it is. Such power never goes unnoticed. Such power never goes unused. But Carvolo does not care…

For a silver schilling he will join a troop, wrapping his minstrel's cloak about the soldiers of the enemy no matter who they are. To the proud folk of Cygnar or the zealots of Menoth, he sells his services cheap—but never to Khador. A bull of solid gold could not buy a note for such "treacherous weasels."

What does one receive for their mercenary coin? What tunes in his repertoire might be of use to a commander of the field? Why the Piper's March, of course. Summoning all the subtle menace of a poisoned nursery tale it may go something like this:

"See, children, how the forest parts at the sound of the Piper's March? See the scrub laid flat and the thorny brambles twist aside to let the Piper pass? But,

do not dally my sweet children, my brave soldiers. You must keep up, lest the demons of twig and thorn find you alone and drag you down and fill your sobbing throat with clumps of rotting leaves. March in double time to the Piper's tune, and see how the fleetness of his melody grants you the element of surprise. Strike once, strike twice before your enemy can raise his guard, and laugh and weep as you skip into battle, for the melody of misery compels you."

"And what next, Piper of Sorrows?" the braying ranks beseech. "Squeeze out a tune to give us courage!"

The Piper's eyes gleam with tears as he pipes the Heroic Call, a tune to lift a warrior's heart beyond fear and reason. Driven by the exultation of Carvolo's refrain, they will grip their weapons and charge forth even into the face of certain death. Though weapons pierce their flesh, still they will fight, for the power of the Heroic Call will not let them be still—not until the piping stops or the body is broken. Only then will the poor wretches who appealed for courage desist, lie still, and die.

"Something for the advancing ranks," say the commanders of the field. "Play something for them, Carvolo. Something to protect them and confound the enemy's aim."

Then shall he gather the men about him and play the Dirge of Mists, and as the cold slime of the piper's aegis runs clammy on their skin, the unit will advance. Pity the enemy then, for in all the realm of Cryx there are no more terrible sights than those that swim in the vomit fog of the Piper's song. The enemy does not see a unit of men approaching but a swirling mass of shadows and gibbering madness. In panic, they loose their arrows. In terror, they fire their guns. However, few attacks find their mark, for the Piper of Sorrows denies them. Lost in the reverie of the damned, Carvolo marches ever on with tears on his cheeks and tunes too horrible to mention resounding in his mind.

⟨Sword Knights⟩

⟨Cygnar 1,000 Point Army⟩

≫ALT. STRYKER≪

≫COMMANDER ADEPT NEMO≪

≫STORMBLADE≪
STANDARD BEARER

≫STORMBLADE≪
CAPTAIN

≫SWORD KNIGHT≪

≫STORMSMITH≪

Cygnaran
Military Ranks

Sergeant

Lieutenant

Captain

Major

Colonel

Commander

General

Lord General

Warmaster
General
(aka General
of the Crown)

Cygnaran Mage
Ranks

Apprentice of
the Art

Journeyman

Magus

Adept

Prime

CYGNAR PAINTING TECHNIQUES

One of the key color areas of Cygnar warjacks is the rich gold colored metal work, and this is really quite simple to achieve. The following example is over a black undercoat and all the colors are from the Citadel range.

STAGE 1

Base coat with Brazen Brass. Aim for a neat, even coverage.

STAGE 2

This stage is optional but it can give some nice depth to the detail. Wash with a mix of blue, green, and brown ink and aim for a dirty turquoise color. This should be thinned with water and applied fairly liberally, but not so it forms into deep pools.

STAGE 3

If you followed the optional instructions in stage 2, you will need to follow up with this. Re-coat and tidy with Brazen Brass, leaving the wash color in the deep areas of the model.

STAGE 4

Highlight the edges and raised details with a mix of Brass and Shining Gold. This can either be dry-brushed carefully if you are painting quickly, or the highlights can be painted on.

STAGE 5

Top highlight by adding a tiny spot of Mithril Silver to the first highlight color and repeat the instructions from stage 4.

CENTURION

STORMCLAD

FORT FALK GARRISON COMBAT DRESS

The customary light gray colors of the Fort Falk garrison came into use in 560 AR when a Llaelese designer of utilitarian apparel named Alio Mergevine received the commission for uniform design. The Royal Assemblage noted the choice of color at the time as "Neither significant to the eyes of hostility nor inauspicious aim, yet becoming of smart dress as sharp as Cygnar's regal blue." The choice of yellow for cuffs and piping represents the Falk Trust - a commission that awards valor in combat or astute diligence with golden Cygnaran Crowns. Those who wear the gray and yellow are eligible for the trust as long as they serve under Falk's commander.

In modern times those stationed at the Fort Falk garrison wear the colors as part of their battle dress while they serve as guardians of the Black River and the railway that runs along the market line. Because assignments to serve at Fort Falk are greatly desired, troopers from other garrisons refer to the bright yellow Swan of Cygnar emblazoned on the uniforms of Falk as "the chuffed duck".

PAINTING TIPS

Caine's warband has been painted with flat grey military colors. A mix of black and white or GW Codex Grey with white can be used for this. When you are painting miniatures in neutral tones, it is a good idea to use a strong color as a contrast, and in this case we used a bright golden yellow. Weathering on the lower parts of the clothes, especially the greatcoats, gives the appearance of an army that has been in the field for a while and is made up of hardened veterans. This is pretty easy to achieve. Just complete all the shading and highlighting first and then add a warm mid-brown color to the appropriate areas. This can either be gently dry brushed or carefully blended for a more subtle effect.

CYGNAR ALTERNATE COLOR SCHEME

Flameguard Cleansers

Protectorate of Menoth 1,000 Point Army

KOMMANDANT IRUSK

MAN-O-WAR
KOVNIK

IRON FANG
KAPITAN

IRON FANG
STANDARD BEARER

GREYLORD KOLDUN

ALT. SORSCHA

KHADORAN MILITARY RANKS	SERVICE MARKINGS
SERGEANT	EACH PAIR OF SLASHES INDICATES FIVE YEARS OF SERVICE
LIEUTENANT	KHADORAN MAGE RANKS
KAPITAN	UCHENIK
KOVNIK	RASTOVIK
KOMMANDER	MAGZIEV
 KOMMANDANT	KOLDUN
SUPREME KOMMANDANT	OBAVNIK
 PREMIER	

KHADOR PAINTING TECHNIQUES

Highlighting bright red can be tricky to get just right. The overall effect can either come out too orange or too pink, depending on the highlight mix you use. There is one trick that can fix these problems and give you a really good rich red. it's called glazing and is covered in more detail in the Advanced Techniques section. Here is the best way to apply this technique to red areas. You can use any brand of waterproof, light fast artist's inks.

STAGE 1
Once all of the highlights are applied you should let them dry thoroughly. For the best finish it's worth making the highlights quite a salmon pink color.

STAGE 2
Mix red and yellow ink and aim for a fiery orange color. Water the mixture down considerably before applying it. When glazing you are aiming to apply a thin, even coat so that the color below is just tinted. Let each stage dry before applying another glaze.

STAGE 3
Add a little more red ink to the mix and apply as above, being careful to make sure the ink is dry between applications.

STAGE 4
Use pure red ink (still watered down, but not as much as above) to add some depth to the surface. Only apply it to the areas where you want to deepen the color.

◄DEVASTATOR►

◄KODIAK►

THE 5TH BORDER LEGION

Khador's 5th Border Legion, or the "Enforcers", is one of the Motherland's most feared regiments. Charged with the defense of the great nation's southern border, the 5th Border Legion has a history of violent boundary skirmishes with Cygnar that spans nearly a century. Grim-faced and determined, the soldiers of the Legion attend to their work while keenly aware that the security of all Khador rests upon their shoulders.

Notorious for their brutality and tenacity, the Legion wear drab green uniforms that inspire a powerful sense of foreboding in their frequently-raided enemies. Their uniforms are as utilitarian as their arms and are ideally suited to blend into the environs of the Thornwood. Border wars often degenerate into sniper campaigns and the Legion's drab green color fairs far better than the reds worn by other Khadoran regiments.

PAINTING TIPS

Traditional military colors like this can be used to great effect on WARMACHINE armies and are especially appropriate in this case – the drab olive color contrasts quite well with the usual bright red of the Khador force. Notice how the Khador Red has been used on each miniature. This not only gives some contrast and interest to the scheme, but it also ties the 5th Border Legion miniatures in with the regular Khador army. These sorts of military colors can easily be mixed by adding a spot of brown to a regular deep green, and highlighting with a little grey helps to keep the color neutral and not too bright.

➤KHADOR ALTERNATE COLOR SCHEME➤

Revenant Crew of the Atramentous

Cryx 1,000 Point Army

GORESHADE AND DEATHWALKER

ALT. DENEGHRA

NECROSURGEON AND STITCH THRALLS

PISTOL WRAITH

MACHINE WRAITH

Cryx Animation Glyphs

Necromancy achieves the animation of the dead through ritualistic application of ancient, arcane glyphs. Branded, tattooed, or carved into the dead flesh—each necromantic glyph adds power and ability to the undead thrall.

Authority Ranks

Thrall Warrior

Thrall Lieutenant

Thrall Captain

Mark of Asphyxious

Animation Glyphs

Basic Animation

Aggression

Strength

Protection

Intellect

Stealth

Arcane Power

Cryx Painting Techniques

One of the most striking features of Cryxian warjacks is the unearthly green glow that emanates from beneath the armored hull and it is really quite straightforward to achieve. It's best to do this before painting the surrounding areas. The colors mentioned here are from the Citadel range.

STAGE 1

Working over a black base coat, apply a layer of Scorpion Green mixed with a little Sunburst Yellow. This should be applied quite thickly to make sure the color is strong. Don't worry too much about getting the paint on adjacent areas. This is supposed to represent light that could illuminate the areas around it. Too much over-spill can easily be cleaned up.

STAGE 2

Mix more Sunburst Yellow into the base mix and apply to the center of the area.

STAGE 3

Add Skull While to the above mix and apply to an even smaller area.

STAGE 4

Tidy up around the edges with Chaos Black.

Seether

Leviathan

Cryx Alternate Colors

THE JADE MOURN

Dressed in a deep verdant green, the Jade Mourn are Cryxian warriors and helljacks that operate in and above the waters of the Broken Coast. Goreshade chose the colors for aesthetic reasons, and they represent the dark green of the depths that claims the dead for Cryx and returns them to their shores. While the uniforms themselves hold no special meaning, it is interesting to note that the color is similar to the hue used for some martial orders of Ios. Goreshade has probably perverted the color to his own purposes, and it no doubt symbolizes some obscure elven reference.

The Jade Mourn typically operates as coastal raiders and slavers, wreaking havoc amidst settlements and villages along the Broken Coast. It is a typical tactic for them to deploy a league or more off shore, plung into the deep, and walk inland in order to attack by surprise at night.

PAINTING TIPS

Tying the color of a particular warcaster to a small warband really helps to give a visual key that this is his personal force. This becomes especially true when the smaller warband is attached to a larger force. In this case the scheme was taken from Goreshade and used on a unit of Bane Thralls and a Leviathan. We applied deep green to all the armored areas, but notice also how we used red quite subtly on the miniatures and kept the gold areas to a similar tone. Small touches like this can really help to give a coherent look to an army.

CRYX ALTERNATE COLOR SCHEME

⟣Devil Dogs⟣

⟣Mangler⟣

⟣Ghordson Driller⟣

MAGNUS THE TRAITOR

GRUNDBACK GUNNER

GORTEN GRUNDBACK

RENEGADE

RHUPERT CARVOLO

TALON

Todd Arrington's Cryx Army

All of the painted miniatures depicted in this book show the official colors of the Iron Kingdoms armies. When you paint your own miniatures it's really up to you whether you want to follow these schemes or not. Todd Arrington decided to come up with an original scheme for his Cryx army – pale natural tones that were inspired by some of the maritime scenery of the Pacific Northwest where he lives.

Advanced and Difficult Assembly

There is a huge and ever increasing number of miniatures in the WARMACHINE line that ranges from the smallest Stitch Thrall to the mighty Khador Devastator. Many of these miniatures consist of single pieces that merely need to be attached to a base, while others can have upwards of ten pieces that need to be carefully cleaned and assembled. While this might seem like an onerous task it is a necessary part of the hobby. A well-assembled miniature is going to be easier to paint and far more resistant to damage. All WARMACHINE miniatures are designed with ease of assembly in mind, but inevitably there are some that will provide a certain amount of challenge to even the most skilled hobbyist. However, by employing a few techniques the difficulty can be kept to a minimum.

Let's start with some universal rules that should be applied when putting any miniature together:

• Always make sure that the areas that you are joining are properly cleaned. Any casting marks should be filed off, and both surfaces should be lightly rubbed with abrasive paper (600 grit wet and dry is ideal). This removes any oxidation from the metal and provides a far stronger join. This will also help the glue set quicker.

• Check the fit between the pieces – small imperfections can often develop over the course of a mold's life and these are transferred to the casting. If the join is a 'peg and hole' type, make sure that the peg fits snugly into the hole – you might have to file a little away to make sure it goes in properly.

• Clean all the pieces before you assemble them. If you glue the miniature together first and then attempt to file away the mold lines, there is a good chance that the pieces will come apart again.

• Remember that the larger the surface areas that meet, the stronger the join will be. If the join occurs between two flat surfaces, make sure that they are as flat and smooth as possible. There is a trick that you can use on larger surfaces to see how close the join is. Cover one surface with a very thin layer of paint, then hold the pieces together and twist the join very slightly. When you pull the pieces apart again, the areas where the paint has worn off show where the two pieces meet – file some material away and try again until the join is as flat as possible.

• If you are joining three pieces together – such as the arms on a Stormblade or Exemplar, join two of the pieces together first - like the two arms- then make sure they are dry before attaching them to the body.

• Always use super-glue (cyanoacrylate) – it gives the best bond and dries quickly. Follow the safety instructions on the packaging carefully.

• Don't apply too much glue – it takes longer to form a bond and you are more likely to make your fingers a permanent part of the miniature…

• You can greatly speed the bonding process by using an accelerator such as Zip-Kicker. Just spray a little onto the join area and the glue dries instantly. Be very careful using accelerator sprays – always use in a well-ventilated area and be careful to spray away from yourself (and not toward anyone else). Avoid using on painted miniatures – it can re-wet the surface.

• Fill any gaps left with putty. This may seem like a waste of time but it will make the join many times stronger in the long run. Two-part epoxy putties like green stuff work best. Just mix a tiny amount, roll into a thin sausage and apply to the gap. It can be worked in and smoothed out with a dental-style modeling tool or even a tooth-pick.

• If you know there is going to be a gap that needs filling, it is possible to add the green stuff while you are actually joining the two pieces. Just add a tiny (much less than you think you are going to need) amount of green stuff to one half and a spot of glue to the other. The pieces will join instantly and once the putty is dry the bond will be super-strong. You have to leave the miniature alone completely while the putty is drying though. A great example of where to use this technique would be on the horns of the Satyxis. Apply a tiny (and I really mean tiny – like the size of a rivet…) ball of putty to the indentation in the head. The put a spot of glue on the end of the horn and push the two pieces together.

PINNING

The best way to strengthen joins that are likely to take a lot of weight or leverage– such as the hand/ weapon on a Man-O-War - is to add a strengthening pin. This is a simple process but can turn a join that is likely to break into a rock-solid bond. I am going to use the Leviathan as an example as the long limbs can be prone to coming apart if handled roughly.

Here is the process broken down into simple stages:

• Before you start doing anything, do a 'dry-fit' to see how the miniature goes together and what pose you are aiming for. With a large and complex miniature such as the Leviathan, there are several different poses that can be achieved. You should know what you want to do with it before you start the actual assembly.

• Clean all the pieces thoroughly making sure to take the surface off the join areas with wet and dry.

• File the top of the rounded pegs flat. This will make it easier to drill a pin hole.

• Drill the hole as close to the center as possible. Start the hole by gently twisting the point of a craft knife into the surface.

• Drill into the opposing piece at the deepest point of the rounded hole.

• Cut a pin that fits neatly when the two pieces are held together and make sure it is not too long. Glue this into the smaller of the two pieces and let the glue dry before moving on.

• As an optional stage if there is going to be a gap in the join, add a tiny amount of green-stuff on the flat part of the join area.

• Apply a small amount of glue to the larger of the two pieces and press them together.

• The arms are assembled differently – it is not a very easy area to pin, so it's best to use a variation of the green-stuff/superglue technique. Apply a small amount of putty into the arm socket then push the arm into it. To make the bond instant run a tiny spot of glue into the join.

• The carapace can be attached by adding a small amount of green stuff to one side and glue to the other. This will create the best bond.

ADVANCED PAINTING TECHNIQUES

Miniature painting is something you can happily do at practically any level. It doesn't really matter if you are just painting simple flat colors or spending hours of painstaking work on each miniature. One thing is almost always true: once you start painting, you generally strive to get better. It really won't be long before you are looking at other people's miniatures and try to work out how certain effects are achieved. In the next couple of pages we're going to try to take some of the guesswork out of it and go over a few so called "advanced" techniques.

PAINTING FACES

The face is the focal point of a figure – the place to which your eye is drawn as soon as you look at the miniature. It's also the place that gives you a real opportunity to add some life and character to a piece. Whether it's pale and sickly tones for the living or undead minions of Cryx or frost-tinged faces for the troops of Khador, both are easy to achieve and can really place a miniature firmly in a setting. The Iron Kingdoms has many women fighting for their lands, and it's pretty straightforward to emphasize the differences between them and their male counterparts. In general female faces should be treated with a little more subtlety. Colors should be a little lighter and warmer and the shading should be a little less harsh. You can also add some color and character to female faces by adding a little make-up, though this needs to be handled with care or your Sorcsha will look like she is more at home in one of the brothels of Five Fingers!

Let's look at a couple of stage-by-stage examples of female and male faces. It doesn't really matter at what stage you paint the face on a miniature – some people prefer to do this first and some as the very last thing. Whatever works for you is just fine.

STAGE-BY-STAGE SORSCHA ~ PAINTED OVER A BLACK UNDERCOAT

- Basecoat with flesh that has a spot of brown to add a little depth. Make sure the coverage is even and the paint is reasonably thin so it doesn't fill any of the detail or features.

- Add a spot of brown ink to flesh (Higgins water proof drawing ink is ideal), and carefully wash this over the whole face. Don't apply too much here – you are just aiming to add shading for depth.

- Using a standard flesh color, start to add some highlights. Apply the paint to the cheek bones first and blend down onto the lower jaw area. The forehead and nose are next – be careful to leave the creases dark or you will have to go back in with a deeper tone later.

- Use the same flesh color to paint the upper lip and chin.

- Add a little grey to a flesh color and paint between the top of the eye and the brow. It's not easy to see this on Sorscha, but it can clearly be seen on the other female faces shown in this book.

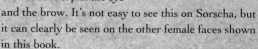

- Black in the eyes and mouth.

- Mix a lighter flesh color and apply to the cheek bones, bridge of nose, chin, and brows. With the cheek bones, blend the color down onto the cheek

- Mix basic flesh with a spot of bright red for the cheeks. Apply the color just below the cheekbones and blend into the cheeks. Be careful to be subtle here.

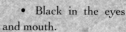

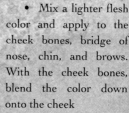

- Add a little more red to this mix for the lips. This is just added to the lower lip. If you

paint the upper lip as well she'll look like a lady of "ill repute."

- Less is more with the eyes. If you paint in too much white she'll look like she's staring (*or in extreme cases, Marty Feldmen*). On Sorscha a tiny spot of a bone color was added to one side of the eyes.

- The final stage is to clean up around the face.

VARIATIONS

Cryx females can be painted with overall lighter tones, even with a spot of blue added to cool down the colors. You can also use a deep shade beneath the eye as well as above to give a harsher feel. A deeper lip color also gives a harsher, less natural feel.

STAGE~BY~STAGE KOSSITE WOODSMAN ~ PAINTED OVER BLACK UNDERCOAT

This uses the same techniques and stages as Sorscha unless noted.

- Start with a deeper flesh tone than with the female face. Add slightly more brown or tan to the flesh color and paint evenly over the face and ears.

- Mix a dark flesh color with a spot of brown ink and wash over the face evenly.

- Use a dark flesh color to paint the forehead, nose, and cheek bones – blend down onto the lower cheek. Let this dry and then pick out the jaw line and blend this up onto the cheek. This emphasizes the jaw line and gives a stronger profile.

- Paint the upper lip, chin, and ears in a dark flesh color.

- Mix a lighter flesh tone and paint onto the forehead, bridge of nose, and cheekbones. Don't forget the ears also!

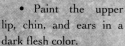

- Paint black in the eyes and mouth if open.

- On male faces, instead of adding color to the cheeks, five o'clock stubble can be added. Add a spot of black and brown to your flesh color and apply thinly to the lower face areas and upper lip. Add a touch of flesh to this mix and highlight the jaw line again.

- Add a spot of red and brown to your flesh color and paint the lower lip. Make sure this color isn't too red.

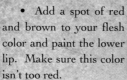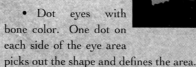

- Dot eyes with bone color. One dot on each side of the eye area picks out the shape and defines the area.

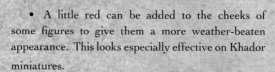

- A little red can be added to the cheeks of some figures to give them a more weather-beaten appearance. This looks especially effective on Khador miniatures.

BLENDING

Once you have mastered the basics of painting – such as neatness, highlighting, and shading - you will be itching to add some subtlety and depth to your work to make it really shine. There is one technique above all others that, once mastered, will make a huge difference to the look of your miniatures. That technique is blending. There are really two subdivisions here: blending highlights and blending shade colors, but the technique is the same for both. In the example below we will just cover blending highlights.

The theory is that you blend colors as you put them onto the miniature and create a subtle gradation from light to dark tones. There are several different ways to achieve this, but the one we are going to look at here is the two-brush technique. There are a few points to remember that are vital to perfecting this technique of good blending.

- Always apply paint to a surface that is totally dry. If you are trying to blend a highlight over a color that is still wet you will end up with a mess. (There is a technique that blends two wet colors together, but

it's practically impossible with acrylic paint and is far more suitable for oils and enamels where the drying time is far longer.)

• The consistency of the paint is key. You want to use a fairly thick paint – the mistake that most people make is to have the paint too watery thinking that it will make it easier to blend. This actually makes it dry faster when applied and the results will always be patchy.

• Work in small areas. If you try and work on too much at a time you will find it difficult and the paint will dry before you finish.

• Work fast. Once you have the highlight color mixed, try to work as quickly as possible. As soon as you apply the highlight to an area, blend it right away before it has a chance to dry.

• Don't over-work an area; try to keep it simple. If you make a mistake it's usually easier to go back and fix it later rather than keep on trying to get the blend perfect.

The basic technique itself couldn't be more simple – you apply the highlight color with one brush and immediately use the other (which is just damp, not wet) to blend the edge. As mentioned previously, you are not trying to blend the two colors together – this is impossible as the one you are painting over is dry. You are using the second brush to fade the edge of the highlight color. It's best to keep the second brush (the one with no paint on it) held in your mouth so you can swap as soon as the color is applied.

That's it! Once the color is dry you can mix a lighter highlight and repeat the process but cover a smaller area. As with normal highlighting the more shades you apply, the more subtle the finished effect

will be. For really top quality display miniatures it's not uncommon to apply 8-10 layers of highlights, each one blended.

Once an area is finished you can go back and tidy up using a mid tone that is half-way between the base color and the highlight. If you want to add more depth to the shading, just blend a deep color into the recesses. Inks are ideal for this but you can also use deep paint.

Once you have started highlighting and blending an area, it's good to see it through to the end. That way you don't have to mix colors later. This shows the gradation of highlight color that you might use on a chosen area. It's best to start with far more paint than you think you will need; it's better to have too much rather than run out.

FREEHAND DECORATION

There is one area of miniature painting that people seem to be more nervous about than any other – painting freehand decoration such as symbols, runes, and tattoos. While this should probably be considered an advanced technique, with a few tips it's really not that difficult to become proficient. There are a few things to remember that will make life much easier:

• Half the work is in the planning. Making an accurate sketch (to the same size) will make life far easier. Draw out an accurate representation of the area on which you are painting the symbol and then carefully

Facing such iron vengeance, the Winter Guard soldiers pull out of the city square, leaving behind only a few badly wounded individuals who huddle helplessly behind the slim cover of the fountain's edge. One frenzied warjack charges the hurt men and begins pummeling them into unrecognizable pieces.

"Damn it!" yells Jakob. Seven of his nine warjacks pursue the fleeing Khadorans as Jakob pulls his awareness back to himself. He runs to the center of the square and shouts orders all around, gesticulating like a madman. "After them! Jaxin, Retnus, gather your squads and pursue, double quick! Don't give them a chance to regroup! Raven Company, with me!"

Cullyn grabs the commander's arm just above the elbow. "I don't like it, sir," he yells over the din of shouted orders, stamping boots, and the occasional gunshot. "You need to call your 'jacks back!"

The warcaster rounds on him, one fist raised to strike. "You questioning my orders?!"

"'Course not!" Cullyn backs up a bit. "It's just too bloody easy! Winter Guard don't nip off like that."

"That's 'cuz they wasn't bloody expectin' the 'helms to kick their bum-fluff out the front door, now, ain't it?" boasts Jakob jubilantly.

"Sir, I—"

"Forward!" bellows the commander. "Let's go, boyos!" He charges out of the square, leading a wedge of nearly two-hundred soldiers and his two remaining 'jacks in the wake of his other cobblestone-pounding warjacks. Flushed with excitement, he rushes ahead, not waiting for Jaxin or Retnus to ready their troops.

A block away, Winter Guard units turn and engage at key points along the city streets, only to crumble as soon as Jakob's van of warjacks smash through their defenses. The warcaster and his Raven Company keep the pressure on, until at last they push the Winter Guard out of the town.

The mercenary warcaster pauses for a moment to catch his breath. He assesses perhaps a hundred men lost and three of his warjacks were down. The Khadorans gave a decent fight, but it wasn't even close. As Jakob turns to coordinate the pursuit, Cullyn appears at his side. "I'm tellin' you, sir, something's still not right," he says.

Jakob looks out at the Winter Guard, routed and fleeing across the open fields. He had a feeling Cullyn was on to something, after all. "You may be right, boyo. They're probably planning on bushwhacking us at the tree line. Jaxin! Retnus!..."

"Retnus is dead, sir," a mercenary with a bloody gash on his face replied. "I'm his second."

"Very well. Form your men up here. We're moving out in close order! Pickets out front! They may try to stand up to us at the woods, but we'll force 'em out!"

"Hold on. I'm not sure that's a good idea, sir," Cullyn protests, but the officers move off to arrange the men. "I told you about those explosions! We don't know yet what made them or where in the hells they're coming from."

"Nonsense! Sappers is what we're dealing with. Snuck up and placed charges on the barracks. These blokes couldn't guard an overfilled outhouse on a summer day. That's why they hired us. Now, get in ranks, soldier. Forward!" Jakob waves his troops on and begins advancing on the scattered remnants of Winter Guard troopers.

The Thunderhelms begin crossing the open fields at the edge of town, and Jakob's smile grows with every passing step. Bloodshed. Victory. Glory. And a bloody huge bonus from the government for saving Laedry from a Khadoran raid.

If things keep going like this, he thinks, my mercenary days are over! I'll retire and—

Suddenly he senses the strange tug of powerful magic, and the ground softens to mush beneath his feet. He pushes forward, but his feet sink in the mud, and he stumbles.

He hears deep, bass thumps coming from somewhere in the drizzle. The troops begin to murmur, and he senses the rising panic. Above, somewhere in the clouds, he hears a few faint whistles. He looks around for Cullyn, but the man is nowhere to be seen.

The whistles grow in volume, and then Jakob finally remembers every detail of what Cullyn described. He was just too battle-eager before. Too impulsive. "Morrow help us," the warcaster murmurs, and then starts to yell something to his troops…

…But there is nothing more.

Behind their firing walls at the west end of town, the Llaelese troops watch the Winter Guard troopers pull back from the far end of Laedry. The soldiers begin to rally their courage, although continued fire by the Widowmakers keeps them pinned.

Then a mass of Thunderhelm Irregulars march out from the cover of the town, perhaps four hundred

men and several miscellaneous warjacks resolutely pursuing the retreating Khadorans. The Llaelese soldiers cheer. They begin to rally, ready to charge, Widowmakers or no, and drive the bastards back to Khador, but suddenly, across the battlefield, a Khadoran warcaster appears, casting a potent arcane spell. The Thunderhelm mercenaries stall and, a few scant breaths later, the ground erupts in massive fiery explosions, altogether consuming the mercenaries.

After a stunned moment, a Llaelese trooper murmurs, "What in the world was that?"

"Beats me," answers another. "Some new mechanika?"

"Aye, mayhap they got a bunch of them whaddayacall 'jacks hidden in the woods," posits a third.

"Destroyers, I think they calls 'em. Bloody guts! Heavy artillery to the right, Widowmakers to the left, can this get any worse?"

Then, behind them, the hiss and thump of steam-powered warjacks become evident. The soldiers turn to see over a dozen great machines each brandishing a pair of huge axes and, in their midst, a solitary human attired in ancient, plate armor. Raw magical power arcs from his hands.

"Surrender," says the newcomer, his voice like black satin.

"Right," says a soldier. "That sounds reasonable, eh lads?"

The Llaelese soldiers nod, then their pikes and muskets clatter noisily upon the cobblestone streets.

It has been nearly a week since the fall of Laedry. The sky is leaden, the rain heavy as it beats down on a solitary rider emerging from the Widower's Wood along the Great Northern Trailway. The horse keeps slipping into a trot or a walk, whereupon the rider whips it into a gallop once more. Moments after the rider draws within sight of the lights of Corvis, the steed collapses, tumbling them both off the road, down a scree-coated embankment, and into a muddy ditch.

The man groans and sits up. He gazes for a moment at his steed lying dead mere feet away, its great heart obviously spent in the exhaustive effort of a long, hard ride. Second bloody horse in seven bloody days, he thinks, then checks himself over for wounds or broken bones, but finds he is merely scraped up a bit.

The man crawls to the dead steed and loosens a saddlebag, throws it over his shoulder and clambers back up the sloppy embankment to the rutted, muddy road. He pulls his tattered soggy coat about his shoulders, and begins sloshing toward the city at a trot.

Soon, it is nightfall. He has slogged in the rain for what seems an eternity until finally he comes alongside the wide and swift running Black River and, shortly thereafter, arrives at the north gates of the City of Ghosts. Soaked to the bone, the man nevertheless hunches beneath an archway in a brief respite from the rain, gasping for air. The great gates are shut so he pounds on the door of the outer watch tower.

"Open up!" he bellows. "Urgent news from the north!"

He bangs some more but still no answer. "Urgent news!" he yells yet again, but after waiting a few more moments, he refills his pistol, praying that the rain hasn't dampened his powder, and discharges it. The report is loud, but not the same as thunder.

"Bloody hell!" descends a voice from above him. "Who goes?!"

The man peers up and shields his eyes from the falling rain. A lone watch guard leans over a railing, looking down. He takes a deep breath to focus the last of his energy and yells, "Open up, you poxy wanker!"

He sags against the arch and slowly sinks to the ground. At last, a small trap in the watch tower door opens, and a suspicious face peers out. "What's all this riot then, wot?"

"Urgent news," he gasps, "for your commander. Is there… who's the ranking officer here?"

"Right," says the watch guard, "but if yer yankin', it's the pillory for you, especially discharging an arm like that." He opens the door and steps out. "You hurt or somethin'?"

"Just… mostly tired," the man replies. "My horse dropped a couple leagues back. I've run quite a ways."

The guard bends and helps the man up. "Let's see you inside, then."

Moments later, the guard deposits the man in a chair near a roaring fire while other armed men fetch a blanket, some hot mulled wine, and their leaders. Not long therafter, several military officers enter the room. One man, bedecked in housecoat and slippers, with a shock of white hair and a thick white moustache, seats himself behind a desk and addresses the drenched messenger. "I am Commander Adept Nemo," he says, peering down his nose over the rims of his spectacles. "I am the senior officer presently here in Corvis, so state your name and speak your mind, and be quick. I'm missing dinner."

"My name is Cullyn Lopryssti, commander adept," says the messenger through chattering teeth. "A mercenary of the Thunderhelm Irregulars. Well, that is if the 'helms still exist... Simply put, it's war, sir. Khador has attacked Llael in greater numbers than ever before, men and 'jacks. And they've got some sort of heavy ordnance that drops shells from far off and wherever they damn well please. They swept in completely by surprise. The city didn't stand a chance."

The commander adept eyes the messenger. "You are certain of this?" he asks, leaning forward.

Cullyn nods slowly, as if even moving his head is a grueling struggle. "I was there when Laedry fell. Saw it with my own eyes. Passed around Merywyn as it was under siege on my way here and had a damn time of it. They'll take the entirety of Llael before the snow is knee deep, at this rate."

"This is tripe," observes one officer. "Beg your pardon, but he's having one on us, sir. Mayhap trying to lure us out so his band can winter in our own beds and drink our drafts."

"Agreed, sir," says another. "How is this pocketeer privy to more than our entire spy corps, eh?"

Cullyn imparts a caustic stare at the aides, then sips at the mulled wine. "This here's the extent of the 'helms knocking back your bloody drafts this season... and possibly for all time, as far as I know... sirs." He spits after uttering the last word, as if clearing his mouth of something distasteful.

"Look here, now..." begins one of the officers, taking a step forward.

"All right, gentlemen. Enough." Nemo says with a severe tone that culls the situation. "I'll have none of this. Now, Lopryssti, is it? Tell me more."

Cullyn relates to the commander adept everything he's seen and endured the past seven days, the men he's seen die, the men he's killed, but most importantly the hordes of Khadoran soldiers and warjacks that are even now washing over Cygnar's ally. When he's finished, Nemo and his aides sit silent and brooding as they absorb the dire news. If what the messenger speaks is true...

"All due respect," says one of Nemo's aides in hushed tones. "I don't buy it, sir. How can this be? We've received no word of such a thing—"

"I'm telling you now," Cullyn murmurs.

The man continues, ignoring the messenger, "...and the campaigning season is over."

"Campaigning season?" says Nemo. "Hells, man. You think a change in the weather will halt the Khadorans?"

"It has before, sir."

The wispy-haired commander adept fixes the officer with a hard stare. "Well, not this time, captain. This time what's gone before counts little indeed."

The room is silent for a few moments, then one of the other aides asks, "Then what shall we do, sir?"

"First, have our associates in the Order confirm our friend's news here and, if what he speaks is truth, we muster an attack," Nemo states emphatically. "And we must do so immediately. If we don't move on this, our own ally shall unwillingly reinforce Khador's bid for a restored Khardic Empire, Morrow forbid."

"But sir," protests the aide, "we're far from mobilized. Most of our troops are on winter leave or committed to civic efforts."

"Hmm. Well then, I suggest we kindly ask the good Queen Ayn to suspend her offensive for a month or two while we prepare. We'll call them to arms, captain. Immediately."

Nemo rises and paces the room. "They planned this, know that for certain. They chose the moment and the battleground. Contentious. Conditioned. Tenacious people. I've always said as much. No. They'll endure winter's bite. Make no mistake, they're counting on us to do as we've always done—wait for good weather; for the 'campaigning season' as we so aptly put it. But, not this time. If we wait, they'll dig in and all their forces shall be arrayed against us come the spring. No, we must act, and now."

"Sir," offers one of the aides, "if the wizards confirm this man's claim, we must get sanction from the Assembly. Only a royal order can muster the army. Attacking without endorsement from—"

"Do you understand what I'm saying, captain?" interrupts the aged warcaster. "There is no time! We must act now. The king can make his mark on a piece of paper later. No, gentlemen, the Khadorans have forced us into a new season of war. They think us unready, unwilling to act against them, but we must prove to them that Cygnaran pride is sterner stuff than Khadoran iron."

Nemo signals for some mulled wine, then starts dispensing orders. "Captain Reardan, fetch Abra—

fetch Lord General Skirvin, wherever he is. Inform him his presence is required immediately, then I want a supply train with the barest necessities ready to go upriver as soon as can be. In order to act quickly, we must travel light. Captain Vale, notify city command of our intentions to head upriver, requisition as many worthy civilian vessels as you can, and then see to it that every soldier within a dozen leagues is mustered, equipped, and ready to march. Also send riders to Stonebridge and Falk and tell them Corvis requires a full regiment each. If Khador thinks to make downriver and take this city, they are sorely mistaken. Captain Gorlick, I want every 'jack inspected immediately. Rouse the mechaniks. They can sleep after we've departed. Which brings me to you," he concludes, pointing to the messenger. "You're in no shape to ride. I want a dictate of your full report so we can make dispatches afore this night is through."

A heavy wool blanket draped over his shoulders but still shivering, the messenger named Cullyn Lopryssti nods.

Nemo sighs. "A full invasion in the middle of winter," he says, more to himself than anyone else. "Madness. This war, gentlemen, shall have no respite, and mayhap only darkness at the finish. Let us pray for the mettle to endure what's to come."

"War, sir?"

"Oh, yes. Make no mistake."

A rapping sounds at the door. "Enter," Nemo replies.

A damp guard steps inside the room to be greeted by the hard looks of its inhabitants.

"Begging your pardon, sir… captains… but more visitors have arrived at this late hour, led by Lord Lorimer Kex of the Fraternal Order. He has a dire way about him, sirs. Says he's sensed his attention is needed tonight?"

Nemo reflects the concerned looks of his aides, and then glances at the messenger. He nods knowingly. "I believe confirmation has just arrived, gentlemen. Show him in."

Khadoran troop ships glide slowly along the chill waters of the Black River, cautiously searching their way through dark winter's night. Longboats ply nearest the riverbank, with lookouts doing what they can to locate landmarks of any sort. Unfortunately, lanterns have little impact in the heavy snow, other than to brightly illumine the annoying white veil that conceals the shore.

The ships sail in heavy silence, broken only by the creaking of oars and the occasional call of a lookout or helmsman. Even these signals are muffled in the heavy snowfall, so that the flotilla seems to be in a world all its own.

At last, the lookout in the lead boat calls for the troop ships to back the oars, and the cry echoes from ship to ship. The boat pulls up to a pier, icy and deserted, and a lone Khadoran climbs out, clumsily ascending the ladder in his heavy greatcoat. A compatriot hands up a lantern by supporting it on a pole, and the soldier takes the lantern and moves carefully to a sign at the end of the dock. He brushes away the snow that clings to its face, holds the lantern up, and reads the inscription. He smiles.

"Northguard," he calls back. "We are near, comrades! Bring in the ships!"

He swings his lantern back and forth to signal the location of the dock. Orders pass among the vessels, and one of the ships begins poling in, its lanterns ghostly in the snowy darkness.

The guard is happy to swing the lantern, for the activity helps him warm up. He only stops when the tip of a spear suddenly erupts from his chest.

He catches a glimpse of flaxen hair before he dies.

Then a trio of Defender warjacks opens up their heavy barrels, aiming towards the murky lights that mark the locations of the troop ships. In an instant, screams and cries fill the night. A Sentinel 'jack takes a step into the icy river's shallows and its chain gun showers the nearest ship with a hot hail of inch-wide pellets. Her fingers crackle with energy as the warcaster, Victoria Haley, blindly fires arcane lightning into the darkness, hoping it will ground itself out through Khadoran flesh.

Within a minute, the only illumination left is the flames of three sinking troop ships. Somewhere in the darkness, Khadorans frantically propel their boats away, trusting it to be safer in navigating the river blindly than to force a landing in the face of enemy warjacks.

Somewhere in the snowy blackness, floundering soldiers cry in helpless dread, struggling to keep their heads above the bitter water.

Haley turns away and walks off the dock.

"Let 'em drown," she snarls. "We'll be sending more of 'em to join their comrades at the river's bottom soon enough."

Forces are on the move to rekindle ancient enmities and settle old grudges, hurtling the realms and peoples of the Iron Kingdoms into an immense, world-changing conflict. The Kings, Nations and Gods Campaign gives players the chance to experience the shifting tides of war in western Immoren. From simmering hostilities to the boiling point of all-out war, this campaign has true consequences for both victory and defeat. Kings, Nations, and Gods takes players through the events of this all-encompassing storyline and immerses them in the struggle for dominance and survival in the Iron Kingdoms.

It begins with the great northern kingdoms of Khador and its winter invasion of the country of Llael. The Campaign takes players through dark days as war breaks out across western Immoren as a result of this invasion. A true Menite prophet, the mysterious one known only as the "Harbinger," guides the Protectorate of Menoth to prepare its legions for a great crusade to restore the glory of the One Faith. Meanwhile, Cryxian forces stalk the kingdoms under cover of darkness, seeking horrific new weapons and a foothold on the mainland. Caught between the hammer and the anvil, Cygnar, the Jewel of the Iron Kingdoms, girds itself for a desperate fight to keep a hold on its very existence!

CAMPAIGN RULES

Kings, Nations and Gods is ideal for groups of four players, each playing a separate faction, though play with more or fewer players is possible. Please see **Duplicate Faction and Large Group Play, page 136,** for rules for groups with more than four players.

At the start of the Campaign, each player chooses one of the four factions: Cryx, Cygnar, Khador, or the Protectorate. Players must continue to play with the same faction throughout the Campaign, though they may include mercenaries alongside their faction forces if they wish.

The Campaign is divided into four seasons which set the tone and location of the major events. Each season focuses on the machinations of a particular faction, spotlighting the faction's ambitions and storyline.

There are three Acts in each season. Act I, is the leading scenario of the season where players play a 500-point group game and vie for control of a major strategic point in the contested region. During Act II, players are paired off in 1000-point scenarios. These scenarios are key missions and events that must be played in chronological order to preserve the storyline and game balance. In the climactic final battle of Act III, the player scoring the most wins during Act II of a season faces off against the next highest scoring player from a different faction.

CUSTOMIZATION

Players should feel free to customize the scenarios and rules to make sure their group has a great time. For example, if the scale of the scenarios is too large for your local group, cut 1000-point games down to a more manageable level.

Even players who do not play through the entire Campaign will find it to be an invaluable resource for play. Players can pick and choose from among the many scenarios and easily modify them to suit their needs. Seven of the scenarios are ideally suited for competitive play. See Index for Competitive Play Scenarios. The Weather Tables found on page 137-138 can also be adapted to play outside the context of the Campaign.

CAMPAIGN TERRAIN

Some of the scenarios in the Kings, Nations and Gods Campaign dictate terrain required for play. Players are encouraged to build terrain for scenarios if possible, but in a pinch, terrain features can easily be improvised. Cut paper can be used to mark the route of a river. Old paint cans make suitable towers. If you are in a rush, cut building floor plans out of paper. Be sure to mark doors and windows on the floor plans. When in doubt, rely on your imagination.

RECIPE FOR DISASTER

Start with a bitter stew of Khador's unrealized expansionistic ambition bound by outdated treaties. Simmer over the heat of contempt and fanatical nationalism. Add a weakened neighbor unable to defend its borders and allied to a hated rival. Spice with the prophetic call of the Menite faithful to a great Crusade. Chill with the Dragon's breath as Toruk turns his attention to the rising power of the kingdoms of men. Note: This is not a dish favored at Cygnaran tables!

PLAY CONDITIONS

Play conditions are special rules that modify some scenarios in the Campaign. Play conditions can be anything from randomly rolled weather conditions to cowering penalties for models that do not leave their starting deployment zone. Look for the Play Conditions icons indicating the conditions in effect throughout each scenario. Icons are listed below scenario titles.

Play Conditions follow:

 Camping: Camping is for cowards! A model or unit remaining in its deployment zone after the third round must pass a CMD check during each of its controller's maintenance phases or flee the table.

 First Blood: The first army to cause damage to any model in an opposing army gains +1 on all attack rolls on the controlling player's next turn.

Hammertime: When the hammer falls, you are done. After a number of rounds described in the scenario, a random chance exists in which the game concludes at the end of each additional round. At the end of the last player's turn of the round described, one of the players (sometimes specified in the scenario) should roll a d6. On a result of 1 the scenario ends. Otherwise, players continue to play until the end of the next round. At the end of each additional round, roll to see if the hammer falls. The chance of the scenario ending is increased by +1 each additional round until the third round. From the third additional round on, the game concludes on a roll of 1-3.

For example, James and Rob are playing the Wrath of Summer's Heat Act II scenario, Lawgiver. Rob is the first player. After 7 rounds, either Rob or James rolls a d6 at the end of each of James's turns. At the end of round 7 the game ends on a roll of 1. At the end of round 8, the game ends on a roll of 1 or 2. Starting at the end of round 9, the game ends at the end of any round on a roll of 1-3.

 Terrain: This scenario uses a special piece of terrain that might require additional set-up.

 Timed Game: This scenario lasts a predetermined number of rounds and ends after the final round.

 Warcaster Casualty: The victory conditions for one or more players

are met if all warcasters from the indicated factions are destroyed or removed from play. See the scenario's Victory Conditions section for details.

 Weather Condition: Players must roll a weather condition on the table from the current season. If both players agree, their armies can "wait out the weather" and play the game without the weather condition in effect. See Weather Conditions on page 137-138 for details.

TABLE SIZE

Most scenarios described in this campaign are intended to be played on a 4'x4' table. Some scenarios will dictate a smaller or larger play area.

PLACING TERRAIN

Since every group has access to different terrain features, there are no hard and fast rules on terrain placement. Instead, players have to rely on guidelines and common sense. Terrain features should be moderately sized, no larger than 6" across unless mandated by the scenario. A player may place one large terrain feature instead of two smaller ones. Large terrain features should be no larger than 12" across.

When placing terrain features, begin by rolling to determine which player places first. Players then alternate placing terrain, each taking a turn placing one terrain feature at a time.

VICTORY POINTS

Victory Points are used in several ways throughout the Campaign. The specific use of Victory Points is detailed in the text of each scenario. For example, the total number of Victory Points scored determines the winner of some scenarios. In other scenarios, Victory Points determine the scale of a player's reward for winning.

Players should track their total number of Victory Points throughout Act II scenarios of a season. Victory Point totals are used to break ties when determining which player moves on to Act III of the season.

Players also gain a Survival Bonus based on the Victory Point total of their remaining forces after each Act II scenario. Survival Points are later added to the point total of the player's army if they play in the Act III scenario of that season.

WARCASTER CASUALTIES

Warcasters are pivotal characters throughout the Campaign. Though a warcaster may fall in combat during the course of play, his hard-bitten

In addition to tracking warcaster deployment, the Kings, Nations and Gods Campaign Record Sheet, found on Page 220, will help you track scenario outcomes, Victory Points, Survival Bonuses, and records for each season in the Campaign.

To begin filling out the sheet, record your name, the current Campaign season, and your faction. After playing the Act I scenario of the season, record the placement of each player and use it to determine the order in which players will deploy their warcasters. Once you are ready to move onto Act II of the season, write down the scenarios you will be playing as well as the warcasters you deploy. After each Act II game, fill in the pertinent information below the scenario's column including Victory Points, Survival Points, any rewards earned, and whether or not you suffered a warcaster casualty. If your army suffers a warcaster casualty, place an "X" over the warcaster's name in the Warcaster Deployment area. This will help you remember to double the point cost of that warcaster if you want to use him in your next game.

In larger campaigns where you will play the same scenario against more than one player, mark the Final Result Yes for the game you wish to count toward your record. If you have a warcaster embark on his side quest, you can record any rewards he returns and whether or not he survives as well.

Finally, mark down any results from the Act III scenario if you participate in it. With all your game results recorded in one handy reference sheet, determining the outcome of your campaign should be a snap.

determination usually means that he survives what would otherwise be a deadly conflict. If a warcaster is destroyed or removed from play during a Campaign game, the controlling player must pay double the warcaster's point cost to use the warcaster in the player's next game.

ACT I SCENARIOS

Act I scenarios are 500-point group games, in which several factions come together to battle over control of a particular area or resource. One player from each faction represented in the Campaign plays in the Act I scenario. Once a player loses his warcaster, his forces flee the table and he is eliminated from play. The outcome of the Act I scenario for a season determines the order players reveal their warcaster deployments in Act II of the season.

ACT I MERCENARY WARCASTERS

Players may use mercenary warcasters in Act I scenarios in place of faction warcasters. The mercenary warcaster has been hired by the player's faction and represents his faction in the game. If a mercenary warcaster is used, all models in the army must be mercenaries that will work for the player's faction.

ACT II SCENARIOS

Act II scenarios form a series of battles fought over a given season. They are the real meat of the conflict and lay out the course of action for each faction. Act II scenarios are played in chronological order.

Each scenario in Act II is a 1000-point game in which each player fields two warcasters.

ACT II WARCASTER DEPLOYMENT

Sure, they are powerful, but warcasters cannot be everywhere at once. The demands of the battlefield call upon warcasters to lead faction forces into combat or execute secret missions in remote locales. Throughout the Campaign, players assign their warcasters marching orders by deploying them to various Act II scenarios.

After completing Act I of a season, each player deploys at least one warcaster to each Act II scenario he will play. Deployed warcasters are assigned to the scenario and must be used each time the scenario is played during the season. Warcaster deployments are recorded on the Campaign Record Sheet, page 220.

The order in which players deploy their warcasters is determined by the outcome of the Act I scenario of the relevant season. The order begins with the player who placed last in the scenario and ends with the winner of the scenario. Once a player deploys his warcasters, he must inform the other players of his assignments. In groups larger than two, players are only required to deploy a single warcaster to each scenario - the second will be chosen at the time of play. If only two players are playing through the Campaign, both warcasters must be deployed to the one scenario played each season.

For example, after finishing the Icy Grip of Winter Act I scenario, the Battle for Riversmet, Kevin (Protectorate), Jason (Cryx), Alex (Cygnar), and Rob (Khador) are ready to deploy their warcasters for the Winter Act II scenarios. Each player must deploy one warcaster to each Act II scenario beginning with Kevin since he was the first player eliminated. Kevin deploys Kreoss to the Well of Truth, Feora to Over the River & Through the Woods, and the High Reclaimer to You Can Run. Next, Alex deploys his warcasters, then Jason, and finally Rob, the scenario winner.

In another example, Adam (Cryx) and Brian (Khador) play a Campaign. Adam wins the Icy Grip of Winter Act I scenario, the Battle for Riversmet. Because there are only two players participating in the Campaign, Adam and Brian will only play one Winter Act II scenario, Within the Dark Soil. Brian lost in the Act I scenario, so he deploys his warcasters first choosing Sorscha and Irusk. Adam then deploys his warcasters, Deneghra and Goreshade.

If a player only deploys one warcaster to each scenario, he chooses his second warcaster when he builds his army. During Act II, a warcaster may not be used in an army before playing the scenario to which he was initially deployed. Players may not assign mercenary warcasters in place of faction warcasters, but mercenary warcasters may be included in the army as the second warcaster.

For example, having deployed Kreoss to the Well of Truth scenario, the first Protectorate scenario in the Icy Grip of Winter Act II, Kevin must include Kreoss in his 1000-point army but cannot include any warcasters that he deployed to later Act II scenarios that have not yet been played. Since both Feora and the High Reclaimer have been deployed to later scenarios, Kevin must either use Grand Scrutator Severius or a mercenary warcaster as his second warcaster in the scenario.

ACT II REWARDS

When a player wins an Act II scenario, he gains the rewards detailed in the description of the scenario. A reward gained from an Act II scenario may be used once in a single scenario of the season. Player's must declare the use of a reward before the start of a scenario and may use multiple rewards during the same game.

Some rewards give the winning player bonus models or units; however, bonus models and units cannot exceed the normal field rating for the models. Other rewards are strategic bonuses that affect the Act III game of the season.

Act II rewards cannot be used during side quests and do not carry over from season to season.

ACT II SURVIVAL BONUS

Players earn a Survival Bonus for their models and units that were not destroyed or removed from play during each Act II scenario. A Survival Bonus represents forces remaining from earlier battles that may be re-deployed later in the season. Obviously, the more troops and warjacks that survive a battle, the more assets a commander will have at his disposal.

After an Act II scenario, each player who participated in the game totals the victory point value of his surviving models. Warjacks survive a scenario if they are not inert, disabled, or wrecked at the end of the game. The player then multiplies his total by three to get his Survival Bonus for the scenario.

A player's Survival Bonus is added to his army point total in the Act III scenario of the season. Survival Points can only be used in the season they were earned. Regardless of the number of Survival Points earned, players cannot field more than two warcasters in the Act III scenario.

ACT II SIDE QUESTS

Each season, a player has the option to send a certain warcaster on a side quest. Taking place between the major events of the Campaign, side quests are special scenarios that focus on individual warcasters and advance the story and often the development of the character. If the warcaster succeeds in his side quest, he gains a reward that lasts for the rest of the Campaign.

Each warcaster's side quest takes place during a particular season. During that season, a player may send his warcaster on the side quest after winning an Act II scenario in which the warcaster participated and was not destroyed or removed from play. Side quests are optional and a player can choose not to play

them. After a player wins an Act II scenario with a warcaster during his side quest season, the player may choose to play through the side quest after completing any Act II scenario. If the player intends to play a side quest, the player must undertake it before progressing to Act III.

Side quests are very small engagements that often pit a lone warcaster against a small force of enemy models. The enemy force in the side quest may be controlled by anyone participating in the Campaign, though it is recommended that someone playing the faction described control the opposing force. Side quest army compositions are described in the scenario text.

Each side quest is a specialized scenario that dictates the dimensions of the play area. Players do not gain Survival Points for side quests and side quests do not add to a player's victory point total for Act II. Players may not use Act II scenario rewards during a side quest. If a warcaster is destroyed or removed from play during a side quest, he cannot be used during the Act III scenario of the season, but also does not suffer the normal warcaster casualty penalty.

ACT III SCENARIOS

The Act III scenario is the culminating battle of the season. The battle is fought between the faction players with the most wins from Act II of the season. The Act III scenarios of the winter, spring, and summer are two-player games, but the Fall's Bitter Harvest Act III scenario, the Harvest, is the immense four player climax of Kings, Nations and Gods.

During winter, spring, and summer, the player with the most wins throughout Act II of the season plays against a player from a different faction with the next highest total number of wins. To break a tie, players compare their Victory Point totals for Act II of the season. To get his Victory Point total, a player adds together the Victory Points he scored in each Act II scenario of the season. The player with the highest Victory Point total throughout Act II of the season breaks the tie and moves on to the Act III battle.

For example, when the dust clears at the end of the Icy Grip of Winter Act II, Rob (Khador) has three wins, Kevin (Protectorate) has two wins, Jason (Cryx) has one win, and Alex (Cygnar) has no wins. Rob and Kevin go on to play in the Icy Grip of Winter Act III Scenario, the Ruins of Riversmet.

CALCULATING YOUR SURVIVAL BONUS

Use the following formula to calculate your Survival Points at the end of each Act II scenario:

Victory Point Value of your surviving models x 3 = Survival Bonus

For example, having played the Icy Grip of Winter scenario, Throat Cutter, Mark totals his surviving models after the game. He has Stryker (5 VPs), Caine (5 VPs), a Defender (3 VPs), a Lancer (2 VPs), a Long Gunner squad with three remaining models (2 VPs), and a Gun Mage Captain Adept (1 VP) for a total of 18 Victory Points. Mark then multiplies this total by three to get his Survival Bonus of 54 points, which may be added to his army in the Winter Act III scenario, the Ruins of Riversmet.

ACT II VICTORY POINTS

Remember to track your total Victory Points through Act II of each season. When determining which players move onto Act III of the season, Victory Points are used to break ties between players who win the same number of games.

In another example, at the end of Winter Act II, Adam (Cryx), Mark (Cygnar), and Brian (Protectorate) each have won two games, leaving James skunked with no wins. To determine which players advance to the Act III battle, Adam, Mark, and Brian must compare their Victory Point totals for Act II of the season. Adam scored 38, Mark scored 32, and Brian scored 45. Adam and Brian go on to play in the Icy Grip of Winter Act III Scenario, the Ruins of Riversmet.

DUPLICATE FACTION AND LARGE GROUP PLAY

Though the Campaign is optimized for groups of four players, larger groups can customize it to suit their needs. Very large groups should consider playing the Campaign in smaller groupings, if possible, to satisfy the needs of all the players. Alternatively, players may form faction teams and scenarios may be divided up between a team's players.

ACT I LARGE GROUP OPTIONS

Only one player from each faction participates in the Act I scenario of each season. All players playing the same faction face off in a 350-point multi-player duel to determine which player plays in the Act I scenario. The winner of the duel plays in the Act I game.

For example, a large group begins playing through the Campaign. Jason and Adam play Cryx. Eric, Matt, and Mark play Cygnar. Alex and Rob play Khador. Kevin is the lone Protectorate player. The Cryx, Cygnar, and Khador players all play in 350-point duels against the other players of their faction to determine who goes on to play in the Act I scenario of the season. Jason beats Adam and advances to play for Cryx in the Act I scenario. Matt trounces Eric and Mark, and goes on to play for Cygnar. Rob handedly beats Alex and represents Khador in the Act I game. As the only Protectorate player, Kevin moves on to represent the Protectorate in the Act I game.

ACT II LARGE GROUP OPTIONS

After playing the Act I scenario of the season, players have to deploy their warcasters before moving onto Act II scenarios. Large group warcaster deployment varies slightly from the system detailed previously. Players who did not play in the Act I game simultaneously deploy their warcasters for the Act II games of the season before the players who participated in the Act I scenario deploy their warcasters. Once the players who did not participate in the Act I scenario have completed their deployment, those who did participate deploy their warcasters in the order determined by the Act I results.

Based on the example above, after the Act I scenario is completed, players must deploy their warcasters for Act II. The players that did not participate in the Act I scenario—Eric, Mark, and Alex—simultaneously deploy first. Once the first warcaster deployments have been revealed, the remaining players—Jason, Matt, Rob, and Kevin—deploy their warcasters in the order determined by the outcome of the scenario.

Players deploy their warcasters by filling out their Campaign Record Sheet, found on page 220, in secret. Once all players who did not participate in the Act I battle have filled out their Campaign Record Sheets, the deployments are revealed to the players who did. The Act I players then deploy their warcasters according to the results of the Act I game.

During Act II, each player will face off against each other player using the scenario pertaining to their matched factions. For example, if a group has three Cygnar players and two Cryx players, both of the Cryx players will have to play each of the Cygnar players individually in the Cryx vs. Cygnar scenario of the season. In this case the Cryx vs. Cygnar scenario will be played a total of six times.

Because every player in the group must play every other player during Act II, players playing the same faction must face off in basic 1000-point games. If both players agree, they may play a scenario from WARMACHINE: Prime instead of a basic game. Same faction games can be played at anytime during Act II of a season. Players cannot use rewards earned during Act II of the current season in games against other players playing the same faction. Players do not gain rewards or Survival Points for same faction games, but should keep track of their Victory Point totals and wins.

For example, if Alex, Eric, Mark, and Matt are all playing Cygnar in the same Campaign, Alex will have to play separate 1000-point games against Mark and Matt during Act II of each season.

Rather than winning scenario rewards each time the same scenario is played, players must choose which game will count toward his score. The scenario winner, reward, and Survival Bonus will all come from the same game. A player can only earn a scenario reward and Survival Bonus once for any scenario, regardless of the number of times the scenario is played. Rewards won during a given scenario may not be used in the same scenario if the player must play it again against another opponent during the season. All scenarios played still add to a player's Victory Point total whether the outcome of the scenario affects the player's wins or Survival Bonus.

For example, Rob beats Matt in Throat Cutter, scoring 15 Victory Points and 54 Survival Points. He then loses to Mark, scoring 12 Victory Points and 69 Survival Points. Rob has his choice of which game's results to keep and he chooses his victory over Matt, scoring a win, the scenario, and 54 Survival Points. Rob scored a total of 27 Victory Points for the two games.

NEW TERMS

Starting Roll: The roll made in the Beginning section of each scenario.

Hold: A player may Hold a location if he controls all models within the space described during his maintenance phase. Models that are engaged in melee combat cannot be used to Hold a location. Neither warrior models with CMD stats of 1 or less nor Incorporeal models can Hold a location.

WEATHER CONDITIONS

Weather can have an unpredictable effect on the fortunes of war. Heavy snowfall can utterly disrupt battle plans, dense fog can cover the movement of whole armies, and heavy rain can turn roads to mud overnight, disrupting the vulnerable supply lines required to keep warjacks fueled in the field.

If a scenario calls for a random Weather Condition, roll 2d6 and consult the corresponding season's table. Roll for Weather Conditions after terrain is placed, but before players deploy their armies. If both players agree, their armies can "wait out the weather" and play the game without the Weather Condition in effect.

Weather Conditions last the entire battle unless the description specifies otherwise.

TABLE 1-1:
THE ICY GRIP OF WINTER
WEATHER CONDITIONS

2D6	RESULT
2	**Blizzard** Ranged and magical attacks against any model from greater than 5" away automatically miss.
3-4	**Cold Snap** All warrior models that did not move or are not engaged in melee, suffer a POW 6 damage roll at the end of their controlling players turns. Warjacks suffer 1 DEF.
5-9	**Clear Skies** No special weather effects.
10-11	**Ice Storm** Any models that are hit by a successful Slam or Throw power attack are moved +2. A knocked down model must roll a d6 anytime it attempts to stand up. On a roll of 1 or 2, the model slips and falls on the ice and remains knocked down.
12	**Deep Snow** All non-Khador models without All Terrain, Incorporeal, or Pathfinder suffer 1 movement but can still charge and slam.

TABLE 1-2:
THE STORMS OF SPRING
WEATHER CONDITIONS

2D6	Result
2	**Flash Flood** Roll a d6 each round before the first players turn. On a roll of 1 or 2, the battlefield is flash flooded. All non-elevated terrain becomes Shallow Water for the round. See Shallow Water, WARMACHINE: Prime, page 61, for details.
3-4	**Heavy Rains** All models suffer 2 RAT from decreased visibility and wet powder. Living models suffer an additional 1 CMD.
5-9	**Clear Skies** No special weather effects.
10-11	**Powerful Winds** All AOE ranged attacks that miss their targets deviate one extra inch and have no minimum deviation range. All cloud effects leave play at the end of each turn.
12	**Thunderstorm** All Cygnaran models gain +1 CMD. Generator Blades, Lightning Rods, Storm Rods, and Storm Glaives gain +1 POW on melee and blast or burst attacks. Ball Lightning, Chain Lightning, and Electrify spells gain +1 POW. Stormsmiths gain +1 POW to all Stormcall special actions.

TABLE 1-3:

THE WRATH OF SUMMER'S HEAT WEATHER CONDITIONS

2D6	RESULT
2	**Cyclone** Place a 5 cloud effect in the center of the table to represent the cyclone. At the beginning of each players maintenance phase, the cyclone moves 1d6 in a random direction determined by the deviation template. Direction one on the template always faces the direction the template last moved in. Any model touched by the cyclone is thrown 1d6 in a random direction determined by the deviation template with the same effect as a Throw power attack, suffering a POW 12 damage roll. See Throw, WARMACHINE: Prime, page 43, for details. Any cloud effect touched by the cyclone leaves play. The cyclone leaves play when any part of the template moves off the table.
3-4	**Flash Fire** A flash fire begins on a randomly determined table edge to the right or left of the deployment zones. At the beginning of each players maintenance phase, the flash fire moves 1d6 toward the opposite table edge in a line running the length of the table. Any model crossing or crossed by the flash fire line suffers a POW 12 damage roll.
5-9	**Clear Skies** No special weather effects.
10-11	**Dust Storm** Roll a d6 each round before the first players turn. On a roll of 1 or 2, a dust storm hits the battlefield. All models suffer 1 on ranged attack rolls. Models cannot give or receive orders. The dust storm lasts for one round.
12	**Heat Wave** Any Non-Protectorate model that runs must forfeit its movement on its next turn. All non-Protectorate warrior models suffer -1 DEF.

TABLE 1-4:

FALL'S BLIGHTED HARVEST WEATHER CONDITIONS

2D6	RESULT
2	**Corpse Candles** Divide the table into 4 separate quadrants, assigning each a number from 1-4. Roll a d6 each round before the first players turn. On a roll of 1-4, corpse candles appear in the quadrant with the number corresponding to the die. On a roll of 5 or 6, nothing happens. All non-Cryx models in the quadrant where corpse candles appear must pass a CMD check or flee. Corpse candles remain in play for one round.
3-4	**Creeping Mist** All models gain Concealment.
5-9	**Clear Skies** No special weather effects.
10-11	**Stygian Wind** All living models suffer 1 STR and ARM.
12	**Baleful Moon** All undead models gain Tough. Whenever a Tough model takes sufficient damage to be destroyed, the controlling player rolls a d6. On a 5 or 6, the model is knocked down instead of being destroyed. Models not destroyed are reduced to one wound. If this Condition has been rolled already this campaign, roll another Weather Condition and ignore this result.

GORIM 3RD, ASHTOVEN 604 AR

The icy grip of winter seizes the nations of western Immoren, and Khador begins a year of conflict the Iron Kingdoms will never forget. Queen Vanar, supported by the kayazy merchant nobility, sets her eyes upon reclaiming lands unjustly lost when the Council of Ten signed the Corvis Treaties almost 400 years ago. The queen commands the nation's most loyal warcaster, Kommandant Irusk, to lead her forces and bring what was once part of the mighty Khardic Empire back into the arms of the Motherland.

Under Irusk's command, Khadoran forces victoriously seize the Llaelese cities of Laedry and Elsinberg. As the Khadoran siege on Riversmet and Redwall begins, Llael's own armies route and flee in the face of terrible losses, unable to stand against the might of the Khadoran war march. Within days, the stunned kingdom of Llael finds itself in the beginning stages of Khadoran occupation.

Cygnar receives word of the advance days after the fall of western Llael. Fearing Cygnaran interference, Khadoran forces out of Ravensgard attempt to cut off the Black River, but Cygnaran battle groups, desperate to keep open the flow of coal and trade supplies from Rhul, rush to stop the enemy from crippling them before the Royal Assembly in Caspia can react to the war movement. If Llael falls under Khadoran rule, Cygnar will have failed a valuable ally and perhaps as importantly, be cut off from the nation of Rhul and summarily weakened.

Meanwhile in the south, the Harbinger of Menoth — born to Caen as the daughter of Menoth, a divine savior in the flesh of a mortal woman — utters a demand for the faithful to serve the Protectorate and gird its armies for a holy crusade. The Harbinger has become a guiding light and pilgrims desert their homelands to heed her clarion call. Thousands prepare to uproot their families and homes to journey to the Protectorate, while Menite warcasters and warjacks seek out ancient secrets or move to protect the influx of new worshippers.

Under cover of darkness, Cryx, the island of Nightmare, the treacherous nation of the Dragonfather Lord Toruk, senses the change and turmoil. His plan unfurls as the great dragon moves to blind the powers of the Iron Kingdoms, while also intending to destroy and consume His own hidden and treacherous dragon brood. First, His black legions of thralls move to the shores then travel inwards to clutch at the reins of control, tentatively measuring the responses of the other factions. His is a measured game. Eons of patience and planning will finally bestow unto him the chance to strike down his own children and become the god he once was.

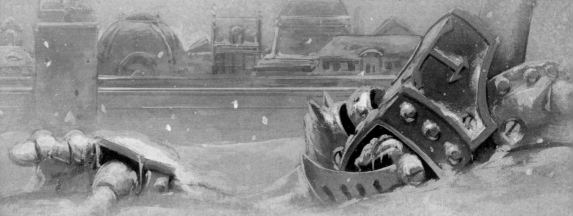

The Icy Grip of Winter Act I

Scenario 1, Battle for Riversmet

Multiplayer Game, 500 points

Donard 2nd, Glaceus 605 AR—Riversmet, the Three Rivers Town, is where two rivers—the Rangercliffe Run and the Oldwick River—converge and create the mighty Black River. Two large bridges span the confluence, and they are key strategic positions. Khador covets these passageways to the rest of Llael. Once across them, Khadoran forces can send troops along the northeastern corridor of Llael and raid deep into the nation's center without resistance. Luckily, Cygnaran forces have managed to make their way from a military summit at Horgenhold to meet the Khadorans at the edge of the Riversmet Bridges.

Protectorate forces, caught in the midst of the occupation by surprise, are in the process of securing alchemical reagents and volatile liquids to supply their army. Shipping from Leryn and sailing south in a small fleet of steamships, their course passes directly under the twin bridges. Fearing the fleet's vulnerability in the river's waters, the Protectorate commander dispatches all of the warjacks accompanying the fleet to meet the other factions at Riversmet. The gambit relies on surprise; the unexpected appearance of Protectorate warjacks will draw the attention of other forces while the vital supplies pass by unnoticed.

Fortified with necrotite harvested from ancient battlefields, Cryx moves under the cover of night. Their incursion is a typical probing tactic to test the mettle of the other factions. Skillfully placed, the Cryxian force arrives just as the remaining three factions meet. The dead are expendable, and Lord Toruk's workshops can produce no end of bonejacks and mechanikal monstrosities. For Him, this is simply a game, a test of skill for His warcasters, and a measure of the enemy's resolve.

Special Rules & Set Up

For a two-player game, see two-player map. A river approximately 8" wide runs directly through the middle of the 4' by 4' table. A bridge 8" wide and 10" long spans the river at the center of the table.

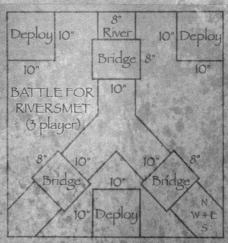

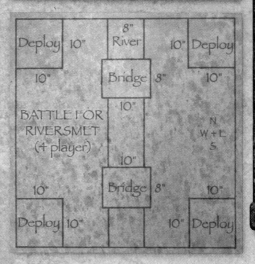

For a three-player game, see three-player game map. A river 8" wide runs through the table, forking at the center to cut the table into thirds. Three bridges 8" wide and 10" long span the center of each river.

For a four-player game, see four-player map. The 8" wide river runs directly through the center of the 4' by 4' table. Two bridges 8" wide and 10" long cut the river into thirds.

Call to War

Gorim 5th, Ashtoven 604 AR

Cygnar declares war on Khador immediately following the fall of Laedry and Rynyr. In the days to come, both Ord and Rhul declare their neutrality, although the Rhulic ambassadorial staff to Khador is recalled.

A Tough Blow

Llael is western Immoren's foremost producer of blasting powder and firearms. Not only is the Order of the Golden Crucible the largest producer of blasting powder and a powerful order of alchemists and wizards based in Leryn, but the mines of Rynyr also provide much of the raw materials for powder. In years past, the Order of the Golden Crucible controlled the manufacture and distribution of blasting powder across the Iron Kingdoms. Over time, their stranglehold over powder has waned as Cygnar and Khador have developed their own production centers in recent years. The Crucible evolved to dominate the trade of powder rather than monopolize its production, and although the capture of Rynyr is a huge prize for the Khadoran war effort, it is not as crippling as it might have been a generation ago.

Players take turns placing up to two (2) terrain features each. Terrain features may not be placed within 3" of another terrain feature, including the bridge or river. Terrain features may be placed on hills.

Kossite woodsmen may only come into play in Khador's deployment zone.

BEGINNING

At the start of the game, each player rolls a d6. The player who rolls highest chooses to go first or last. The player who rolls second highest then chooses to go first or last from among the remaining spots in the play order. The third highest roller does the same and so on until the lowest roller takes the final spot. The first player gets his choice of deployment zones and takes the first turn. Each player deploys in a 10" by 10" area of the table determined by the scenario map.

For example, Rob, Jason, Matt, and Doug roll to determine the order of play. Matt rolls highest and chooses to go last. Doug is the second highest roller, so he may choose to go first or third. Doug chooses to go first. As the third highest roller Jason can choose to go second or third and decides to go second. Finally Rob, as the lowest roller, takes the final spot and will go third.

VICTORY CONDITIONS

Whoever has the last surviving warcaster in play wins. When a player loses his warcaster, his remaining models are routed and must be removed from the table.

REWARDS

• **Warcaster Deployment:** The outcome of The Battle for Riversmet determines the order the players reveal their warcaster deployments for Winter Act II. Beginning with the first player knocked out of the game and ending with the winner of the scenario, each player deploys one warcaster to each Icy Grip of Winter Act II scenario. In a two-player game, the losing player must inform the winner of both warcasters he intends to field during the Winter Act II game.

• **Gaining the Initiative:** The winning player also gains control of key bridges throughout the winter season and gets a +1 bonus on all Starting Rolls during all Winter Act II scenarios.

The Icy Grip of Winter Act II

Scenario 2, Throat Cutter

Khador vs. Cygnar, 1000 points

"Look at these fools. Why do they swim? Do they not know they are already dead? Wait. See that one there? He is shot twice, but still he swims. A stubborn duzka. Hand me my rifle."

—Kapitan Beleskova Tzavarov, Widowmaker sharpshooter

Description

Gorim 3rd, Glaceus 605 AR—Desperation grips the Cygnaran military as Khadoran forces methodically invade deeper into Llael. With the hopes that sheer numbers can forestall the advance, Cygnar makes the measured risk of rushing in more warjacks by barge, road, and rail. Now the warjacks need coal, and supplies are running low. The one thing that can provide relief is a bulk re-supply of coal brought in from Rhul.

Using scouts and spies Cygnar gets a request for aid to Rhul, but there is a problem: Kommandant Irusk's strategic planning has cunningly predicted this tactic, and a warcaster battle group has taken troops to the Black River and set up a massive chain called the Throat Cutter. Acting as a barricade, the chain proves lethal to oncoming ships.

When the first of the Cygnaran coal barges, the Belching Mary, approached the barricade, its captain made the unfortunate decision to ram through the Throat Cutter. The ship hung up on the links of the massive chain, crushed its own prow, and sunk within mere seconds. Widowmakers waiting on shore mercilessly sniped at the crew as they swam away from the wreck and all hands were lost. Since then a handful of ships have unsuccessfully tried to pass the barricade, but their wrecks and crews rest silently as well in the cold, dark waters of the Black River.

The responsibility of the Khadoran battle group is to guard the Throat Cutter until troops from Ravensgard can arrive and relieve them. Cygnar must destroy the chain's guardhouse and lower the barricade so that they can replenish their dwindling supplies before Khadoran fortifications are staunchly in place. Timeliness is a factor, as Cygnar has lost a handful of coal ships already and more are on the way even now, unknowingly headed toward a cold and bitter end.

Special Rules

See map. A 4" wide river spans the rear of the Khadoran deployment zone on the south side of the battlefield. See Deep Water, WARMACHINE: Prime, pg. 61 for details.

Khadoran forces garrison a guard tower housing the machinery that controls the slack of the great chain. Place a tower measuring approximately 4" x 4" in the middle of the Khadoran deployment zone so that one edge borders the river. The tower has one door facing east, but has no other doors or windows. The door is big enough to accommodate medium-based models. The door has ARM 16 and can take 10 points of damage. The guard tower has ARM 18 and can take 10 points of damage per inch. The tower will collapse when 8" or more of its surface has been destroyed. See Damaging and Destroying Structures, WARMACHINE: Prime, pg. 62 for details.

If Cygnar forces Hold the guard tower, any model inside the tower can forfeit his action to pull a lever to release the slack from the chain. The chain is dumped into the water, allowing the merchant vessels to once more traverse the Black River.

The game goes into Hammertime at the end of round 8. If the game ends before Cygnaran forces destroy the guard tower or pull the lever, Khadoran reinforcements arrive and drive off the Cygnaran attackers.

Set Up

Players take turns placing three (3) terrain features each. The Khador player may not place terrain within either player's deployment zone. The Cygnar player may not place terrain within the Khador player's deployment zone. Terrain features may not be

The History of Throat Cutter

The Throat Cutter scenario was inspired by the real world events in 1452 when the Ottoman Turks laid siege to Constantinople. Six miles from the city, the Turks built a great fortress called Throat Cutter at the mouth of the Black Sea to keep ships from reaching the city during the siege. However, the Christian defenders were not without their own naval blockade. They stretched a heavy chain across a small waterway leading to the city known as the Golden Horn. Any invader ships that tried to cross into the city were torn apart by the chain. Eventually, the Turks had enough of the siege and actually dragged their ships overland to bypass the chain. In no time, the sultan's elite Janissaries had stormed Constantinople, much to the horror of Christendom.

143

placed within 5" of another terrain feature, including the guard tower and the river. Terrain features may be placed on hills.

Beginning

The Khador player deploys first by placing his models up to 6" from the river. The Cygnar player then deploys his forces on the opposite table edge by placing his models up to 10" from the edge. After set up, each player rolls a d6. The high roller chooses who goes first.

Victory Conditions

The Cygnar player wins if the guard tower is destroyed or if the lever is pulled to release the chain.

The Khador player wins if all Cygnaran warcasters are destroyed or removed from play, or if the Cygnar player has not won by the end of the game.

Rewards

- **Supply Ships:** If the Cygnar player wins the game, the merchant ships escape down the river and supply Cygnaran forces. Once during any single Icy Grip of Winter scenario, the Cygnar player pays 10 points less for warjacks.

- **Captured Ships:** If the Khador player wins the game, the merchant ships are captured and the Cygnaran supplies are commandeered by Khadoran forces. Once during any single Icy Grip of Winter scenario, the Khador player pays 10 points less for warjacks and Man-O-War units.

Scenario 3, The Well of Truth

Protectorate vs. Cryx, 1000 points

Gorim 6th, Glaceus 605 AR — For long centuries, Menites have scoured western Immoren for the Well of Truth, a long-lost relic said to have safeguarded pilgrims in ages past. In ancient accounts, the well is described as a brass bowl engraved with scripture from the Canon of the True Law. When water is poured into the basin, it is said to hide the faithful from an enemy's detection. The Well was lost during the Orgoth Occupation after the Prophet Cassian used it to conceal the exodus of refugees after the destruction of Laedry at the hands of the invaders. Although periodic rumors of its discovery have circulated over the years, none have been substantiated.

Long feared lost forever, the approximate location of the Well of Truth was revealed to Hierarch Voyle in a vision in which he was told to seek the relic at the ruins of an ancient Menite temple south of Leryn, a place known to Protectorate scholars. The Menites have waited for the opportunity to investigate the site for decades but have been unable to secure permission from Llael's Court of Nobles. Now, they feel, is the time to act, as the distractions of war have provided the perfect opportunity to recover the artifact.

However, as the Menites walk through the dark woods of the nearly forgotten ruin, the attentions of Toruk's thralls fall upon their passage. Cryxians, as well, have been searching the ruins for signs of some long-forgotten thing, and they have set aside their own mysterious motives after managing to capture and interrogate an unfortunate Protectorate trooper who strayed too far from the others. His lips sorrowfully and painfully rasp the secrets of the Menites' purpose. Granting the trooper swift death as his reward, the thralls and bonejacks then move to interfere with the excavations. They will seize the artifact for themselves and haul it away in their own bloodstained talons.

Special Rules and Set Up

Players take turns, each placing three (3) ruined buildings within 12" of the center of the table. Ruined buildings may be up to 4" x 5" with gaps or doors large enough to accommodate large-based models. Ruined buildings may not be placed within 3" of another ruined building. Each player then places an additional terrain feature at least 3" away from any other terrain feature, including the ruined buildings.

The Well of Truth is hidden within one of the ruined buildings. Players roll a d6 during their Maintenance Phase for each ruined building their models Hold. On a 6, the Well is found. A player's models Hold a ruined building if all models within the ruined building are controlled by that player during his Maintenance Phase. Models that are engaged in melee combat cannot Hold a ruined building. Warrior models with CMD stats of 1 or less, or Incorporeal models, cannot Hold a location.

When the Well of Truth is found, it must be assigned to one of the models Holding the building. The assigned model is considered to be carrying the artifact and cannot run. A friendly model in base-to-base contact with the model carrying the well may forfeit his action to take the artifact, but any model carrying the well is unable to run. Incorporeal models cannot carry the well. If the model carrying the well is destroyed or removed from play, the artifact remains at the model's last location. A model in base contact with the Well of Truth may forfeit his action to pick it up and carry it.

Both armies are desperate to gain possession of the Well of Truth. If either player can get the artifact back to his deployment zone, he wins.

BEGINNING

At the start of the game, each player rolls a d6. The high roller chooses who goes first. The first player gets his choice of deployment zones and takes the first turn. Players deploy their forces up to 10" from the table's edge.

VICTORY CONDITIONS

Whoever gets the Well of Truth back to his deployment zone wins.

REWARDS

• **The Well of Truth:** The winning player may use the Well of Truth once during any single Icy Grip of Winter scenario. The player must declare the use of the well before the start of the game and assign it to a faction warcaster—the artifact is much too valuable to entrust to a mercenary. The Well of Truth may be used once during the game. It may only be taken into battle once during the Campaign and, whether or not it is utilized, it cannot be used again. The warcaster cannot run during the game until the well is used. To use the well, the warcaster must forfeit his activation to pour water into the basin. He then remains absolutely still to keep from spilling a single drop. Once the Well of Truth is activated, all friendly models in the player's army that are not currently engaged become Invisible for one round. While Invisible, models cannot be targeted by ranged or magical attacks, cannot be charged, and gain +4 DEF against melee attacks. If the model moves or takes any action during its turn, including using feats, casting spells, or channeling spells, it loses the benefits of Invisible. Invisible models do not block line of sight or provide screening.

SCENARIO 4, WITHIN THE DARK SOIL

KHADOR VS. CRYX, 1000 POINTS

Vendarl 4th, Casteus 605 AR—The movement of enemy troops behind Khadoran lines has caused much concern in the upper echelons, so units have been patrolling the rear flanks, especially along the borders of Llael, Cygnar, and Khador. Their goal is to monitor any reports of movement by enemy troops along the forward flank of the Llaelese line. It is of little surprise that reports come back from an elite team of scouts serving the Bryzatski Kompani, or the "Wild Boar Company." What does take Khadoran officers by surprise is that the ones observed are not Cygnaran battle groups, but rather a growing Cryxian force preparing to mine for necrotite in the ancient battlefields known as the Willow Barrens.

The Khadoran High Kommand passes down the order to eliminate Cryx from the region and ensure that neither bilious thrall nor uttering witch survives. However, Greylord intelligence has posited a major concern: when the mining efforts go into full swing, pulverized necrotite dust could potentially fill the air. These plumes of toxic dust have horrendous properties, and every graveyard downwind for dozens of leagues could end up teeming with re-animated corpses called "risen." Haste is necessary. With so many mass graves of soldiers and dead civilians around Llaedry, Rynyr, and lands between, possible epidemics of walking dead are the makings for a catastrophe to Khador's important supply lines.

SPECIAL RULES

The Cryx player places four (4) mining rigs between the forward edge of his deployment zone and the center of the table. The mining rigs are cylindrical in shape approximately 2" in diameter and stand 3" high. The mining rigs have ARM 16 and 15 damage points. See Damaging and Destroying Structures, WARMACHINE: Prime, pg. 62 for details.

After seven (7) rounds, the toxic fumes from the mining rigs force Khador off the field and the game ends.

SET UP

Taking turns each player places three (3) additional terrain features outside his opponent's deployment zone and not within 3" of another terrain feature, including the mining rigs. Terrain features may be placed on hills.

KOMMANDANT IRUSK,

It is my regret to inform you that your suspicions have been confirmed. However, the nature of the threat is not Cygnaran. The intruders are more sinister than we had anticipated. Moreover, we lack the expertise required to remove them from the area.

Three scouts have confirmed observations of Cryxian forces operating in the fog of war surrounding the Willow Barrens. Two of them fell terribly ill; I suspect due to overexposure to necrotite dust. For the safety of my kompania, I have put them to the sword.

I respectfully request a battalion to neutralize the Cryxian operation. It is a grim thing I have had to witness, and I would wish none of this on our own dead. The winds at this time of year prevail to the north and west, toward the theater of battle. I suspect you know what this could mean.

I look forward to your wisdom, Kommandant.

For the Motherland,

Kapitan Misori Niederzof, Winter Guard 4th Border Patrol

EAT HEALTHY & BUILD TERRAIN

When looking around for suitable mining rigs, we suggest trying your refrigerator. Most yogurt containers — we like Yoplait — make excellent mining rigs once they are emptied of their contents and rendered suitably Cryxian.

BEGINNING

At the start of the game each player rolls a d6. The high roller chooses who goes first. The first player sets up and takes the first turn. Players deploy their forces up to 10" from the table's edge.

VICTORY CONDITIONS

Khador wins the game if all mining rigs are destroyed.

Cryx wins if there is at least one mining rig that has not been destroyed after seven rounds.

REWARDS

• **Territorial Dominance:** If the Khador player wins, Khador remains in control of the territory after forcing back Cryxian forces. The Khador player may exert his dominance once during any single Icy Grip of Winter scenario, allowing him to place one additional terrain feature and keeping his opponent from using the Advance Deployment ability during the scenario. Placed terrain must follow the guidelines of the scenario.

• **Mined Necrotite:** If the Cryx player wins, the mined necrotite reduces the cost of each of his bonejacks and helljacks by 10 points once during any single Icy Grip of Winter scenario.

SCENARIO 5, OVER THE RIVER & THROUGH THE WOODS

CYGNAR VS. PROTECTORATE, 1000 POINTS

"I have no idea how in Urcaen they expect us to slog cargo through that territory! We may as well paint our 'jacks bright yellow and chain their knees together. I, for one, am hiding behind the biggest warjack I can find…"

— Journeyman Warcaster Albrecht Jaimes, before receiving orders to lead the march

Malleus 5th, Casteus 605 AR—Caught off balance by the aggression and sheer audacity of Khadoran tactics, Cygnar has found it difficult to respond to the demands of a shifting frontline. Dashing madly into Llael to assist isolated troops and to retake fallen outposts, Cygnaran forces have found their supply lines torn ragged. Widowmakers have been blowing the heads off of anyone who seems to be giving orders, Manhunters have crept into camps and slain officers in their tents, and Khadoran warjacks have trenched roads and dug pitfalls along the supply lines. Among these underhanded tactics and a series of hit-and-run ambushes, Cygnar is bleeding dry along the northern front.

With supplies running low across the frontline, the Black River dominated by Khadoran snipers and patrols, and time falling short, Cygnar must resort to using warjacks like mules to haul in crates of food, clothing, and ammunition so that their soldiers have a chance against the Khadoran onslaught.

Having crossed the Black River, the supply train must traverse open ground with little terrain to conceal the passage of the warjacks and the black columns of coal smoke rising from their furnace stacks. Khador will have time to prepare ambushes, and Cygnar's encumbered warjacks will have to persevere and push through any traps in their path.

Lying in wait along one of the less-protected paths in the Glimmerwood lurks a Protectorate force waiting to ambush Khadoran or Cygnaran forces. Either will do, since what the Menites need are scraps of 'jacks and any surviving converts they can till from the soil of battle. As a Cygnaran contingent heads for a re-supply depot, the Protectorate forces strike and reap the rewards of Khador's tactics without having taken any of the risk.

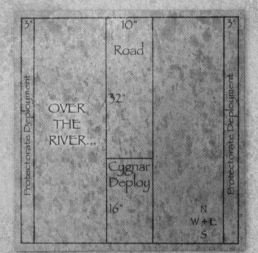

SPECIAL RULES

Cygnar must get as many friendly warjacks to safety as possible by moving them off the table through the Escape Edge. Models that move off the table by crossing the Escape Edge survive the battle, but cannot return to play. If a warcaster leaves play via the Escape Edge, his warjacks do not become inert, but they can no longer be allocated focus. If a 'jack marshal leaves play via the Escape Edge, his warjacks become autonomous, but do not become inert The Cygnar player earns Survival Points for all models that exit the table through the Escape Edge.

All warjacks controlled by the Cygnar player are heavily burdened with supplies and suffer -1 SPD. Warjacks can still charge despite the SPD penalty.

Cygnar must spend at least 300 points on warjacks.

SET UP

See the map. A road runs through the center 10" of the table from the rear edge of the Cygnar player's deployment zone to the Escape Edge. Players take turns each placing three (3) terrain features. No terrain can be placed on the road or within the Cygnar deployment area. The Cygnar player cannot place terrain within the Protectorate deployment areas. Terrain cannot be placed within 3" of another terrain feature, including the road. Terrain features may be placed on hills.

BEGINNING

The Cygnar player deploys his forces first.

The Protectorate player takes the first turn.

Malleus 4th, Casteus 605 AR

Landon,

Praise Menoth you have escaped the eyes of the blasphemous Greylords! You have been of great service to His Glory, and it is my hope that you will be of greater service to us in the times and trials to come.

I have read your missive and understand your situation. The man carrying this message has orders to deliver you to us. He shall lead you to a larger force performing its duties at the northern edge of the Glimmerwood. Should harm befall him, he will be carrying instructions on how you might locate the group and signal them for your rescue.

I know that you are accustomed to comfort, Landon, but you must brace yourself. The times ahead will not be easy. I know you have endured much before now, but remain strong. Recite the Prayer of Trials and ready your mind for the challenge ahead. I often find consolation and focus with the scourge and wire. Perhaps they will do the same for you.

Menoth guide you,

Scrutator Avistus Mercarr

Victory Conditions

The game ends when all Cygnaran warjacks have either exited the table from the Escape Edge or have been disabled or wrecked. The player who scores the most Victory Points wins the game. For the purposes of determining a winner, in addition to his normal Victory Points, the Cygnar player also receives an amount of Victory Points for each model or unit that makes it off the Escape Edge equal to the value printed on the model or unit's stat card.

Rewards

• **Fresh Supplies:** Win or lose the Cygnar player gains additional army points for each warjack that leaves the table through the Escape Edge. Once during any single Icy Grip of Winter scenario, the Cygnar player gains 10 additional army points for each heavy warjack and 5 additional army points for each light warjack that exits the table. Additional points must be spent on the same scenario and cannot be split between scenarios.

• **Liberated Supplies:** Win or lose the Protectorate player gains 10 additional army points for each Cygnaran heavy warjack and 5 additional army points for each Cygnaran light warjack that ends the game disabled, wrecked, or inert. The additional points may be used once during any single Icy Grip of Winter scenario. Additional points must be spent on the same scenario and cannot be split between scenarios.

Scenario 6, You Can Run...

Khador vs. Protectorate, 1000 points

Donard 3rd, Casteus 605 AR—For years the Protectorate has supplemented its production of warjacks by smuggling cortexes out of Khador with the help of Menite loyalists. Khador once ignored the problem, believing that a strong Protectorate military stretched Cygnar's resources thin. Occasionally

Khador has even gone so far as to ship parts covertly to the Protectorate through various agencies. However, recent troubles between the two nations have resulted in a Khadoran crackdown to end the practice of smuggling. The Greylord Covenant has been the primary agency seeking out Menite smugglers, their observing eyes taking in every detail they can through magic and coercion. Despite the redoubled efforts of the Greylords, the wily leader of the smugglers has so far evaded capture.

Landon Trellayne is a Menite sympathizer, a skilled alchemist, and a Llaelese merchant of mixed descent. As the head of a secret society known as Menoth's Trust, he has organized efforts to provide covert assistance to the Protectorate by shipping cortexes in crates disguised with the mark of the Order of the Golden Crucible. At least he did, until the Greylords infiltrated the organization and slaughtered or imprisoned nearly every member of his group.

With Khadoran forces searching for Trellayne, he has grown desperate to evade capture and execution. Through his remaining contacts, he has managed to arrange a rescue by Protectorate forces in the area. He needs to escape, and quickly. The alchemist knows the locations of several smuggling caches along the Black River, and he commands a formidable knowledge of explosives and the refining process used to manufacture Menoth's Fury. A valuable asset to the Protectorate, Trellayne desperately rushes for the safety of his Protectorate rescuers while a Khadoran force follows closely behind.

Special Rules

Both Protectorate and Khadoran forces are attempting to escort smuggler and would-be defector, Landon Trellayne, off the table. Trellayne does not begin the game on the table. He is placed during the

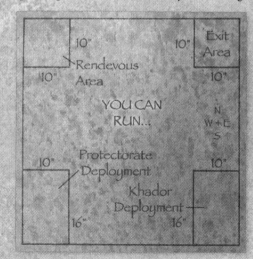

first Protectorate Maintenance Phase in which the Protectorate force Holds the Rendezvous Area. When Trellayne appears on the table, the Protectorate player may place him inside the Rendezvous Area within 3" of any table edge.

Landon Trellayne has the following stats: SPD 5, STR 3, DEF 12, ARM 11, and CMD 5.

Trellayne is an independent model under the control of the Protectorate player. Both hungry and exhausted, he is in far from fit condition. During each of his activations while under the control of the Protectorate player, the smuggler may move up to 10" directly toward the nearest Protectorate warcaster within 12". If there is not a Protectorate warcaster within 12", Trellayne forfeits his activation.

Khador can Capture Trellayne by getting two or more friendly warrior models into base-to-base contact with him anytime he is not also in base-to-base contact with a Protectorate model. The Khador player must assign Trellayne to one of the capturing models and this model becomes his captor. Once he has been captured, Trellayne can move up to 10" during his captor's activation and must end movement in base-to-base contact with the captor. If either the smuggler or his captor are moved out of base-to-base contact with each other for any reason outside of normal movement, or if the captor model is destroyed or removed from play, Trellayne is freed and returns to the Protectorate player's control.

Any player ending his turn controlling Trellayne within the Exit Area wins the game. If the smuggler is destroyed or removed from play, both players lose the game and forfeit their Survival Bonus for the scenario.

Kossite woodsmen may not come into play on the West table edge.

SET UP

See the map. The Protectorate player may place one terrain feature within the Rendezvous Area. Players then take turns, each placing three (3) additional terrain features. Players may not place terrain features within their opponent's deployment zone or within 3" of another terrain feature. Terrain features may be placed on hills.

BEGINNING

The Protectorate player deploys first and takes the first turn.

VICTORY CONDITIONS

The Protectorate player wins the game at the end of any turn he controls Landon Trellayne within the Exit Area.

The Khador player wins the game if either the Protectorate loses its last warcaster or if Landon Trellayne is under Khadoran control within the Exit Area at the end of the Khador player's turn.

If Landon Trellayne is destroyed or removed from play, both players lose the game and forfeit their Survival Bonus for the scenario.

REWARDS

• **Spare Parts:** If the Protectorate wins, spare parts carried by Landon Trellayne are used to repair a damaged warjack. During the Icy Grip of Winter Act III scenario, The Ruins of Riversmet, the Protectorate player may purchase a single light warjack for half the normal point cost rounded up.

• **Commendation:** If Khador wins the scenario, his forces receive additional troops as a commendation for success on the mission. During the Icy Grip of Winter Act III scenario, The Ruins of Riversmet, the Khador player may purchase a single Iron Fang Pikeman, Kossite Woodsman, or Winter Guard unit for half the normal point cost rounded up.

SCENARIO 7, DEAD BY DAWN

CYGNAR VS. CRYX, 1000 POINTS

Gorim 1st, Casteus 605 AR—Hungry, depleted, and harassed at all ends, forward elements of the Cygnaran army charged with reconnaissance of the Llaelese countryside have been bloodied and beaten to the breaking point, yet their strength of purpose stands true in their hearts. When heavy snowfall threatens the mission, Cygnaran forces vow to wait out the storm. Their new home, a quickly assembled firebase codenamed Keepers Dig, provides a modicum of shelter from the brutal snows that impede their progress. The battle groups rest in the Dig under the watch of cannons manned by Cygnaran artillerymen. The cannons are silent thanks to the impeding winds of a raging blizzard, but as the storm abates, the Cygnarans begin to warm the guns and make sure they can be fired as soon as the blizzard ends.

In the night, the void-like silence of snowfall gives way to ominous noises. Ever nervous and fearing the worst, the group readies itself. Just before dawn, troopers hear the unmistakable roar of 'jack furnaces in the distance. As the sounds move closer, a chill runs down the spines of the Cygnarans. Their enemy is not some bold Khadoran company. Instead, they see the baleful green light pouring from the furnaces of helljacks. They hear the shambling footsteps of thralls. Through the snow, the dark bristling shapes of Cryx emerge just before the dawn arrives, just before the hope of a new day. Cryx has come to call on Keepers Dig, and they have brought enough pain for everyone. Their time is short however, for the Cygnaran guns will soon be ready.

SPECIAL RULES

This scenario takes place under cover of darkness. The LOS of all models is limited to 6".

The Cygnar player must spend at least 250 points on warjacks.

The game ends after 6 turns, when dawn arrives and the Cygnaran artillery drives the Cryxian forces from the field.

SET UP

The Cygnar player may place two (2) low wall sections and two (2) other terrain features within 10" of the center of the table. Players then take turns, each placing up to two (2) additional terrain features outside 10" of the center of the table and not within 3" of another terrain feature. Terrain features may be placed on hills.

BEGINNING

The Cygnar player deploys first, placing his models within 6" of the center of the table. The Cryx player then deploys his models within 3" of any number of table edges.

The Cygnar player takes the first turn.

VICTORY CONDITIONS

The game ends after 6 turns. The player who scores the most Victory Points wins the game.

REWARDS

• **Recon:** The winning player's forces are able to complete reconnaissance of the area. During the Icy Grip of Winter Act III scenario, The Ruins of Riversmet, the winning player may extend his deployment zone by 4".

THE ICY GRIP OF WINTER ACT II SIDE QUESTS

HEAD IN HAND, CRYX SIDE QUEST

GORESHADE THE BASTARD

Of all the darkest fiends to send to the lands of the Protectorate, Goreshade the Bastard is perhaps best suited for meeting Menites in the field. Charged with invading the sacred reliquary of the Scrutator Marius Grummel, Goreshade must retrieve the recently departed cleric's skull in order to interrogate him on the nature of the Harbinger. Such dark matters and the desecration of hallowed ground are areas of Goreshade's expertise. Suited for the task, he heads to the site of the Scrutator's remains within the Shrine of Marius.

Waiting for him are the funerary Flameguard known as the Somber Guard. Ostensibly, their primary duty is to keep the most fervent of the flock from straying away with pieces of the blessed Scrutator. Even the smallest finger bone is a blessed item to his followers, but removal of any part of the Scrutator's body would desecrate his remains.

SPREAD TOO THIN

Cryx players need to fight the temptation to spread their forces too thin. While it may be novel to surround your enemy, Cygnaran forces are not nearly as helpless as they may seem.

the Menite cleric's body while his soul takes a journey of passage through the gates of Urcaen. The soul of Marius must cross the treacherous regions of Urcaen as befits a scrutator. For 77 days and nights, the Somber Guard must stand vigilant over his remains, as during that time his spirit is vulnerable to necromancy.

A handful of troops are waiting nearby to support the Somber Guard in case they sound the alarm. Admittedly, this heavy of a guard for the remains of one faithful scrutator is unusual, and it is a mystery why the Hierarch insisted on such precaution. Undeniably, Goreshade will not have an easy time completing this task.

DARK MUSINGS

With a splash, the heavy form of Goreshade the Bastard sank into water so cold and black under the night sky that it lent no light to the eldritch's descent. The heavy shackles of iron clamped to his feet urged his descent ever quicker into the depths of the sea, until after a count of twenty his feet finally touched bottom.

The darkness surrounding him belied a peaceful calm, although above him the sea roiled in anger. One way or another, he still would have preferred to disembark at shore, but he had not dared contradict the wishes of the Iron Lich, Asphyxious. As much as he admired that evil creature, he despised him as well, but Goreshade would do this small errand for the lich and laugh all the while, murdering as he goes.

As he trudged through the blackness among the silt and the rocks of the sea floor, the eldritch reviewed his mission. His first objective was to gather information on this "Harbinger," the being to whom the Menites flocked and revered. In order to find truly useful information, Goreshade needed to interrogate an advisor or close attendant of this holy vessel. However, only a select few would have attended the Harbinger, and Asphyxious had provided a list of the key candidates. To Goreshade, the recently dead were better targets than living ones, who would be protected within the Protectorate's fortress-like cities and towns.

One name on the list was that of a scrutator who had recently died. The rites of such clerics included long and onerous journeys during which the soul is particularly vulnerable to necromancy. All Goreshade required was the seat of the cleric's conscious mind to use as a focus—his brain or his skull perhaps. With either, he could plunge into the man's spirit as easily as he had plunged into the dark waters.

Goreshade found it convenient that the clerics of Menoth were so eager to sacrifice anything in the name of their deity, sometimes even mortifying their own flesh. This particular cleric scourged himself to death to keep his own vile thoughts

enjoyment in peeling so many dirty secrets from the man's soul.

After what seemed like an eternity of marching toward the shore, Goreshade's body slowly took form as it emerged from the murky depths. By the time he reached solid ground, the storm that had raged above had become a quiet breath of wind and the rains had given way to calm and starry skies. Amidst the jutting rocks of the coastal bay, he brushed the withered seaweed and sand from his armor. Night would soon pass, and he sensed the sun already gnawing at the edges of dawn, eager to light the world.

Looking up at the stars, the eldritch quickly gathered his location and pulled a map from the sealed scroll tube at his belt. Making quiet thoughtful noises as he read the map, he looked about and began to walk. He supposed the lich had some grand scheme in place, but it mattered not. Goreshade hoped he would gain enough favor in the eyes of his master and eventually take a place beside Asphyxious; it was all a matter of taking advantage of this opportunity.

"Never send a wolf to gather sheep…" his voice grated against the night sky. There was a long walk ahead of him, and Goreshade would have plenty of time to think.

CRYX ARMY COMPOSITION

Goreshade the Bastard

PROTECTORATE ARMY COMPOSITION

Temple Flameguard unit with 1 Captain and 9 troopers

200 points spent on Knights Exemplar, Flameguard Cleansers, Holy Zealots, additional Temple Flameguard units, or a Paladin of the Wall

SPECIAL RULES, SET UP, AND BEGINNING

Place the shrine of Scrutator Marius Grummel in the center of the table. The shrine is a structure approximately 6" x 3" with a single entrance on the 3" side. The entrance is large enough to accommodate a medium-based model. The shrine has ARM 18 and can take 10 points of damage per inch. The shrine will collapse when 9" or more of its surface have been destroyed. See Damaging and Destroying Structures, WARMACHINE: Prime, pg. 62, for details.

Players then take turns, each placing up to two (2) additional terrain features. Players cannot place terrain features within 3" of another terrain feature,

FORENSIC NECROMANCY

Long ago, necromancers along the Broken Coast and the Scharde Islands learned that questioning the dead was often easier than interrogating the living. For centuries, Toruk's agents had scoured the gravesites of western Immoren for the remains of the exceptionally gifted dead. Cryx has restlessly relocated the bones of many arcane mechaniks and strategic thinkers in order to strip them systematically of their secrets. The greatest success of the forensic necromancers was unlocking the secrets of the arc node before Cygnar even realized the tombs of its most venerated inventors had been desecrated. As a result of this practice, Cygnar's best and brightest are currently interred under great slabs of stone and guarded by arcane wards, constructs, and other measures that can challenge the might of several warjacks combined.

including the shrine. Terrain features may be placed on hills.

The Protectorate player deploys one unit of Temple Flameguard within 3" of the shrine. Goreshade is then placed anywhere at least 18" from the shrine. Goreshade takes the first turn.

Once Goreshade enters the shrine, the remaining Protectorate forces are immediately placed within 12" of any table edge.

If Goreshade Holds the shrine, he may forfeit his action to remove the head of Scrutator Marius Grummel. Once he removes the head, Goreshade carries the head for the rest of the game. If Goreshade moves off any table edge with the head in his possession, the Cryx player wins the game.

VICTORY CONDITIONS

Cryx wins if Goreshade moves off any table edge with the head of Scrutator Marius Grummel.

The Protectorate wins if Goreshade is destroyed.

REWARDS

• **Prophetic Visions:** If Cryx wins the game, Goreshade makes off with the severed head of Scrutator Marius Grummel. After animating and thoroughly questioning the head through the application of necromancy, Goreshade may consult the head before the start of any battle. In games in which Goreshade is used, the Cryx player sets up his models after all his opponents' models have been placed, including models with the Advance Deployment ability. The order of play remains unchanged.

DEUS EX MACHINA, CYGNAR SIDE QUEST

COMMANDER ADEPT NEMO

Commander Adept Nemo is fascinated with the Cult of Cyriss and his knowledge of their religion is quite extensive. While battle groups advance into Llael, Nemo moves along the front in search of a temple rumored to have been abandoned by the cult hundreds of years ago. Within the temple rests the secrets of manufacturing advanced mechanika, including arcane coils of tremendous potency. A researcher into the secrets of voltaic science, Commander Adept Nemo would be able to command the forces of lightning with incredible accuracy if the

Cygnaran military had possession of these powerful coils. After assembling a small team, Nemo takes a brief leave from the frontlines to investigate rumors of the site.

After some exploration, Nemo discovers the Stele of Cyriss—great mechanikal devices that act as the lock and key to what can only be the Cyrissist temple. Unless Nemo forces the devices to work, he will have little chance of opening the great temple doors set into the earth. Conduits, cogs, gears, pistons, and various other mechanika litter the earth surrounding the ruined temple, and crawling amidst these heaps of scrap iron are necrotechs, unaware of the treasures they might discover if their own undead minds were only slightly more inquisitive. Nemo is faced with a challenge and his time has almost run out. He must make for the temple entrance or abandon his quest altogether. With war on the winds, he is unsure if he will ever have another chance to explore this site.

WEIRD SCIENCE

One of the finest minds ever to grasp the concepts of mechanika, Commander Adept Nemo threw the wrench with all his might at the warjack in front of him. Rather than ringing against the spot Nemo had aimed—the middle of the 'jack's heavy hull—the iron and steel wrench was drawn to the warjack's shield and clanged against its massive voltaic barrier with a resounding ring. The wrench had stuck fast.

"Aha! The accumulo-voltaic flow is maximized by the passing of electricity through the sub-coils. Perfect!" The joy in the warcaster's voice was obvious. Once again he had found a more efficient way to get a warjack system operating. "Now, I need to recalibrate the reflex triggers around the cortex to make sure it doesn't list to the left. Bad battle form, I'd say. Opens it up after a swing. Makes it vulnerable. Easier to pull over if the shield locks to something too big…" His mind slipped into momentary contemplation as he wondered if he could scavenge some reliable triggers from the scrapped Nomad out in the yard. The entrance of an assistant suddenly disturbed his musing.

"What is it, Jeoffrey?" Nemo glanced at the young man. Jeoffrey was talented with minuscule sparks of genius, but the lad was a bit of a dimwit when it came to articulated systems. "You look like you've been pinched by a river clam."

"There's a… man here to see you." The youth seemed flustered, a hint of uncertainty in his voice. "He says he's an adventurer you hired."

Nemo raised his right eyebrow in excitement. "That would be Master Craske. He and I have some talking to do. Send him in, lad."

The white-haired warcaster seemed to forget all about the

warjack and his voltaic experiment. Crinnebule Craske was an expert at uncovering hidden places, and Nemo had hired the skilled mage to do some research for him. With the maps and diagrams Craske had promised to deliver, the Commander Adept could locate the renowned Tellurian Forge before heading off to battle once more. The lost temple of Cyriss was not ancient, but an experiment some years ago had gone awry, and since that time, the cultists had abandoned it leaving it to rot and ruin.

Purported to be within the Tellurian Forge was mechanika that could twist electrical forces unlike anything Nemo had ever seen. He looked over at the 'jack and willed the Centurion into dormancy. The wrench fell from the shield and landed on the ground with a clatter. It was sometimes hard to pry facts from an adventurer of this sort; they could be a little protective of secrets. Not to mention the various critters and conditions they ran across could warp their minds and bodies—especially with so many Cryxians about—so Nemo left the Centurion's battle systems charged just in case. It was all but a wary afterthought. The warcaster was confident he could reason with the man as he hefted a sack filled with crowns onto his worktable.

"You know how to get to a man's heart faster than a farrow's spear, Nemo." The voice of Craske was mirthful, but with an undertone that spoke of how dangerous the man could be. "I've been looking into matters for you, and this ought to be your ticket."

Nemo turned to see what the man was holding. Craske looked like a chewed boot, ragged and ugly, but Nemo knew better. A former companion of Professor Viktor Pendrake's, Craske had a reputation for delving into dangerous places and leaving intact, with valuables to boot. Right now, the man was holding a small pyramidal object.

Nemo nodded a terse greeting as he peered at the relic. "What have you got there?" The Commander Adept could spy the symbols and markings on it, and he could clearly discern it was something Cyrissist-made.

"A key," the adventurer smiled. "But more importantly, it is also a compass…"

CYGNAR ARMY COMPOSITION

Commander Adept Nemo

Journeyman Warcaster

1 Field Mechanik unit with a Crew Chief and 3 Goblin Bodgers

CRYX ARMY COMPOSITION

1 Necrotech

4 Scrap Thralls

1 Bane Thrall unit with 1 Lieutenant and 5 Troopers

1 Mechanithrall unit with 1 Lieutenant and 5 Troopers

SPECIAL RULES AND SET UP

The Stelae of Cyriss are great mechanikal pillars 1" in diameter and 3" high. Place the four stelae of Cyriss in a 12" square at the center of the table with two of them on each side of the table. The stelae are indestructible. To activate a stele, Nemo or the Journeyman Warcaster must be in base contact with the stele and forfeit his action. A Crew Chief or a Goblin Bodger may attempt to activate a stele. To attempt to activate the stele, the mechanik must be in base contact with one and pass a repair check. Activating a stele is a special action. Goblin Bodgers may assist the chief in the roll. When all four stelae are operable, the temple doors open and Cygnar wins the game.

Destroyed Cryx models and units return to play during each of the Cryx player's Maintenance phases. Models are placed within 3" of the Cryx table edge. Units are returned to play only if all models in the unit have been destroyed.

The Cryx player places two (2) light warjack wreck markers and one (1) heavy warjack wreck marker anywhere on the table at least 3" from a table edge or a stele. Players then take turns, each placing three (3) additional terrain features. Players cannot place terrain features within 3" of another terrain feature, including one of the Stelae of Cyriss and warjack wreck markers. Terrain features may be placed on hills.

BEGINNING

At the start of the game, each player rolls a d6. The high roller chooses who goes first. The first player gets his choice of deployment zones and takes the first turn. Players deploy their forces up to 10" from the table's edge.

VICTORY CONDITIONS AND RESOLUTION

Cygnar wins the game if all four stelae are activated.

Cryx wins the game if Nemo is destroyed.

REWARDS

• **Weather Manipulation:** If Cygnar wins, Nemo enters the temple. Once inside he discovers an ancient

THE CULT OF CYRISS

Cyriss is the mysterious goddess of machinery and mathematics. From within her cult's hidden temples, her priests strive endlessly to unravel the secrets of the universe. These temples are vast receptacles of arcane knowledge, and any self-respecting arcane mechanik would trade his eyeteeth for a mere glimpse at them. Indeed, to uncover an abandoned temple is akin to discovering the mother lode for scientists and mechaniks alike.

YOU SAY STELA, I SAY STELE

Stele: also ste·la (stl) pl. steles, also ste·lae (-l) An upright stone or slab with an inscribed or sculptured surface, used as a monument or as a commemorative tablet in the face of a building.

mechanikal device that allows him to manipulate local weather patterns. For the rest of the Campaign, the Cygnar player may modify Weather Condition rolls by up to +2 or –2 in games in which Nemo is used. For example, if Nemo is used during the Spring Act II scenario Collateral Damage, he can influence the Weather Condition roll for the scenario. If the roll is a 3, Heavy Rains, Nemo can add or subtract up to 2 from the die roll, either increasing the roll to 5, Clear Skies, or lowering it to 2, Flash Floods.

- **Arcane Coils:** Nemo also discovers arcane coils that may be used to supercharge his electrical powers for a short time. Once during any single scenario in which Nemo is used, the Cygnar player may activate the coils. The player must declare use of the coils before the start of the game. For the duration of the game, Nemo gains +1 POW on all Lightning Rod, Electrical Burst, Ball Lightning, Chain Lightning, and Elecritical Storm damage rolls.

CHARGE OF THE WINTER GUARD, KHADOR SIDE QUEST

KOMMANDANT IRUSK

Despite the inexperience of its young kapitan, the Vlastrykia Kompania has performed relatively well due to the leadership of its sergeants. However, the prospect of taking Saldon Tower from Llael's allies, a stubborn company of Cygnaran soldiers, on the outskirts of Riversmet has proven too great a challenge for the company and they find themselves pinned down.

Those who led the initial charge against Saldon Tower are now dead. The remaining troops have taken what little cover is available. Constant fire from Cygnaran trenchers, their chaingun, and two journeymen warcasters along with their warjacks are wreaking havoc on the Khadoran troops, and the few who have attempted to flee from cover are cut down by bullets, spells, and cannon fire.

In an effort to save his company, the Kapitan has requested a warcaster and warjacks to cover his men so that they can move to a safer position and regroup. However, the battle elsewhere in Riversmet is so desperate that resources are at the breaking point. While making a tour of the various efforts around the city, Kommandant Irusk comes upon the Kapitan and reminds him of his duty. Inspired by the words of his commanding officer, the young Kapitan makes a courageous but ill-fated charge to rescue his men. He falls.

With the remainder of the company cornered and no other leaders in sight, Kommandant Irusk realizes the gravity of the situation. If the Cygnarans retain control of Saldon Tower, then reinforcements can approach and create a rallying point. Using the tower as shelter, Llaelese skirmishers and Cygnaran soldiers may be able to regroup and repel them.

Without hesitation, Kommandant Irusk charges into the field. Accustomed to the chaotic climate, he rushes to Vlastrykia Kompania's aid, all the while bellowing orders and inspiration.

DUTY

Endless shots churned the muck and mire surrounding Saldon Tower. Stutters of chaingun fire snapped into the puddles of bloody mud like deadly rain. A warjack's cannon went off and a unit of Winter Guard troopers became a ragged pile of flesh, canvas, and broken metal.

Time was running out. Kommandant Irusk gazed upon the faces of Vlastrykia Kompania. The men huddled behind low walls as the pressure of battle etched upon them, dampening their resolve. Damn that Cygnaran chaingun!

The biggest problem Irusk faced was that Llael's allies already had such weaponry on the field. Hunkered down around the tower, Khador's enemy was doing a good job of denying his men the field of battle and laying waste to these young patriots.

Looking at the young man beside him, Irusk spoke briskly. "Kapitan, do you plan to leave your men out there to wait for the cover of night?"

Each of the soldiers trapped out there was a loyal subject of the Motherland willing to lay down his life for the cause. Meanwhile, this indecisive coward seemed incapable of making a clear tactical decision. "You are fortunate these are but journeymen you face. I suggest you solve this problem at once, Kapitan."

"Kommandant, the range of our guns is too short! What can be done?"

The Kapitan, obviously assigned out of necessity to fill a gap in the advancing lines, was unprepared for a cover and fire situation. This was supposed to be one of the softer objectives of the campaign, and now it had turned into a crucial point. Such were the unpredictable fortunes of war. Irusk noted that the man wore a noble crest on his uniform which meant his appointment to station was due to privilege rather than service, and the hard-bitten sergeants trapped out there in a forward position were probably a decade this noble's senior.

"Staying here and doing nothing is suicide, Kapitan; not to mention consigning your officers to a bloody death at the hands of their lessers. Action under pressure is the only way to success. If you allow the enemy to maintain a firing alley along those walls with their superior range, your men will remain trapped. Gather your men and run them under covering fire to the foremost wall." He emphasized his point by gesturing towards the Khadoran position with his sword cannon, Onslaught. "But you must time the charge correctly and rally the men to follow, understood?"

The Kapitan nodded and contemplated Irusk's words for a moment. After snapping a salute, the young officer began to charge and yell to his men for covering fire. Winter Guard troopers snapped shots at the Cygnarans in an attempt to create a covering blanket of blunderbuss fire, but the enemy was tenacious, dug in, and out of range. Irusk watched as rifles trained on the officer and fire from the chaingun snapped at his feet like a hungry wolf. Miraculously, the Kapitan landed out of their sight, safely behind one of the walls protecting his troopers. He had timed his charge correctly.

"There's hope for you yet," Irusk smiled. He watched as the Kapitan rallied the soldiers. The group rose from cover to cross the distance between their wall and a nearby wall where more troops were hiding, but Irusk became disappointed as the Kapitan led them too close to the range of the enemy guns.

A single shot caught the noble Kapitan in the upper torso. Surprised, he staggered aside, and the Cygnaran chaingun roared. The youth was torn apart in a shower of bloody chunks. The troopers around him were spattered with gore and they turned and ran. Gunfire trailed them back to the safety of the wall from where they'd just charged—none of them had fallen except the noble Kapitan, but the soldiers were back where they had started, huddled behind the low stone.

With more troopers trapped further out and closer to the objective, Irusk could see he was the only chance they had to take the tower. Losing the noble Kapitan was a sad occurrence; he could have molded the young man into a competent officer, but there was nothing to be done for it now. The Kommandant raised Onslaught aloft and charged the first group of pinned down soldiers, yelling for cover as his jackboots pounded the muck and mire surrounding Saldon Tower.

KHADOR ARMY COMPOSITION

Kommandant Irusk

3 Winter Guard units each with 1 Sergeant and 5 Troopers

CYGNAR ARMY COMPOSITION

2 Journeyman Warcasters

1 Trencher Unit with 1 Sergeant and 5 Troopers

1 Trencher Chaingun Crew

Each Journeyman controls one of the following warjacks: Charger, Defender, Hunter, Lancer

SPECIAL RULES AND SET UP

See the map. Place two 12" long high walls 12" forward from the Khador deployment zone with one wall bordering the west table edge and the other bordering the east table edge. Place a third 8" long high wall in the center of the table.

The Cygnar player places all of his models on the table, including models with the Advanced Deployment ability.

The Khador player then places one unit of Winter Guard behind each wall. The Winter Guard should not be placed within the LOS of the Cygnar models. The Khador player then deploys Irusk within the Khador Deployment Zone.

The Winter Guard units begin the game shell-shocked and must be rallied by Irusk before they can activate. Each Winter Guard unit within Irusk's command range during the Khador player's Maintenance Phase can make a command check to steel its nerve. Once it passes a command check, the unit can activate normally for the rest of the game.

The game goes into Hammertime at the end of round 5. If the game ends before Khadoran forces destroy the two Journeyman Warcasters, Llaelese and Cygnaran reinforcements arrive and drive the Khadorans off the field.

BEGINNING

The Khador player takes the first turn.

VICTORY CONDITIONS AND RESOLUTION

Khador wins the game if both Journeyman Warcasters are destroyed.

Cygnar wins if Irusk is destroyed or if the game ends before both Journeyman Warcasters have been destroyed.

REWARDS

• **Motivator:** If Khador wins the game, Irusk becomes a living example of valor to his men. For the rest of the Campaign, all friendly troopers within Irusk's command area gain +1 movement.

MORNING SERVICE, PROTECTORATE SIDE QUEST

HIGH EXEMPLAR KREOSS

High Exemplar Kreoss has traveled many leagues, and in Llael he seeks respite at a small shrine dedicated to Menoth known as the Temple of the Eye. Along with his seneschal, he has been traveling through the kingdoms carrying word of the Hierarch's call. He urges the faithful to make pilgrimages to the south to the Protectorate. Staying near the various temples, he speaks of faith and devotion to fellow Menites and of the wrath of Menoth's hand upon those who doubt His calling.

One morning before heading to battle, Kreoss and his guards make the short trip to the Menite shrine for daily supplication. Their arrival draws a small flock of zealot converts from Llael who have come to pray in the High Exemplar's company. Their offerings are suddenly interrupted as the swings of fell blades and the chant of Orgoth steel mark the arrival of Doom Reavers, no doubt dispatched to murder Kreoss and anyone found with him. Heeding the call, Kreoss must fulfill his duty to protect the faithful and stop Menite blood from spilling on holy ground.

INSPIRATION

Faithful servants of Menoth gathered around the High Exemplar as he walked through the snow towards the tiny shrine. They had all come through ice and snow to witness his presence and to heed the Creator's call. As Kreoss moved towards the crowd, he inspected them. They were huddled in woolen cloaks and scarves, many of them with hands and faces made blue from the bitter cold. Truly these were faithful Menites willing to endure discomfort in order to offer prayer to the Lawgiver. Kreoss felt a stirring of honor within his heart.

Kreoss paused; his seneschal behind him halted as well. The High Exemplar turned to address the masses, his voice ringing strong and loud. "I am pleased you have come to pray with me before my battle against the unbelievers. It is good to see your faith is stronger than your fear of tyranny. If there are ill among you, Menoth shall heal you. If there are doubters here today, I will allay your uncertainty.

"The call is for all of good faith. None are unseen. All that is asked is that you place your trust in the Hierarch. Very soon, the time will come to pass when we will be a whole people, united in prayer, not fractured by the borders of petty rulers and despots interested only in ungodly coin and the rule of their false law.

"Now let us gather about the shrine in prayer. We call upon you, Menoth, for strength." He paused for a moment, allowing the people around him to absorb his words. "Here, we are nothing to the rulers of these godless lands. But in our Protectorate, we have a home, a place to worship you, a way to prove our undying faith in your great name and, above all, a secure place beside your grandeur in Urcaen.

"All of you here and now, gather your faith. It is your armor. Ready yourselves and go south. The Hierarch welcomes Menoth's faithful with open arms.

"Now, let us enter the shrine and pray for guidance in the long journeys to come…."

Just as Kreoss and his seneschal stepped a few feet toward the shrine, he sensed something awry: a lingering evil clouded from the edges of his sight. Nodding to his guards, he made a symbol with his right hand. The warriors readied to draw their weapons as Kreoss murmured a small prayer to summon his armor. He did not wish to alarm the faithful, but danger was near, and interrupting an exemplar in prayer was a deadly prospect.

PROTECTORATE ARMY COMPOSITION

High Exemplar Kreoss

Exemplar Seneschal

Holy Zealots unit representing the Menite Faithful with 9 Zealots and no Priest

KHADOR ARMY COMPOSITION

Doom Reaver unit with 1 Lieutenant and 5 Troopers

Manhunter

SPECIAL RULES

See the map. This scenario takes place inside the shrine, a circular chamber 30" in diameter. A 2" diameter pillar stands in the center of the room.

The Holy Zealots represent nine Llaelese Menites. The Zealots are independent models and do not have to maintain unit coherency. Use the stats for Zealots; there is no Priest present. The Zealots cannot make Fire Bomb attacks during this scenario. When a Zealot flees, instead of moving, he becomes a stationary model until he is rallied.

SET UP

There is no additional terrain in this scenario.

BEGINNING

See the map. The Protectorate player deploys his models anywhere on the Protectorate half of the table.

The Khador player then deploys all his models within the 5" x 6" area shown on the map.

The Protectorate player takes the first turn.

VICTORY CONDITIONS AND RESOLUTION

The Protectorate wins if all Khadoran models are destroyed before more than four (4) Menite Faithful are destroyed.

Khador wins if either Kreoss or five (5) or more Menite Faithful are destroyed.

REWARDS

• **Disciples:** If the Protectorate player wins, word of Kreoss' selfless defense of the Llaelese Menites circulates far and wide and his fame begins to grow to legendary proportions. For the rest of the Campaign, any time Kreoss is used in a scenario the Protectorate player gains an additional Holy Zealot unit made up of a Priest and 5 Troopers representing Kreoss' faithful disciples.

THE ICY GRIP OF WINTER ACT III

SCENARIO 8, RUINS OF RIVERSMET

TWO-PLAYER GAME, 1000 POINTS

Vendarl 3rd, Trineus 605 AR—As the harsh winter campaign wears on, supplies run low. With stockpiles of fuel, food, and shot dwindling, one by one, the demands of war are forcing rival factions to pull back and lose hard-won territory. In the end, only two forces remain poised for a final desperate showdown at the scorched ruins of Riversmet.

The site of countless battles over the past months, the former Three Rivers Town has all but burned to the ground. In fact, some weeks ago Khadoran troops made sure the destruction of Riversmet was complete by setting the city ablaze in order to drive out remaining enemy forces and to send a warning to the

Order of the Golden Crucible in nearby Leryn.

Amidst the charred ruins, burnt out hulks, and cremated troopers, not a living thing has been spared in this former city; however, resources still remain. At the epicenter of the conflict is a storage vault filled with coal beneath the ruins of the previous Crucible chapterhouse. Sheltered from the harmful flames by the order's own protective measures, the coal is still usable and protected in a fortified position. The bomb-blasted grounds still hold plenty of supplies in the depths of the chapterhouse's catacombs that wait to be plundered by anyone who can hold Riversmet long enough to gain access to the vaults. In addition to tons of coal, the chapterhouse is purportedly a treasure trove of alchemical lore as well.

After days of burning, the fires have mostly subsided. Confident that there is no longer a threat other than opposing forces, both armies march in unaware of the other. Damage to Crucible laboratories has resulted in a volatile mixture of unstable alchemical compounds. As the battle begins, once-sealed alchemical reagents begin to intermingle and activate. When the forces collide, sudden fierce explosions erupt from the ground as the vapors of the Crucible laboratories react from exposure to the hot air above!

SPECIAL RULES

The Ruins of Riversmet is a two-player scenario between the player with the most wins throughout The Icy Grip of Winter Act II and the player from another faction with the next highest total number of wins. In case of a tie, compare each player's Victory Point total throughout Winter Act II.

Players take turns, each placing three (3) ruined Crucible buildings within 15" of the center of the table. Assign each ruin a number between one and six. The ruined Crucible buildings must be at least 3" x 5" with gaps or doors large enough to accommodate large based models. A ruin may not be placed within 5" of another Crucible ruin.

At the start of each player's Maintenance Phases, the player rolls a d6 to determine if volatile chemicals within one of the ruins explode. If a 1 is rolled then one of the buildings will explode and the player must roll again to determine which one goes up in flames. The building that corresponds to the number of the second roll explodes. If the building corresponding to the roll has already exploded, nothing happens. When a ruin explodes, remove the ruin from the table. Any model that was inside the ruin is thrown 1d6" in a random direction determined by the deviation template with the same effect as a Throw power attack, suffering a POW 14 damage roll. See Throw, WARMACHINE:

Prime, pg. 43, for details. Any model within 2" of the ruin is knocked down.

A treasure trove of alchemical lore, inside one of the Crucible buildings is an experimental elixir. A player can roll a d6 during his Maintenance Phase for each building his models Hold. Make this roll after determining if any ruins explode. On the roll of 6, the elixir is found. A player's models Hold a ruined building if all models within the ruined building are controlled by that player during his Maintenance Phase. Models that are engaged in melee combat cannot Hold a ruined building. Warrior models with CMD stats of 1 or less and Incorporeal models cannot Hold a location.

When the elixir is found, it must be assigned to one of the models Holding the building who then carries it. A friendly model in base-to-base contact with the model carrying the elixir may forfeit his action to take it. If the model carrying the elixir is destroyed or removed from play, the elixir remains at the model's last location. A model in base contact with the elixir may forfeit his activation to pick it up.

SET UP

Players take turns, each placing 2 additional terrain features. Terrain features may not be placed within 3" of another terrain feature, including the Golden Crucible ruins. Terrain features may be placed on hills.

BEGINNING

At the start of the game, each player rolls a d6 and the high roller chooses who goes first. The first player gets his choice of deployment zones and takes the first turn. Players deploy their forces up to 10" from the table's edge.

VICTORY CONDITIONS

The player with the last surviving warcaster in play wins the game.

REWARDS

• **Fit Condition:** After seizing control of the coal vault, the winner's forces remain in fighting condition throughout the winter. The winner may add up to 25 points to the size of his army in the Storms of Spring Act I scenario, the Battle for Aliston Yard.

• **The Elixir:** Win or lose the player whose model carries the elixir at the end of the game keeps it. If no model was carrying the elixir at the end of the game, nobody gets it. The elixir can be used once during any single Campaign scenario. The player must declare its use before the start of the game and assign it to a faction warcaster. Whether or not the elixir is used during the scenario, it cannot be used again. It may be used once during the game during the warcaster's activation. When used, the warcaster's power field is completely regenerated and all damage points sustained by the warcaster are removed.

THE CRUCIBLE'S SURRENDER OF LERYN

Pressured by Cygnar's Royal Assembly to maintain trade ties and keep their own significant resources and assets in check, the Order of the Golden Crucible's leaders replied to the Greylord envoys sent to intimidate them with a simple "No."

Unwilling to concede or accept Khadoran authority, the Order of the Golden Crucible further antagonized the High Kommand by using their own arcane talents to cripple warjacks, obliterate troops, and establish the core of a hardened resistance. Khador's reaction was unmistakable: they burnt Riversmet to the ground.

After this drastic retort to the Golden Crucible's defiance, the leaders of the order bowed their heads and complied with Khador's demands. On Vendarl 1st, Cinten 605 AR, Khador dispatched 8,000 soldiers to Llael's Proud City of Leryn. As part of their compliance, the Crucible ensured that the city that once held off the Orgoth longer than any other aside from Caspia surrendered without a fight. With Riversmet's fate in mind, the Crucible leaders ordered their forces to stand down, pulling the Crucible Guard from Leryn's walls. Shortly after the surrender, the order signed a contract to supply blasting powder exclusively to Khador's military. Leryn remains intact, although occupied now by Khadoran forces.

A handful of Crucible leaders refused to be cowed, but they and their families were summarily executed. Clemency was extended to all of the organization's conforming members as long as they agreed to bow in fealty to the Motherland. Still, several Crucible alchemists fled south, bearing their alchemical secrets, materials, and trade with them, and the Cygnarans welcomed the exiles, promising to safeguard them from their enemies and put them to immediate use.

GORIM 2ND, TRINEUS 605 AR

Winter fades and spring's thaw melts away the icy cloak that buried the torn bodies of troops and the ruined wrecks of warjacks during the cold months. The Black River swells from the melting mountain snows and envelops roads and waterways as the Black River Valley becomes a vast floodplain. Khador has claimed most of the nation, but their occupation has been challenged by Cygnar's military persistence. The deep waters of the flood have not washed away the violence, nor prevented further battles; they serve only to hinder the movement of Khadoran troops for a short time.

The lands between the Khadoran stronghold of Ravensgard and its somber Cygnaran counterpart, the fortress of Northguard, are full of activity. Trenchers, warjacks, and Winter Guard troops clash incessantly in tug-of-war battles. The bodies of the dead and wounded are literally crushed under the boots of soldiers and the stomping feet of warjacks as titanic weapons clash amidst waves of blood, magic, and fire.

Elsewhere, Protectorate forces are frantically directing Menite pilgrims to the relative safety and isolation of their own lands. The pilgrims are often armed, and the chants and prayers are those of a religion ready to wage war upon an entire world of faithless heathens. Whipped into frenzy, the Protectorate is at the brink of bursting. Scrutators and priests ready themselves for a Holy Crusade upon all of Immoren, for soon the Protectorate will bring the full might of Menoth to bear on the west, subjugating all heretics and delivering them to righteousness.

Meanwhile, Cryx is busier than ever with the sweet harvest of battlefields that yield untold dead. The bodies of troops and the wreckage of warjacks present a feast for the Necrotechs. As if responding to some terrifying plan, thralls rise and gather up the wasted dead and bring them to the necrofactoriums for conversion. The armies of Cryx bloat with the blue-black dead of winter and grow ever stronger as the attrition of war bolsters them with the harvest of loss.

Caught in the midst of this turmoil, Cygnar readies itself; the proud nation must rely on its military might and the skill of its warcasters if it is to survive this great war of wars. The storms of spring have come and with them, the thunder and lightning that Cygnar hopes will lend them the strength to persevere and destroy those who seek to tear their great nation apart.

THE STORMS OF SPRING
ACT I

SCENARIO 1, THE BATTLE OF ALISTON YARD

MULTIPLAYER GAME, 500 POINTS

Vendarl 4th, Tempen 605 AR—Ceaseless spring storms falling on the lowlands of Llael have flooded the Black River Valley. Isolated hills and high ground have become islands amidst a sea of floodwater. Outside of the capital city of Merywyn, four armies fight to hold high ground or perish in the flowing floodwaters around them.

Khadoran forces have routed the defenders and Merywyn has fallen to Khadoran occupation. Cygnaran forces, hoping to lend aid to the city, have been forced to give up ground in hopes of establishing some kind of foothold and waiting out the weather. Due to the thaw of a hard winter and the endless spring downpours, the flooding in the lowlands has caused the Black River to rise to dangerous levels. The vast wash has also caught Cryxian and Protectorate incursions unprepared as they scramble for high ground. Now, all four forces are staring down each other's throats as the rain soaks them to the bone.

Aliston Yard is a vantage point over the Black River just north of Merywyn. Not only does it offer a commanding view of the river, it is also one of the few patches of semi-dry land in the entire long valley. As the forces of each faction make their way through the flood lands, fighting breaks out for control of Aliston Yard.

SPECIAL RULES AND SET UP

Place a hill no larger than 10" across in the center of the table. Each player then places an additional hill no larger than 10" across anywhere on the table outside of 3" from another hill or table edge. Players alternate placing two (2) ruin terrain pieces on any of the hills. A ruin cannot be placed within 3" of another ruin.

With the exception of the hills, Shallow Water covers the entire battlefield. See Shallow Water, WARMACHINE: Prime, pg. 61, for details.

The first player to Hold two hills simultaneously for two consecutive rounds wins the game. A player Holds a hill if all models on the hill are controlled by that player during his maintenance phase. Models that are engaged in melee combat cannot Hold a location. Neither warrior models with CMD stats of 1 or less nor Incorporeal models can Hold a location.

Kossite Woodsmen may only come into play in the Khador deployment zone.

BEGINNING

At the start of the game, each player rolls a d6. The player who rolls highest chooses to go first or last. The player who rolls second highest then chooses to go first or last from among the remaining spots in the play order. The third highest roller does the same and so on until the lowest roller takes the final spot. The first player gets his choice of deployment zones and takes the first turn. Each player deploys in a 10" by 10" area in a corner of the table.

VICTORY CONDITIONS AND RESOLUTION

The first player to Hold two hills for two rounds wins the game. The ranking of the other players is determined by the amount of Victory Points each player scores during play. A player's standing determines the order he must reveal his warcaster deployments for Spring Act II.

REWARDS

• **Warcaster Deployment:** The outcome of The Battle of Aliston Yard determines the order that players will reveal their warcaster deployments for the Storms of Spring Act II scenarios. The losing player with the fewest Victory Points begins the process by revealing his warcaster deployments for each Spring Act II scenario The losing player with the next fewest victory points reveals his warcaster deployments and so on with the winner of the scenario revealing his warcaster deployments last. In a two-player game, the losing player must inform the winner of both warcasters he intends to field during the Storms of Spring Act II game.

• **Gaining the Initiative:** The winning player also gains control of most of the dry land remaining in Western Llael and gets a +1 bonus on Starting Rolls during all Storms of Spring Act II scenarios.

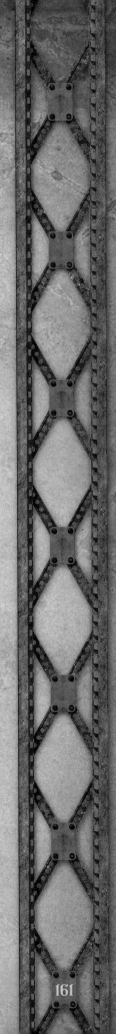

THE STORMS OF SPRING ACT II

SCENARIO 2, COLLATERAL DAMAGE

CYGNAR VS. PROTECTORATE, 1000 POINTS

Malleus 2nd, Tempen 605 AR—Cygnaran troops have been on the lookout for Protectorate forces running raids against merchant and military caravans carrying supplies for the war. In addition to the supplies and refugees appropriated by the Menites, they have also somehow managed to seize a surplus of Cygnaran 'jack parts. These supplies could help Cygnar recover from the assaults of winter.

After some detailed reconnaissance, Cygnaran forces have discovered the location of a secret Protectorate fueling depot near the northeast edge of Widower's Wood. Of course, the Protectorate has established the base on the site of a Menite monastery,

and this location presents two obstacles: first, the Menite monks are caring for wounded Llaelese civilians and if harm comes to them, Cygnar would be cast in a very bad light, and, second, the monks have a tank full of deadly explosive chemicals capable of destroying not only the Cygnaran troops, but the entire monastery as well. Before Cygnar can claim the supplies and "liberate" the refugees, they must disable the tank of explosive chemicals and neutralize the threat posed by the Protectorate presence.

Cygnaran forces need to move in, engage the enemy, and locate the tank of Menoth's Fury. The only way to remove the threat safely is to empty the contents of the tank and use a special alchemical reagent, a rare material known as "firebane," to neutralize the volatile liquid. The tank must be opened and emptied. With a vial of firebane mixed into the spilling contents, the fuel will no longer be able to burn. The potent alchemical reagent can disrupt the volatile properties of the fuel long enough for the Cygnarans to destroy the Protectorate forces and safely evacuate the refugees. Unfortunately, there's not a lot of time, as two more Protectorate battle groups will be returning shortly. Cygnaran troops must move before their chance is lost.

SPECIAL RULES

Place the monastery in the middle of the table bordering the forward edge of the Protectorate deployment zone. The monastery is a stone structure approximately 5" x 6". It is heavily barricaded and cannot be entered. The monastery walls have ARM 16 and can take 10 points of damage per inch. The monastery will collapse after 11" or more of its surface has been destroyed. See Damaging and Destroying Structures, WARMACHINE: Prime, pg. 62, for details.

Place a tank of Menoth's Fury that is 2" in diameter and 3" high in contact with the monastery, centered behind it, and inside the Protectorate deployment zone. The tank has ARM 16 and will explode if it takes one or more damage points. If it explodes, the monastery will be destroyed, killing all the civilians inside and causing all models within 10" to suffer a POW 16 damage roll.

If the monastery is destroyed, both players lose the game and forfeit their Survival Bonus for the scenario.

Any Cygnar model in base contact with the tank can forfeit its action to unchain the tank's valve. After the valve has been unchained, any Cygnar model in base contact with the tank can forfeit its action to open the valve and release the tank's contents and mix the Firebane with the fuel as it spills. The Cygnar player wins if the tank's valve is fully opened.

The game goes into Hammertime at the end of round nine. If the game ends before Cygnaran forces open the valve on the tank of Menoth's Fury and neutralize its contents, Protectorate reinforcements arrive and drive off the Cygnaran attackers.

SET UP

Players take turns, each placing three (3) terrain features. The Protectorate player may not place terrain within either player's deployment zone. The Cygnar player may not place terrain within the Protectorate player's deployment zone. Terrain features may not be placed within 3" of other terrain features including the monastery or tank. Terrain features may be placed on hills.

BEGINNING

At the start of the game, each player rolls a d6 and the higher roller chooses who goes first. The first player sets up and takes the first turn. Players deploy their forces up to 10" from the table's edge.

VICTORY CONDITIONS

Cygnar wins the game if the valve on the tank is opened and its contents neutralized.

The Protectorate wins if Cygnar loses its last warcaster or if Cygnar has not won by the end of the game.

If the monastery is destroyed either by damage to the monastery walls or because the tank explodes, both factions lose the game and forfeit their Survival Bonus for the scenario.

REWARDS

• **Fuel Depot:** If the Cygnar player wins, the Menites are driven off and the site is converted into a supply and fueling depot. Once during any single Storms of Spring scenario, the Cygnar player pays 10 points less for his warjacks.

• **Arms Cache:** If the Protectorate player wins, the Menoth's Fury is moved to a new hiding spot and saved for a later battle. Once during any single Storms of Spring scenario, the Protectorate player may purchase a single Deliverer, Flameguard Cleanser, or Temple Flameguard unit for half normal point cost rounded up.

SCENARIO 3, NEEDLE IN A HAYSTACK

KHADOR VS. CRYX, 1000 POINTS

Malleus 4th, Tempen 605 AR—Spring thaw has brought with it a horrid harvest for eager Cryxian hands. The thaw and the rushing floodwaters have uncovered corpses buried by ice and snow, and the rushing waters of the flood have torn mass graves apart. The dead have been uncovered, and soon they will no longer rest. Amidst the now silent battlefields, Stitch Thralls process the bodies while Necrosurgeons convert them into the various types of thralls that serve the vile motives of Lord Toruk.

However, the dead still carry secrets, and a single Khadoran officer fallen on the battlefields around Merywyn carries battle plans for their spring efforts. This parchment, if discovered, will compromise the entire war effort and force the Motherland's army to alter its tactics drastically. Amid the receding floodwaters outside of Merywyn, the armies of Cryx and Khador clash, and while Cryx scrambles like a murder of crows over the bodies of the dead, Khador must find one single waterlogged corpse amidst the teeming mass of thralls, leeches, maggots, and fear.

SPECIAL RULES AND SET UP

See map. A Shallow Water river approximately 8" wide runs through the center of the table. See Shallow Water, WARMACHINE: Prime, pg. 61, for details.

Players take turns, each placing three (3) terrain features. Terrain features may not be placed within 3" of another terrain feature, including the river. Terrain features may be placed on hills.

Once terrain is set up, players take turns, each placing four (4) corpse tokens within the river. Corpse tokens cannot be placed within 5" of another corpse token.

Khadoran warcasters can search a corpse token as a special action. Roll 2d6. If the roll comes up doubles, the plans are discovered and picked up by the searching warcaster. The last corpse token in play always has the plans. A Khadoran warcaster ending movement within base contact of the last corpse token picks up the plans.

Remove the corpse token from play once searched. If the warcaster carrying the plans is destroyed or removed from play, the plans remain in the place the model last occupied. A Khadoran warcaster ending movement within base contact with the plans picks them up. The plans can only be picked up by a Khadoran warcaster. If a Khadoran warcaster carries the plans into their deployment zone, Khador wins.

Any Cryx model, except an Incorporeal model or a bonejack, may pick up a corpse token in base-to-base contact by forfeiting its action. Small-based models can pick up a single corpse token and move at half their normal movement rate while carrying the token. Medium based models can carry up to three (3) corpse tokens without penalty. Large based models can pick up an unlimited number of corpse tokens without penalty. Corpse tokens carried into the Cryx deployment zone are removed from the table. If a model carrying a corpse token is destroyed or removed from play, the token remains in the place the model last occupied. A model can drop a corpse token at any time. Dropping a corpse token does not require an action. When dropped, the token is placed on the table in base contact with the model that dropped it.

BEGINNING

At the start of the game, each player rolls a d6 and the high roller chooses who goes first. The first player gets his choice of deployment zones and takes the first turn. Players deploy their forces up to 10" from the table's edge.

VICTORY CONDITIONS AND RESOLUTION

Khador wins if one of their warcasters carries the plans into the Khadoran deployment zone.

Cryx wins if the plans have not been discovered before the last corpse token is taken off the table or if Khador loses their last warcaster.

REWARDS

• **Battle Plans:** If the Khador player wins the game, the plans prove valuable to the continuing war effort. Once during any single Storms of Spring scenario, he may place all the terrain detailed in the text of the scenario. The terrain must be placed legally.

• **Fresh Meat:** Win or lose, the dead carried off by the Cryxian forces provide fresh meat for the Dragon's charnel army. Once during any single Storms of Spring scenario, the Cryx player may add 10 additional points to the size of his army for every corpse token carried into the Cryx deployment zone. Additional points must be spent on the same scenario and cannot be split between scenarios.

SCENARIO 4, SOUL MILL

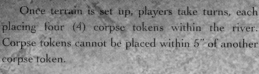

CYGNAR VS. CRYX, 1000 POINTS

Gorim 6th, Tempen 605 AR—The number of Cygnaran soldiers missing in action has swelled since the final days of winter. At first military officials attributed these disappearances to the dead lost beneath the snows or misplaced by the Black River's treacherous current. Then again, recently, hundreds of homesick deserters have been rounded up and offered the chance to return to the frontlines or face the hangman's noose. Still, with the thaw, scouts have discovered forward positions completely unmanned; whole units abandoned without signs of struggle, guard towers empty of all but the haunting winds whistling through open windows and cold meals left half eaten. Though it was common for Cryxian forces to make off with the remains of the dead, the absence of any sign of resistance has been perplexing.

Troops out of Northguard have confirmed the worst: a single man wandering alone near the ominous Thornwood; the only sign of his fealty is a tattered outfit marking him as a Trencher. Amidst his ranting and lunatic interludes, he is calm enough to relate his escape from his tormenters. Taken by surprise through fell magic, Cryxians seized the soldier and his comrades from their camp before they could bring arms to bear. Chained and hauled away by thralls answering the call of the witch Deneghra, the man was taken to a secret camp on the outskirts of the Thornwood. There with other soldiers abducted from the front, he witnessed Necrotechs feeding men to a nightmarish engine that tore away their very souls and distilled them into some sort of fuel for Cryxian helljacks. He remembers little about his escape—only that the camp lies northeast of Deepwood Tower somewhere within the fringes of the eerie marshes of Bloodsmeath.

After only a few minutes of speaking with the man, military advisors send the necessary orders. The military dispatches a strike force to find the camp, free the living, and destroy any sign of the Cryxian dark necromagic.

SPECIAL RULES

The Cryx player must include at least one Necrotech in his army.

The Soul Mill is a dark and ugly Cryxian construction designed to draw souls from the living. Place the Soul Mill in the center of the Cryx deployment zone touching the forward edge of the zone. The Soul Mill is approximately 3" in diameter and at least 3" high. The Soul Mill has ARM 18 and 30 damage points. See Damaging and Destroying Structures, WARMACHINE: Prime, pg. 62, for details.

If the Soul Mill is destroyed, it explodes catastrophically and ends the game. If the Mill explodes, both players lose the game and forfeit their Survival Bonus for the scenario.

The Cryx player then places a row of six (6) Cygnaran captives in base contact with the Soul Mill. The captives are chained together and must remain in a row with each model in base-to-base contact. During each Cryx turn, one Warcaster or Necrotech within 2" of the row of captives may forfeit its action to attempt to feed a captive into the Soul Mill. When the attempt is made, the Cryx player rolls a d6. On a roll of 1 the captive fights off the Necrotech and remains in play. On a roll of 2-6 the captive is fed to the machine and removed from play. Remove captives fed to the Soul Mill from the back of the line as all captives are forced to take a step forward toward the Soul Mill.

The Cryx player wins the game if all six captives are fed to the Soul Mill.

A Cygnar model in base-to-base contact with any captive model in the row may forfeit his action to free the captives at anytime there is not also a Cryx model also in base-to-base contact with a captive model in the row.

The Cygnar player wins the game if the captives are freed.

The captives have DEF 11, ARM 10. The captives cannot move or be moved.

Any player who destroys or removes a captive from play, except by feeding him to the Soul Mill, loses the game.

SET UP

The Cryx player places two (2) terrain features within his deployment zone. Terrain features may not be placed within 3" of another terrain feature. Terrain features may be placed on hills. Players then take turns, each placing two (2) additional terrain features. These terrain features may not be placed within an opponent's deployment zone or within 3" of another terrain feature. Terrain features may be placed on hills.

BEGINNING

At the start of the game, each player rolls a d6 and the high roller chooses who goes first. The first player sets up first and takes the first turn. Players deploy their forces up to 10" from the table's edge.

VICTORY CONDITIONS

Cygnar wins if the captives are freed or if all Cryxian warcasters are destroyed or removed from play.

Cryx wins if all six captives are fed to the machine or if all Cygnaran warcasters are destroyed or removed from play.

Any player that destroys or removes a captive from play loses the game.

REWARDS

- **Soul Fuel:** If the Cryx player wins the game, the distilled souls may be used to fuel Cryxian warjacks once during any Storms of Spring scenario. During each of the Cryx player's control phases, any bonejack or helljack allocated one or more focus points by a Cryxian warcaster receives one additional focus point from the distilled soul fuel. Soul fuel cannot be used to give a warjack more than three total focus points.

- **Freed Prisoners:** If the Cygnar player wins the game, the Cryxian death camp is demolished. Additional prisoners are located in the surrounding area and soon many are able to return to active service. Once during any single Storms of Spring scenario, the Cygnar player may purchase a single Long Gunner, Sword Knight, or Trencher unit for half normal point cost rounded up.

BLIGHTS EVE

Malleus 6th, Cinten 605 AR—The origins of Blight's Eve extend back to when the dragon Toruk's presence first began to warp the warriors of the Isle of Satyx. It began as a holy night when chanting and sacrifices were offered in order to stave off the effects of dragonblight. However, many Satyxis felt the blight made them stronger, and soon they began cavorting in a reverie of arcane rites and passions as feral and fearsome as any druidic ritual to enhance the blight's effects.

Now the evening marks all manner of celestial events and portents. While drunken Schardefolk see it as a time to pillage, rape, and murder, it is of much more importance to the cunning mages of Cryx. The Lich Lords, the Satyxis, and a handful of witch covens realize the hidden significance of the holiday. Due to celestial forces, the dark magic of Cryx is made malleable; enchantments during this time gain a resistance to fading. The streets are filled with drunken celebrations as dark work is done, often at the expenditure of the souls of revelers too ignorant to notice something dire is about to befall them.

SCENARIO 5, RUN FOR THE BORDER

KHADOR VS. PROTECTORATE, 1000 POINTS

Malleus 3rd, Cinten 605 AR—Hot on the trail of Protectorate cortex smugglers fleeing Llael, Khador tracks them to a secret base on the Black River where a barge sits fully loaded with warjack parts taken from the battlefields. The barge is bound for the Protectorate where the parts will help fuel the Menite war effort. Before the barge can set sail, the Khadoran forces make their presence felt.

SPECIAL RULES

See the map. The Protectorate forces are loading a barge from the Loading Dock, a 4" x 10" area centered in the Protectorate deployment zone bordering the rear table edge. The Khador player must stop the barge from setting sail within eight (8) rounds. The Khador player can stop the barge by activating one or more of his models within the area of the Loading Dock. After eight rounds, the barge sets sail down the river.

SET UP

Players take turns, each placing three (3) terrain features. Players cannot place terrain within their opponent's deployment zone or within the Loading Dock. Terrain features must be placed at least 3" from another terrain feature. Terrain features may be placed on hills.

BEGINNING

At the start of the game, each player rolls a d6 and the high roller chooses who goes first. The first player sets up and takes the first turn. Players deploy their forces up to 10" from the table's edge.

VICTORY CONDITIONS

Khador wins if they can keep the barge from setting sail within eight rounds.

The Protectorate wins if the barge has not been stopped within eight rounds or if Khador's last warcaster is destroyed or removed from play.

REWARDS

• **Warjack Parts:** The winning player ends the scenario in possession of the barge loaded with warjack parts. Once during any single Storms of Spring scenario, the winning player pays 10 points less for his warjacks.

SCENARIO 6, PENDULUM

CYGNAR VS. KHADOR, 1000 POINTS

Donard 2nd, Cinten 605 AR—While most of Llael has fallen, the true bastion of Cygnar in the north has held fast. The mighty fortress of Northguard stands against the relentless forces of the Khadoran Ravensgard division. The sentinels of Northguard fight day and night, trenching the ground and turning the fields between them and Ravensgard into a virtual wasteland of muck, barbed wire, death, and steam.

The battlefield between Ravensgard and Northguard resembles a vision of hell. The dead are sprawled amidst the muck, and men struggle for hours to gain a few feet of territory. Once again war has come to the trenches, and both sides are feeling the fatigue of the prolonged battle. Acting decisively, Cygnar seeks to regain lost territory. The order is issued: push the Khadorans back to the gates of Ravensgard at all costs. Spare no prisoners, grant no quarter, and answer their treachery with the lightning of Cygnar's might.

SPECIAL RULES

Divide the table in half with a line running west to east through the center. Using a piece of string is a good method for marking the centerline. The objective of Pendulum is for a player to get one or more of his models across the centerline onto his opponent's side

of the table while keeping his opponent's models from crossing the centerline onto his side of the table. The first player to have models on his opponent's side of the table while there are none of his opponent's models on his own side for three (3) consecutive rounds wins the game.

For example, Matt and Rob play the Pendulum scenario. Matt wins if he has models on Rob's side of the table while Rob has no models on Matt's side of the table for three consecutive rounds.

SET UP

Players take turns, each placing five (5) low wall, ruin, sandbag, or trench terrain features. Terrain features must be placed at least 3" from another terrain feature or the centerline.

BEGINNING

At the start of the game, each player rolls a d6 and the high roller chooses who goes first. The first player gets his choice of deployment zones and takes the first turn. Players deploy their forces up to 10" from the table's edge.

VICTORY CONDITIONS

To win the game, a player needs to have models on his opponent's side of the table while none of his opponent's models are on his own side for three consecutive rounds.

REWARDS

• **Held Territory:** The winner of the game seizes control of the territory and may deploy his forces 4" further forward once during the Storms of Spring Act III scenario, Death in the Deepwood.

SCENARIO 7, INCOMING

PROTECTORATE vs. CRYX, 1000 POINTS

Gorim 3rd, Cinten 605 AR — For the better part of a decade Cryxian agents have been searching for signs of the infamous Deathjack — a black steel horror of unfathomable power. Should the hell-wrought 'jack ever fall into the grasp of the Dragonfather, it would prove a dark day for the nations of western Immoren.

Pursuing a rumored sighting of the Deathjack, a Cryxian expeditionary force travels under cover of night to scout near the Sea of Graves north of Elsinberg. Arriving before dawn, they trust the morning mists to obscure their movements before Khadoran forces in the area discover them. They do not know a Protectorate force has camped on the ancient battlefield just after a terrifying kettle-black fiend decimated their forward position the evening before. Unaware of any Khadoran threat and rattled by the predations of the dark warjack, the Protectorate troops hold fast to their position and remain vigilant in case the enormous black armored 'jack stalks them.

Unknown to either force, Khadoran troops are situated on a well-defended vantage with Irusk's long-range siege guns targeted on the battlefield. After observing both Cryx and Protectorate troop movements below them, the Khadoran Kommander decides to hold fire until the two forces engage. He is happy to take the chance to kill two enemies with one complete stratagem. He issues orders to the gun crews: once the mists clear, the shelling begins.

SPECIAL RULES

See map. Place a pillar of rock, an approximately 8" x 8" obstruction standing at least 8" high, in the middle of the table 8" forward from the north table edge.

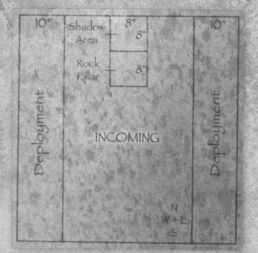

A continuous Khadoran artillery barrage pounds the battlefield during this scenario. To determine the points of impact for the artillery blasts, each player nominates a point on the table at the start of each of his maintenance phases. The blast then deviates 2d6" inches from this point in a direction determined by the deviation template. Center a 5" AOE blast on the point of impact. All models within the AOE suffer a POW 12 damage roll.

The pillar shadows a small area of the table from the Khadoran bombardment. The Shadow Area is an 8" x 8" space between the pillar and north table edge. Players may not nominate artillery points of impact with the Shadow Area.

The first player to Hold the Shadow Area for three consecutive turns wins the game. A player Holds the Shadow Area if all models within the Area are controlled by that player during his Maintenance Phase.

SET UP

Players take turns, each placing three (3) terrain features. Terrain features must be placed at least 3" from another terrain feature. Terrain features may be placed on hills.

BEGINNING

At the start of the game, each player rolls a d6. The high roller chooses who goes first. The first chooses a deployment zone along the east or west table edge and takes the first turn. Players deploy their forces up to 10" from the table's edge.

VICTORY CONDITIONS

The first player to hold the Shadow Area for three consecutive turns wins the game.

REWARDS

• **Battle Ready:** The winner of the game escapes in fit fighting condition and may deploy his forces 4" further forward during the Storms of Spring Act III scenario, Death in the Deepwood.

The Storms of Spring Act II Side Quests

Dirty Deeds, Cryx Side Quest

Warwitch Deneghra

As a Cryxian warwitch, Deneghra has always craved power—her twisted upbringing saw to it. Satyxis courtesans trained her for battle and necromancers gave her incantations and sweet cantrips to seduce men, but no matter how sufficient her power, she wants more. Thus, her sights are fixed on that opposite reflection of her own dark self, her twin sister. Deneghra is convinced her sibling is a path to greater power. While arcane abilities closely link their two souls, their minds and motives could not be more opposed. Using a private network of spies and informants—and her own powers of seduction and intimidation—the warwitch has managed to uncover the identity of her twin: the Cygnaran warcaster, Victoria Haley.

The plan Deneghra has formulated is so twisted yet simple that it speaks of her inborn brilliance. She must release the soul of her sister by causing her to die through some noble act then draw it into her own body through necromancy. To do this, the warwitch must place a trinket on her twin's body and see to it that she dies fighting a hero's battle.

The warwitch wishes nothing more than to use her own hands to snuff out the life in her sister's eyes. She wants to reveal the truth to her sibling, but the ritual forbids it, so Deneghra plans to do the next best thing. Betrayal will suffice as a sweet enough message. Through spies, Deneghra has learned of a young officer just recently ordered to Haley's staff. Seeking to set a trap that may take months to bring to fruition, she wishes to locate the man, as even the most loyal soldier is no match for her dark powers of seduction. Once she has broken him with the manipulations of her dark magic, her sister's officer will be more than happy to play his part in her designs.

Best Laid Plans...

A curl formed at the corner of the Warwitch's mouth. Her eyes closed halfway in an expression of self-satisfaction—the kind that comes from the realization of a flawless plan. Soon, she would be complete.

Deneghra gazed into the inky blackness within the chamber of the soul cage. One more time, her cold fingers traced the arcane symbols she had etched along its frame. She read them by touch and visualized them in her mind. Woven into the complex description of a spell designed to trap a specific soul was the name of her prey: Victoria Haley.

Her sister's identity was a surprise, though hardly a disappointment. Haley was a renowned Cygnaran warcaster. It was a shame such potential was squandered on a life of servitude to a mundane cause, but it would be a pleasure to release her twin sister's soul from her mortal prison and claim it for her own.

The trapping of a specific soul was not an easy task. It would take precision and the coordination of an exquisitely-timed plan. This single cage, a simple vessel for such potent force, was the key to her design, yet there was much more to set in motion.

A light tap at the door shifted her attention. Her spy had returned and, as always, the little man's timing was perfect. Deneghra called for him to enter and turned toward the door with the soul cage still in her hands.

The henchman stepped into the dimly lit chamber, eyes downcast. He averted his eyes from the warwitch as often as he could. It was a rare occasion that she allowed anyone to see her without helm or armor in place, and she knew her haunting sensuality stirred emotions in the living, for the warwitch could wield weapons of desire as effectively as any arcane magic.

"I have the information you asked for, my mistress," the spy said softly. "Deployment orders for Cygnaran infantry under Captain Haley. Assignments and marching orders… exact numbers and identities… down to the last soldier."

"Excellent." Deneghra caressed the little man's face, running her fingertips down his rough-shaven jaw line. She was visibly pleased. "Come. Tell me everything."

Cryx Army Composition

Warwitch Deneghra

Cygnar Army Composition

3 Long Gunner units each with a Sergeant and 5 Troopers

1 Trencher unit with a Sergeant and 5 Troopers

1 Journeyman Warcaster

1 Sentinel Light Warjack

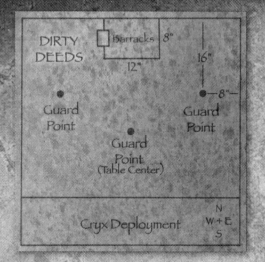

SPECIAL RULES AND SET UP

See map. Place a barracks, a brick structure approximately 8" x 12", in the middle of the table bordering the northern table edge. The barracks has a single door large enough to accommodate a small-based model facing the western table edge. The barracks is too solid a building to be destroyed within the confines of this scenario.

Each Long Gunner unit stands watch around a Guard Point. One point is located 8" from the west table edge and 16" from the north table edge.

Another is 8" from the east table edge and 16" from the north table edge. The third is located in the center of the table. The Cygnar player must place one Long Gunner unit around each Guard Point and all models must be placed within 5" of the Point.

This scenario takes place during a dark and misty night in which the moons of Caen shed no light. Under these conditions, all models are limited to 8" LOS. The war witch's natural stealth is further enhanced by the darkness and only models within 5" of Deneghra have LOS to her.

Cygnaran models without LOS to Deneghra or a model under the Cryx player's control may not make ranged attacks.

Long Gunner and Trencher units may only activate if a model in the unit has LOS to Deneghra or a unit under the Cryx player's control. The Journeyman and Sentinel may activate normally.

Deneghra is attempting to enter the barracks to seduce a sleeping officer. If she enters the barracks, Cryx wins the game. If any model makes a ranged attack before Deneghra enters the barracks, an alarm wakes the sleeping officer and Cygnar wins the game.

The game goes into Hammertime at the end of round six. If the game ends before Deneghra enters the barracks, she is spotted by a patrol and forced to flee the camp.

BEGINNING

The Cygnar player begins by placing one Long Gunner unit around each Guard Points. All models in the unit must be placed within 5" of the Point.

The Cygnar player then places the unit of Trenchers around the barracks so that all models are within 5" of the structure.

Finally the Journeyman Warcaster and Sentinel are placed anywhere within 12" of the north table edge.

The Cryx player places Deneghra within 5" of the southern table edge.

The Cryx player takes the first turn.

VICTORY CONDITIONS

Cryx wins the game if Deneghra enters the barracks.

Cygnar wins if Deneghra is destroyed, any model makes a ranged attack, or if the game ends before Deneghra enters the barracks.

REWARDS

- **Traitors:** If the Cryx player wins the game, Deneghra lays the groundwork for her dark machinations and begins a campaign of seducing officers to expand her network of pawns throughout the enemy armies. In any game Deneghra is used, the Cryx player may add any one solo from any other faction to his army free of cost. The solo is controlled by the Cryx player but is not a Cryx model and none of the information on his stat card is altered. A Journeyman Warcaster or 'jack marshal may not begin the game controlling warjacks. Models with the Field Officer special ability do not allow Cryx to play with additional non-Cryx models. For example, if Deneghra is used in a game, the Cryx player could add a Man-O-War Kovnik to his army. However, the Kovnik cannot begin the game controlling warjacks, nor can the Cryx player use the Kovnik's Field Officer ability to take a unit of Man-O-War.

THE BIG HIT, CYGNAR SIDE QUEST

LIEUTENANT ALLISTER CAINE

After trading favors with a mysterious stranger, Lieutenant Allister Caine sets out on a grim task of redemption. His target is a kapitan in the Khadoran military and a man with whom Caine has dealt before in the mists of his own nebulous past. It seems that whatever happened between these two men has left a vendetta hanging over their heads. Whether the motives are business or personal is something that only Caine knows as he treks off to unload a month's worth of ammunition into the man and his companions.

The ploy is simple. Through mercenary contacts, Caine has arranged a meeting between the Kapitan and his returning brother, who was believed lost in the Menite exodus to the Protectorate. The Kapitan awaits his brother's return, not knowing his sibling is dead somewhere at the bottom of the Black River. Along with a group of gun mages in disguise, Allister Caine has taken the brother's place and is convincingly garbed in rags and chains. He hopes to get close enough to pay the Khadoran back for their past bad dealings, and to ensure no witnesses survive to tell the tale.

A MAN WALKS INTO A BAR

The barroom door creaked open and a man in a rain-drenched greatcoat stepped into the room. He kept his face covered by a high collar, his head held low. It was not the grand entrance of a hero, but rather the unassuming ingress of a lone man preferring to remain anonymous. There were dozens of these shanty watering holes in the riverside berg, but this one had the desired luxuries: chiefly a door, a roof, and an out-of-the-way location.

A large man hunched at a rickety table furthest from the entrance. Suspended from hooks below the uneven rafters of the low ceiling, guttering lanterns cast flickering shadows in the dim room. Nestled amongst shadows the large man's presence was still tangible, even from within his shroud of darkness. With a motion slowed by the wear of war, the figure's jack-booted foot slid a chair a few inches in the newcomer's direction. Metal clinked as he did so.

"It's been a long time, Lieutenant," said the nebulous figure with a voice like gravel on a rusted 'jack hull.

"Aye," replied the new arrival. Water poured off his coat and collected in a dirty puddle on the floorboards beneath him. He leaned forward carefully. "You have what I came for?"

The shadowy figure lifted a tarnished tankard to his mouth and spoke more into the drink than to his guest. "You bring my book?"

"Blagged it. Dead simple. In the stockade strong room, just like you said. I don't think they've touched that junk since... you know when." The Lieutenant reached beneath the breast of his greatcoat and produced a small, leather-bound book with cracking yellow pages. Stamped on the weathered tome was a simple sigil, the Sunburst of Morrow. The book was no ornate arcane text, just a simple commoner's copy of some Enkheiridion scriptures. "I never took you for a churchie."

The hunched-over hulk of a man reached forward. Steam pistons hissed and a metal fist thrice the size of any normal human hand emerged from the shadows to pluck the holy book from the Lieutenant's grasp. The man's other hand, normal except for calluses and scars, reached out with an envelope sealed with a waxen sigil. He placed it in the Lieutenant's outstretched hand. "From someone... special."

"I've risked a lot to get your little prayer book to you, so this information better not be dodgy." There was a measured threat hidden in the deep waters of the Lieutenant's voice. He tore open the envelope and looked inside.

"It's all there, Caine. I've taken the liberty of arranging a meeting. Of course, I don't think the poor Kapitan will be expecting to see you." The grin on the man's face was intimidating and ugly, like that of a dracodile.

"Better not be," the Lieutenant replied as he stood up.

"Caine," the hunched figure said in a voice suddenly level and without threat. "I've heard from him."

Caine paused to listen. The Lieutenant knew that the man was talking of someone different now, someone more important. "He's coming back. This time for real. Corvis was nothing. A training mission. You don't want to be on the wrong side this time. Come with me and I'll make sure you get a good place at his table."

"I'll let you know," Caine called back, already heading toward the door. "Right now I have other business."

"Don't wait too long," the large man called after the Lieutenant as he vanished into the rain.

CYGNAR ARMY COMPOSITION

Lieutenant Allister Caine

1 Arcane Tempest Gun Mage unit

KHADOR ARMY COMPOSITION

1 Manhunter

1 Man-O-War unit with 1 Kapitan and 2 Troopers

1 Widowmaker unit

1 Winter Guard unit with 1 Sergeant and 5 Troopers

1 Winter Guard unit with 1 Sergeant and 9 Troopers

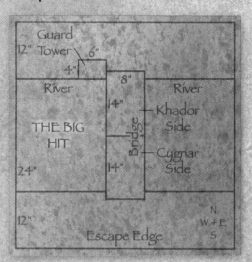

SPECIAL RULES

See map. A river 24" wide runs through the center of the table. Spanning the middle of the river is a stone bridge 8" wide and 28" long. The bridge is much too strong to be damaged during this scenario. Any models slammed past the edge of the bridge will fall into the river. Any model falling off the bridge is removed from play.

Standing against the northwestern side of the bridge is a small stone building that has been made into a Khadoran check point. The structure is approximately 4" x 6" and has one door facing east and a single window facing the bridge. The door is big enough to accommodate small-based models. The door has ARM 16 and can take 10 points of damage. The building has ARM 18 and can take 10 points of damage per inch. The building will collapse when 10" or more inches of its surface have been destroyed. See Damaging and Destroying Structures, WARMACHINE: Prime, pg. 62, for details.

Khadoran forces have arrived on the scene to buy back a Khadoran prisoner. Allister Caine pretends to be the prisoner and intends to kill the Winter Guard Kapitan who is overseeing the exchange. Convincingly costumed in chains and rags, Caine hopes to get close enough to the Khadoran Kapitan to drop him where he stands with one shot.

Plans start going wrong when the Kapitan sends a subordinate in his place to make the exchange. Instead the Kapitan watches the events as they unfold from the relative safety of the stone-walled check point. An absolute coward, the Kapitan will not leave the checkpoint for any reason. Caine must assassinate the Kapitan and the rest of the Winter Guard unit that witness the act and then move safely off the table across the southern table edge.

SET UP

The Khador player may place three (3) terrain features anywhere on the table. Terrain cannot be placed within 3" of another terrain feature, including the bridge or check point. Terrain features may be placed on hills.

BEGINNING

The Khador player must place the ten-man Winter Guard unit on the north side of the bridge within 5" of the center of the table. The Man-O-War may be placed anywhere north of the center of the table outside of the checkpoint.

The second Winter Guard unit is placed within the checkpoint. The unit's Sergeant represents the Kapitan.

The Cygnar player then places Caine and the Arcane Tempest Gun Mage unit anywhere on the southern half of the bridge.

Finally, the Khador player may place the Manhunter and Widowmaker unit anywhere on the table, off the bridge.

Cygnar gets first turn.

VICTORY CONDITIONS

Cygnar wins when the Kapitan and his unit within the checkpoint have been destroyed and Caine moves off the southern table edge.

Khador wins if Caine is destroyed or removed from play.

REWARDS

• **Practice Makes Perfect:** If Cygnar wins, Allister Caine is left pondering the events that led up to the assassination of the Winter Guard kapitan. He clears his head by practicing for hours with his Spellstorm pistols, temporarily turning from drink. Slowly, he not only begins to formulate his plans, but he also refines his control over the pistols. For the rest of the Campaign, if Caine voluntarily forfeits his movement by not changing position or facing, he gains a +2 bonus to magical attack rolls on spells cast directly from him that are projected through his pistols. Additionally, Caine gains +1 to all magical attack damage rolls on spells cast directly from him. Channeled spells do not gain either benefit.

CHURCH & STATE, KHADOR SIDE QUEST

BUTCHER OF KHARDOV

Largely free from many of the ethnic and religious conflicts that have plagued other kingdoms, Khador has prided itself on the loyalty of its people. Largely a Menite state, Khador is also home to a huge population of Morrowans, but nationalistic pride generally comes first to most Khadorans. Faithful adherents of Menoth have seen themselves as Khadorans first and Menites second, but as relations between the Protectorate and Khador strain and break, many Menite citizens have begun to question their loyalties.

As the war intensifies and brings Khadoran forces into direct conflict with the Protectorate, Menite visgoths start calling for a mass exodus to the Protectorate where the faithful can better serve the Creator. Adding weight is news of the Hierarch's call for pilgrimage, and ignoring the emissary of Menoth's will is not a wise thing to do. With the first signs of spring, refugee flocks gather their families and belongings to make the trek south escorted by Paladins of the Wall at the behest of the Menite visgoths.

Queen Ayn has long prided herself on the loyalty of her people. Such insolence demands immediate action. Encouraged by her advisors in the High Kommand, the Queen sends word to Kommander Orsus Zoktavir, the infamous Butcher of Khardov. She requests assistance in reminding her people of the consequences of treason, and being a true patriot, the Butcher always answers the call.

The Butcher comes upon a caravan of pilgrims departing their community and he lets loose with a terrible howl. He charges them, wading through the crowd cutting men down with each and every step. Paladin escorts call for a small retinue of holy zealots to attempt to hold back the Butcher while the pilgrims make their escape.

THE SLAUGHTER

Bloodshot eyes stared unblinking at the doors of the secret Menite sanctuary a hundred yards away. Puffs of steam vented from the breathing holes in the Butcher's iron cuirass as the sorrowful words of his hot breath touched the icy air.

"Lola…"

He mumbled the name over and over again, his thick accent weighing it down like iron. They never should have taken her from him. Sometimes when the grief came over him, all he could see was the color of rage and the blackness of hate. He could feel the edges of that dark precipice closing in on him now as he continued to mumble the name.

"Lola…"

The man named Orsus Zoktavir, the Butcher of Khardov, stood at the edge of the quad, his bulk a veritable barricade for the single path leading up to the sanctuary doors. The queen had requested his assistance in discouraging a sudden exodus of Menite faithful. It was a request he was happy to fulfill.

Small snowflakes danced on the air as the doors opened. Khadoran pilgrims laden with provisions for their long journey began filing out. These religious devotees had renounced their country, and the Butcher had come for them. In two gauntleted fists he clutched his massive mechanikal axe Lola.

"Wake up, pretty," the Butcher whispered to the weapon. "It's time to do her work again." He lowered his head and charged, bellowing like a bull.

"Go to Lola!" The Butcher hefted his axe. "Go to Lola NOW, pigs!" He sliced a handful of fleeing pilgrims into ruins of flesh and torn cloth.

"Run, pigs! Scream! The Butcher take you!" The crowd reacted chaotically to the mad warcaster suddenly among them. They knew the man. His very name invoked fright, and his presence summoned a kind of frantic, animal horror - the kind felt by prey as it realizes a predator looms over it.

At the far end of the hall, a few men gathered their wits and prepared to stand against him. Fighting the Butcher only made his job easier. Suddenly, some twisted thing inside of him resembling joy filled his heart. "Stupid creatures," he said with a grin.

Nearly a score of armed men and a Paladin of the Wall prepared to fight him. Their heads would roll then the rest of the pilgrims would die bleeding in the mud like the worthless herd they were. The fools would pay dearly for turning away from the Motherland. With a mighty roar, the Butcher charged. His mind fell into a black pit, and he lost thoughts of all else but slaughter.

KHADOR ARMY COMPOSITION

Butcher of Khardov

PROTECTORATE ARMY COMPOSITION

1 Paladin of the Wall

2 Holy Zealot units each with 9 Troopers

SPECIAL RULES

See the map. This scenario is played on a 10" x 24" table.

The Holy Zealots represent Menite pilgrims preparing their journey to the Protectorate. Only trooper models are used in this scenario. The models are independent rather than part of a unit. The Zealots cannot make Fire Bomb attacks during this scenario.

The Protectorate player must get as many Holy Zealots off the table as possible by moving them across the southern table edge, or Escape Edge. Models that move off the table by crossing the Escape Edge are pilgrims that have escaped to safely. Fleeing Holy Zealots move toward the Escape Edge rather than the Protectorate Deployment Edge.

All Protectorate models that have been destroyed or that exit the table by moving across the Escape Edge are put back into play during each of the Protectorate player's maintenance phases. These models are placed within the Protectorate deployment zone and may activate on the turn they come into play.

The game lasts for five (5) rounds. The Khador player must destroy 20 or more Protectorate models to win the game.

SET UP

Players take turns, each placing two (2) terrain features. Terrain features must be placed at least 3" from another terrain feature. Terrain features may be placed on hills.

BEGINNING

The Protectorate player deploys his forces up to 5" from the north table edge. The Khador player then deploys the Butcher up to 5" from the opposite table edge.

The Khador player takes the first turn.

VICTORY CONDITIONS

Khador wins if 20 or more Protectorate models are destroyed before the end of the game.

The Protectorate wins if the Butcher is destroyed or if the game ends before 20 Protectorate models have been destroyed.

REWARDS

• Infamy: If Khador wins the game, the Butcher gathers the heads of the slaughtered pilgrims and sends them down the river on a barge bound for the Protectorate as a warning to those who would betray the Motherland. In the coming days, the Butcher's reputation reaches new heights of infamy. In any game the Butcher is used, all enemy models suffer –1 CMD.

MALEDICTOR, PROTECTORATE SIDE QUEST

FEORA, PRIESTESS OF THE FLAME

Months ago while traveling to the frontlines, Feora, Priestess of the Flame, and her Flameguard escorts sought refuge from a harsh winter storm at a tiny Menite enclave in southern Llael. Myrr is an isolated village of Llaelese Menites, and its residents have long welcomed pilgrims passing through the area. When the villagers met Feora and her troops, they were overjoyed. They provided warm meals and a place to rest, and though their stay was brief, Feora was touched by Myrr's generosity and unquestioning faith.

Early in spring, news reached her that the Myrrans had extended the same hospitality to Cygnaran troopers mere weeks after her forces departed. The enemy then claimed the settlement as a base of operations and the residents happily hosted soon as she were able, she would purify the village with holy fire.

Recently, a short lull in hostilities provided the Priestess with the opportunity to return to Myrr. Having called upon a unit of loyal Flameguard Cleansers, Feora prepared for the task of absolving the village of its fatal flaws. She intends to drive the Cygnarans from the village and reduce it to ash.

FURY

Feora watched the procession of Flameguard proudly as they performed a spear fighting drill. Assembled in ranks, these faithful were her charge, her children, and her group of warriors. Hierarch Sulon had founded them to protect the temples, but Feora had refined their training. Now, the Flameguard were an elite group without reproach. They were as loyal to Menoth as they were to her. Watching her troops, she felt fearless and defiant. Feora was proud.

A Flameguard warrior stepped into the room. The crest of a burning menofix on his shoulder pad indicated his station. He was one of her personal guard. "I have five cleanser volunteers, Priestess. They are ready."

Feora nodded, her eyes narrowing and her countenance growing grim. "Make sure they know to be discrete." Her heart beat with anger. "If we are going to cleanse Myrr and remove the presence of the heretics, we can afford to let no one know of it."

"They are aware, Priestess. Four of the men were with us in Myrr when we stopped there. They know what has happened and are eager to aid us. The fifth, I am not sure." The guard hesitated. "I think he has never seen Cygnarans in combat, and he merely wishes to do so."

Feora smirked. "He'll have his chance then, won't he?" The soldier would have a story or two to tell after this. "Very well."

She turned again to witness the Flameguard spinning their spears in unison, their movements precise and fluid. "We'll make sure no traitors remain and that the Myrrans join our holy Creator in Urcaen, then we'll burn the village. Better to obliterate the faithless than allow betrayal to linger and fester."

She remembered the welcoming smiles of the villagers. After the news of their welcome of the Cygnarans, Feora could not stomach the memory of their false faces. Menoth's Fury shall wipe their countenances clean. Harboring the enemies of the Protectorate was an act of treason, not to mention a blasphemy. It was a pity she could not wrack them all. One day, perhaps, she would make such judgments, Menoth willing.

PROTECTORATE ARMY COMPOSITION

Feora, Priestess of the Flame

1 Flameguard Cleanser unit with 1 Arms Master and 5 Cleansers

CYGNAR ARMY COMPOSITION

1 Gun Mage Captain Adept

2 Trencher Units each with 1 Sergeant and 5 Troopers

SPECIAL RULES AND SET UP

Players take turns, each placing five (5) buildings, approximately 4" x 6", anywhere on the table. The buildings cannot be placed within 5" of another building.

Players then take turns, each placing two (2) additional terrain features. The terrain features may not be additional buildings. Terrain features may not be placed within 3" of another terrain feature, including the buildings. Terrain features may be placed on hills.

To win the game, the Protectorate player must set all the buildings on the table ablaze. Protectorate models within 8" of a building may forfeit their action to set the building on fire. Any model that moves into a burning building, ends its activation within a burning building, or occupies a building when it catches fire suffers a POW 12 damage roll. A building continues to burn throughout the game once it has been set on fire.

The game goes into Hammertime at the end of round five (5). If the game ends before all buildings have been set on fire, Cygnaran reinforcements arrive from the nearby area and push Protectorate forces off the table.

BEGINNING

The Cygnar player deploys his forces first and places them anywhere on the table. The Protectorate player then chooses a table edge and deploys his forces within 10" of the edge.

The Cygnar player takes the first turn.

VICTORY CONDITIONS

The Protectorate wins when all buildings on the table have been set on fire.

Cygnar wins if the game ends before all buildings have been set on fire or if Feora is destroyed.

REWARDS
- **Divine Example:** If the Protectorate player wins, Feora becomes an example of excellence for all Menites to follow as stories of her deeds circulate throughout the Protectorate's armies. For the rest of the Campaign, all troop models within Feora's command range gain +1 to attack rolls. Additionally, in games Feora is used, all friendly models gain +2 movement on their first activation of the game.

THE STORMS OF SPRING ACT III

SCENARIO 8, DEATH IN THE DEEPWOOD

TWO-PLAYER GAME, 1000 POINTS

Gorim 7th, Cinten 605 AR—Deepwood Tower is especially vital to Cygnaran security as Khador begins to move greater concentrations of forces along the border. However, the fighting in Llael has badly drained Cygnaran military strength to the point that they lack sufficient numbers to continue to operate the tower's defenses. The troops that should garrison the tower re-deploy to Northguard, while another contingent defends Merywyn. In order to ensure its enemies cannot use it against them, Cygnaran forces prepare to scuttle the tower.

Not knowing the present state of Deepwood Tower, Khador is preparing an assault against the tower defenders. If the tower falls, Khador will have little trouble bypassing Northguard and flanking Merywyn. Should Khador manage to outflank Cygnaran positions, they will cut off supplies to Merywyn and easily surround the city.

Khador and Cygnar are not the only factions with a stake in the site. For Cryx, Deepwood Tower is an easily-defensible position within close proximity to vast quantities of necrotite and endless fields of corpses. Because of its nearness to the Thornwood, controlling this tower would be like controlling the toll gate of an open road.

The Protectorate's interest in the tower is one of operation and acquisition. Not only can they use the tower to observe Khadoran movements south, but it can act as a vital smuggling point for cortex materials and other crucial supplies for the Protectorate's war efforts, in addition to being an ideal staging point for pilgrims and converts.

At least two of the forces manage to make their way to the tower. The others, tied up by the battles they encounter along the way, do not make it in time to lay siege. Whoever gets there first is the most likely to gain its use until Cygnar can regroup and concentrate its efforts on reclaiming or destroying it.

SPECIAL RULES

Death in the Deepwood is a two-player scenario between the player with the most wins throughout The Storms of Spring Act II and the player from another faction with the next highest total number of wins. In the case of a tie, compare each player's victory point total throughout Spring Act II.

Place a hill in the center of the table. The first player to Hold the hill in the center of the table for three consecutive rounds wins the game. A player Holds the hill if all models on the hill are controlled by that player during his maintenance phase. Models that are engaged in melee, warrior models with CMD stats of 1 or less, and Incorporeal models cannot Hold the hill.

Place a watchtower on the center of the hill. The watchtower is approximately 4" in diameter and 6" tall. No model may enter the watchtower during the game. The tower walls have ARM 20 and can take 20 points of damage per inch. The watchtower will collapse after 8" or more of the surface has been destroyed. See Damaging and Destroying Structures, WARMACHINE: Prime, pg. 62, for details.

If Cygnar is playing in this scenario, Cygnaran forces have not yet scuttled the watchtower. The Cygnar player may place one unit of Long Gunners with 1 Sergeant and 5 troopers on top of the watchtower. The Long Gunners benefit from cover (+4 DEF) and will not flee during the battle.

SET UP

Players take turns, each placing four (4) terrain features. Terrain features must be placed at least 3" from another terrain feature, including the watchtower. Terrain features may be placed on hills.

BEGINNING

At the start of the game, each player rolls a d6. The high roller chooses who goes first. The first player sets up in his deployment zone and takes the first turn. Players deploy their forces up to 10" from the table's edge.

VICTORY CONDITIONS

The first player to Hold the hill in the center of the table for three (3) consecutive rounds wins the game.

REWARDS

• **Border Control:** After seizing control of Deepwood Tower, the winning player gains a foothold in the Thornwood and is able to move men and supplies across the Cygnar-Khador border with ease for the time being. The winner may add up to 25 points to the size of his army in the Wrath of Summer's Heat Act I scenario, the Wrath of Menoth.

• **Observation Post:** Deepwood Tower stands at a strategic point along the Cygnar-Khador border and is a valuable observation post. The winning player may use the Observation Post reward once before the start of any single Campaign scenario. The winning player then gets to look at his opponents' final army composition and make changes to his own army composition before the start of the game. An opponent may not alter his army composition once he declares it as his final composition.

THE FALL OF MERYWYN

Malleus 5th, Rowen 605 AR—Following the battle for Deepwood Tower, Cygnar is forced to re-assess its troop deployments. At the beginning of the war, troops were rushed from Cygnaran border garrisons to the frontlines to defend the Llaelese capital of Merywyn. Reinforcements continued to flood into Merywyn and Northguard to counter the Khadoran siege but at the cost of leaving Cygnar's borders poorly defended. When Khador attempts to outflank the defenders of Merywyn by crossing the border and marching around Northguard, it becomes apparent that the security situation has grown critical.

Ultimately, Cygnar is forced to choose between its own internal security and the defense of Merywyn. A substantial force is re-deployed from Merywyn to shore up border defenses, while at the same time Khador renews its offensive against the city. In the weeks to come, Merywyn is the site of the fiercest fighting to date. Khador slowly breaches the walls of the capital and suffers horrendous losses in the process. Ultimately, the defenders are forced into a rout as the city falls to Khadoran armed forces.

The Wrath of Summer's Heat

VENDARL 2ND, SOLESH 605 AR

Amassing on the eastern borders of Cygnar, Protectorate ranks fill with pilgrim zealots dedicated to the defense and expansion of the Menite faith. Heeding the Harbinger's call, warcasters have formulated their battle plans and built their armies. The Protectorate readies itself for the march to bring the faithless to heel. In spite of the sweltering desert heat, faithful Menites are spurred onward by the Harbinger of Menoth, her divine proclamations moving them rapturously toward battle.

Cygnarans grow increasingly nervous as the rumblings of the Protectorate army become more evident. Soldiers throughout Cygnar are called to Caspia in an effort to fortify and defend the city should Menoth's army strike. This depletes defenses elsewhere and, along the coasts, village after village has become an abattoir, grounds flowing red with the work of Cryxian raiders.

Llael is lost. Khador's troops occupy the capital city of Merywyn. Its walls display the severed heads of many among the Council of Nobles, save the former Prime Minister Deyar Glabryn who declares his support for a renewal of the Khardic Empire. While some resistance is still attempted here and there by Llaelese nobility and token rebel groups, most of the kingdom is within the tight grip of the Motherland's fist.

The Khadorans have set their sights on Cygnar's northern borders. Using the ability to traverse the Black River at will, they have made incursions into Cygnar to raid various villages and supply depots. Worse yet, Cygnaran troops have left many of the northern communities undefended by pulling away to fortify the east from the Protectorate threat.

The weather itself seems to conspire against Cygnar. A heat wave withers crops, dries the fields with drought, and kills livestock by the hundreds. The people of the Protectorate are accustomed to the heat, living as they do at the edge of the Bloodstone Marches. The walking dead among the Cryxian forces, too, are affected little—save for thick clouds of flies flitting amidst the thralls. Whereas the Menite forces are primed to begin their Holy Crusade, the focus of Lord Toruk's hordes are on setting up massive excavation operations near old battlefields where veins of necrotite are thick with death.

The Wrath of Summer's Heat Act I

Scenario I, The Cistern of Asherius

Multiplayer Game, 500 points

Malleus 4th, Solesh 605 AR—Hot winds blow in from Meredius, colliding with even hotter winds from the Bloodstone Marches. Heat distorts the atmosphere as the Protectorate summer smolders like a blasting furnace. Stationed at the refinery known as the Cistern of Asherius, many zealot converts and newly-arrived pilgrims work all hours drilling for Menoth's Fury, the volatile oil that fuels many of the Protectorate's powerful weapons. In the high heat of this especially hot summer, the fumes of the thick oily substance turn the area near the cistern into a toxic wasteland where filtering masks provide little protection from the noxious vapors.

Some Cygnaran troops have decided to attempt to liberate "religious captives" from the Menite work camp. They harbor hopes that by rescuing the ill-treated converts, they will be able to retrieve useful intelligence from them. Khadorans are in the area as well, but they are motivated more by vengeance than mercy; they wish merely to destroy the operation.

A heavy contingent of Menite troops are assigned to the grounds. Menoth's Fury is a crucial resource in the Protectorate war effort, so these troops serve to protect the cistern and motivate the relocated faithful to toil in the sweltering heat. Due to the prospect of violent conflict and the movements of troops along the Black River, the Hierarch has ordered warjacks and warcasters to ensure the cistern's safety until pilgrims produce a sufficient surplus.

As the various factions are spurred toward conflict, they must tread carefully amidst the battlefield. The hazards in the fields surrounding the cistern can alter the balance of battle just as easily as a well-placed shot.

Special Rules and Set Up

The Cistern of Asherius is a major production center of Menoth's Fury and is the location of many oil wells. Before the start of the game, the Protectorate player places three (3) wells anywhere within 15" of the center of the table. The wells are structures approximately 2" in diameter and 5" high. Wells have ARM 12 and 5 damage points. See Damaging and Destroying Structures, WARMACHINE: Prime, pg. 62, for details.

When a well is destroyed, it explodes catastrophically. All models within 3" of an exploding well suffer a POW 16 damage roll, catch Fire, and are knocked down. Fire is a continuous effect that sets the target ablaze. A model on fire suffers a POW 12 damage roll each turn during its maintenance phase until the fire expires on a d6 roll or 1 or 2.

Next players take turns, each placing two (2) terrain features anywhere on the table. Terrain features cannot be placed within 3" of another terrain feature, including wells. Terrain features may be placed on hills.

After terrain is placed, the Protectorate player places three (3) more wells anywhere within 15" of the center of the table. These wells may be placed in close proximity to other terrain features.

Kossite Woodsmen may only come into play in the Khador deployment zone.

Beginning

At the start of the game, each player rolls a d6. The player who rolls highest chooses to go first or last. The player who rolls second highest then chooses to go first or last from among the remaining spots in the play order. The third highest roller does the same and so on until the lowest roller takes the final spot. The first player gets his choice of deployment zones and takes the first turn. Each player deploys in a 10" by 10" area in each corner of the table.

Victory Conditions

The player with the last surviving warcaster in play wins the game. When a player loses his warcaster, his remaining models are routed—completely remove them from the table.

Rewards

• **Warcaster Deployment:** The outcome of The Cistern of Asherius determines the order players reveal their warcaster deployments for Summer Act II. Beginning with the first player eliminated from the game and ending with the winner of the scenario, each player deploys one warcaster to each Wrath of Summer's Heat Act II scenario. In a two-player game, the losing player must inform the winner of both warcasters he intends to field during the Summer Act II game.

• **Gaining the Initiative:** The winning player pushes back his enemies and gets a +1 bonus on all Starting Rolls during all Wrath of Summer's Heat Act II scenarios.

The Wrath of Summer's Heat Act II

Scenario 2, Cleansing Waters

Khador vs. Protectorate, 1000 points

Donard 5th, Solesh 605 AR—Khador has begun to suffer the predations of Protectorate forces as they make headway south along the Black River. The influx of zealot converts supplies the Protectorate with a constant stream of reinforcements and allows them to fight with freshly supplied—although green and relatively inexperienced—troops. Khador is growing tired of this constant fight, and Khadoran kommanders are looking for a way to make a decisive and final strike against the zealot guerillas and battle groups that have been harassing convoys and supply ships.

Using the situation to its advantage, the Protectorate has decided to exploit Khador's ire. Knowing that the Khadorans will take a good opportunity when they see it, Protectorate forces have vacated a firebase located at the center of the Ausperine valley just a half day from the Black River along the eastern side. The Protectorate has also leaked information about a depleted battle group under the command of a wounded warcaster. Khadoran intelligence believes

that this would be an excellent opportunity to strike. What the forces of the Motherland do not know is that this is simply bait. Once lured into the trap, the Protectorate will attack the Khadorans and force them into the valley while it is flooded with water diverted from a tributary of the Black River.

By taking the high ground and holding it, the Protectorate hopes to wash the sinners clean in the eyes of Menoth.

Special Rules

See map. Place a hill with a radius of approximately 16″ in the northwest corner of the table. This is the Escape Hill. A second hill with an 8″ radius is placed on top of the first hill.

Models may move off the table through an escape passage on the second elevation of the Escape Hill. Up

Protectorate Deployment

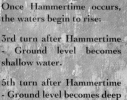

Tidetables

Once Hammertime occurs, the waters begin to rise:

3rd turn after Hammertime - Ground level becomes shallow water.

5th turn after Hammertime - Ground level becomes deep water.

7th turn after Hammertime - First elevation becomes shallow water and ground level remains deep water.

9th turn after Hammertime - First elevation becomes deep water, ground level remains deep water, and second elevation level becomes shallow water.

180

to one model or unit may use the passage to leave the table during each player's turn. Models that use the passage to move off the table cannot return to play. If a warcaster leaves play via the passage, his warjacks do not become inert, but can no longer be allocated focus. If a 'jack marshal leaves through the passage, his warjacks become autonomous but do not become inert. Players earn Survival Points for all models that exit the table through the escape passage.

The game goes into Hammertime at the end of round three, but the game does not end when the hammer falls. Instead, floodwaters begin to rise across the table (see callout, Tidetables). Two rounds after Hammertime is rolled, floodwaters cover the ground with shallow water. Four rounds after Hammertime, the ground level is covered with deep water and low hills are covered in shallow water. At the end of the sixth round, the floodwaters crest and cover the ground and the bottom hill elevation level with deep water and the second hill elevation level with shallow water. For the effects of shallow and deep water see WARMACHINE: Prime, pg. 61.

Kossite Woodsmen may use the Ambush ability to come onto the south or east table edges.

SET UP

Players take turns, each placing one (1) hill anywhere on the table. Hills cannot be placed within 3" of another hill. The hills are approximately 16" in diameter and 1" high. A smaller hill 12" diameter and 1" high is then placed in the center of each of the first hills. Finally, a third hill 8" diameter and 1" high is placed in the center of the second level hills.

Players then take turns, each placing three (3) low wall, ruin, or tree base terrain features anywhere on the table level. Terrain features may not be placed within 3" of another terrain feature. Players may not place terrain features on hills.

BEGINNING

The Protectorate player deploys his forces first and places his models anywhere within 10" of the north or west table edges but not on the Escape Hill.

The Khador player then deploys his models in a 10" x 10" area in the southeast corner of the table.

The Protectorate player takes the first turn.

VICTORY CONDITIONS

The Protectorate wins if either both Khadoran warcasters are destroyed or if they Hold the second elevation level of the Escape Hill for two consecutive rounds beginning at the end of the sixth round after Hammertime.

Khador wins if either both Protectorate warcasters are destroyed or if they Hold the second elevation level of the Escape Hill for two consecutive rounds beginning at the end of the sixth round after Hammertime.

REWARDS

• **Hardened Supply Lines:** If Khador wins, the Menites are driven back allowing Khador to harden its supply lines against future attacks. Khador can then rush more parts and fuel to the front free of harassment. Once during any single Wrath of Summer's Heat scenario, the Khador player pays 10 points less for his warjacks.

• **Pilgrim Recruits:** If the Protectorate wins, the Menites gain ground and pilgrim immigrants swell the Protectorate ranks. Once during any single Wrath of Summer's Heat scenario, the Protectorate player may purchase a single Deliverer, Holy Zealot, or Temple Flameguard unit for half normal point cost rounded up.

SCENARIO 3, THE REAVERS

CYGNAR VS. CRYX, 1000 POINTS

Gorim 2nd, Solesh 605 AR—As tensions along Cygnar's border with the Protectorate intensify, the Cygnaran military begins recalling troops from across the country to reinforce defenses at Caspia. Taking advantage of weakened defenses, Cryxian raiders strike up and down the coastline at will. Confident in their plans, Cryx begins making bold raids against undefended coastal towns in Cygnar, seizing supplies and the living or dead, as needed. Lately, raids have intensified as Toruk's army prepares for a long war during the summer and fall seasons. The actions of Cryx have started to sting Cygnar, so the Crown dispatches an entire regiment to deal with the threat.

At Clockers Cove, a small village becomes the site of an embittered conflict as Cryx discovers they are not in control. Cygnar has caught the armies of the Dragonfather off guard by laying a complex ambush in the village just off the edge of the deep waters of the cove. In order to succeed in their ploy, Cygnar must delay Cryxian forces from signaling a reaver vessel waiting offshore.

Cygnar is waiting for two frigates to arrive to sink the reaver ship and assist in the capture of the raiders. If the frigates arrive in time, Cygnar will win the battle. Storms have delayed the frigates' arrival though, and as the battle begins, it is uncertain which

force will prevail as Cryx tries to get a signal to the waiting reaver vessel. If the Cygnaran navy sinks the black ship, the Cryxian battle groups will have a long walk home, assuming, of course, that they can outrun Cygnar's guns.

SPECIAL RULES

See the map. The western table edge is divided into four 12" x 12" sections of dock. The Cryx player wins the game if he can Hold two or more dock sections simultaneously for three consecutive rounds, allowing transport vessels from the blackship to pull into port. A player Holds a dock section if all models on the section are controlled by that player during his maintenance phase. Models that are engaged in melee combat cannot Hold a location. Warrior models with CMD stats of 1 or less and Incorporeal models cannot Hold a location.

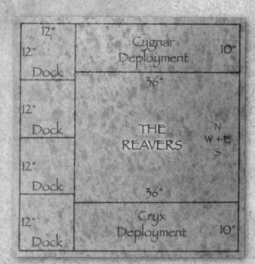

The Reavers scenario takes place on the Cygnaran coast, many miles away from the deserts of the Protectorate. Roll a weather effect from the Spring Weather Condition table rather than the Summer table.

Revenant Pirate units, Satyxis Raider units, and Leviathan helljacks gain the Advance Deployment ability during this scenario. Place models with the Advance Deployment ability after normal deployment, up to 12" beyond the established deployment zone.

The game goes into Hammertime at the end of round seven. If the game ends before Cryxian forces Hold two dock sections for three consecutive rounds, Cygnaran cannon fire forces the Cryxian blackship out of port before the main body of attackers can disembark.

SET UP

Players take turns, each placing three (3) buildings anywhere on the table outside the dock sections. Buildings can be up to 6" x 8". Buildings cannot be placed within a deployment zone or within 3" of another building, dock section, or table edge. All buildings have ARM 15 and can take 5 points of damage per inch. Building doors have ARM 14 and can take 5 points of damage. See Damaging and Destroying Structures, WARMACHINE: Prime, pg. 62, for details.

Players then take turns, each placing two (2) additional terrain features. Players cannot place terrain within a deployment zone or within 3" of a table edge or another terrain feature, including the dock sections or buildings. Players can place terrain features on hills.

BEGINNING

The Cryx player deploys first by placing his models within 10" of the south table edge but outside the dock section.

The Cygnar player then deploys his forces within 10" of the north table edge but outside the dock section. Up to one Cygnaran unit or solo may be deployed in any building as a part of normal deployment.

Players may place models with the Advance Deployment ability on dock sections. Cryx models may not Advance Deploy inside buildings.

The Cygnar player takes the first turn

VICTORY CONDITIONS

Cryx wins the game if they Hold two dock sections for three consecutive rounds. Cryxian transport vessels then arrive and the town is overrun by thralls. The Cygnaran guns are overrun before they can drive off the ship.

Cygnar wins the game if both Cryxian warcasters are destroyed or removed from play or if Cryx has not won by the end of the game. Cygnaran cannons open fire and drive the blackship from port.

REWARDS

• **Press Gang:** If Cryx wins, their forces overrun the town and drag many inhabitants back to the blackship. The lucky ones drown on the way, but all are turned over to the necrosurgeons. Once during any single Wrath of Summer's Heat scenario, the Cryx player may purchase a single Bile Thrall, Mechanithrall, or Revenant Crew unit for half normal point cost rounded up.

• **All Quiet:** If Cygnar wins, Cryxian forces scale back their attacks and watch the coast, allowing Cygnar time to build up its defenses. Once during any single Wrath of Summer's Heat scenario, the Cygnar player pays 10 points less warjacks.

SCENARIO 4, LAWBRINGER

PROTECTORATE VS. CYGNAR, 1000 POINTS

Vendarl 6th, Octesh 605 AR — For months, if not years, the Protectorate has prepared its Holy Crusade. By the Hierarch's decree, it is Menoth's will the task begins against the Cygnarans who have long held the Protectorate in unjust servitude. Once Cygnar has fallen, all of the Iron Kingdoms shall follow.

The key instrument of the Hierarch's will is a weapon—a mighty engine designed to bring down the walls of the Cygnaran throne city of Caspia. The Lawbringer is a mighty ballista of brass and steel that throws enormous explosive shells over great distances. With its construction finally complete, the Protectorate prepares to attack. Though unprepared for a full-on assault, the Menites intend to show that, if they wish, they can bring down the walls of Caspia—something never accomplished in history. All night the Menites toil. Through faith, sweat, and loss, they ferry the massive creation and its volatile ammunition across the river and assemble it on the Cygnaran shore, and at dawn's first light, the walls of Caspia shudder.

Cygnaran forces within the city instantly race to their battle stations, but they can do little from the city walls to stop the fiery bombardment raining down. Warcasters and their battle groups rush to the waterfront to destroy the weapon before it does too much damage to the mighty walls of Caspia.

SPECIAL RULES

Lawbringer takes place on the waterfront outside the massive Cygnaran capital city of Caspia. Protectorate forces must hold back the Cygnarans long enough to breach the city's walls. Once they fall, the Protectorate will declare a great victory and halt the attack. Cygnaran forces must overrun Protectorate positions and destroy the cannon before the walls crumble.

Lawbringer is a ballista approximately 6" x 12" and 8" high positioned in the middle of the Protectorate deployment zone bordering the north table edge. The ballista has ARM 16 and can take 80 damage points before becoming inoperable. See Damaging and Destroying Structures, WARMACHINE: Prime, pg. 62, for details.

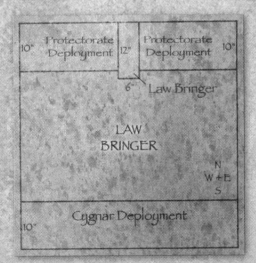

Lawbringer towers over the battlefield. LOS to the ballista is not blocked by trees or cloud effects.

Any attack that causes damage to Lawbringer has a chance of detonating its volatile ammunition. Anytime the ballista is damaged, the Protectorate player rolls a d6. If the ballista suffered 1-5 points of damage from the attack, it explodes on a roll of 1. If it took 6-10 points of damage from the attack, it explodes on a roll of 1 or 2. If it took 11+ points of damage from the attack, it explodes on a roll of 1-3. If the ammo explodes, Lawbringer is destroyed and all models within 8" suffer a POW 15 damage roll.

The Cygnar player wins the game if either the cannon is rendered inoperable or is destroyed.

The game goes into Hammertime at the end of round seven. If the game ends before Cygnaran forces have rendered the Lawbringer inoperable or destroyed it, the ballista blasts through Caspia's walls and the Menites claim victory.

Smoke from the repeated explosions of the bombardment gives all models concealment.

SET UP

Players take turns, each placing three (3) low walls or ruins outside their opponent's deployment zone and not within 3" of another terrain feature, including Lawbringer.

BEGINNING

The Protectorate player deploys first by placing his models within 10" of the north table edge.

The Cygnar player then deploys within 10" of the south table edge.

The Protectorate player takes the first turn.

VICTORY CONDITIONS

Cygnar wins if Lawbringer is made inoperable or destroyed.

The Protectorate wins if the game ends before the ballista is rendered inoperable or destroyed.

REWARDS

• **Security:** If Cygnar wins, Lawbringer is silenced long enough for them to make a punitive strike against Sul. The attack temporarily cripples the Protectorate war effort and gives Cygnar time to recover and extend its defenses. With no attack imminent, Cygnar re-distributes its forces and frees up much needed resources. Once during any single Wrath of Summer's Heat scenario, the Cygnar player pays 10 points less for units.

• **War Effort:** If the Protectorate wins, the damage done to Caspia's walls forces Cygnar into a defensive posture. For weeks while the walls are rebuilt, the Protectorate is able to focus on its own war effort and build great numbers of warjacks. Once during any single Wrath of Summer's Heat scenario, the Protectorate player pays 10 points less for warjacks.

SCENARIO 5. SPAWNING GROUND

KHADOR VS. CRYX, 1000 POINTS KHADOR AND 1500 POINTS CRYX

Malleus 4th, Octesh 605 AR—At first, Khadoran kommanders scoffed at rumors of raids along their borders, but significant lapses in supply lines started them looking into the matter nevertheless. Something had been undermining the transfer of weapons, food, and clothing to troops in Llael. Working with Greylord ternions, they discovered Cryxian forces deploying from some point along the border and laying waste to Khadoran convoys.

Initially the Cryxian source was unknown, but troopers assigned to monitor the activity of Menites in a small village near the border soon revealed a devious ruse. The denizens of the village, seemingly going about their business, were nothing more than re-animated husks manipulated by dark magic and made to appear to have some semblance of life. The village itself was a front for a Cryxian base where necrotechs and necrosurgeons toiled in the dark tunnels beneath the town to create fresh nightmares.

After the survivors of the tunnel expedition reported back to Khadoran officers, it was clear that this dubious ploy needed ending. Khador has sent an armed force sufficient to level the village and ensure nothing escapes. What they do not know is the extent of the Cryxian invasion, nor what they have planned for anyone who comes to the village seeking to destroy it.

SPECIAL RULES

The Cryx player places five (5) buildings, each approximately 4" x 6", on his half of the table. The buildings must be placed outside the Cryx deployment zone and not within 5" of another building or table edge. The buildings are dilapidated brick structures rotted through from the necromantic energies of the Cryxian industry below. The buildings have an ARM of 14 and 5 points of damage per inch of wall. See Damaging and Destroying Structures,

WARMACHINE: Prime, pg. 62, for details.

The Cryx player receives 1500 points to build his army, but is still limited to two warcasters. The player deploys no models at the start of the game; instead, models emerge from the buildings remaining in play. During each of his maintenance phases, the Cryx player may place one (1) model or unit on the table for each undestroyed building remaining in play. A model must be placed inside or within 3" of the building that spawned it. Emerging models and units activate as normal.

A warcaster cannot allocate focus until he has been placed on the battlefield.

Once all buildings have been destroyed, the Cryx player cannot put any additional models in play. At the end of the game, the Cryx player gains a Survival Bonus for all models remaining on the table and does not gain a Survival Bonus for models that were not put into play.

SET UP

Players take turns, each placing two (2) additional terrain features. Players cannot place additional buildings. Terrain features cannot be placed within an opponent's deployment zone or within 3" of another terrain feature, including the buildings. Terrain features may be placed on hills.

BEGINNING

The Khador player deploys his forces within 10" of his table edge.

The Cryx player takes the first turn.

VICTORY CONDITIONS

Khador wins if, at the end of their turn, all Cryx models in play are wrecked or inert.

Cryx wins once both Khadoran warcasters have been destroyed or removed from play.

REWARDS

• **Necrofactorium:** If Cryx wins the game, a large number of horrific bonejacks and helljacks are assembled on the mainland before Khador manages to shut down the operation. Once during any single Wrath of Summer's Heat scenario, the Cryx player pays 10 points less for helljacks and 5 points less for bonejacks.

• **Recruitment Drive:** If Khador wins, propagandists have a field day with the events of the Spawning Ground scenario. Great numbers of patriots, outraged that Cryx would dare assault the Motherland, immediately re-enlist. Once during any single Wrath of Summer's Heat scenario, the Khador player may purchase a single Iron Fang Pikeman, Kossite Woodsman, or Winter Guard unit for half normal point cost rounded up.

SCENARIO 6, DUST STORM

PROTECTORATE VS. CRYX, 1000 POINTS

Donard 6th, Octesh 605 AR—For days Cryxian forces have closely trailed a large group of Menite pilgrims as they make their way down the Black River and across the treacherous Bloodstone Marches toward the Protectorate. Near the end of their arduous journey, scouts among the faithful uncover the threat that trails them and the pilgrims make haste toward the Tower of Judgment. Realizing their quarry is attempting to escape their clutches, Cryxian forces make their move, but they are suddenly scattered when a great dust storm blows across the wastes. Praising Menoth, the pilgrims make their way into the tower and huddle in the sanctity of its walls.

Deciding to use the storm to their advantage, Protectorate forces garrisoning the tower elect to

regroup. They plan to use the dust storm to screen their advance.

SPECIAL RULES

No models on either side may use Advance Deployment.

Each round before the first player's turn, roll a d6 to determine if a dust storm kicks up. On a roll of 1 or 2, a storm hits the battlefield. All models suffer –1 to ranged attacks rolls. Models cannot give or receive orders. The dust storm lasts for one (1) round.

SET UP

Players take turns, each placing three (3) terrain features. Players should choose terrain features common to a desert setting and avoid such features as rivers and forests. Terrain features cannot be placed within 3" of another terrain feature. Terrain features may be placed on hills.

BEGINNING

Players roll to determine who chooses his deployment point first and then alternate choosing deployment points anywhere on the table. Each player chooses three (3) deployment points, but a player may not choose a point within 12" of a point selected by his opponent.

Players then alternate arranging one (1) unit or battle group at a time anywhere within 6" of one of their deployment points. When deploying his solos, a player must deploy all of his solos at once instead of setting up a unit or battle group. Players arrange

deployment points. After all forces are deployed the players roll again, and the high roller chooses who goes first.

VICTORY CONDITIONS

The player with the last warcaster in play wins the game.

REWARDS

• **Safe Passage:** After destroying their enemies in the dust storm, the victorious faction is able to navigate the eastern side of the Black River free of enemy forces. During the Wrath of Summer's Heat Act III scenario, Smoke on the Water, the winning player may choose to go first or last.

SCENARIO 7, SILENCER

KHADOR VS. CYGNAR, 1000 POINTS

DESCRIPTION

Gorim 1st, Octesh 605 AR—With much of Llael occupied and controlled, Khador has initiated a plan of attack on soft targets down the Black River Valley. Khador intends to strike southward with a river-borne fleet of gun ships. Before Khador can begin its attacks, however, Cygnaran ordnance overlooking the river must be silenced. Three heavy guns are trained upon the Black River and are calibrated to

186

bombard any unauthorized ships attempting to pass. The cannons—named Terrata, Defiant, and Gaius—have capable range and can destroy a river vessel with a single well-placed shot.

Making their way by land, a Khadoran strike force prepares to assault the emplacements north of Corvis. The Khadorans must destroy the three heavy cannons so that their own gun ships can come into range. They have to do this before Cygnaran reinforcements arrive from downriver, for the Cygnaran soldiers have signaled for more troops.

SPECIAL RULES

The Cygnar player places the three (3) gun emplacements on hills between the forward edge of his deployment zone and the center of the table. The gun emplacements are structures approximately 4" x 4" standing 4" high and their barrels aim high over the battlefield and are not obstacles to play. The guns are slow to use and trained on the river, so they cannot be used during the scenario. The gun emplacements have ARM 18 and can take 15 damage points before becoming disabled. See Damaging and Destroying Structures, WARMACHINE: Prime, pg. 62, for details.

Khador wins the game if all three gun emplacements are disabled.

The game goes into Hammertime at the end of round five. If the game ends before Khador disables all three gun emplacements, the Cygnaran guns open fire on the Khadoran ships and force them back upriver.

SET UP

The Cygnar player places two (2) low walls and two (2) other terrain features anywhere on his side of the table. Low walls may be placed in contact with the guns. Other terrain features cannot be placed within 3" of another terrain feature, including gun emplacements and walls. Terrain features may be placed on hills.

The Khador player then places two (2) terrain features on his half of the table. Terrain features cannot be placed within 3" of a terrain feature, including walls or gun emplacements. Terrain features may be placed on hills.

BEGINNING

At the start of the game, each player rolls a d6 and the high roller chooses who goes first. The first player gets his choice of deployment zones and takes the first turn. Players deploy their forces up to 10" from the table's edge.

VICTORY CONDITIONS

Khador wins when all guns have been disabled.

Cygnar wins if all Khadoran warcasters have been destroyed or removed from play, or if Khador has not disabled all three guns by the end of the game.

REWARDS

• **Preparation:** The winning player has time to prepare his force's movements along the river. Once during the Wrath of Summer's Heat Act III scenario, Smoke on the Water, the winning player may either choose to add 2" to his barge movement or not move the barge at all. He may decide after rolling the die for barge movement.

THE WRATH OF SUMMER'S HEAT ACT II SIDE QUESTS

TURNS OF TREACHERY, CRYX SIDE QUEST

PIRATE QUEEN SKARRE RAVENMANE

Skarre Ravenmane, Pirate Queen and reaver witch, views the world through omens, portents, and divinations. Renowned for her dark gifts, Skarre's visions are accurate enough to draw amusement from the Lich Lords themselves. However, as summer wanes, ill omens seize the satyxis witch: a vision that all is not well becomes an obsession. Unable to discern the exact nature of this portent, she sets her sights upon the culprit most clearly pictured in her mind's eye. It is an interesting figure…

The Iron Lich, Asphyxious.

Guided by something more than instinct, Skarre has secretly pursued the skarlock thrall Silshade, an agent of the Iron Lich, to a remote island. Along the way, she has taken great care to remain undetected, following the thrall's small craft with her own blackship, the Widower. Disembarking, the Pirate Queen and a group of raiders stalk through the deep jungle forest to the site of a long-forgotten Orgoth ruin.

From a short distance away, Skarre observes the skarlock ordering mechanithralls to lift heavy blocks of stone and slide them into place, attempting to restore the ruins and make them appear undisturbed. Silshade then begins a malefic rite and, soon enough, the ruins begin emitting a haunting glow. Visions

assail the Pirate Queen—images of a gateway to Urcaen. Though the exact purpose of the rite remains a mystery, Skarre is certain she must act quickly. Whatever Asphyxious' plans might be, she is convinced they are not in the interests of the Dragonfather, and she must not allow the Iron Lich to succeed in whatever devious plot he has set in motion. It is clear. Skarre must destroy this skarlock, destroy the mechanithralls, and reduce the Orgoth ruins to nothing more than shattered debris.

VISIONS OF A DARKER DAY

Deep in the sanctuary, Skarre the Pirate Queen knelt in contemplation. The stone and obsidian room was tiled with the bones of men who had mated with satyxis. In the center, the reaver witch began delving into the omens of the future. A crystalline orb set in the midst of steaming stinking entrails acted as her focus. The blood of the sacrifice made the visions thick, and the incense that burned in the censers lent strength to her talents. She knelt and began to let her mind drift, billowing to the distant shoals of prophecy that she so often visited in her trancelike state.

Her eyes closed and her hands clutched at her brow just below the long horns jutting from her skull. Suddenly, her head throbbed with scarlet lightning. Wave after wave of visions assailed her. In her eyes one sole visage glowed with a fiery intensity: the powerful aura of a being so clear it almost burned her eyes as if she had stared too long at the wicked sun.

"Asphyxious…" the words left her mouth like bitter ashes.

The overtones of foreboding and danger in the vision swept through her like a sickness and she moaned and swayed. Her attendants prepared to catch her if she swooned, but Skarre held fast. She straightened herself, drawing a sigil of ancient design in the air, and her mind calmed.

With a second sweep of her hand, Skarre built a complex enchantment that gave her surcease from the omen's strength. Mumbling words of warding and taking a drop of rare oil, she traced a symbol between the horns on her brow. All of these measures put her to ease. The pain began to subside, and the clarity of the vision became distant as if it were but a remembered dream.

Now centered and in control of the portent, Skarre dove further into it looking for a tangible point to anchor her thoughts. Her mind sought some person, place, or thing that would lead her to the source of her vision. As if through a distant window, she saw one of his most trusted skarlocks: Silshade. The thrall was boarding a ship crewed with bleached bones and tattooed thralls. Its destination was a dim and angry darkness in the southern isles of the Broken Coast. Whatever Asphyxious was up to, it was dire.

Skarre beckoned to one of her entourage, and a single satyxis with long dark hair moved close to her. "Yes, O Queen?" The reaver witch's first mate was calm, having witnessed such visions before, although none so consuming as this. She was there merely to serve and heal, if need be.

"Ready the Widower." Skarre's voice was strong, but the pain still ebbed beneath her enchantment; somewhere it waited like a caged rabid dog. Whatever Asphyxious was up to, he made the souls of even the ancients cringe. The twisted path of his plan threaded through the warring nations of the mainland. It was a plot so complex that, although she could sense it, she could not perceive every step. Skarre could only see but one of the Iron Lich's strides, but she knew that it was in her interest to impede as many steps as she could.

Skarre looked at her first mate who was preparing to follow her order. "Have the crew equip for battle," she said softly. "There is dark work to be done."

The first mate nodded and smiled.

CRYX ARMY COMPOSITION

Pirate Queen Skarre

1 Satyxis Raider unit with 1 Dominatrix and 5 Troopers

CRYX ARMY COMPOSITION

1 Skarlock Thrall

2 Mechanithrall units each with 1 Lieutenant and 9 Troopers

SPECIAL RULES

The scenario takes place on a 3' by 3' table.

The Orgoth shrine is a ruin approximately 6" by 6" in the center of the table. The ruin has ARM 16 and can take 30 damage points before being destroyed.

The spiritual energy surrounding the Orgoth ruin affects Silshade in two ways. First, the spiritual energy protects the Skarlock and keeps it safe from harm. Until the ruins have been destroyed, Silshade cannot be damaged in any way. Second, the energy fuels the skarlock's Spell Slave ability. Throughout the scenario, Silshade may cast spells as if he were within Asphyxious' control area. Silshade must remain nearby the ruins to retain these abilities and loses them anytime he is more than 3" from the ruin.

SET UP

Players take turns, each placing two (2) additional terrain features. Players cannot place terrain within 3" of another terrain feature including the ruins. Players can place terrain features on hills.

TRUST

"But there are three of them, Prince. We know so little of their capabilities…" Sorscha's voice trailed off as her gaze returned to study the trio of iron terrors seemingly trapped in the courtyard of a ruined village. The Khadoran Kommander and Prince Vladimir Tzepesci had been observing the unknown helljacks for over an hour from the safety of a bluff above the site of a recent confrontation with the Cryx.

Seethers, they called them. On the outside, they had much in common with the Slayer Helljack—an opponent with which the Khadoran warcasters had become quite familiar over the past months—but these abominations contained a vile intelligence and a twisted motivation beyond the capacity of any warjack ever seen. Their necrotite-burning furnaces smoldered, conserving fuel until their Cryxian masters could recover the abandoned 'jacks. Nevertheless, rage continued to boil beneath their cold metal skins as brief spasms of fury manifested in the form of cuffs and shoulder checks that sluggishly knocked each other about like wild beasts squaring off for territory. The homes of a Llaelese village had collapsed around them, corralling the Seethers like so many cattle while the Khadoran army finished the job of repelling the remaining Cryx back to their hidden safeties.

"They are not so different from other Cryx," the Prince said after watching the 'jacks during Sorscha's pause. "So approach them as you would any other Cryx. Strike accurately and viz force, and leave them viz no chance to return attack."

"Our jacks are too damaged from the engagement. I will summon the guard," replied Sorscha as she rose slowly from her crouch to avoid attracting the attention of the helljacks. "We can decimate them from the tops of —"

"No, Kommander," Vladimir interrupted. Sorscha always addressed the Prince formally, but he rarely did the same. His words, no longer affable, were clearly an order. "I vant you to dispatch these monsters yourself."

"Alone?" The woman's expression betrayed her uncertainty, but the Prince turned away to continue watching the strange Cryxian warjacks. The hiss of venting steam below interrupted Sorscha's hesitation. "Very well, my lord. I will strike swiftly."

"You rely on speed too much, Kommander. It may not all-vays be there for you," the Umbrean warcaster continued. His tone was that of a mentor, not a comrade. "You have a great aptitude for sorcery, yes, but you must employ other strengths. Most importantly, your strength as a varrior."

Sorscha's face was tense. She hoisted her battle scythe Frost Fang from its resting place on her shoulder. She turned to move toward the shuffling black carapaces below. Stopping to stand a moment, she contemplated her approach to the aberrant helljacks.

The Dark Prince contemplated the woman from behind with deep, brooding eyes. For all her courage, her stamina, her ability as a warcaster, her battlefield experience, and her lifetime as a soldier, she had not been weathered. She remained unsullied by the strife around her, as perfect and innocent as a child. War was ripping the world apart, but Sorscha bore not one scar. Sensing her uncertainty, he offered an assuring word.

"Do not fear, muya dorogaya…," Vlad said softly. He used the term of endearment even more rarely than her title. "I am here."

Sorscha looked over her shoulder at the Prince. Frost Fang pulsed, and a trail of glittering shards of ice fell from its blade. Her fear was gone, and her eyes reflected only trust. Gripping the scythe, she evenly and confidently strode down the bluff, ready for whatever the helljacks could deliver.

KHADOR ARMY COMPOSITION

Kommander Sorscha

Vladimir Tzepesci

CRYX ARMY COMPOSITION

3 Seether Helljacks

SPECIAL RULES

This scenario is played on a 3' x 3' table.

The Khador player loses the game at the end of any turn in which Sorscha casts Wind Rush or Vladimir activates.

The Seethers are low on necrotite and therefore less aggressive than usual. They will not attack each other under any circumstances. A Seether will always charge the nearest Khadoran model within LOS unless it is already engaged.

SET UP

Players take turns, each placing two (2) terrain features. Terrain features cannot be placed within 3" of another terrain feature. Terrain features may be placed on hills.

BEGINNING

The Cryx player deploys his models first and places them within 5" of the center of the table.

The Khador player then chooses a table edge and deploys Sorscha and Vladimir within 5" of the edge.

The Khador player takes the first turn.

VICTORY CONDITIONS

Khador wins when all three Seethers have been disabled.

Cryx wins at the end of any turn in which Vladimir activates or Sorscha casts Wind Rush. The Cryx player also wins if Sorscha or Vladimir is destroyed.

Rewards

- **Inspiration:** If Khador wins, Sorscha completes her tutelage under Vladimir and becomes one of Khador's greatest leaders. An inspiration to the soldiers under her command, Sorscha grants +2 MAT and an additional melee attack to any friendly Khador trooper or solo that ends its charge movement within Sorscha's command range in a turn Sorscha charged.

Gone Fishing, Protectorate Side Quest

Grand Scrutator Severius

War has intensified, and the Protectorate has had to extend the manufacture of its warjacks with salvaged parts from battlefields. Indeed, Protectorate efforts have redoubled in order to create a larger, stronger fighting force, though one major problem persists: the Menites have a multitude of 'jacks ready for cortex imprinting and deployment, but a massive shortage leaves them with no cortexes to mount. This is a problem the Hierarch has decreed must be solved within the span of a fortnight or heads will roll, literally.

Realizing the importance of the situation and tempering the Hierarch's fervor for results, the Grand Scrutator Severius collects intelligence from Khadoran pilgrims and military defectors. With this knowledge he has tracked the efforts of the Greylord ternions, knowing that these wizards have the secret of cortex manufacture. The Grand Scrutator intends to capture a Greylord with such knowledge.

Severius knows of a Greylord with strong ties to the Menite faith, and he has set out to find the man and persuade him to aid the Protectorate. Expecting some resistance, the Grand Scrutator plans to resort to his gifts of persuasion in order to subjugate the wizard. Severius is prepared should the man prove unwilling to betray his country. He expects the wizard will have mixed feelings between duty to his nation and duty to his faith and, while he can easily handle a few mages, the Grand Scrutator has taken along a personal exemplar seneschal guard to ensure he is not harassed excessively during this important mission.

Fear Forgiveness

The pilgrim cringed and panic filled his eyes. As the young man cowered, the Grand Scrutator Severius snorted in disgust. "You would do well to stand tall and speak with the tongue of a Menite rather than snivel like a lowly dog."

The derision in his voice ran thick like a rolling flame. "Now, tell me the name of your uncle. From what I have learned, he is a koldun of the Greylord Covenant, correct?" Physically, Severius was frail in comparison to the strong youth, but he nevertheless emanated the presence of a titan. His thin frame contained such immense power the youth could not hope to hold his tongue.

"Yes, yes, Scrutator. He is —" His voice trailed off as he realized he had betrayed a family member.

"Fear not, young man. Once you have imparted this knowledge, I shall personally see to it you are forgiven for withholding your words." The voice of the Grand Scrutator suddenly shifted and his charisma exuded an air of forgiveness and compassion. "Menoth does know mercy, and it is not always the mercy of the lash. Now, fulfill your duty and tell me of your uncle. His name, his appearance… most importantly, is he a good Menite? Does he still attend service?"

The young man looked puzzled. To enlighten him, Severius slapped the boy across the face with his gauntleted palm.

"Answer my inquiries or I will have your family sent to mine salt for Kregor Rock." Severius had little patience for uncertainty, especially when the information this boy held could aid the Protectorate. "Tell me. Does your dear uncle attend service?"

"Regularly… my lord," the youth sobbed. "He has a personal confessor… in Korsk." Tears streamed from the boy's eyes.

The Scrutator smiled. "Very good. That is what I needed to hear, young man. Now, write his name down on this parchment, his appointed station… and whatever else you can think of…"

The youth complied. Better to betray an uncle than to face the wrath of the Grand Scrutator.

Severius looked on as the boy wrote his death sentence. The knowledge the youth was committing to parchment could not fall into anyone else's hands. After a moment, the boy handed over the parchment with a quaking hand.

The Grand Scrutator accepted the document and smiled at the youth. "The wrack," he said to his guards, and the young man's eyes widened. The youth fell to his knees pleading, but suffering was the only true way Menoth could forgive this young man for his weakness. Severius tucked the parchment into his robes and replaced his mask as the boy, screaming for the very mercy he would soon receive, was dragged away.

PROTECTORATE ARMY COMPOSITION

Grand Scrutator Severius

2 Exemplar Seneschals

KHADOR ARMY COMPOSITION

1 Man-O-War Kovnik

1 Greylord Ternion unit

1 Berserker Heavy Warjack

SPECIAL RULES

This scenario is played on a 3' x 3' table.

The Grand Scrutator must use the Convert spell to take control of a Greylord and then get the converted model back to his deployment zone.

The Khador player may not target friendly models with attacks. If a Greylord makes a Frost Bite attack that overlaps another Greylord model, the attacker forfeits his action rather than casting the spell.

SET UP

Players take turns, each placing three (3) terrain features. Terrain features cannot be placed within 3" of another terrain feature. Terrain features may be placed on hills.

BEGINNING

At the start of the game, each player rolls a d6. The high roller chooses who goes first. The first player sets up in his deployment zone and takes the first turn. Players deploy their forces up to 6" from the table's edge.

VICTORY CONDITIONS

The Protectorate wins if the Grand Scrutator Severius converts a Greylord using his Convert spell and gets him back to his deployment zone.

Khador wins if the Grand Scrutator Severius is destroyed, or if the last Greylord model is destroyed or removed from play before the Protectorate wins.

REWARDS

• **Secrets of the Cortex:** If the Protectorate wins, the converted Greylord divulges his secrets to Severius and grants him new insights into cortex defense protocols. For the rest of the Campaign, during his activation Severius may spend a point of focus to shut down the cortex of up to one warjack within his control area. The warjack may not be allocated focus for one round.

THE WRATH OF SUMMER'S HEAT ACT III

SCENARIO 8, SMOKE ON THE WATER

TWO-PLAYER GAME, 1000 POINTS

Vendarl 6th, Katesh 605 AR—Cygnar built barge crossings on the Black River to facilitate traffic along the Great Northern Tradeway. With the war in Llael, barge crews have grown used to military traffic coming and going from Cygnar. However, the dangers of war have crept up on them. Due to the barge dock's proximity to Widower's Wood, crews have had to rely on mercenaries to keep marauding patrols of Khadoran, Cryxian, and Protectorate forces at bay. Unfortunately, Cygnar is only protecting the southern end of the barge line and has not provided either side with a full warcaster contingent.

The barges on the Cygnaran side have poorly-protected walls and roads, and several docks and barges have no security. Access to the barges is

unhindered in most cases since engineers built the docks with an emphasis on traffic, not protection from invading forces. It is of little surprise when enemy forces commandeer a barge and use it to ferry their own troops.

This, of course, sets the stage for a vicious river battle as two barges loaded with opposing forces come within proximity. Warjacks smash and wrestle above the cold waters of the Black River while troopers and warcasters attempt to thwart their enemy's plan safely to attain the docks on either side of the river. These docks are the only alternative to drowning in the depths of the murky waters and becoming food for dracodiles and dragonfish or ending up as salvage for junker crews who routinely dredge the river for cogs, gears, and whatever else that can be found in the muck below.

SPECIAL RULES

This scenario is a battle between rival forces passing by each other on barges over deep water. See Deep Water, WARMACHINE: Prime, pg. 61, for details.

See map. Each barge is approximately 12" x 24". One barge is placed bordering the north table edge 12" from the west table edge. The second barge is placed bordering the south table edge 12" from the east table edge.

Each player deploys his forces on one barge, and the barge upon which a player deploys moves d6" directly toward the opposite table edge during each of his maintenance phases. The barges will then slowly pass each other and create no end of mayhem. Care should be taken to align the barges to make sure they do not collide. A barge has ARM 16 and cannot be damaged by ranged attacks below POW 14, unless the attack also inflicts continuous fire or corrosion. Barges suffer fire and corrosion continuous effects in the same manner as models. Melee, magic, and area of effect attacks all do full damage to the barges.

When the barges line up to pass one another, they will be close enough for models to move from one barge to the other without movement penalty. Models can likewise be thrown from one barge to another. A model Slammed or Pushed past the edge of the barge will fall into the water. Any models falling into the water are removed from play.

When a barge moves, any model straddling both barges must be moved by its controlling player to one barge or the other. The model must be placed touching the edge of the barge. If there is no room to accommodate the model's base, it falls into the water and the model is removed from play.

Once either barge reaches the opposite table edge from its starting position, the barges stop moving for the rest of the game and the barge that has taken the most damage sinks. All models on the barge fall into the water and suffer the effects described above.

The game ends when one player Holds the last barge in play. A player Holds the barge if he controls all models on the barge during his maintenance phase. Models that are engaged in melee combat cannot be used to Hold a barge. Warrior models with CMD stats of 1 or less and Incorporeal models cannot Hold the barge.

Fleeing models move to the back edge of the barge on which they are currently standing.

Models cannot use the Advanced Deployment ability in this scenario.

Kossite Woodsmen cannot use the Ambush ability in this scenario.

Gorten Grundback may not use his feat during this scenario.

SET UP

Players take turns, each placing three (3) terrain features on their barge. Players can place crates, barrels, or anything else that may be found on a barge. Terrain features may be targeted. Each feature has ARM 20 and is removed from the table if it takes any damage.

BEGINNING

At the start of the game, each player rolls a d6 and the high roller chooses who goes first. The first player deploys his models on his barge and takes the first turn.

VICTORY CONDITIONS

The player who Holds the last barge in play wins the game.

REWARDS

• **Waterway:** After the river battle, the winner takes control of a valuable river waterway and is easily able to fortify his positions. The winner may add up to 25 points to the size of his army in the Fall's Blighted Harvest Act I scenario, the Balebrand.

• **Reserves:** The winning faction takes control of a vital river crossing. Once during the Campaign in a single scenario, the winning player may put one (1) unit into play during any of his maintenance phases after the first round. The unit may be worth up to 100 points and is in addition to the player's point total for the scenario, but it may not exceed normal field allowance. The unit is placed on the table within the player's deployment zone. The Reserves reward may only be used in scenarios in which the winning player has a deployment zone bordering a table edge. The player does not have to declare the use of Reserves before the game.

WHAT ABOUT MY LEVIATHAN?

All models that fall into the water are removed from play, even the Leviathan. While it is likely the Leviathan scuttles up onto the riverbank a few hours later, the barges and the battle will be long gone. Between the current and the river depth, you might as well put your helljack's face on milk cartons.

MAKING BARGES

While some of you will no doubt build highly detailed barges out of balsa, others may not be quite so inclined. A warning to the lazy: if you intend simply to cut out a barge floor plan for this scenario, use foam core or card board and not paper. When it comes time to move your barge, you will appreciate the foam a lot more than you would paper.

Fall's Blighted Harvest

MALLEUS 1ST, GOLOVEN 605 AR

Lord Toruk has begun His move to sunder the Iron Kingdoms, and Cryx has unleashed another diabolical weapon in its arcane arsenal. The Balebrand is a creation of dark magic born out of the schemes of the Lich Lords in collusion with the witch covens of Cryx. The brand consists of a distillation of necromantic energy brewed during the celestial alignment of dark bodies in the heavens in conjunction with the maddening moon Laris. Thralls deployed to the frontlines in Cygnar are enchanted with the Balebrand. These legions of undead form the vehicle for the weapon's mystical contagion—a toxic element that infects through skin contact. Upon contact with a living target, the enchantment begins its life-siphoning work by eating away at the victim and sapping his will.

Cryx begins its move throughout western Immoren and spreads the brand among the living. The infected return to their homes and armies, apparent survivors of deadly conflicts, and are welcomed with open arms. However, once the stars re-align and Laris becomes full once more, a warcaster or mage with the proper knowledge can activate the devious mark, suddenly wresting full control over the infected unfortunates. At this crucial moment, Cryx must make its move or the secretive effects of the brand may dissipate and fade into nothingness, thus releasing those formerly consumed by its dark enchantment.

Cygnar, haggard from war, is in much need of a hero. The Jewel of the Iron Kingdoms is on the brink of fracturing under the pressure of its mounting problems. With strife in the Royal Assembly, the capital city of Caspia under assault, and various cities under attack by Khadoran, Protectorate and Cryxian forces, King Leto Raelthorne is desperate for a solution. In the face of dwindling supplies, Cygnar's military is tasked with not only fighting a war on all fronts, but also protecting its civilian populace at all cost.

In the north, Khador has started to feel the strain of overextending its military. Cygnarans are familiar with the terrain of their own lands and are employing effective hit-and-run strikes on Khadoran supply lines. The High Kommand's war effort may have been too overconfident, and their battle on Cygnaran soil has not been as successful as planned. Indeed, the legendary Kommandant Irusk is contemplating the withdrawal of troops in order to regroup and begin a new stage of assaults.

Frenzied and eager just months ago, the Protectorate of Menoth has simmered down with summer's fading. The notion that their Holy Crusade must be conducted differently has dawned on them. Cooler heads have prevailed, calling for extended planning, strategy, and caution. While numerous Menites still do not agree, Hierarch Voyle has issued that Menoth's will must be meted out with patience and replenished toil. Tearing down the walls of Caspia is hard work and requires dedication—qualities exemplified by Menoth's flock. The faithful will rise to take their appointed place in time.

Further incursions by Cryx had seemed to be slowing, but their methods have merely shifted. Rather than sneaking around the countryside by night anymore, their forces have been moving during the day. This change can only mean one thing: Cryx is ready for open war, and the harvest for which they have come is ripe for the reaping.

FALL'S BLIGHTED HARVEST ACT I

SCENARIO 1, BALEBRAND

MULTIPLAYER GAME, 500 POINTS

Malleus 7th, Goloven 605 AR—In the waning days of the year, the longer nights have fortified the Cryxian advance. Everyday Toruk's legions grow bolder, striking deeper and deeper into Cygnaran heartland. Unknown to all, Cryx prepares to unleash a terrifying weapon that threatens to wrest control of the populace and sow utter chaos. As the moon Laris comes into its fullest phase, Cryxian necromancers and witches re-focus their efforts to act upon their long months of planning.

Simply known as the Balebrand, its infection is no mere contagion but the product of endless hours of demented Cryxian experimentation. As this insidious enchantment spreads, it leeches living energy and slowly devours men from the inside out. Cryx spreads the necromantic sigil through skin contact in battle. Wounded soldiers then carry the Balebrand home where they will wait, concealing the mark until summoned when the time is right and the moon Laris becomes full again.

Agents of the Dragonfather have carefully laid the groundwork for a chance meeting between the rival factions in a Corvis bourg called Drewlin's Grove. Cygnaran scouts discover secret Khadoran battle plans for an upcoming offensive to strike at the town, Menite loyalists harbor troops there for a campaign around the City of Ghosts, and it is merely a matter of creating an opportunity for all three factions to meet on the field of battle. Once gathered, branded thralls will sweep across the field and infect their enemies at will.

Lord Toruk and his Lich Lords hope the Balebrand will be the insidious lever to their plot. Seeking to use the roiling sea of conflict to sail them into power, the Cryxian armies intend for the Balebrand to act as the major device to ensure their victory.

SPECIAL RULES

All undead Cryx models begin the game infected with the Balebrand. Any living model beginning its activation in base-to-base contact with a model infected by the Balebrand becomes infected and is marked with a brand marker.

Kossite Woodsmen may only come into play in the Khador deployment zone.

SET UP

Players take turns, each placing two (2) buildings anywhere on the table. Buildings can be up to 6" x 8". Buildings cannot be placed within 3" of another building or table edge. All buildings have ARM 15 and can take 5 points of damage per inch. Building doors have ARM 14 and can take 5 points of damage. See Damaging and Destroying Structures, WARMACHINE: Prime, pg. 62, for details.

See Damaging and Destroying Structures, WARMACHINE: Prime, pg. 62, for details.

THE BALEBRAND

The devious necromantic sigil known as the Balebrand can express itself only a few times in the life of its enchantment. Over weeks, the diabolical brand begins to lay doubts and thoughts in the mind of the carrier of its dark plague and wears away at his will with nightmares and terrifying visions. Once the proper conjunction occurs and Laris is close enough to extend her energies, the sigil can reactivate one last time. A mage with the proper training or a warcaster skilled in necromancy can easily command a single individual carrying the brand to manifest. However, if this brief window of opportunity passes, the sigil—an almost living enchantment—begins to fade, and the infected individual returns to normal, scarred only by the terrors of the ordeal and perhaps a bit worse for the wear.

Players then take turns, each placing one (1) additional terrain feature. Players cannot place terrain within 3" of a table edge or another terrain feature, including the buildings. Players can place terrain features on hills.

BEGINNING

At the start of the game, each player rolls a d6. The player who rolls highest chooses to go first or last. The player who rolls second highest then chooses to go first or last from among the remaining spots in the play order. The third highest roller does the same and so on until the lowest roller takes the final spot. The first player deploys in a 10" by 10" area in his choice of table corners. The other players then chose their table corners and deploy in the order of play.

VICTORY CONDITIONS AND RESOLUTION

In games with only two players, the Cryx player wins the game outright if 10 or more of his opponent's models in play are infected with the Balebrand at the end of his turn. In games with three or more players, the Cryx player wins the game outright if 5 or more models in play from each faction are infected with the Balebrand at the end of his turn.

If the Cryx player does not win outright, the player with the last warcaster in play wins the game. When a player loses his warcaster, his remaining models are routed—completely remove them from the table.

REWARDS

• **Warcaster Deployment:** The outcome of Balebrand determines the order players reveal their warcaster deployments for Fall's Blighted Harvest Act II. Beginning with the first player eliminated from the game and ending with the winner of the scenario, each player deploys one warcaster to each Fall's Blighted Harvest Act II scenario.

• **Gaining the Initiative:** The winning player pushes back his enemies and gets a +1 bonus on all Starting Rolls during Fall's Blighted Harvest Act II scenarios.

• **The Brand:** If the Cryx player wins the game by infecting enemy models with the Balebrand, the arcane contagion spreads far and wide before the end of fall. During the Fall's Blighted Harvest Act III scenario, the Harvest, each Cryx warcaster in play may take control of enemy models with the Balebrand instead of a single warcaster chosen by the Cryx player before the start of the game.

FALL'S BLIGHTED HARVEST ACT II

SCENARIO 2, SCORCHED EARTH

CRYX VS. CYGNAR, 1000 POINTS

Donard 3rd, Goloven 605 AR—At the onset of the harvest season, Cryxian forces begin targeting the very thing that keeps the nation vital: food.

Cryx is intent on destroying the now ripe crops of the Cygnaran folk in an attempt to create starving conditions for the coming winter. Not only will the mass starvation of entire towns and villages cripple Cygnar, but the dead will serve as more grist for the armies of Cryx. Moving methodically through the passes of the Dragonspine Peaks, Cryxian forces are destroying every farm, grain silo, and animal herd they encounter.

In an attempt to secure grain and resources for the military, a company has ridden hard from Point Bourne to garrison the outlying village of Murrow's Bluff west of Bainsmarket in order to fortify and protect its important grain silos. The troops' orders are simple: defend the grain.

The troops arrived before the Cryxians and set up heavy defenses, thus deterring a direct assault. The Cryxians have elected to attack at dawn before Cygnaran forces have a chance to change the guard. In the pre-dawn the nightmarish throng attacks, and the Cygnaran soldiers rush to their battle stations while the bulk of the company races to assemble gear and activate inert warjacks.

Special Rules

Place a grain silo in the center of the table. The Cygnar player then places two (2) additional silos anywhere on the same half of the table as his deployment zone. The grain silos are 2" in diameter and 6" high. Each grain silo has ARM 16 and can take 15 points of damage before being destroyed. The silos are full of grain and cannot be entered by models. See Damaging and Destroying Structures, WARMACHINE: Prime, page 62, for details.

The game goes into Hammertime at the end of round five. If the game ends before Cryxian forces destroy the last grain silo, Cygnaran reinforcements arrive and drive off the Cryxian attackers.

Set Up

Players take turns, each placing three (3) terrain features. Terrain features cannot be placed within 3" of another terrain feature, including grain silos. Terrain features may be placed on hills.

Beginning

At the start of the game, each player rolls a d6. The high roller chooses who goes first. The first player sets up in his deployment zone and takes the first turn. Players deploy their forces up to 10" from the table's edge.

Victory Conditions

Cryx wins when all three grain silos are destroyed.

Cygnar wins when either all Cryx warcasters have been destroyed or removed from play, or if a grain silo has not been destroyed by the time the game ends.

Rewards

• **Starvation**: If Cryx wins, Cygnar begins to suffer a dire shortage of food. Matters only get worse as the days grow shorter. Cryxian forces claim the starving dead across Cygnar and add them to their numbers. Once during any single Fall's Blighted Harvest scenario, the Cryx player may purchase a single Bane Thrall, Bile Thrall, or Mechanithrall unit for half normal point cost rounded up.

• **Food Stores**: If Cygnar wins, ample food stores will remain for the harsh winter. Wounded troops are fed well and recover more quickly. Once during any single Fall's Blighted Harvest scenario, the Cygnar player pays 10 points less for units.

SCENARIO 3, KREGOR ROCK

KHADOR VS. PROTECTORATE, 1000 POINTS

Gorim 5th, Goloven 605 AR—The facility at Kregor Rock is the Protectorate's major alchemical refinery. Here the Protectorate manufactures a vast quantity of Menoth's Fury, where workers mix the resinous oil with salts harvested from the Bloodstone Marches. This process changes the oil into a viscous and volatile fluid, and distilled into a thinner fluid, Menoth's Fury becomes the fuel for Repenter flamethrowers and Vanquisher Flame Belchers. Kregor Rock also manufactures Skyhammer propellant, rocket explosives, and firebombs favored by zealots.

The Khadoran military has decided to strike a crippling blow against the Menites by destroying Kregor Rock. Using a logistical flaw in the facility's design, the Khadorans intend to blow up the plant, for stacks venting volatile fumes are its major vulnerability. Protectorate troops have managed to respond just barely in time. Crews have attempted to shut the stack vents with remote cranks, but the residue on the closing mechanisms of the stacks have jammed them, so an emergency crew must shut them manually. If the Khadorans reach the smokestacks before them, a single incendiary device could potentially destroy the entire facility.

SPECIAL RULES

The Protectorate player places three (3) smokestacks outside his deployment zone up to 14" from the back table edge of his deployment zone. The smokestacks must be placed in a row at least 5" apart. The smokestacks are 2" in diameter and 3" high. Each stack has ARM 18 and can take 10 points of damage before being breached, but it will not collapse. See Damaging and Destroying Structures, WARMACHINE: Prime, pg. 62, for details.

All Khadoran warrior models carry satchel bombs that may be dropped down smokestacks once they have been breached. To drop a satchel bomb down a smokestack, a Khadoran warrior model must begin its activation in base contact with a breached smokestack and forfeit its activation to drop a charge down the shaft. If a Khador model successfully drops a charge down the smokestack, the Khador player wins.

The game goes into Hammertime at the end of round seven. If the game ends before a Khadoran warrior can drop a satchel charge down a breached smokestack, Protectorate forces shut down the refinery to keeping an explosion from occurring.

SET UP

Players take turns, each placing a single terrain feature due to the sparse terrain around Kregor Rock. Players should choose terrain features common to a desert setting and avoid such features as rivers and forests. Terrain features cannot be placed within 3" of another terrain feature, including the smoke stacks. Terrain features may be placed on hills.

BEGINNING

At the start of the game, each player rolls a d6. The high roller chooses who goes first. The first player sets up in his deployment zone and takes the first turn. Players deploy their forces up to 10" from the table's edge.

VICTORY CONDITIONS

Khador wins when a warrior drops a satchel charge down a breached smokestack.

The Protectorate wins if Khador has not won by the end of the game.

REWARDS

• **Secure Supply Lines:** If the Khador player wins, Khadoran supply lines will be open for the rest of the season. Once during any single Fall's Blighted Harvest scenario, the Khador player pays 10 points less for warjacks.

• **Refinery:** If the Protectorate player wins, the Kregor Rock facility continues to refine Menoth's Fury at full output. Once during any single Fall's Blighted Harvest scenario, the Protectorate player may purchase a single Deliverer, Flameguard Cleanser, or Temple Flameguard unit for half normal point cost rounded up.

SCENARIO 4, SEEKER

CRYX VS. PROTECTORATE, 1000 POINTS

Malleus 2nd, Doloven 605 AR—Thus far Cygnar has borne the brunt of the Cryxian incursion, but now Lord Toruk has turned His attentions to the Protectorate. With the advent of fall, the strength of Toruk's dark army has grown as has the boldness of His warcasters. Delving deep into the borders of the Protectorate in search of the Harbinger, the deathless army has made itself known. Targeting a shrine of Menoth, Cryxian forces hope to slaughter temple priests and drag them off for animation and questioning.

Unknown to Cryx, faithful Menites observe their movements and report back to Protectorate forces, so just before the assault begins in proper a garrison is dispatched to defend the shrine.

SPECIAL RULES

At the center of the board, place a 6" by 4" stone structure to represent the shrine. The shrine has one door large enough to accommodate medium-based models. The door has ARM 16 and can take 15 points of damage. The stone walls of the shrine have ARM 16 and can take 10 points of damage per inch. The shrine will collapse when 10" or more of its surface have been destroyed. See Damaging and Destroying Structures, WARMACHINE: Prime, pg. 62, for details.

Place three (3) models representing Menite priests inside the shrine. The priests are independent models under the control of the Protectorate player. Priests have the following stats:

SPD 6, STR 4, DEF 12, ARM 10, CMD 8

If the priests flee, they will run toward the shrine instead of the Protectorate table edge.

When a priest model is destroyed, mark the location of its body with a corpse token. Any Cryx model, except an Incorporeal model or a bonejack, may pick up a corpse token in base-to-base contact by forfeiting its action. Small-based models can pick up a single corpse token and move at half normal movement rate while carrying it. Models with medium or large bases can carry any number of corpse tokens without penalty. If a model carrying a corpse token is destroyed or removed from play, the corpse token remains in the place the model last occupied. A model can drop a corpse token at any time. Dropping a corpse token does not require an action. When dropped, the token is placed on the table in base contact with the model that dropped it.

SET UP

Players take turns, each placing three (3) additional terrain features. Players should choose terrain features common to a desert setting and avoid such features as rivers and forests. Terrain features cannot be placed within 3" of another terrain feature. Terrain features may be placed on hills.

BEGINNING

At the start of the game, each player rolls a d6 and the high roller chooses who goes first. The first player gets his choice of deployment zones and takes the first turn. Players deploy their forces up to 10" from the table's edge.

VICTORY CONDITIONS

Cryx wins if they can get one or more priest corpse tokens into their deployment zone.

The Protectorate wins once both Cryxian warcasters have been destroyed or removed from play.

REWARDS

• **Forensic Necromancy:** If Cryx wins, the priests are reanimated and tortured for information, providing insight not only into the Harbinger but also Protectorate troop movements. Cryxian forces are easily able to move even their largest helljacks unseen. Once during any single Fall's Blighted Harvest scenario, the Cryx player pays 10 points less for helljacks and 5 points less for bonejacks.

• **Vassals of Menoth:** If the Protectorate wins, Hierarch Voyle doubles the number of vassals servicing the warjacks of his victorious warcasters. Once during any single Fall's Blighted Harvest scenario, the Protectorate player pays 10 points less for warjacks.

SCENARIO 5, THE EXILES

KHADOR VS. CYGNAR, 1000 POINTS

Donard 6th, Doloven 605 AR—For months, desperate Llaelese fighters have led a savage guerilla war against the Khadoran occupation in spite of overwhelming odds. Hungry and low on ammunition, their ragtag bands have slowly fallen back across the Cygnaran border to regroup and rest. Sympathizers in numerous settlements have done what they can for the resistance leaders by treating their wounds and re-supplying their troops.

Khadoran forces have made it a point to make examples of such communities whenever they come across them. A Widowmaker squad was recently dispatched to pursue the ill-fated Lord Antonin di Rhys and his men to a safe house. They slaughtered most of the group and tracked a handful of wounded stragglers to an unassuming hamlet. The following day, the Widowmakers arrived with greater numbers and a will to level the entire village.

The game goes into Hammertime at the end of round six. If the game ends before the Khador player destroys or searches all five buildings, Cygnaran troops arrive in force and rout the Khadorans from the field.

As it happens, a large Cygnaran border garrison has set up a firebase nearby. Having detected the dull rhythm of mortar fire, a full company was deployed to investigate, but it will take time before they arrive in force. Most of their warjacks have not yet heated up to optimal fighting condition.

SPECIAL RULES

The Cygnar player begins by placing five (5) buildings within 12" of the center of the table. The buildings can be no larger than 4" x 6" and must be placed at least 3" apart. Each building must have at least one door large enough for a medium-based model. The doors of the buildings have ARM 16 and can take 8 points of damage each. The building walls have ARM 16 and can take 8 points of damage per inch. Each building will collapse when half of its surface in inches has been destroyed. See Damaging and Destroying Structures, WARMACHINE: Prime, pg. 62, for details.

Khador must search or destroy all five buildings. If Khadoran models Hold a building for one (1) round, it is considered searched and its inhabitants killed. To Hold a location, all models within the building must be controlled by the Khador player during his maintenance phase. Models that are engaged in melee combat cannot be used to Hold a building.

SET UP

Players take turns, each placing up to two (2) terrain features at least 3" from another terrain feature, including the buildings. Terrain features may be placed on hills.

BEGINNING

At the start of the game, each player rolls a d6 and the high roller chooses who goes first. The first player gets his choice of deployment zones and takes the first turn. Players deploy their forces up to 10" from the table's edge.

VICTORY CONDITIONS

Khador wins once all the buildings have been searched or destroyed.

Cygnar wins if either all Khadoran warcasters have been destroyed or removed from play, or if the scenario ends before Khadoran forces destroy or search all five buildings.

REWARDS

- **Replacements:** If Khador wins, the Khadoran High Kommand repays its victorious officers with fresh troops. Once during any single Fall's Blighted Harvest scenario, the Khador player pays 10 points less for units.

• **Guerilla Escort:** If Cygnar wins, the Llaelese guerillas keep Cygnaran supply lines clear of harassment. Once during any single Fall's Blighted Harvest scenario, the Cygnar player may purchase a single light warjack for half normal point cost rounded up.

SCENARIO 6, MIRED

KHADOR VS. CRYX, 1000 POINTS

Vendarl 5th, Khadoven 605 AR—With the increase of traffic along the Black River, Khador has had to employ increasing numbers of riverboats to ferry troops south in order to contest Cygnar's hold over the lands above Corvis. In many cases, Khadorans rely on the small channels and waterways that web through the marshes of Bloodsmeath in order to circumnavigate Cygnaran patrols and sentry towers.

One such expedition, a spearhead to establish a base within the marshes, recently ran upon unfortunate circumstances. The steamship's rudder and steering lines collapsed from being dragged along the shallow mire of the swampy channels, and the Khadorans were forced to slog through the swampy lowlands to meet a repair vessel on the banks of the Black River. A Juggernaut warjack was employed to haul a heavy assembly back to the ship, but on the way back to their vessel, the Khadorans encountered Cryxian thralls in the swamp. The sounds of battle rang out in the Bloodsmeath, and additional Cryxian forces were alerted and rushed to the area. Soon, the Juggernaut was mired in a marsh pit and the Khadorans had to fall back.

Now, the crucial component for their riverboat, not to mention an inert warjack, lies in the midst of a Cryxian position. With a limited amount of time to effect repairs and an unknown number of thralls and helljacks in the vicinity, the frazzled Khadorans must meet a deadline or completely abandon their efforts and set out for Ravensgard.

SPECIAL RULES

See map. Place a shallow water marsh pit approximately 8" in diameter in the middle of the table 10" from the north table edge bordering the Cryx deployment zone. See Shallow Water, WARMACHINE: Prime, pg. 61, for details.

Place a disabled Juggernaut model in the center of the marsh pit. The Juggernaut has been knocked down in the pit and the shallow water extinguished its furnace. The Khador player must assign the Juggernaut to the

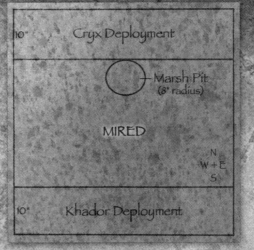

battle group of a Khadoran warcaster. If the warjack's furnace is restarted, the Juggernaut will join that warcaster's battlegroup. This warjack is in addition to the player's army point total.

Any friendly model in base-to-base contact with the Juggernaut may forfeit its action to restart its furnace. The Juggernaut cannot activate in the turn it is restarted.

The Juggernaut is holding the rudder assembly needed to repair the Khadoran steamship. Any warjack with a functional Open Fist in base-to-base contact with the Juggernaut may forfeit its action to pick up the rudder assembly. If a warjack carrying the rudder assembly is knocked down or disabled, the assembly remains at the warjack's last location. A warjack with a functional Open Fist in base contact with the assembly may forfeit its action to pick it up.

SET UP

Players take turns, each placing three (3) terrain features. Terrain features cannot be placed within 3" of another terrain feature, including the marsh pit.

BEGINNING

At the start of the game, each player rolls a d6 and the high roller chooses who goes first. The first player sets up and takes the first turn. Players deploy their forces up to 10" from the table's edge.

The Khador player takes the first turn.

VICTORY CONDITIONS

Khador wins if they get the rudder assembly into their deployment zone.

Cryx wins when all of Khador's warjacks with open fists have been totaled, or when both of the Khadoran warcasters have been destroyed or removed from play.

REWARDS

- **Gaining Ground:** The winner of the game pushes back his enemy's forces and may deploy his forces 4" further forward during the Fall's Blighted Harvest Act III scenario, The Harvest.

SCENARIO 7, TERMINAL POINT

CYGNAR VS. PROTECTORATE, 1000 POINTS

Donard 1st, Khadoven 605 AR—The impressive Marchbridge crosses a gap known as the Marchbank Ravine in the Upper Wyrmwall mountains. It is a major rail bridge that supports traffic between Fharin and Steelwater flats, and because of military activity it has become a significant link in terms of supply traffic between Corvis and Caspia. The bridge helps accelerate armed forces, goods, and other vital services such as mail, communiqués, and orders to and from Fharin, the waypoint between the two cities.

The Protectorate has decided to deliver a crippling blow to Caspia by destroying the Marchbridge. If successful, the Protectorate will also campaign along the rail line to destroy trains, raid the wrecks, and, of course, purify the survivors with flame. Massing at the Marchbridge, the Protectorate troops plan to sabotage the tracks along the line to make Marchbank Ravine impassable for rail traffic and derail transit attempting to cross. They do not know, however, that Cygnaran scouts have observed their troop movements. Just as the Protectorate forces arrive at the bridge, Cygnaran soldiers appear to engage them. Massing on opposite sides of the bridge the two forces square off, waiting to see who will make the first move.

SPECIAL RULES AND SET UP

See map. The huge ravine spans the entire table. A rail bridge 48" long and 12" wide runs north-south and spans the middle of the ravine. Any model falling off the bridge and into the ravine is removed from play.

The Protectorate player is attempting to destroy the bridge, but it was built to last and is able to take a massive amount of punishment. The bridge's weakest spot is its center where it is not as fortified. The only part of the bridge that may be damaged is a 12" x 12" area in the center. The bridge has ARM 18 and may be damaged by ranged attacks with POW 14 or greater and all melee attacks. AOE ranged attacks inflict full damage regardless of POW. Continuous effects do not affect the bridge.

Once the bridge suffers a total of 60 damage points, the bridge supports begin to wrench apart and create a 3" hole in the center of the bridge. A model completely within the area of the hole falls into the ravine and is removed from play. Any model falling through the hole is likewise removed from play. The bridge begins to collapse once it has suffered a total of 100 damage points.

When the bridge collapses, the Protectorate wins and both faction forces rush off the table to safety.

The game goes into Hammertime at the end of round seven. If the game ends before either faction has won the scenario, a train barrels across the bridge, all models still on the table are removed from play, and Cygnar wins.

BEGINNING

During this scenario, players do not deploy all their models at the start of the game. Instead, players deploy in waves as their forces make their way onto the bridge. At the start of the game, each player may place as many models on the table as he has room in his deployment zone. A player may deploy his models up to 3" from the rear of his table edge on the bridge.

During his maintenance phase, a player may put additional models in play provided he has room inside his deployment zone to accommodate them. All models in a unit must be placed at the same time.

Models with the Advance Deployment ability may use the ability normally at the start of the game. After the game starts, models with Advance Deployment must be placed on the table as described above.

A warcaster may not allocate focus until he is placed on the table.

The Protectorate player chooses a table edge and deploys his forces first.

The Protectorate player takes the first turn.

VICTORY CONDITIONS

Cygnar wins once both Protectorate warcasters have been destroyed or removed from play or if the scenario ends before the Protectorate wins.

The Protectorate wins if the Marchbridge collapses.

REWARDS

• **Gaining Ground:** The winner of the game pushes back his enemy and may deploy his forces 4" further forward during the Fall's Blighted Harvest Act III scenario, The Harvest.

FALL'S BLIGHTED HARVEST ACT II SIDE QUESTS

SEEDS OF DESTRUCTION, CRYX SIDE QUEST

ASPHYXIOUS THE IRON LICH

Having executed most of his vile plot Asphyxious the Iron Lich readies for his masterstroke, but first he must ensure that his theories about the Thornwood are correct. Within the deep and twisted wood, a dire and ancient Orgoth ruin stands as an anomalous merging of arcane rite and divine focus. The Umbral Cairn is a prison, an entropic snare for souls that has permeated the Thornwood preventing spirits that depart their physical form in the region from ever making their journey to the hereafter. The Orgoth ruin is most certainly why the Thornwood is such a warped, dangerous place.

Asphyxious intends to study the workings of the Umbral Cairn firsthand, and he requires victims for his experiment in the transference of soul energy. His theories about a perfect and incredibly powerful soul cage must be confirmed, after all, and by trapping living essence within the area of the Umbral Cairn, Asphyxious can put his presumptions to a true test. To quantify the different qualities of usage and storage of this vital energy, he is determined to discover how the Orgoth created the cairn.

Through his own significant network, he has managed to feed rumors of a dangerous Cygnaran effort within the Thornwood to act as a precursor to his trap. He intends to bait some nearby Khadoran troops—a heavily armed scouting party from the 5th Legion. When the Khadorans stumble upon the Orgoth ruins near the Umbral Cairn, Asphyxious intends to engage them in a game of cat and mouse. Little does he know that the Iosan mage hunter named Eiryss has been tracking him through the Thornwood for days, biding her time to attack at the most opportune moment. While Asphyxious positions the Khadorans where he needs them, Eiryss lurks amidst the ruins and stalks the hunter as he toys with his prey.

SOULS TORN FREE

Asphyxious marveled at the sight before him. Although the Orgoth ruin was beyond the perception of any mortal, his undead senses could detect the tangible aura of power within. The ornate altars and troughs set in a macabre arrangement formed a design familiar to the Iron Lich. Sacrifice and bloodletting were the purposes of this ruin. The altars were a place of slaughter designed to produce the reservoir of power Asphyxious sensed. The Orgoth were incredibly advanced in soul magic, and Asphyxious was impressed.

In the darkness of the night, this ruin in the Thornwood felt haunted and abandoned by the gods of Caen. Carved stones and leering faces stared emptily over a reservoir; perhaps it was some form of prison or cage. Asphyxious could see the ancient soul energies were weary from millennia of imprisonment.

Each glowing blue mote that floated in the night air was a single soul. At the edge of the reservoir was the potential for vast power, yet it was nearly empty. Only a few imprisoned souls were held fast, no doubt killed in some final moment by an Orgoth overlord making sacrifice. They orbited the ruin and drifted like errant stars.

If Asphyxious could have expressed his delight, he may have laughed aloud or yelled in exultation, but such sounds were distant memories to him now. Instead he growled in satisfaction. The purpose of the place was unclear; the mysteries of the Orgoth were lost even to one of his considerable knowledge. All he knew was that among every Orgoth site he had uncovered throughout western Immoren, this was unquestionably the largest.

Invisible to the human eye, the heart of the Umbral Cairn was a spherical area floating in space above the dais of the sacrificial altars. It was invisible to Asphyxious as well. He could only feel where it should be like a buzzing in his head, suspended somewhere above the vast black tablets of obsidian and slate.

The pillars with their leering faces, overgrown with centuries of ivy and flora, stared into the silence. The vines and flowers around Asphyxious' body, however, rotted and marked his spoiling presence with a stain. He approached

the pillars and the ivy wilted away as the thralls around him busily excavated, cutting rotten vines and plants loose and clearing away fallen debris.

The souls themselves attempted to drift away from the area only to be drawn towards it again, as if pulled back on some spectral leash. Their spiral pattern seemed to indicate that the pull was inconstant, but it never waned for long. The vital energies here could not escape the pull of the Umbral Cairn.

Asphyxious reached out and grasped a soul in his hand, willed it still, and forced it into a soul cage at his belt. Vapors of the soul's suffering drifted from the perforations of the cage like wicked incense. Asphyxious could sense the madness within the soul that would only make it more potent for his magic. He could utilize the energy around the ruin; he had tested that theory already. Now he would have to lure souls close enough to see the Umbral Cairn in action. How would it react to freshly drawn souls? Would it absorb them or simply draw them in? He must test it.

Adventurers in this wood were rare. With the war most of the living had taken to lying low and waiting for a victor to be declared, much like carrion birds waiting for a man to die. Luring that sort to the ruin would not be easy. The military however, in all its paranoia, could be drawn into such an intricate ambush if the right bait were dangled.

Asphyxious considered the strategy and necessary motions needed to set such a test into being. So delicately balanced were his ploys that if he emphasized too much danger a full-blown battalion might arrive. No. He needed subtlety and quiet. In the midst of the dark woods, sitting on a ruined stone where bloody victims once prayed for swift death, the Iron Lich began to think through the details of his experiment.

Yes. He required the living. He required victims…

CRYX ARMY COMPOSITION

Asphyxious the Iron Lich

1 Skarlock Thrall

KHADORAN ARMY COMPOSITION

1 Man-o-War unit with 1 Kapitan and 2 Troopers

1 Man of War Kovnik

2 Winter Guard units each with 1 Sergeant and 9 troopers

Eiryss, Mage Hunter of Ios

SPECIAL RULES

See the map. The Umbral Cairn is a low stone dais surrounded by six (6) carved obelisks and dominates the table. Place the stone dais, a low stone slab approximately 5" diameter, in the center of the table. Next, place the six obelisks 12" from the dais in a symmetrical pattern. Use the Deviation diagram to determine the proper alignment for the obelisks. The obelisks are approximately 1" in diameter and 3" high.

Any living model destroyed during play is replaced with a soul token. All soul tokens in play move 3" directly toward the dais during each player's maintenance phase. Remove any soul tokens from play that reach the dais.

After moving, the Iron Lich or Skarlock Thrall may collect any soul tokens within 2". Collected soul tokens are used in the same way as those trapped by the model's Soul Cage ability.

SET UP

No additional terrain is placed in this scenario.

BEGINNING

The Khador player deploys his forces within 10" of the north table edge.

The Cryx player then deploys his forces within 10" of the south table edge.

The Cryx player takes the first turn.

VICTORY CONDITIONS

Cryx wins if the Iron Lich and Skarlock Thrall can capture at least ten soul tokens during play.

Khador wins if the Iron Lich is destroyed or if the Iron Lich and Skarlock Thrall do not capture at least ten soul tokens during play.

If the Iron Lich is destroyed or removed from play, he may still be used in the Fall's Blighted Harvest Act III scenario, The Harvest, but the Cryx player must spend twice his normal point cost.

REWARDS

- **The Warding:** If Cryx wins, Asphyxious learns to manipulate the necrotic energies around the Umbral Cairn to create an impenetrable barrier around the dais. This arcane knowledge may be used during the Fall's Blighted Harvest Act III scenario, The Harvest. During his activation, if Asphyxious Holds the dais he may spend three soul tokens to use The Warding. Asphyxious may Hold the dais if he is the only model completely within the area of the dais during his maintenance phase. Asphyxious cannot Hold the dais while he is engaged in melee combat. After warding the dais, Asphyxious may not move off and no model may move onto the dais for any reason for one round. A model on the warded dais cannot be damaged in any way by models that are not also standing on the dais. While the dais is warded, Asphyxious may not make melee attacks against models not on the dais, but he may still cast spells normally.

HEART OF DARKNESS, CYGNAR SIDE QUEST

COMMANDER COLEMAN STRYKER

The tides of fortune have turned against the Cygnaran people, especially in the north where war has struck hardest. Cryxian raids and the summer drought followed by a harsh fall have limited the crops needed to survive the winter months. Food and fresh water have become scarce, and refugees both Cygnaran and Llaelese have been flooding into fortresses, supply stops, and the city of Corvis to receive stipends from the military.

Commander Coleman Stryker has set out from Fort Falk to check on the relief efforts in the north and ensure that refugees are supplied as they relocate southward. Khadoran forces, currently in the process of advancing their siege south, have come upon the flood of refugees, and their officers have decided to harass Corvis by taking advantage of the bedraggled civilians. Protectorate troops west of the Black River, however, have also witnessed the heathen refugee camps setting up south of Corvis and have decided to exploit the situation. They act quickly to descend on the camps in force. A Khadoran squad discovers the attack and, not wanting to lose the advantage in striking at Corvis, joins the fray and clashes with the Menites amidst the terrified civilians. Cleansers and zealots make no distinction between faithless heathens and viable military targets, and the bodies of innocent men, women, and children soon lay under the rubble of wrecked buildings, their blood staining the ground when Commander Stryker arrives. He only manages to save a handful of survivors from execution at enemy hands.

RUIN

Stryker clutched the reins, his knuckles white with despair and his head low over the mare's neck. He hated riding, but there was no faster way to reach the refugee camp south of Corvis. He rode fast, for news of an attack on the camp had come to him by signal lanterns at a guard station several leagues south of Corvis along the Black River.

The heavy morning mists made visibility difficult. Apparently during the night, a Protectorate detachment put the refugee camps to the torch. The blaze had attracted the attentions of patrolling Khadorans—damn them all!—who quickly moved to engage the Protectorate units.

Stryker could only imagine the ensuing fight had slowed the zealots' plans for the camp, but the report stated they could not last much past dawn. The warcaster kicked the flanks of his steed, urging it on to greater speed in spite of the mist and muddy conditions, and he hoped against hope that he was in time to lend whatever help he could. He hoped that Corvis may have seen the fires and sent some units to investigate. He hoped for anything and all things.

A great plume of smoke a quarter-league ahead filtered the first rays of dawn, choking them in the blackness of soot and casting a shadow over the landscape to the west. Stryker loosened the holster strap over his hand cannon then grasped the hilt of his blade, Quicksilver. Through his armored glove he could feel the vibration of the arcane accumulator as the sword hummed to life, ready for battle.

As he entered the fringes of the smoldering community, Stryker leapt from the back of the horse. He could clearly detect a change in temperature. The heat was rising, and embers pelted him in the face. Shouting came from his left where a pair of Winter Guard soldiers burst from clapboard shack—someone's home—carrying sacks and boxes. Pillage torn from the lives of innocents. "Put that down, you bastards!" Stryker bellowed.

The Khadoran soldiers suddenly stared at Stryker in disbelief, dropping their loads and reaching for their blunderbusses. Suddenly, a burst of flame from one side engulfed the men. A Menite cleanser had not yet seen Stryker and he afforded the warcaster a precious moment to close the gap between them as he continued spraying gouts of flame at the Winter Guard.

Stryker moved in and swept the cleanser's legs with the flat of his blade. The Menite landed with a resounding crack and the man's back arched unnaturally over the tank strapped to it. Stryker stomped the cleanser's firing wrist and *kicked the incinerator away, the flame snuffing out in the dirt. Then the warcaster ripped the helm from the Menite's head and placed Quicksilver's heavy edge across his throat. "How many of you are there?" Stryker demanded through clenched teeth. "How many Khadorans? Where are the people?"*

The cleanser looked up at Stryker, his face blackened by soot except for the rings around his eyes where his goggles had been. The eyes were light blue and they glared at Stryker with obvious hate. "Your heretic countrymen are dead, Cygnaran. Only those in the blasphemous church structure remain, and they too will fall. Menoth wills it!"

Stryker's rage grew and his grip tightened. The weight of the massive battle blade slid across the man's throat, ending his life, and blood spattered across the warcaster's armor. Lifting his head, he peered into the smoking ruins around him and discerned the charred corpses of the victimized civilians. Some were grown men and women; others were not.

He swallowed his nausea at the thought of these poor people. Tears welled in his eyes and mixed with clinging ash, dripping down to mingle with the blood of the Menite on his breastplate. Hatred was the price Cygnar paid for tolerance. Ruin was the price Cygnar paid for diplomacy. Destruction was the reward earned for sending aid to Llael when they should have fortified their own borders. Stryker had been wrong about many things.

The warcaster's face became grim, and he stoked his armor's furnace. Taking his pistol in his left hand and Quicksilver in his right, Stryker set out toward more figures rummaging in the gray haze and flickering flames. As he began to gather his focus, his teeth clenched with rage. It was much too late to right the wrongs done here, but the souls of the victimized would not go to Urcaen alone this day.

CYGNAR ARMY COMPOSITION

Commander Coleman Stryker

OPPOSING ARMY COMPOSITION

1 Winter Guard unit with 1 Sergeant and 5 Troopers

1 Widowmaker Kapitan model

1 Temple Flameguard Cleanser unit with 1 Arms Master and 5 Troopers

SPECIAL RULES

This scenario is played on a 3' x 3' table.

See map. Place a church of Morrow in the middle of the table bordering the north table edge. The church is a hearty wooden structure approximately 4" x 6". The surviving villagers have barricaded themselves inside and no model may enter it. The church has ARM 14 and can take 12 points of damage per inch. The church will collapse when 10" or more of its surface have been destroyed. See Damaging and Destroying Structures, WARMACHINE: Prime, pg. 62, for details.

The player controlling the opposition forces plays with both Khadoran and Protectorate models. These rival factions are not working together, but they are both in Stryker's warpath. The Temple Flameguard Cleansers are attempting to burn down the church while Khadorans set about capturing whatever is left of the village.

The opposition player wins if the church is destroyed.

SET UP

Players take turns, each placing two (2) terrain features. Players should choose terrain features common to a war-torn makeshift camp such as small wood buildings, tents, and ruins. Terrain features cannot be placed within 3" of another terrain feature, including the church. Terrain features may be placed on hills.

BEGINNING

The opposition player places his models first. The Temple Flameguard Cleansers may be placed anywhere within 5" of the Church of Morrow. The Winter Guard unit and Widowmaker Kapitan may be placed anywhere within 5" of the center of the table.

The Cygnar player may deploy Stryker anywhere within 10" of the south table edge.

Stryker takes the first turn.

VICTORY CONDITIONS

Cygnar wins when all enemy models have been destroyed or removed from play.

The opposition wins when either Stryker or the church is destroyed.

REWARDS

- **Steeled Vengeance:** If Cygnar wins, Stryker channels his rage and desperation into his attacks. For the rest of the Campaign, Stryker may boost both his attack and damage rolls by spending one focus point.

DEATH'S DOOR, KHADOR SIDE QUEST

VLADIMIR TZEPESCI

Vladimir Tzepesci was no stranger to the matters of the arcane. He had as deep an understanding of magic as any seasoned Greylord. When his talent for reading omens was triggered by a vast black cloud to the south, he realized something evil was about to take place.

Within the hour, a lone scout from the dark regions near the fringes of the Thornwood straggled into his encampment. Choking and gasping for air, with his dying breath the soldier spoke of Cryxian horrors and a deadly black cloud over the land near the Bloodroot battlefields. Legions of dead rested within the ancient sepulchers within those barrows. If Cryxian necromancers called upon the dead within, they might turn the dormant remains into countless thralls.

Vladimir guessed that the dark magic over the Bloodroots had mixed with the foul humors of the barrows, creating some form of necrotic miasma. As the vile cloud had increased in size so had Vladimir's sense of impending doom, and though the position held by his kompania was vital to the Khadoran effort, he knew he could not ignore the deadly black cloud.

The Dark Prince ordered his troops to withdraw and rejoin their forces in the north. During his contemplation of the storm, Vladimir realized he must stop whatever was transpiring. As the death cloud spread, he feared that the souls of his soldiers, as well as any of those who encountered the cloud, would be drawn into the Thornwood where something lurking within would grow stronger and more powerful with every victimized soul.

Standing alone before the spreading vapors, Prince Vladimir Tzepesci drew a final breath of fresh air and entered its murky banks. He knew he must do whatever needed done to cut off the source of energy powering this dark and deadly fog.

LAST WORDS

"Get them out of here!" Vladimir yelled, slapping a horse on the rump and sending it trotting. His men, stubborn and loyal to the end, had refused to leave. His words, as desperate as they were meaningful, could not impel these loyal fools away from here. "Your very souls are at risk!"

"My Lord, we stand beside you no matter what," stated one of the defiant and courageous soldiers, his face like slate.

Not only was his overwhelming sense of doom sending him into a near panic, but his soldiers also taxed his patience. He had no time for heroics, though he had to resort to some of his own. "You vould gladly give your soul to Cryx, then? You vould leave your vife and children nothing but a shambling corpse to call husband or father? Listen to your prince! I order you to report to Kommander Kratikoff at Khybreski! Regroup and inform her of vot has come to pass here." His voice grew grim, his visage even more so, and they slowly began to leave. The rage in Vlad's face was as tangible a threat as a drawn and bloody sword.

"Karlof! Come here." One of the soldiers, a man named Karlof Omirov, was a trusted adjutant and swordsman. He hurried over to his kommander.

"Yes, my Prince!" He snapped a quick and formal salute.

"This scroll. Ensure Lady Sorscha receives it." Vladimir handed the man an ornate tube made of ivory and gold. It was marked with the house of Umbrey and sealed with a light blue arcane sigil.

"Of course, my lord…" the man hesitated. "Should we not go with you?"

"No. You are to follow her orders as you would my own. She will guide you as I have in the past. Gather this group together and guard her dearly. There are hard choices ahead for her." The Prince hoped he would live to see Sorscha again. He was unsure what awaited him in the Thornwood.

"Tell her… Karlof, tell her I will see her again soon. Now, you must go as fast as you can. The cloud must not overtake you if I fail. If that happens there will be no one for you to serve except perhaps…" Vladimir peered in the distance at the ominous cloud, then looked again at Karlof. "…the Dragonfather."

With that, Prince Vladimir Tzepesci clapped the soldier on his shoulder. "Go."

The soldier saluted once more, turned on his heels, and departed the encampment.

Vladimir faced the oncoming mass of black vapor. Swiftly, he left the camp behind. He ran toward the rolling cloud faster than any man could hope to run. As his feet crossed the gap of distance in bounds and leaps, his fears wrestled with his courage. Within the darkness, a feeling of hatred incarnate awaited him. The Umbrean prince armored himself with the love he had for his men and for his country and, not least of all, with memories of a beloved woman as beautiful as a doll and as fierce as winter itself.

KHADOR ARMY COMPOSITION

Vladimir Tzepesci

CRYX ARMY COMPOSITION

6+ Bane Thrall Lieutenants

SPECIAL RULES

The Cryx player places five (5) markers anywhere on the table to represent the ancient tombs. Tomb markers are approximately 2" in diameter. Markers must be placed at least 5" from a table edge or another tomb marker.

Vladimir must seal all five tombs in order to keep his men safe from the necrotic cloud. On any turn Vladimir casts Blood of Kings, he can seal a tomb in base contact by forfeiting his action.

During each Cryx maintenance phase, the controlling player may place one Bane Thrall Lieutenant in play. The Bane Thrall Lieutenant must be placed within base contact of an open tomb marker. All Bane Thralls are considered to be independent models and are not required to maintain unit coherency.

Vladimir suffers a POW 12 damage roll at the end of each Khador turn from the effects of the noxious cloud.

All models on the battlefield have concealment from the noxious cloud.

SET UP

Players take turns, each placing two (2) terrain features. Terrain features cannot be placed within 3" of another terrain feature, including the tomb markers. Terrain features may be placed on hills.

BEGINNING

The Cryx player places one Bane Thrall Lieutenant in base contact with each tomb marker.

The Khador player then places Vladimir within 3" of any table edge.

The Khador player takes the first turn.

VICTORY CONDITIONS

Khador wins if Vladimir seals all five tombs.

Cryx wins if Vladimir is destroyed.

Regardless of which side wins, Vladimir Tzepesci disappears within the dark cloud and is not seen again. The Khador player may not field Vladimir during the rest of the Campaign.

REWARDS

• **Sacrifice**: If Khador wins, Vladimir sacrifices himself to interfere with Cryx's plans. As a result, Cryx warcasters cannot use the Balebrand to take control of Khadoran models in the Fall's Blighted Harvest Act III scenario, The Harvest.

DELIVERANCE, PROTECTORATE SIDE QUEST

THE HIGH RECLAIMER

The Knights Exemplar often perform clandestine missions for the good of the Protectorate, relying on a network of faithful that extends throughout Cygnar, Khador, and what was formerly the sovereign nation of Llael. During a mission to investigate Khadoran activity in the Thornwood, a group of knights have gone missing. This has caused much concern among the Protectorate's tactical warpriests. If exemplar knights have been taken, the Khadorans must have a great number of forces in the area.

The High Reclaimer sensed the passing of the missing knights but felt their souls held fast, caged at the edge of some boundary that would not release them. From within the depths of his monastic cloister, he detected their suffering and calls for aid. Only he could free them, for his vow of silence prevented him from voicing their dilemma.

The High Reclaimer took up his mace, Cremator, and headed north. Compelled by his visions, he delved into the depths of the haunted Thornwood, slaying the beasts that accosted him in the heavy woods and glades. Driven by his mission to reclaim souls at Menoth's behest, the High Reclaimer had no choice but to find the knights, return them to life, and take them to the Harbinger. Such was the nature of his vision.

RECLAMATION OF THE FAITHFUL

Cremator burned with Menoth's fury and so did the thrall at the Reclaimer's feet—yet another corpse smashed into burning flesh. The warcaster's iron mask ran thick with the ichor of his enemies; he had been in a constant state of battle since making his way into the woods. The massive man had spent hours fighting the forest, fighting the creatures within it, and now fighting these undead that lie in his path. Sweat and grime ran down the corded muscles of his arms and his mighty chest heaved with the breath of exertion. Stepping over the ruined corpse of the thrall, he moved toward the clearing ahead. The keening of many souls called out to him.

He entered a sudden clearing and took in a grisly sight. Souls floated in the air, and mounds of bodies were heaped all around him. Countless souls were held fast in this place, suffering from some force he could not sense. Within the clearing he could make out dolmens of obsidian—ruins from some tremendous age.

He spied a skarlock, a vile Cryxian servant of the damned, harvesting souls in the center of the dark ruin. Thralls suddenly erupted from all around and the High Reclaimer did not hesitate to charge them. He brought down Cremator in vast arcs, slamming and crushing undead bodies with magnificent force. Beyond the combat, the skarlock was motioning and gathering souls for some unknown purpose. The High Reclaimer crushed more thralls and moved toward the ruin, making his approach to gather the souls of the faithful trapped therein.

In his mind's eye, a vision unfolded. One of the exemplar knights had witnessed something that should not be. The

knight's words must reach the ears of the Harbinger. The High Reclaimer could not carry those words—his tongue was silenced by his own oath—so the knight must return to the lands of the faithful. The High Reclaimer would guide those souls back to safety, and they, in turn, would ensure he prevailed over this creature of darkness.

PROTECTORATE ARMY COMPOSITION

The High Reclaimer

1 Knights Exemplar unit

CRYX ARMY COMPOSITION

3 Skarlock Thralls

5+ Bane Thrall Lieutenants

SPECIAL RULES

See the map. The Umbral Cairn, a low stone dais surrounded by six (6) carved obelisks, dominates the table. Place the stone dais, a low stone slab approximately 5" diameter, in the center of the table. Next, place the six obelisks 12" from the dais in a symmetrical pattern. Use the deviation diagram to determine the proper alignment for the obelisks. The obelisks are approximately 1" in diameter and 3" high.

Models may not move onto or move off of the dais for any reason during the scenario. A model on the dais cannot be damaged in any way by models that are also not standing on the dais.

There are 16 soul tokens that move from the obelisks to the dais throughout the scenario. During each player's maintenance phase, roll a d6 to determine from which obelisk a soul token moves. When it enters play, the soul moves 3" from the obelisk directly toward the dais. All soul tokens already in play also move an additional 3" during each player's maintenance phase. Soul tokens that reach the dais are placed on it.

The High Reclaimer may reclaim a soul token if he ends his movement within 2" of it. The High Reclaimer may not reclaim soul tokens once they reach the dais. Collected soul tokens may not be replaced with focus points in this scenario. Instead, once the High Reclaimer has reclaimed six soul tokens, he may use his feat to put a Knights Exemplar unit into play anywhere within his control area. The knights may be placed on the dais when they are put into play.

Place the Skarlock Thrall Perfido and three soul tokens on the dais. During each of the Cryx player's turns, Perfido may remove one soul token from the dais to put a Bane Thrall Lieutenant into play. The Bane Thrall model must be placed within base contact of the dais, but may not be placed on the dais. Creating a Bane Thrall does not require an action.

Throughout the scenario, Skarlock Thralls may cast spells as if they were within Asphyxious' control area.

SET UP

No additional terrain is placed in this scenario.

BEGINNING

The Cryx player places the Skarlock Thrall Perfido on the dais and then places two (2) Skarlock Thralls within base contact of the dais, but not on it. The Bane Thralls do not begin the game in play.

The Protectorate player then places the High Reclaimer within 3" of any table edge. The Knights Exemplar unit does not begin the game in play.

The High Reclaimer takes the first turn.

VICTORY CONDITIONS

The Protectorate wins when Perfido is destroyed.

Cryx wins if the High Reclaimer fails to reclaim six soul tokens, or if he is destroyed.

REWARDS

• **Soul's Deliverance:** If the Protectorate wins, the High Reclaimer gains greater insight into the boundaries between Caen and Urcaen. For the rest of the campaign, anytime the High Reclaimer uses his feat, he rolls 4d6 instead of 2d6 and keeps the two highest dice rolled to determine the number of models returned to play.

FALL'S BLIGHTED HARVEST ACT III

SCENARIO 8, THE HARVEST

MULTIPLAYER GAME, 1000 POINTS

Vendarl 2nd, Ashtoven 605 AR—When it comes to destroying their enemies, Cryxians can be patient. Most of them are already dead, so they have time on their side. This is most evident in the ploys they have used to draw western Immoren into bloody conflict. Networks of spies, arcane enchantments, eldritch research, and dark magic all contribute to the same insidious purpose. The timing is right for a deadly battle. The Iron Lich Asphyxious controls the circumstances and the field, and he plans to make use of the Umbral Cairn in the Thornwood. Seeking to weaken the armies of the Iron Kingdoms, he has assembled a vast group of thralls, bonejacks, and helljacks ready for war. Relying on the best warcasters at his disposal, Asphyxious is ready to make his move. This shall not be the last battle, but it shall be a deciding one.

Cryx has woven an intricate web. With treacherous seeds planted by Deneghra's cautious agents, the plot takes root in the form of false leads intercepted by enemy intelligence. Khadorans learn that Cygnar plans to build a base in the Thornwood, and the Cygnarans hear that Khador plans to do the same. Compelled by this news, the Khadorans come seeking to bring the Cygnaran plot to heel under their mighty iron boots while, in turn, Cygnaran troops trudge with swords and storm glaives at the ready, eager to spoil Khador's plans. Protectorate forces have gathered here as well, the only ones moving forward with an inkling of what is at stake. Even though the Harbinger is not ready for battle, warcasters of Menite faith rush to enter the Thornwood and face the evil of the Iron Lich and his Umbral Cairn.

Unknown to all, the warring factions are not the only ones concerned with the wars and how they have progressed in the past months. Hidden sentinels within the Thornwood watch silently. They are observers to a struggle fought with flesh, steel, fire, and spell, and as these mysterious spectators witness the carnage, they too ready themselves for the conflict to come.

DARK WOODS

The already still forest went even more still, if such a thing were possible, as the Iron Lich Asphyxious approached his leading warwitch. He towered over her, and she could hear the necrotite hissing in his kettle-black furnace. Soul cages at his waist were stuffed with humming and hissing souls, and the Lich looked more dangerous than ever. His baleful skull face looked down at her with malevolent intelligence. She could understand why others found him so terrifying, but Deneghra met her mentor's gaze calmly.

"So, we sit here, deep in the lands of our enemies… for what purpose?" Her voice carried the edges of inquisition. Hers was the cold analytical voice of a woman seeking truth behind reasons. She had used her own spy network at his behest to lure their enemies into the wood, but he had not fully explained why.

"Thou art here to witness a gift left behind by the ancient enemies of our adversaries. Thou art here to see it twisted to our own will." Cryptic as ever, but something in his dread voice betrayed an emotion that sounded much to her like anticipation. She must have been imagining it. The Iron Lich's mechanikal heart had no place for such things. "Thou must follow me to yon clearing ahead."

Deneghra became more surprised with Asphyxious' tone. It was unusual for him to speak so quickly and concisely. He had a destination in mind, and as they made their way through the warped wood, Deneghra contemplated. Obviously whatever was ahead was of great import. The effort Asphyxious had expelled to conceal their passage to the Thornwood spoke of much caution. The Iron Lich had plans in motion, plans that had taken him many years—decades in fact—to bring to completion, and she had a feeling something essential was set to unfold.

The dark pair entered the clearing where thickets gave way to an old path of broken stone. Along the path at the center of the clearing, a massive collection of black obsidian obelisks displayed deeply carved Orgoth runes. The standing stones were arranged at the points of a hexagram and in the center, a dais of smooth black stone bore more Orgoth sigils. Deneghra immediately felt the power resonating in this place. Then, with her witch eyes, she saw even more: captive souls flitted through the air as tiny wisps of desperate light.

"In this place, I sense Orgoth magic… powerful as the day it was cast. Altars of sacrifice… and these stones, the sigils…" Her voice trailed off and she looked at Asphyxious. "It is a massive soul cage! An Umbral Cairn!"

The Iron Lich's skull face seemed to grin. "Thine knowledge in such matters pleases me, my warwitch. These dolmens, carved from ensorcelled basalt, are an anchoring point."

The lich gestured toward the simple construction, with one massive iron gauntlet. "Thou art correct. 'Tis a cage, but on a much grander scale." He began moving toward the construction and beckoned her to follow.

"You are using this to harvest and store souls?" Deneghra measured the concept in her mind. Why would he gather souls in a place where focusing them in an arcane device would be laborious and mind numbing? Even as she watched a skarlock gathered souls in a cage, but the process was inefficient. Why bother with this when they could simply gather the souls in the battlefield? A smile crept across Deneghra's face when she suddenly worked it out and realized the full extent of the Lich's plan.

Asphyxious chuckled; it was the gurgle of a hanging man. "I doth see the wheels turning in thine beautiful skull, my warwitch. Thou hast discerned the nature of my plan. Thou art an apt pupil."

He made for the center of the monument, and Deneghra walked at his side. She observed that all around them, thralls toiled and labored to increase the size of the clearing. The area was expanding. They could erect a camp—no, an entire town—around this ruin! No one would know until it was too late. Asphyxious was building a staging area.

"As the armies fall, we shall leadeth our forces south. The nations of western Immoren are no longer a threat. Shaken and fraught with war, they art blind to the true threat amongst them. They are but sheep."

"Does Lord Toruk know of this place?" Deneghra asked.

"Lord Toruk must only hear of victory. Nothing more."

The war witch nodded.

"With this cairn, the energies released by the deaths of our enemies shall be caged. Unlimited power. With it, we will harvest and control even the mightiest souls." Asphyxious made a broad gesture with his hands, expanding them outward. Dozens of souls flew to him, passed through his body, and swirled about his form. The Iron Lich rose on shadowy wings above the ruin, and the blue motes that teemed around him suddenly shifted in color to a dark, bloody red. They were pulled into his soul cages, and he swayed in flight, his skull face beaming down.

Deneghra smiled wickedly. She was honored. Sharing his plan with her showed an uncommon trust. Asphyxious was not merely talking about the simple collection of wayward souls. No, he was after much more than that. No mortal soul of a man or woman or even the potent soul of a warcaster would do.

Asphyxious wanted something more. He wanted the Harbinger.

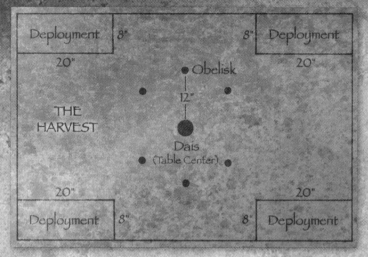

SPECIAL RULES

See the map. This game is played on a 4' x 6' table.

The Umbral Cairn is a low stone dais surrounded by six carved obelisks and dominates the middle of the table. Place the stone dais, a low stone slab approximately 3" in diameter, in the center of the table. The dais does not provide cover or hinder movement in any way. Next place the six obelisks 12" from the dais in a symmetrical pattern. Use the Deviation diagram to determine the proper alignment for the obelisks. The obelisks are approximately 1" in diameter and 3" high. Neither the obelisks nor the dais may be damaged during this scenario.

Place a soul token on the dais anytime a living model is destroyed whose base is at least partially within the area of the obelisks, and his soul token is not claimed by another model.

A Cryx warcaster within the area of the dais may remove any number of soul tokens from the dais during the model's activation. During the Cryx player's next control phase, replace each soul token with a focus point.

A Cryx warcaster within the area of the dais may also channel spells through the obelisks. The range of a spell channeled through the obelisks is doubled.

During The Harvest scenario, the Cryx player may utilize the Balebrand spread in Fall's Bitter Harvest Act I. At the start of the game, the Cryx player nominates a single warcaster who will be able to utilize the Balebrand throughout the game. If the Cryx player won the Act I scenario by infecting enemy models with the Balebrand, both Cryx warcasters can utilize the Balebrand.

A Cryx warcaster capable of utilizing the Balebrand may, for one round, take control of one enemy unit or solo within his control area during his activation. The same unit or solo may not be controlled by the Balebrand for two consecutive rounds. The Balebrand may not be used on character units or character solos.

If Vladimir Tzepesci succeeded in his sidequest, the Cryx player may not utilize the Balebrand to take control of the Khador player's models.

The Cryx player must use the Iron Lich Asphyxious in this scenario. If Asphyxious was destroyed or removed from play during his Fall Side Quest, the Cryx player must pay double the point cost to use him in this scenario.

Kossite Woodsmen may only come into play in the Khador deployment zone.

SET UP

Players take turns, each placing two (2) terrain features. Terrain features cannot be placed within the area of the Umbral Cairn or within 3" of another terrain feature, including the obelisks.

BEGINNING

At the start of the game, each player rolls a d6. The player who rolls highest chooses to go first or last. The player who rolls second highest then chooses to go first or last from among the remaining spots in the play order. The third highest roller does the same and so on until the lowest roller takes the final spot. Each player deploys in an 8" by 20" area in one corner of the table.

VICTORY CONDITIONS

The player with the last warcaster in play wins the game.

REWARDS

Victory: After a year of seemingly endless conflict, the winning player has emerged victoriuos from the first great battle of the war. Though this is a day for celebration, the festivities will be short-lived. Across the Kingdom the march of great armies heralds a new age of bloodshed. Peace is a fading memory.

EPILOGUE

Two of King Leto's elite Stormguard stand to either side of the elaborately sculpted double doors of the Royal Assembly Hall, their charged mechanikal halberds held crossed in front of the doors, and their blue-enameled armor reflecting the light of the braziers. The familiar but tattered figure of Coleman Stryker approaches. As he nears, the guards snap their heels to attention and retract their weapons. The doors open from within, and the battle-weary commander, still caked with the blood-soaked grime of a dozen consecutive battles, walks into the chamber, his heavy footfalls echoing with the weight of his demeanor.

At the far end of the long hall, King Leto Raelthorne, the Younger, sits in his throne of office, several steps above the main floor on a dais of white rose marble. To the king's right stands the General of the Crown, Olson Turpin, second only to the king in command of Cygnar's armed forces. To the king's left stands an older man who seems illuminated with a divinity from within, the Primarch Arius of the Church of Morrow; but even the presence of Leto's warmaster general and his lifelong friend and mentor, the Primarch, cannot dispel the look of consternation upon his face as one of Cygnar's most famed warcasters closes the long space between them.

At the foot of the dais, a dozen advisors representing as many interests—from commerce and trade to arcane research and development—have gathered, as well. They part as the grim Stryker comes near. He stops at the foot of the dais and draws his blade, Quicksilver, then drops to one knee in formal genuflection. "Your Majesty. Holy Father," the warcaster speaks the words levelly and without emotion. "My lords."

Before any of them can return the greeting, Stryker stands, hoists his battleblade, and flings it at the feet of the throne. The king and warmaster general both start as the heavy sword clangs upon the stone steps, shattering the air of formality like a hammer upon a crystal vase and stopping every person in the hall in frozen silence. Only the Primarch does not show surprise, for the man seems to nearly always expect all things as if the ascendants themselves attend and whisper in his ear—and perhaps they do.

Stryker fixes his gaze on King Leto. The two men have grown close over the years, but such flagrant abandonment of etiquette is staggering. Letos' posture stiffens, but he places a restraining hand on General Turpin, whose flushed expression has foretold his response. The warcaster has never been so contumacious, and the king, for the sake of their personal relationship, is willing to hear him out.

"My lord king…" the words strain to come out of Stryker's mouth. "I am a warrior. A knight of Cygnar. I have sworn to protect this land, its people, and its king from any threat, may my life be forfeit in the cause. I have taken an oath to preserve honor in battle, to act with humaneness, even in warfare. The Primarch has taught us that all men are beloved by Morrow, and deserve to be treated with compassion and mercy be they brother or enemy."

"But I now *know* our enemies, my king, better than I should ever care to." Still paralyzed, the members of the Royal Assembly scarcely take a breath as the warcaster's eyes become moist. Stryker pauses and tears suddenly stream freely down his cheeks, creating rivulets on his battle-stained face. "No amount of description can convey the most remote idea of the hardships I've seen. I have witnessed horrible things that I will never forget as long as I live. Such… such utter disregard for human life! I have observed such greed and hatred… such willingness to destroy everything before them in their own self-serving goals.

"We are alone, my king. Surrounded on all sides by the jackals of this world. They will stop at nothing… until they have gorged on our flesh. We are trapped between imperialism, intolerance, and unbridled evil! We have been too kind… and it is too late to reinforce our borders. They have crumbled. Our enemies are well past our doorsteps. They have burned and pillaged our homes. They have rent families apart. They have despoiled our churches.

"This war has only begun, my king… and it will only end with our fall. Cygnar is doomed. *We* are doomed—" Upon hearing this, the members of the Royal Assembly begin to buzz with words sotto voce and heated grumblings. They shift about uncomfortably, some of them imparting the warcaster with hard looks, others appearing fearful to hear such a sinister proclamation from one of their national heroes.

Stryker looks at them and continues. "Doomed for our arrogance! We all thought our way of life was embraced. We all believed humanity was valued beyond our borders. We felt safe in our noble regard and just treatment of those outside our realm. We were wrong! So very wrong…"

The warcaster looks once again at the men upon the dais, his blood and soot-stained countenance imparting them with his remorse, and says, "I can

no longer uphold the code of the Knights of Cygnar. I can no longer honor Morrow with compassion toward all men. Should I take up the sword again, it shall be for feelings other than patriotism or duty; my only true purpose shall be to mete out unremitting vengeance, and that blade shall be ever stained with the blood of our enemies until such time there is not a soul—not one!—left on all of Immoren to threaten the people of this kingdom or pollute its soil with their footsteps!

"So, before this assembly, I must resign my station as a commander of the Royal Cygnaran Army, lest what I have said be your wish, my king, as well."

Somewhere in the belly of a cold, dimly lit cave, a broken warrior lays face down, unmoving on a makeshift pallet of leaves and straw. Infected scars cover his back, a lattice of black wounds, and his broken limbs are arranged in unnatural positions. The air is heavy with the stench of strong unguents. Candlelight flickers ominously in the juts and hollows, and battered pieces of ancient red armor, a now-worthless heirloom of a bloodline heritage as long as the Iron Kingdoms are old, are strewn about the cavern.

Beside the broken warrior, a cloaked figure hunches, making poultices by dipping strips of cloth in clay bowls and whispering in a tongue not heard in Immoren for hundreds of years. Metal claws, each the length of an assassin's dagger, protrude from the stooped stranger's covered mass, delicately peeling soaked strips of bloodied cloth from the warrior's body and replacing them with unguent-slathered bandages.

"Rest now, *moy dorogoy...*" the dark figure's voice rasps softly to the unfeeling, unhearing warrior. "Take your sleep. The Old One vatches over you now. Vee shall repair the damage and vait, my child. The Motherland is not yet ready to face her doom...."

In the Menite holy see known as the Sovereign Temple of the One Faith in Imer, a massive leaded-glass, bevel-cut window shaped in the image of the Holy Menofix filters the first rays of dawn into the massive Ordinance Chamber. The light breaks low off the eastern horizon, casting a long shadow upon the gilded tile floor, and the shadow's size contrasts with the small form that casts it.

She turns toward the light in the great ornamental window, just a wisp of a girl, her body pirouetting slowly, toes never touching the ground. "Every day is a new opportunity to serve the will of Menoth, Hierarch."

"May he be pleased with our work," responds Garrick Voyle, looking up from the stillness of the sanctuary. He sits at a lectern, a quill in hand. He has been endorsing various holy writs to be carried out this day to further the splendor that is Menoth, but becomes taken with the vision of the girl hovering five full spans in the air. With the dust-speckled rays of light behind her, she is little more than a silhouette, but with a glorious aureole of light about her form which calls to mind Visgoth Var Bodalin's cherished tapestry, Niemiec's "Corona."

Voyle sees that she has turned to face him in spite of her blindfold. A radiant smile dances upon her lips. "Indeed, to die in his name," she says, "is a great honor, but to claim victory in his name is to truly be exalted."

She speaks with a wisdom beyond her years, something that both pleases and unsettles the Hierarch. "The Menite faithful have done well," she continues. "The crusade to restore the glory of Menoth is well underway..."

The girl pauses for a moment, raising her blindfolded face once more to the light, her body arching weightlessly, outlined in a nimbus of light. The Hierarch is acquainted with this sudden rigidity of her form, the gentle lift of her body, and knows she is in thrall to a divine interaction. It is a direct connection with the Shaper of Man, or so she claims, and Garrick Voyle has no cause to doubt.

"He is pleased," he hears her whisper. "Very... very pleased."

The tattered black sails trap the wind like the outspread wings of a raven, propelling the charred blackship the *Widower* down the Dying Strands at speed. Its hold is laden with the spoils of war, although it is a bounty that only those of Cryx can really appreciate: bodies of fallen men stacked like cordwood fifty high from bow to stern.

At the black galleon's helm, the Pirate Queen of the Broken Coast stares across the water, lost in contemplation. Lord Toruk's plan was unfolding, and the results of hundreds of years of strategic plotting were nearly within his mighty grasping talons. The chaos of war wracked the human kingdoms, and every battle fought between them was a victory for Cryx.

And yet, the satyxis witch was unsettled. A web of schemes had revealed itself to her, the design not yet understood, but the goal becoming ever more clear. Asphyxious the Iron Lich had discovered a source of great power—possibly infinite power— and he did not intend to share this revelation with the Dragonfather.

Such hubris in that steaming, glowering skull! Perhaps the great wyrm would reward her when *she* shared the lich's revelation.

Skarre smiles a wicked smile, and then giggles and sighs in one; but the giggle dominates the sigh, for the Pirate Queen had decided what new course she would take. "Helm!" she bawled.

"Aye?" came the reply from the ship's horned steerswoman.

"Plot a new course! Make for the Dragon's Roost!"

gained much ground—most of Llael was occupied, and all in all, in spite of the losses that came along with the costly victories, in spite of Protectorate forces offering unexpected opposition and Cryxian horrors uprearing their ghastly, decaying craniums, it had been a good year.

For the moment, Khador rests. This year, winter will be their shield rather than their spear, protecting them from retaliation by their lessers. Ranks shall be rebuilt, machines repaired and, come spring, the Motherland will be prepared to continue their pursuit of a manifest destiny to rule all of western Immoren.

Irusk reclines in his chair and glances through the semi-translucent glass of his suite window. He can see the shadows of snowflakes drifting on the wind. "It *was* a good year," the kommandant says, reflecting on his trials and successes.

He then sets aside the parchments in favor of tipping the vyatka to his lips. He reposes a few moments more, staring out the window and thinking private things while he drains the glass of its intoxicating contents, and then stands and withdraws to his bedchamber. Servants have already thawed the room with a low fire burning in the hearth, and turned down the layers of his large bed. The warmth beckons.

Time for the bear to retire to his cave, thinks the renowned Kommandant Irusk, and he prepares to sleep for several long, well-earned hours.

Irusk sits at a large desk in his chambers overlooking the Gate of Warvotsk and the imposing towers of the Queen's Palace beyond. He is once again behind the walls of the greatest capital in the world, mighty Korsk. He has dismissed his retinue and, for what seems like the first time in a year, he is alone, dry, clean, and unencumbered by steam-chugging warcaster armor.

The long-faced kommandant pours some of Khador's best *vyatka* in a glass, then pores over reams of reports, mostly scouting observations and loss assessments—men and equipment expended these past twelve months in Queen Ayn's bid for a renewed empire. Thousands of lives sacrificed, a fortune in warmachines, equipment, supplies, and ammunition exhausted. But the Motherland has

Dusk falls over the twisted canopy of the Thornwood. Beneath its autumnal leaves, a trio of shadowy figures stands at the edge of an open field littered with the broken remains of four nations. Mountains of wrecked machinery litter the stained ground still reeking of death. The smoke and fire has gone, but the wounded earth scorched by weapons both man-made and arcane clearly narrates the tale. For those with adept vision—such as the trio of grim-faced observers—disoriented souls can still be seen fluttering in the twisted boughs of the haunted wood, struggling against the binding gravity of the terrible Orgoth creation reincarnated by the meddlesome Cryxian warcasters.

"Brothers," one of the figures speaks in a voice both melodic and bestial at the same time. "Our time draws near. The days of humans will soon be finished. When the beasts emerge from their winter sleep to hunt again, so, too, shall we."

From his vantage atop the northernmost peak of Caerlyss Craig, a scowling warcaster peers across the Greybranch Gap, barely discerning the dim lights of that hovel of a border town called Ternon Crag. Winded from a lengthy hike, the grizzled warrior reaches across his body with his left hand, to massage a cramp from his lame leg held fast in a brace of steel.

Looking across the expanse to the east, he is pleased by the clarity of the air. Winter's thunderheads were beginning to make their trek in from Meredius to the west, but the Marches remained untouched by the changing of the seasons.

Perfect, the traitor thinks, as he loads a flare round into a short musket. He aims and pulls the trigger. The gun's report reverberates down through the gap and a sparkling missile flies skyward, exploding in a shower of fire high overhead.

They will see the signal... and then he will come.

CAMPAIGN RECORD SHEET

PLAYER [_____]   FACTION [_____]   SEASON [_____]

ACT I

WARCASTER [_____]   VICTORY   YES/NO   ACT II DEPLOYMENT ORDER [___]

REWARDS [_____]

ACT II

SCENARIO			
DEPLOYED WARCASTER			
SECOND WARCASTER			
VICTORY	YES/NO	YES/NO	YES/NO
VICTORY POINTS			
SURVIVAL POINTS			
FINAL RESULT	YES/NO	YES/NO	YES/NO
REWARDS			

TOTAL VICTORY POINTS [_____]   TOTAL SURVIVAL POINTS [_____]

ACT II WARCASTER SIDE QUEST

WARCASTER [_____]   VICTORY   YES/NO   CASUALTY   YES/NO

REWARDS [_____]

ACT III

WARCASTERS [_____]   VICTORY   YES/NO

REWARDS [_____]

All Quiet (pg. 183): If Cygnar wins, Cryxian forces scale back their attacks and watch the coast, allowing Cygnar time to build up its defenses. Once during any single Wrath of Summer's Heat scenario, the Cygnar player pays 10 points less warjacks.

Arcane Coils (pg. 154): Nemo also discovers arcane coils that may be used to supercharge his electrical powers for a short time. Once during any single scenario in which Nemo is used, the Cygnar player may activate the coils. The player must declare use of the coils before the start of the game. For the duration of the game, Nemo gains +1 POW on all Lightning Rod, Electrical Burst, Ball Lightning, Chain Lightning, and Elecritical Storm damage rolls.

Arms Cache (pg.163): If the Protectorate player wins, the Menoth's Fury is moved to a new hiding spot and saved for a later battle. Once during any single Storms of Spring scenario, the Protectorate player may purchase a single Deliverer, Flameguard Cleanser, or Temple Flameguard unit for half normal point cost rounded up.

Battle Plans (pg. 164): If the Khador player wins the game, the plans prove valuable to the continuing war effort. Once during any single Storms of Spring scenario, he may place all the terrain detailed in the text of the scenario. The terrain must be placed legally.

Battle Ready (pg. 168): The winner of the game escapes in fit fighting condition and may deploy his forces 4" further forward during the Storms of Spring Act III scenario, Death in the Deepwood.

Border Control (pg. 177): After seizing control of Deepwood Tower, the winning player gains a foothold in the Thornwood and is able to move men and supplies across the Cygnar-Khador border with ease for the time being. The winner may add up to 25 points to the size of his army in the Wrath of Summer's Heat Act I scenario, the Wrath of Menoth.

The Brand (pg. 198): If the Cryx player wins the game by infecting enemy models with the Balebrand, the arcane contagion spreads far and wide before the end of fall. During the Fall's Blighted Harvest Act III scenario, the Harvest, each Cryx warcaster in play may take control of enemy models with the Balebrand instead of a single warcaster chosen by the Cryx player before the start of the game.

Captured Ships (pg. 144): If the Khador player wins the game, the merchant ships are captured and the Cygnaran supplies are commandeered by Khadoran forces. Once during any single Icy Grip of Winter scenario, the Khador player pays 10 points less for warjacks and Man-O-War units.

Commendation (pg. 149): If Khador wins the scenario, his forces receive additional troops as a commendation for success on the mission. During the Icy Grip of Winter Act III scenario, The Ruins of Riversmet, the Khador player may purchase a single Iron Fang Pikeman, Kossite Woodsman, or Winter Guard unit for half the normal point cost rounded up.

Death Omens (pg. 189): If Skarre wins, her prophetic talents grow more powerful. For the rest of the Campaign, Skarre may make a special action to remove a friendly warrior model within 1" from play, divining her future in his innards. After using Death Omens, Skarre suffers no damage or effects from the next attack that hits her that round, after which Death Omens expires.

Disciples (pg. 157): If the Protectorate player wins, word of Kreoss' selfless defense of the Llaelese Menites circulates far and wide and his fame begins to grow to legendary proportions. For the rest of the Campaign, any time Kreoss is used in a scenario the Protectorate player gains an additional Holy Zealot unit made up of a Priest and 5 Troopers representing Kreoss' faithful disciples.

Divine Example (pg.176): If the Protectorate player wins, Feora becomes an example of excellence for all Menites to follow as stories of her deeds circulate throughout the Protectorate's armies. For the rest of the Campaign, all troop models within Feora's command range gain +1 to attack rolls. Additionally, in games Feora is used, all friendly models gain +2 movement on their first activation of the game.

The Elixir (pg. 159): Win or lose the player whose model carries the elixir at the end of the game keeps it. If no model was carrying the elixir at the end of the game, nobody gets it. The elixir can be used once during any single Campaign scenario. The player must declare its use before the start of the game and assign it to a faction warcaster. Whether or not the elixir is used during the scenario, it cannot be used again. It may be used once during the game during the warcaster's activation. When used, the warcaster's power field is completely regenerated and all damage points sustained by the warcaster are removed.

Fit Condition (pg. 159): After seizing control of the coal vault, the winner's forces remain in fighting condition throughout the winter. The winner may add up to 25 points to the size of his army in the Storms of Spring Act I scenario, the Battle for Aliston Yard.

Food Stores (pg. 199): If Cygnar wins, ample food stores will remain for the harsh winter. Wounded troops are fed well and recover more quickly. Once during any single Fall's Blighted Harvest scenario, the Cygnar player pays 10 points less for units.

Forensic Necromancy (pg. 201): If Cryx wins, the priests are reanimated and tortured for information, providing insight not only into the Harbinger but also Protectorate troop movements. Cryxian forces are easily able to move even their largest helljacks unseen. Once during any single Fall's Blighted Harvest scenario, the Cryx player pays 10 points less for helljacks and 5 points less for bonejacks.

Freed Prisoners (pg. 165): If the Cygnar player wins the game, the Cryxian death camp is demolished. Additional prisoners are located in the surrounding area and soon many are able to return to active service. Once during any single Storms of Spring scenario, the Cygnar player may purchase a single Long Gunner, Sword Knight, or Trencher unit for half normal point cost rounded up.

Fresh Meat (pg. 164): Win or lose, the dead carried off by the Cryxian forces provide fresh meat for the Dragon's charnel army. Once during any single Storms of Spring scenario, the Cryx player may add 10 additional points to the size of his army for every corpse token carried into the Cryx deployment zone. Additional points must be spent on the same scenario and cannot be split between scenarios.

Fresh Supplies (pg. 148): Win or lose the Cygnar player gains additional army points for each warjack that leaves the table through the Escape Edge. Once during any single Icy Grip of Winter scenario, the Cygnar player gains 10 additional army points for each heavy warjack and 5 additional army points for each light warjack that exits the table. Additional points must be spent on the same scenario and cannot be split between scenarios.

Fuel Depot (pg. 163): If the Cygnar player wins, the Menites are driven off and the site is converted into a supply and fueling depot. Once during any single Storms of Spring scenario, the Cygnar player pays 10 points less for his warjacks.

Gaining Ground (pg. 204,205): The winner of the game pushes back his enemy's forces and may deploy his forces 4" further forward during the Fall's Blighted Harvest Act III scenario, The Harvest.

Gaining the Initiative (pg. 142, 161, 179, 198): The winning gets a +1 bonus on all Starting Rolls during all Act II scenarios of the season.

Guerilla Escort (pg. 203): If Cygnar wins, the Llaelese guerillas keep Cygnaran supply lines clear of harassment. Once during any single Fall's Blighted Harvest scenario, the Cygnar player may purchase a single light warjack for half normal point cost rounded up.

Hardened Supply Lines (pg. 181): If Khador wins, the Menites are driven back allowing Khador to harden its supply lines against future attacks. Khador can then rush more parts and fuel to the front free of harassment. Once during any single Wrath of Summer's Heat scenario, the Khador player pays 10 points less for his warjacks.

Held Territory (pg. 167): The winner of the game seizes control of the territory and may deploy his forces 4" further forward once during the Storms of Spring Act III scenario, Death in the Deepwood.

Infamy (pg. 174): If Khador wins the game, the Butcher gathers the heads of the slaughtered pilgrims and sends them down the river on a barge bound for the Protectorate as a warning to those who would betray the Motherland. In the coming days, the Butcher's reputation reaches new heights of infamy. In any game the Butcher is used, all enemy models suffer ñ1 CMD.

Inspiration (pg. 192): If Khador wins, Sorscha completes her tutelage under Vladimir and becomes one of Khador's greatest leaders. An inspiration to the soldiers under her command, Sorscha grants +2 MAT and an additional melee attack to any friendly Khador trooper or solo that ends its charge movement within Sorscha's command range in a turn Sorscha charged.

Liberated Supplies (pg. 148): Win or lose the Protectorate player gains 10 additional army points for each Cygnaran heavy warjack and 5 additional army points for each Cygnaran light

warjack that ends the game disabled, wrecked, or inert. The additional points may be used once during any single Icy Grip of Winter scenario. Additional points must be spent on the same scenario and cannot be split between scenarios.

Mined Necrotite (pg. 146): If the Cryx player wins, the mined necrotite reduces the cost of each of his bonejacks and helljacks by 10 points once during any single Icy Grip of Winter scenario.

Motivator (pg. 156): If Khador wins the game, Irusk becomes a living example of valor to his men. For the rest of the Campaign, all friendly troopers within Irusk's command area gain +1 movement.

Necrofactorium (pg. 185): If Cryx wins the game, a large number of horrific bonejacks and helljacks are assembled on the mainland before Khador manages to shut down the operation. Once during any single Wrath of Summer's Heat scenario, the Cryx player pays 10 points less for helljacks and 5 points less for bonejacks.

Observation Post (pg. 177): Deepwood Tower stands at a strategic point along the Cygnar-Khador border and is a valuable observation post. The winning player may use the Observation Post reward once before the start of any single Campaign scenario. The winning player then gets to look at his opponents' final army composition and make changes to his own army composition before the start of the game. An opponent may not alter his army composition once he declares it as his final composition.

Pilgrim Recruits (pg. 181): If the Protectorate wins, the Menites gain ground and pilgrim immigrants swell the Protectorate ranks. Once during any single Wrath of Summer's Heat scenario, the Protectorate player may purchase a single Deliverer, Holy Zealot, or Temple Flameguard unit for half normal point cost rounded up.

Practice Makes Perfect (pg. 173): If Cygnar wins, Allister Caine is left pondering the events that led up to the assassination of the Winter Guard kapitan. He clears his head by practicing for hours with his Spellstorm pistols, temporarily turning from drink. Slowly, he not only begins to formulate his plans, but he also refines his control over the pistols. For the rest of the Campaign, if Caine voluntarily forfeits his movement by not changing position or facing, he gains a +2 bonus to magical attack rolls on spells cast directly from him that are projected through his pistols. Additionally, Caine gains +1 to all magical attack damage rolls on spells cast directly from him. Channeled spells do not gain either benefit.

Preparation (pg. 187): The winning player has time to prepare his force's movements along the river. Once during the Wrath of Summer's Heat Act III scenario, Smoke on the Water, the winning player may either choose to add 2" to his barge movement or not move the barge at all. He may decide after rolling the die for barge movement.

Press Gang (pg. 183): If Cryx wins, their forces overrun the town and drag many inhabitants back to the blackship. The lucky ones drown on the way, but all are turned over to the necrosurgeons. Once during any single Wrath of Summer's Heat scenario, the Cryx player may purchase a single Bile Thrall, Mechanithrall, or Revenant Crew unit for half normal point cost rounded up.

Prophetic Visions (pg. 152): If Cryx wins the game, Goreshade makes off with the severed head of Scrutator Marius Grummel. After animating and thoroughly questioning the head through the application of necromancy, Goreshade may consult the head before the start of any battle. In games in which Goreshade is used, the Cryx player sets up his models after all his opponents' models have been placed, including models with the Advance Deployment ability. The order of play remains unchanged.

Recon (pg. 150): The winning player's forces are able to complete reconnaissance of the area. During the Icy Grip of Winter Act III

scenario, The Ruins of Riversmet, the winning player may extend his deployment zone by 4".

Recruitment Drive (pg. 185): If Khador wins, propagandists have a field day with the events of the Spawning Ground scenario. Great numbers of patriots, outraged that Cryx would dare assault the Motherland, immediately re-enlist. Once during any single Wrath of Summer's Heat scenario, the Khador player may purchase a single Iron Fang Pikeman, Kossite Woodsman, or Winter Guard unit for half normal point cost rounded up.

Refinery (pg. 200): If the Protectorate player wins, the Kregor Rock facility continues to refine Menoth's Fury at full output. Once during any single Fall's Blighted Harvest scenario, the Protectorate player may purchase a single Deliverer, Flameguard Cleanser, or Temple Flameguard unit for half normal point cost rounded up.

Replacements (pg. 202): If Khador wins, the Khadoran High Kommand repays its victorious officers with fresh troops. Once during any single Fall's Blighted Harvest scenario, the Khador player pays 10 points less for units.

Reserves (pg. 195): The winning faction takes control of a vital river crossing. Once during the Campaign in a single scenario, the winning player may put one (1) unit into play during any of his maintenance phases after the first round. The unit may be worth up to 100 points and is in addition to the player's point total for the scenario, but it may not exceed normal field allowance. The unit is placed on the table within the player's deployment zone. The Reserves reward may only be used in scenarios in which the winning player has a deployment zone bordering a table edge. The player does not have to declare the use of Reserves before the game.

Sacrifice (pg. 210): If Khador wins, Vladimir sacrifices himself to interfere with Cryx's plans. As a result, Cryx warcasters cannot use the Balebrand to take control of Khadoran models in the Fall's Blighted Harvest Act III scenario, The Harvest.

Safe Passage (pg. 186): After destroying their enemies in the dust storm, the victorious faction is able to navigate the eastern side of the Black River free of enemy forces. During the Wrath of Summer's Heat Act III scenario, Smoke on the Water, the winning player may choose to go first or last.

Secrets of the Cortex (pg. 193): If the Protectorate wins, the converted Greylord divulges his secrets to Severius and grants him new insights into cortex defense protocols. For the rest of the Campaign, during his activation Severius may spend a point of focus to shut down the cortex of up to one warjack within his control area. The warjack may not be allocated focus for one round.

Secure Supply Lines (pg. 200): If the Khador player wins, Khadoran supply lines will be open for the rest of the season. Once during any single Fall's Blighted Harvest scenario, the Khador player pays 10 points less for warjacks.

Security (pg. 184): If Cygnar wins, Lawbringer is silenced long enough for them to make a punitive strike against Sul. The attack temporarily cripples the Protectorate war effort and gives Cygnar time to recover and extend its defenses. With no attack imminent, Cygnar redistributes its forces and frees up much needed resources. Once during any single Wrath of Summer's Heat scenario, the Cygnar player pays 10 points less for units.

Soul Fuel (pg. 165): If the Cryx player wins the game, the distilled souls may be used to fuel Cryxian warjacks once during any Storms of Spring scenario. During each of the Cryx player's control phases, any bonejack or helljack allocated one or more focus points by a Cryxian warcaster receives one additional focus point from the distilled soul fuel. Soul fuel cannot be used to give a warjack more than three total focus points.

Soul's Deliverance (pg. 212): If the Protectorate wins, the High Reclaimer gains greater insight into the boundaries between Caen and Urcaen. For the rest of the campaign, anytime the High Reclaimer uses his feat, he rolls 4d6 instead of 2d6 and keeps the two highest dice rolled to determine the number of models returned to play.

Spare Parts (pg. 149): If the Protectorate wins, spare parts carried by Landon Trellayne are used to repair a damaged warjack. During the Icy Grip of Winter Act III scenario, The Ruins of Riversmet, the Protectorate player may purchase a single light warjack for half the normal point cost rounded up.

Starvation (pg. 199): If Cryx wins, Cygnar begins to suffer a dire shortage of food. Matters only get worse as the days grow shorter. Cryxian forces claim the starving dead across Cygnar and add them to their numbers. Once during any single Fall's Blighted Harvest scenario, the Cryx player may purchase a single Bane Thrall, Bile Thrall, or Mechanithrall unit for half normal point cost rounded up.

Steeled Vengeance (pg. 209): If Cygnar wins, Stryker channels his rage and desperation into his attacks. For the rest of the Campaign, Stryker may boost both his attack and damage rolls by spending one focus point.

Supply Ships (pg. 144): If the Cygnar player wins the game, the merchant ships escape down the river and supply Cygnaran forces. Once during any single Icy Grip of Winter scenario, the Cygnar player pays 10 points less for warjacks.

Territorial Dominance (pg. 146): If the Khador player wins, Khador remains in control of the territory after forcing back Cryxian forces. The Khador player may exert his dominance once during any single Icy Grip of Winter scenario, allowing him to place one additional terrain feature and keeping his opponent from using the Advance Deployment ability during the scenario. Placed terrain must follow the guidelines of the scenario.

Traitors (pg. 171): If the Cryx player wins the game, Deneghra lays the groundwork for

225

her dark machinations and begins a campaign of seducing officers to expand her network of pawns throughout the enemy armies. In any game Deneghra is used, the Cryx player may add any one solo from any other faction to his army free of cost. The solo is controlled by the Cryx player but is not a Cryx model and none of the information on his stat card is altered. A Journeyman Warcaster or jack marshal may not begin the game controlling warjacks. Models with the Field Officer special ability do not allow Cryx to play with additional non-Cryx models. For example, if Deneghra is used in a game, the Cryx player could add a Man-O-War Kovnik to his army. However, the Kovnik cannot begin the game controlling warjacks, nor can the Cryx player use the Kovnik's Field Officer ability to take a unit of Man-O-War.

Vassals of Menoth (pg. 201): If the Protectorate wins, Hierarch Voyle doubles the number of vassals servicing the warjacks of his victorious warcasters. Once during any single Fall's Blighted Harvest scenario, the Protectorate player pays 10 points less for warjacks.

Veteran Command (pg. 190): If Cygnar wins, Haley removes the threat of future betrayals by exclusively taking command of veteran units she can trust. For the rest of the Campaign, when Haley is used all Long Gunner and Trencher trooper models use their unit sergeant's stat line.

War Effort (pg. 184): If the Protectorate wins, the damage done to Caspia's walls forces Cygnar into a defensive posture. For weeks while the walls are rebuilt, the Protectorate is able to focus on its own war effort and build great numbers of warjacks. Once during any single Wrath of Summer's Heat scenario, the Protectorate player pays 10 points less for warjacks.

Warcaster Deployment (pg. 142, 161, 179, 198): The outcome of the scenario determines the order the players reveal their warcaster deployments for Act II of the season. Beginning with the first player knocked out of the game and ending with the winner of the scenario,

each player deploys one warcaster to each Act II scenario. In a two-player game, the losing player must inform the winner of both warcasters he intends to field during the Act II game.

The Warding (pg. 207): If Cryx wins, Asphyxious learns to manipulate the necrotic energies around the Umbral Cairn to create an impenetrable barrier around the dais. This arcane knowledge may be used during the Fall's Blighted Harvest Act III scenario, The Harvest. During his activation, if Asphyxious Holds the dais he may spend three soul tokens to use The Warding. Asphyxious may Hold the dais if he is the only model completely within the area of the dais during his maintenance phase. Asphyxious cannot Hold the dais while he is engaged in melee combat. After warding the dais, Asphyxious may not move off and no model may move onto the dais for any reason for one round. A model on the warded dais cannot be damaged in any way by models that are not also standing on the dais. While the dais is warded, Asphyxious may not make melee attacks against models not on the dais, but he may still cast spells normally.

Warjack Parts (pg. 166): The winning player ends the scenario in possession of the barge loaded with warjack parts. Once during any single Storms of Spring scenario, the winning player pays 10 points less for his warjacks.

Waterway (pg. 195): After the river battle, the winner takes control of a valuable river waterway and is easily able to fortify his positions. The winner may add up to 25 points to the size of his army in the Fall's Blighted Harvest Act I scenario, the Balebrand.

Weather Manipulation (pg. 153-154): If Cygnar wins, Nemo enters the temple. Once inside he discovers an ancient mechanikal device that allows him to manipulate local weather patterns. For the rest of the Campaign, the Cygnar player may modify Weather Condition rolls by up to +2 or -2 in games in which Nemo is used. For example, if Nemo is used during the Spring Act II scenario Collateral Damage, he can influence the Weather Condition roll for the scenario. If the roll is a 3, Heavy Rains, Nemo can add or subtract up to 2 from the die roll, either increasing the roll to 5, Clear Skies, or lowering it to 2, Flash Floods.

The Well of Truth (pg. 145): The winning player may use the Well of Truth once during any single Icy Grip of Winter scenario. The player must declare the use of the well before the start of the game and assign it to a faction warcaster—the artifact is much too valuable to entrust to a mercenary. The Well of Truth may be used once during the game. It may only be taken into battle once during the Campaign and, whether or not it is utilized, it cannot be used again. The warcaster cannot run during the game until the well is used. To use the well, the warcaster must forfeit his activation to pour water into the basin. He then remains absolutely still to keep from spilling a single drop. Once the Well of Truth is activated, all friendly models in the player's army that are not currently engaged become Invisible for one round. While Invisible, models cannot be targeted by ranged or magical attacks, cannot be charged, and gain +4 DEF against melee attacks. If the model moves or takes any action during its turn, including using feats, casting spells, or channeling spells, it loses the benefits of Invisible. Invisible models do not block line of sight or provide screening.

WARMACHINE: Prime Rules Errata

The following entries present additions, changes, and clarifications for the rules printed in WARMACHINE: Prime. If an entry does not specifically state that it is a replacement or a clarification, treat it as a change to the original text.

p.31: Victory Points

Replace the first paragraph with the following:

Every model and unit is worth a set number of victory points. Award the victory points from a model or unit to the player or team that destroys it, disables it, causes it to become inert, or causes it to be removed from play. If a player accidentally or intentionally eliminates a friendly model, be it his own or a teammate's, award its full victory points to every opposing player or team.

Victory points for models destroyed or removed from play are awarded when the models leave the table. All other victory points for eliminating models are awarded at the end of the game. Once a player has been awarded victory points for eliminating a model or unit, those points are never lost, even if the model subsequently returns to play. If returned models are later eliminated, award victory points for them again.

p.32: Activation Phase

Forfeiting Activation: A model may not forfeit its activation unless required to do so by a special rule.

p.33: Line of Sight

Replace the entire section with the following:

Many game situations such as charges, ranged attacks, and some magical attacks require a model to have line of sight (LOS) to its intended target. A model has line of sight to a target if you can draw a straight, unobstructed line from the center of its base at head height through its front arc to any part of the target model, including its base. Warrior models present a slight exception to this rule. Unlike warjack models, items held in the hands of warrior models - such as their weapons or banner poles - do not count as part of the model for determining line of sight. For example, a Khadoran Widowmaker does not have line of sight to a Menite Temple Flameguard if all he can see is the tip of the Flameguard's spear poking over a wall.

Simply put, having line of sight means that the model can see its target. If a model's line of sight is questionable, it may be easiest for a player to position himself to see the table from his model's perspective. A laser pointer may also come in handy when determining line of sight.

Intervening Models

A model blocks line of sight to models that have equal- or smaller-sized bases. If any line between the center of the attacking model's base at head height and the target crosses another model's base, that model is an intervening model. You cannot draw a line of sight across an intervening model's base to models that have equal- or smaller-sized bases. However, you may still have a line of sight to the target if its base is not completely obscured by the intervening model's base.

An intervening model does not block line of sight to models that have larger bases - ignore it when drawing line of sight.

Screening

A screening model is an intervening model that has an equal- or larger-sized base than the target model and is within 1" of it. The target model is screened by a screening model and gains

+2 DEF against ranged and magic attacks. The target does not gain this bonus if the intervening model has a smaller base, if the attacker's line of sight to the screening model is completely obstructed by terrain, or if the target's base is more than 1" away from the screening model's base regardless of base size. The screening bonus is only applied once regardless of the number of screening models.

Elevation and LOS

When drawing line of sight from a model on a higher elevation than its target, ignore all intervening models on lower elevations than the attacking model except those that would normally screen the target. Additionally, you can draw line of sight through screening models that have equal- or smaller-sized bases than the attacking model, but the target still gains +2 DEF for being screened.

When drawing line of sight to an elevated target, ignore all intervening models on lower elevation than the target. Models on lower elevations do not provide screening to models on higher elevations.

p.34: Movement (Clarification)

The term *normal movement* refers to the movement a model makes during the movement portion of its activation, not to any movement due to other effects such as spells or being slammed. Some rules such as charging and slamming require a model to be able to move its full normal movement. Although a model's SPD stat may be modified during play, the model's unmodified SPD stat determines its *normal movement*. Whether due to a game effect (such as disabled movement), a spell, feat, or weapon effect (such as Crippling Grasp), a terrain effect, or another modifier, a model that suffers any penalty to its SPD or movement (regardless of offsetting bonuses) is unable to move its full normal movement.

p.35: Charging

A model may attempt to charge another model, friend or enemy, in line of sight at the beginning of its normal movement. Declare the charge and its target before moving the model.

p.36: Unit Formation

A unit's leader is always in formation. Other troopers' status is based on their proximity to him or other models in formation with him. If a unit is widely scattered, those troopers in skirmish formation with the leader are in formation and others are not, even if other groupings have larger numbers. If the leader is no longer in play then the largest coherent grouping of troopers is in formation. If two or more coherent groupings have the largest number of troopers, the controlling player chooses which is in formation. A lone survivor of a unit is always in formation.

Formations are not mutually exclusive. Models in tight formation also meet the criteria for being in open or skirmish formation. Likewise, models in open formation also meet the criteria for being in skirmish formation.

A tight formation may consist of any number of ranks, but each rank must be at least two troopers wide.

p.41: Head-butt

A warjack may attempt to head-butt a model, friend or enemy.

p.41: Slam

A warjack may attempt to slam a model, friend or enemy, in line of sight at the beginning of its normal movement. Declare the slam and its target before moving the model.

p.46: Targeting a Model in Melee

Replace the entire section with the following:

A model that makes a ranged or magic attack against a target in melee, either engaged or engaging, risks hitting another model participating in the combat, including friendly models. The standard targeting rules, including line of sight and screening, must be observed in order to target a model that is in melee. Combined ranged attacks cannot target a model in melee - it is impossible to concentrate such firepower against a single target in a swirling fight.

In addition to any other attack modifiers, a ranged or magic attack against a target in melee also suffers a -4 penalty to the attack roll. All of the target's special rules and effects still apply. For instance, an attack targeting a model with the Stealth ability from greater than 5" away still automatically misses, while an attack targeting a model affected by the Death Sentence spell still automatically hits, as normal.

If the attack against the intended target misses, it may hit another combatant. The attacker must immediately re-roll its attack against another model in that combat. Randomly determine which other model in the combat - not including the intended target - becomes the new target. When determining the attack's new target, only the models that are in melee (engaged or engaging) with the attack's intended target and any other models in melee with those models are considered to be in the same combat. Every model meeting these criteria is eligible to become the new target, regardless of line of sight, with two exceptions: a model is ineligible to become the new target if it has a special rule that prevents it from being targeted or if the attacker's line of sight to it is completely blocked by obstructing terrain. If multiple models in the combat are eligible targets, randomly determine which model becomes the new target.

For example, using a d6, if there are three other models in the combat, the first model will become the new target on a 1 or 2, the second on a 3 or 4, and the third on a 5 or 6. However, if the attacker cannot draw a line of sight to one of those models due to an obstruction (e.g., it's around a corner), ignore that model and randomize the attack between the other two: it targets the first on a 1 through 3 or the second on a 4 through 6. If one of those two models cannot be targeted for some reason (such as being under the protection of a Safe Passage battle hymn), then only one model is an eligible target and a random roll is unnecessary.

When re-rolling the attack against a new target, all modifiers affecting the attacker still apply, such as a boost die, aiming bonus, spell effects, and the -4 penalty for targeting a model in melee. All modifiers affecting the newly-targeted model also apply, but ignore those that only applied to the intended target. If the attack against the new target misses, it misses completely without targeting any more models.

For instance, Stryker is in melee with a Revenger affected by the Protection of Menoth spell. A Charger forfeits its movement, aims, and targets the Revenger with its dual cannon and spends a focus point to boost its attack roll. The Charger's attack roll gains a boost die and the aiming bonus, and it suffers the penalty for targeting a model in melee. In addition, the Revenger's DEF against this attack is enhanced due to the spell in play on it. If the attack misses, the Charger re-rolls the attack, this time targeting Stryker, and includes the boost die, aiming bonus, and the penalty for targeting a model in melee. If Stryker is affected by the Blur spell or if he is behind cover in relation to the Charger, then he gains those benefits against this attack. However, if Stryker were affected by the Death Sentence spell, the attack would automatically hit him without having to be re-rolled.

As a second example, Stryker is now in melee with Deneghra and a Deathripper. A Trencher enters the fight from the side and engages Deneghra but not the Deathripper. The Charger makes a ranged attack against the Deathripper and misses. Since Stryker is in melee with the Deathripper and Deneghra is in melee with Stryker, they are both in the same combat as the intended target. The Trencher is not included because it is not in melee with the intended target (the Deathripper) or with another model in melee with the intended target (Stryker - it is far enough from the intended target not to be attacked accidentally. A random die roll determines that Deneghra is the new target. Unfortunately, since Deneghra is more than 5" away from the Charger, her Stealth ability makes the attack automatically miss her without rolling. Even though Stealth prevents her from being hit, she can still be targeted. Since the attack missed both its intended target and the new target, it misses completely with no chance of hitting Stryker or the Trencher.

An area-of-effect attack that misses a target in melee deviates normally instead of following these rules.

p.47: Area-of-Effect Attacks (Clarification)

An area-of-effect attack's point of impact determines the direction of the attack for models receiving blast damage. For instance, suppose an AOE ranged attack targets a trooper benefiting from shield wall from the trooper's front arc, but the attack misses and deviates behind the trooper. Since the point of impact is now behind the model and thus the blast damage attacks its rear arc, it does not benefit from the shield wall.

p.47: Spray Attacks

Terrain that obstructs LOS blocks spray attacks. A model under the spray template cannot be hit by the attack if the attacker's LOS to it is completely blocked by terrain. A model under the spray template does not benefit from being screened.

p.48: Special Combat Situations (Clarification)

Effects with simultaneous timing: If multiple special rules with contradictory effects are triggered at the same time, the attacker's special rule takes precedence. As an example, suppose Kreoss and Severius disagree on the best way to praise Menoth's glory. If Kreoss hits Severius with Spellbreaker, it will dispel Severius' Vision without the spell providing its protection.

Attacks that hit or miss automatically: Some special rules cause attacks to hit automatically or miss automatically. In cases of conflicting special rules, one that causes an attack to hit automatically takes precedence over one that causes an attack to miss automatically. For instance, the Purge special attack hits automatically, which overrides special rules that normally cause an attack to miss automatically, such as the Stealth ability.

p.49: Stationary Targets

Models can never be in melee with stationary models. Stationary models do not engage other models nor does a model engage a stationary model. A stationary model does not have a melee range.

p.49: Knockdown (Clarification)

A knocked-down model does not provide screening or block line of sight, nor does it provide concealment or cover. All attacks against a knocked-down model are to its front arc. A knocked down model may not be thrown.

p.49: Combined Melee Attacks and Ranged Attacks (Clarification)

If the target of a combined melee attack has a special rule or effect in play that affects its attackers (such as Retribution), only the primary attacker - the model making the attack roll - suffers those effects.

p.49: Combined Ranged Attacks (1st print Prime)

The first sentence should read:

Troopers with this ability may combine their ranged attacks against the same target.

p.49: Combined Ranged Attacks (Clarification)

In order to participate in a combined ranged attack, a trooper must be in open formation with all other participants.

If the target of a combined ranged attack can claim concealment or cover in relation to any member of the attacking group, it gets the appropriate bonus against the attack.

When a combined ranged attack targets a model with the Stealth ability, any models found to be more than 5" away from the target do not contribute to the attack and damage roll bonus. All models participating in the combined range attack still perform their action whether or not they contribute to it. If the primary attacker is more than 5" away from the target, the entire combined attack automatically misses, regardless of bonuses.

p.50: Corpse and Soul Tokens

Only destroyed models generate corpse and soul tokens. Models that are removed from play do not generate corpse or soul tokens.

p.50: Damage Rolls (Clarification)

An *attack* is one use of a weapon or offensive spell, even if it generates multiple attack rolls and/or damage rolls. For these attacks, completely resolve all of the attack and damage rolls just like an attack with only one attack and damage roll before applying the targets' special rules. For example, an AOE attack hits three Knights Exemplar. Resolve all three damage rolls before letting the remaining Knights Exemplar benefit from Bond of Brotherhood.

p.50: Recording Damage

Destroyed versus Removed from Play - When a model takes enough damage to eliminate it from play, it is destroyed. A model without damage capacity is destroyed as soon as it takes one damage point. More resilient models are destroyed after all their damage boxes are filled. Destroyed models are cleared from the play area and set aside. It is possible for destroyed models to return to the table during play.

Occasionally models will be outright removed from play. A model removed from play cannot return to the table for any reason.

p.51: Disabling a Warjack (Clarification)

A disabled warjack wreck is still a warjack, and is therefore a model. A disabled warjack has no facing, loses all special abilities, cannot be allocated focus, and does not gain an ARM bonus for functioning shields or bucklers.

Wreck markers, both disabled and totaled, are never intervening models and do not screen, however, they do provide cover. Melee attacks may be made across wreck makers. Wreck markers cannot be slammed, thrown, or moved.

p.53: Warcaster Special Rules (Clarification)

A warcaster can use his feat or cast spells any time during his activation. However, he cannot interrupt his movement or an attack to do so. A warcaster can use his feat or cast spells before or after moving, but not in the middle of his movement. Likewise, he can use his feat or cast spells before and after each attack, but he cannot interrupt an unresolved attack, nor can he use his feat or cast spells between the movement and attack portions of a charge. Spells and feats can be used prior to initiating an attack or after completely resolving an attack, including determining hits, damage, and special effects.

p.53: Control Area (Clarification)

A player may measure his own warcaster's control area at any time. For control area effects against opposing models, a player does not have to measure his warcaster's control area until after the enemy model commits to its movement or action. For example, Haley's player does not have to measure her control area for Temporal Barrier prior to a model entering it as doing so may influence that player's decision. Instead, the opposing player will have to adjust his model's position if it entered her control area and was slowed by the spell.

p.55: Offensive Spells

A magic attack does not suffer the *target in melee* attack roll penalty when the attack's point of origin (warcaster or channeler, as the case may be) is in melee with the target. If such an attack (with a non-AOE spell) misses and there are multiple models in the melee, the attack may hit another random model in the melee, excluding the original target and the originating model - resolve this per the randomization rules on p.46. An AOE spell that misses in this situation will deviate normally.

An offensive spell may not target its own point of origin.

p.56: Channeling

A channeler may be used to channel spells if it engages an enemy model but is not itself engaged by another model.

If the channeler is entirely in the target's back arc at the time an offensive spell is cast, treat the channeled offensive spell as a back strike.

p.57: Command Checks (Clarification)

A model/unit that passes a command check caused by its proximity to a terrifying entity does not make further command checks against that entity as long as it remains inside the range that triggered the check. If these models become separated and encounter each other again later, another command check will be required.

Additional General Rules Clarifications

Leaving the Playing Area: A model that flees off the table is removed from play. A model that would leave the table for any other reason (such as being thrown or compulsory movement like Scramble) will stop at the table edge and remain in play. The table edge does not count as an obstacle; models do not take damage from stopping there.

Inert warjacks: An inert warjack has no facing, loses all special abilities, and does not gain an ARM bonus for functioning shields or bucklers.

WARMACHINE: Prime Models

p.75: Lt. Allister Caine

Crack Shot - Replace text with: Caine's targets do not benefit from being screened.

Thunder Strike - Target model hit by Thunder Strike is slammed d6" directly away from the spell's point of origin with the same effects as a Slam power attack.

p.77: Captain Victoria Haley

Set Defense - Haley gains +2 DEF against Charge and Slam attacks from her front arc.

Temporal Barrier - Temporal Barrier only affects enemy models.

p.80 Arcane Tempest Gun Mages

Arcane Inferno (Clarification) - All participating models must be in open formation with the unit leader, who must also be an eligible participant. Troopers not able to participate in the attack may ignore the order and act normally.

p.83: Cygnar Field Mechaniks

Profile Block (1st print Prime) - Monkey Wrench P+S: 6

p.85: Trencher

Trencher Trooper stat bar - CMD 7, not 6.

p.87: Lancer

Shock Field (Clarification) - Last sentence: When the Lancer attacks with the Shock Shield, mark this damage before making the damage roll.

Set Defense - The Lancer gains +2 DEF against Charge and Slam attacks from its front arc.

p.88: Sentinel

Strafe (Clarification) - A model is ineligible to become the new target if it has a special rule that prevents it from being targeted or if the attacker's line of sight to it is completely blocked by terrain.

Completely resolve each Strafe attack individually, applying the targets' special rules immediately as each attack is resolved.

p.97: Grand Scrutator Severius

Divine Might (1st print Prime) - second paragraph, first sentence: "No spells may be cast or channeled within Severius' control area except by other friendly Protectorate models."

Divine Might (Clarification) - Divine Might prevents all non-friendly Protectorate models with the Focus Manipulation ability from replenishing their focus points normally during

their control phase. It does not prevent a model from gaining focus points in other ways, such as converted soul tokens.

Blessing of Menoth (Clarification) - The affected model can only re-roll a roll that is a result of its own action. Examples include attack and damage rolls, damage location rolls, and deviation. It cannot re-roll a die roll for effects on itself, such as Corrosion, nor for continuous effects that it inflicted on other models, such as Fire.

Convert - Convert can only be cast on non-character troopers. Converted models are independent and cannot run or charge without being ordered to do so, nor rally on their own unless they are unit leaders or officers or are forced to do so by some effect.

p.99: High Exemplar Kreoss

Lamentation - Replace text with: All enemy models in AOE pay double the focus points to cast or upkeep spells.

Retribution (Clarification) - Retribution is not triggered by collateral damage, damage from continuous effects, or damage taken without a damage roll.

p.101: High Reclaimer

Feat: Resurrection - Return 2d6 friendly destroyed Menoth troopers to play, placing them within the Reclaimer's control area. The controlling player chooses which models are returned to play, and models may be returned to their original units or formed into new units of the same type. New units formed cannot be larger than the maximum size allowed for that unit. Resurrected models placed in their original unit cause the unit to lose benefits or effects that it received from the original destruction of the resurrected models. Resurrected models cannot activate the turn they return to play.

p.102: Choir of Menoth

Battle Staff ó add to the Warpriest's and Acolytes' special rules: Reach - 2" melee range.

p.104: Knights Exemplar

Bond of Brotherhood - Replace text with: A Knight Exemplar gains +1 STR and +1 ARM for every member of its unit destroyed. These bonuses are lost if the model is returned to play.

p.106: Temple Flameguard

Shield Wall - Replace text with: When this order is given, every Temple Flameguard who moves into tight formation gains +4 ARM against attacks from his front arc. Models that do not end their movement in tight formation do not benefit from the shield wall. This bonus lasts for one round even if adjacent models are destroyed or removed from play.

Set Defense - A Temple Flameguard gains +2 DEF against Charge and Slam attacks from his front arc.

p.107: Holy Zealots

Critical Fire - On a Critical Hit, every model in the area of effect suffers Fire.

p.112: Vanquisher

Circular Strike (Clarification) - Completely resolve each attack individually and apply the targets' special rules immediately as each attack is resolved.

p.119: Iron Lich, Asphyxious

Shadow Wings (1st print Prime) - Asphyxious moves up to 10", ignoring free strikes and terrain penalties and effects, then ends his activation.

p.121: Skarre

Blood Magic - Replace text with: Give Skarre 1-5 damage points. All friendly Cryxian models currently in her control area, including herself, gain +1 STR and +1 ARM for each damage point she takes, which lasts for one round

Life Drinker - Replace text with: Skarre regains one damage point each time she destroys a living enemy model with Bloodwyrm.

Sacrificial Strike - Replace text with: Remove a friendly Cryx trooper model within 1ì of Skarre from play. A target model within Skarre's control area then takes a damage roll with POW equal to the ARM of the model sacrificed. This damage roll may be boosted.

Dark Guidance - Affects all friendly Cryxian models currently within Skarre's control area.

p.123: Deneghra

Death Rage - Replace text with: When target model takes sufficient damage to be destroyed, Death Rage expires. Target model remains in play for one round and cannot be destroyed during this time. After one round, the model is destroyed.

Stealth - If Deneghra is greater than 5" away from an attacker, she does not count as an intervening model.

Dark Seduction (1st Print Prime) - Can only be cast on non-character troopers.

Ghost Walk (1st Print Prime) - While Ghost Walking, a model cannot charge or slam and ignores free strikes.

p.124: Bane Thrall

Stealth - If a Bane Thrall is greater than 5" away from an attacker, it does not count as an intervening model.

p.125: Bile Thrall

Purge - Replace text with: (★ Attack) - The Bile Thrall sprays out the entire contents of its guts, deflating and automatically hitting all models within 6" of the Bile Thrall's front arc. Terrain that obstructs LOS blocks the Purge attack. A model within range of the Purge attack cannot be hit by the attack if the attacker's LOS to it is completely blocked by terrain. All models hit take a POW 12 damage roll and suffer Corrosion, then remove the Bile Thrall from play. Purge is a ranged attack.

p.127: Necrotech & Scrap Thrall

Immobilize - An immobilized model is released from the Vise Claw if the Necrotech moves, makes an attack against another model, is destroyed, or is removed from play.

Independent Model (1st Print Prime) - An army must include a Necrotech at the beginning of the game to field Scrap Thralls.

Thrall Bomb - Replace text with: When the Scrap Thrall takes sufficient damage to be destroyed, it explodes with a 4" AOE. All models within AOE suffer a POW 8 damage roll. When the Scrap Thrall explodes, remove it from play.

Death Burst - Death Burst is a special action that combines the Scrap Thrall's movement and combat action. Declare that a Scrap Thrall is going to Death Burst when it activates. Move the Scrap Thrall up to twice its SPD (as if it were running), and then perform the death burst. Center the AOE on the Scrap Thrall's target if the attack is successful and on the Scrap Thrall if it is not. The Scrap Thrall is removed from play after performing a Death Burst.

p.128: Satyxis Raiders

Profile Block (1st Print Prime) - The correct point cost for a Satyxis Raider Leader and 5 troops is 64 points.

p.129: Skarlock Thrall

Bound (Clarification) - A Skarlock Thrall may only be bound to a Cryx warcaster. Each warcaster can only have one bound Skarlock Thrall.

Undead(1st print Prime) - A Skarlock is not a living model and never flees.

p.130 Deathripper

Profile Block (1st print Prime) - A Deathripper has a medium-sized base.

p.132 Nightwretch

Damage Grid (1st Print Prime) - Add an additional row of hull boxes to the top of the Nightwretch's damage grid. Its damage grid should be the same as the Deathripper's and Defiler's.

p.133 Reaper

Profile Block (1st print Prime) - A Reaper has a large base.

p.143: Kommander Sorscha

Wind Rush - This spell may be cast once per activation.

p.145: Vladimir, The Dark Prince

Forced March - Only affects friendly Khadoran warjacks currently within Vladimir's control area at the time the feat is used.

Mimic - Replace text with: When making a melee attack with Skirmisher, it may duplicate one special rule from any melee weapon of any warcaster in Vladimir's control area. Declare the special rule being mimicked before each attack.

Parry - Replace text with: Free strikes against Vladimir automatically miss.

Blood of Kings - This spell may be cast once per activation.

Signs and Portents - Affects all friendly Khadoran models currently within Vladimir's control area.

Wind Wall - (1st print Prime) Any ranged attack against Vladimir or a model completely within 3" of him automatically misses.

p.147 Iron Fang Pikemen

Shield Wall - Replace text with: When this order is given, every Iron Fang Pikeman that moves into tight formation gains +4 ARM against attacks from his front arc. Models that do not end their movement in tight formation do not benefit from the shield wall. This bonus lasts for one round, even if adjacent models are destroyed or removed from play.

p.148 Manhunter

Stealth - If the Manhunter is greater than 5" away from an attacker, it does not count as an intervening model.

p.149 Man-O-War Shocktroopers

Shield Wall - Replace text with: When this order is given, every Man-O-War Shocktrooper that moves into tight formation gains +4 ARM against attacks from his front arc. Models that do not end their movement in tight formation do not benefit from the shield wall. This bonus lasts for one round, even if adjacent models are destroyed or removed from play.

p.153: Destroyer

Arcing Fire - When attacking with the Bombard, the Destroyer may ignore all intervening models except those that would normally screen the target.

p.158 Eiryss

Mercenary (1st Print Prime) - Delete the second sentence which reads: "No victory points are gained for models Eiryss destroys." This restriction has been removed from the game.

Invisibility - While Invisible, Eiryss does not block line of sight or provide screening.

p.160: Boomhowler

Mercenary (1st Print Prime) - Delete the second sentence which reads: "No victory points are gained for models destroyed by Boomhowler & co." This restriction has been removed from the game.

Tough - Replace text with: Whenever a Trollkin takes sufficient damage to be destroyed, the controlling player rolls a d6. On a 5 or 6, the Trollkin is knocked down instead of being destroyed. If Boomhowler is not destroyed, he is reduced to one wound.

Stink Bombs - Throwing a Stink Bomb is a special attack.

p.162 Herne Stoneground & Arquebus Jonne

Mercenary (1st Print Prime) - Delete the second sentence which reads: "No victory points are gained for models destroyed by Herne & Jonne." This restriction has been removed from the game.

Slow (1st Print Prime) - Delete "Slow" from the Barrage Arquebus' special rules block.

p.164: Reinholdt

Mercenary (1st Print Prime) - Delete the second sentence which reads: "No victory points are gained for models Reinholdt destroys." This restriction has been removed from the game.

Mercenary (Clarification) - Reinholdt will not work for Cryx or the Protectorate.

Assistant - Remove Reinholdt from play if his warcaster is destroyed or removed from play.

p.177: Glossary

Elevated Target (1st Print Prime) - A model on higher ground than its attacker gains a +2 DEF bonus against ranged or magic attacks from that opponent.

p.183: Glossary

Tight Formation - Delete the last sentence which reads: "Troopers that begin their activation in tight formation cannot run or charge."

Autonomous Warjack (pg. 17): An active warjack without a controller. An autonomous warjack acts normally but may not be marshaled or allocated focus, though it may receive focus from other sources. A warjack must have a controller at the start of the game and may not begin autonomous.

Campaign Record Sheet (pg. 220): Form for tracking warcaster deployment, scenario outcomes, Victory Points, and Survival Bonuses during each season of the Campaign.

Camping, Play Condition (pg. 133): Camping is for cowards! A model or unit remaining in its deployment zone after the third round must pass a CMD check during each of its controller's maintenance phases or flee the table.

Competitive Play Scenarios (pg. 132): Balanced scenarios in which neither player begins with an advantage. Competitive play scenarios are suitable for campaign play. Competitive scenarios include:

Death in the Deepwood (pg. 176-177)

Dust Storm (pg. 185-186)

Incoming (pg. 167-168)

Pendulum (pg. 166-167)

Ruins of Riversmet (pg. 157-159)

Smoke on the Water (pg. 193-195)

Well of Truth (pg. 144-145)

First Blood, Play Condition (pg. 133): The first army to cause damage to any model in an opposing army gains +1 on all attack rolls on the controlling player's next turn.

Hammertime, Play Condition (pg. 133): When the hammer falls, you are done. At the end of the last player's turn of the round described, one of the players rolls a d6. On a result of 1 the scenario ends. At the end of each additional round, roll to see if the hammer falls. The chance of the scenario ending is increased by +1 each additional round until the third round. From the third additional round on, the game concludes on a roll of 1-3.

Hold (pg. 137): A player may Hold a location if he controls all models within the space described during his maintenance phase. Models that are engaged in melee combat cannot be used to Hold a location. Neither warrior models with CMD stats of 1 or less nor Incorporeal models can Hold a location.

Jack Marshal (pg. 17): A non-warcaster model with the ability to control warjacks. A jack marshal may begin the game controlling one or more warjacks. These warjacks are not part of any warcaster's battle group. Each jack marshal has a marshaling range equal to his CMD stat in inches. A controlled warjack within marshaling range of its controller may run, charge, or boost an attack or damage roll once per activation. A warjack gains these benefits even if its controlling jack marshal is stationary. A jack marshal may activate friendly inert warjacks of the same faction in the same manner as a warcaster.

Leaving the Playing Area (pg. 233): A model that flees off the table is removed from play. A model that would leave the table for any other reason (such as being thrown or compulsory movement like Scramble) will stop at the table edge and remain in play. The table edge does not count as an obstacle; models do not take damage from stopping there.

Mercenary Warjacks (pg. 17): Mercenary warjacks may only be included in a battlegroup controlled by a mercenary warcaster or assigned to a mercenary jack marshal. Warcasters belonging to a faction may not control mercenary warjacks. Mercenary warcasters and jack marshals can only control mercenary warjacks and cannot control warjacks belonging to a faction.

Play Conditions (pg. 133): Play conditions are special rules that modify some scenarios in the Campaign. Look for the Play Conditions icons indicating the conditions in effect throughout each scenario. Icons are listed below scenario titles.

Replacing Models (pg.17): When replacing one model with another, place the new model so that the area covered by the smaller of the bases is completely within the area covered by the larger. If two bases are the same size, place the new model in the same location as the one being replaced.

Screening (pg.228-229): A screening model is an intervening model that has an equal- or larger-sized base than the target model and is within 1" of it. The target model is screened by a screening model and gains +2 DEF against ranged and magic attacks. The target does not gain this bonus if the attacker's line of sight to the screening model is completely obstructed by terrain. The screening bonus is only applied once regardless of the number of screening models.

Starting Roll (pg. 137): The roll made in the Beginning section of each scenario.

Survival Bonus (pg. 135): Players earn a Survival Bonus for their models and units that were not destroyed or removed from play during each Act II scenario of the Campaign. After an Act II scenario, each player who participated in the game totals the Victory Point value of his surviving models and multiplies the total by three to get his Survival Bonus.

Terrain, Play Condition (pg.133): This scenario uses a special piece of terrain that might require additional set-up.

Timed Game, Play Condition (pg. 133): This scenario lasts a predetermined number of rounds and ends after the final round.

Unit Attachments (pg 17-18): Unit attachments are made up of one or more models that may be added to a unit specified in the unit attachment's description. A model in the unit attachment with the Officer special ability becomes the new unit leader. If the new unit leader is destroyed or removed from play, the original unit leader regains its Leader ability. A unit attachment increases the victory point value of the unit to which it is added by an amount detailed in the description of the unit attachment.

Warcaster Casualty, Play Condition (pg. 133-134): The victory conditions for one or more players are met if all warcasters from the indicated factions are destroyed or removed from play. See the scenario's Victory Conditions section for details.

Warcaster Deployment (pg. 134): Throughout the Campaign, players assign their warcasters marching orders by deploying them to various Act II scenarios. After completing Act I of a season, each player deploys at least one warcaster to each Act II scenario he will play.

Weapon Crews (pg. 18): Weapon crews are small units, made up of a gunner and one or more crewmen, that operate large or cumbersome weapons. A weapon crew cannot run or charge. The Gunner gains +2" of movement for each Crewman from his own unit in base-to-base contact with him when he begins his activation. If the Gunner takes sufficient damage to be destroyed, a Crewman within 1" can take the destroyed Gunner's place immediately, becoming a new Gunner.

Weather Condition, Play Condition (pg. 133): Players must roll a weather condition on the table from the current season. Roll for Weather Conditions after terrain is placed, but before players deploy their armies. If both players agree, their armies can 'wait out the weather' and play the game without the Weather Condition in effect.

Weather Condition Tables (pg. 137-138)